THE GWR STARS, CASTLES & KINGS

David & Charles Locomotive Monographs

All by O. S. NOCK, B.Sc., C.Eng., F.I.C.E., F.I.Mech.E.,

The Southern King Arthur Family
The Standard Gauge Great Western 4–4–0s, Parts 1 and 2
The Royal Scots and Patriots of the LMS

David & Charles Locomotive Studies

Published titles still in print

Diesel-hydraulic Locomotives of the Western Region, by Brian Reed
The Drummond Greyhounds of the LSWR, by D. L. Bradley
Stanier 4–6–0s of the LMS, by J. W. P. Rowledge and Brian Reed
Sulzer Diesel Locomotives of British Rail, by Brian Webb
AC Electric Locomotives of British Rail, by Brian Webb and John Duncan
The Deltic Locomotives of British Rail, by Brian Webb

The restored and preserved 'King George V' in steam at H. P. Bulmer & Company's
track, Hereford
(from a painting by Terence Cuneo)

DAVID & CHARLES LOCOMOTIVE MONOGRAPHS

THE GWR STARS, CASTLES & KINGS

New Omnibus Edition combining parts 1 and 2

O. S. NOCK, B.Sc., C.Eng., F.I.C.E., F.I.Mech.E.

DAVID & CHARLES

NEWTON ABBOT   LONDON   NORTH POMFRET (VT)

ISBN 0 7153 7977 1
First published in two parts:
Part 1 1967, 1969, 1975
Part 2 1970, 1973
This edition as a revised combined volume published 1980
©O. S. Nock 1967, 1970, 1980
Second impression 1981

Printed in Great Britain
by Redwood Burn Limited, Trowbridge, Wiltshire
for David & Charles (Publishers) Limited
Brunel House Newton Abbot Devon

Published in the United States of America
by David & Charles Inc
North Pomfret Vermont 05053 USA

CONTENTS

PREFACE TO OMNIBUS EDITION

THE span of few British locomotive families has extended over so long a period as that of the 'Stars', 'Castles' and 'Kings' of the GWR, and rarely under the same continuing influence all the time. In this respect this very famous locomotive dynasty differs profoundly from others of equal, or near-equal longevity. And it did not end after Nationalisation. Then, the Great Western itself may have ceased to exist, but the British Railways management, while drafting new standard designs to the Western Region never presumed to dictate alterations to purely Great Western designs. Swindon was allowed to retain complete autonomy so far as ex-GWR classes were concerned. So the story, from its very beginnings, through to the 1930s, and especially from 1948 onwards is straightforward. Inevitably however, over so long a period there were many changes of

detail on individual engines, and, faced with a vast amount of factual data, one has to be careful to distinguish between those changes which were significant, and those that were purely a matter of convenience or expediency in the course of repair work at Swindon. I am indebted to many enthusiasts for a plethora of notes of this kind, some of which have been included in the footnotes to the case histories of the three classes.

As regards the main line of development, which occupies most of the space in this book. I had the privilege, from Mr Hawksworth and his successors at Swindon, of seeing much of the later phases at first hand, with frequent opportunities of seeing tests in progress on the stationary plant, and from the dynamometer car; of studying drawing office and test records, and of riding many thousands of

The Churchward memorial headstone in Stoke Gabriel churchyard

The Churchward window in Stoke Gabriel parish church, South Devon

miles on the footplates of 'Stars', 'Castles' and 'Kings'. I am of, course, very much indebted to S. O. Ell who was in charge of dynamometer car testing after World War II and also to W. H. Pearce, the senior draughtsman who worked out the valve gears of the Churchward locomotives. On the 'running' side my thanks are due to W. N. Pellow, and H. E. A. White, successively Locomotive Running Superintendents, and to the many inspectors who were my guides and philosophers over many thousand miles of footplate travel. My special thanks are due to W. Andress, W. Button, A. Cameron, J. Hancock, A. Jenkins, H. Price and C. J. Pullen.

From the end of World War II until the end of steam traction, when I was travelling regularly and frequently between Bath and Paddington in the ordinary course of business, in addition to making many special journeys to record the locomotive performance, I compiled detailed logs of well over 1000 runs behind 'Stars', 'Castles' and 'Kings'. These engines and their work were not only of great interest to me as a railway enthusiast, but their reliability in service was an important factor in my business life. The background to this book is thus a very extensive experience of the daily work of these engines. Studying it in retrospect, the record of reliability is positively massive. Apart from one or two instances during the glacial winter of 1946-7, when owing to disruption of services, unprepared, or inadequately serviced engines were called upon in emergency, my records in regular business travelling did not include one single engine failure, and the occasions on which any time could be booked against engines amount to less than one per cent of all journeys made.

The indebtedness of the Great Western Railway, and of the Western Region afterwards, to Churchward, is something that his successors never forgot and in the highly modernised dynamometer car of 1955 there was room for a handsome portrait of 'The Old Man'. To add my own modest tribute I have included in this preface two of my photographs taken in the village of his birth, Stoke Gabriel, beside the River Dart.

O. S. NOCK

28 High Bannerdown,
Batheaston, Bath,
February 1980

CHAPTER 1

THE PRELUDE
'By Frenchman out of Albion'

IN the closing years of the nineteenth century the management of the Great Western Railway, finally rid of the encumbrance of the broad gauge, hammered out a policy of such widespread expansion as to constitute a positive resurgence of the spirit of Brunel. New cut-off lines were to be constructed, shortening the main lines to the West of England, to South Wales, and to Birmingham; train schedules faster than ever before were planned, and a new enthusiasm, drive, and sense of renewed purpose was fostered in the staff from end to end of the line. With the passing of the broad gauge there were many older servants of the company who felt that a little 'something' which other railways did not possess had been jettisoned; out of necessity maybe, but a little sadly. But the tremendous upsurge that followed restored, and emphasised to an extent perhaps never previously touched, that inherent Great Western 'pride in the job'.

Nowhere was this spirit more clearly manifested than in the Locomotive Department at Swindon Works. William Dean, Locomotive, Carriage and Wagon Superintendent, was a true industrial autocrat of the late Victorian era. His engines were beautiful to see, and economical to run. Dean on the Great Western, together with S. W. Johnson on the Midland, produced some of the most graceful, exquisitely-styled locomotives ever to run on rails. But then, towards the end of their careers, both engineers began to break with tradition and give their products an entirely new look. Dean began it with the 'Atbara' class of 4—4—0s, dating from 1898, and Johnson followed with his celebrated 'Belpaire' 4—4—0s of 1901. At Swindon, however, the change was undoubtedly due to the rising influence and stature of Dean's principal assistant, George Jackson Churchward, and in the 'Atbara' class 4—4—0s can be seen the first steps towards the great development that was to make

Swindon Works forever famous in the history of steam locomotive engineering.

Churchward was a man of immense vision. Even before he was called upon to take charge of the department he conceived a vast project of standardisation. He looked ahead to the great increases in traffic that were expected to come from the modernisation plans that were being launched by the Board; and just as Daniel Gooch had done when the Battle of the Gauges was at its height he planned to provide the GWR with locomotives, for all classes of traffic, that would be in advance of their time. Standardisation can lead to stagnation, and never more so than in locomotive engineering. But Churchward was looking at least 20 years ahead, when he formulated his historic proposals for no more than six standard classes to work the great bulk of the traffic on the line.

His first approaches to the practical task of setting this plan in action were made while Dean was still in full harness, and were concentrated entirely upon the development of a new design of boiler. Throughout his career Churchward attached an over-riding importance to boiler design, for without a free-steaming boiler a locomotive could not do its work on the road; and equally from the maintenance point of view the boiler could be the most expensive and troublesome part of the locomotive. To those who had delighted in the artistic appearance of Dean's express passenger engines, particularly the 7 ft. 8 in. 4—2—2 singles, the 'Atbaras' with their severe lines, came as something of a shock.

About the turn of the century the directors began to observe with great sadness that Dean's brilliant mind was beginning to give way, and with the utmost discretion they began to place more and more reliance upon Churchward for the management of the department. Never was the greatness of his personal character more finely shown than in those difficult years 1900, 1901 and 1902. He was on the threshold of attaining his life's ambition, in the complete confidence of the directors, yet exercising his delicate assignment with such kindliness and tact that Dean never felt that he was very gradually being superseded. It was in 1901 that the drawing was prepared showing the six standard classes for the future, and the first prototype, the 4—6—0 express passenger engine No. 100, was built in 1902 while Dean was still in office.

One feature was common to all these proposed standard classes. They were all to have two outside cylinders, with Stephenson's link motion inside, and those cylinders were to have the same diameter and stroke on every one of the six classes. All were to have domeless boilers, of varying sizes according to the duties for which the engines were designed, and only three diameters of coupled wheels were proposed. It was a magnificent conception, wholeheartedly endorsed by the Board, and eventually carried through in its entirety, and developed further in later years. Yet within five years of the preparation of that historic outline drawing of the six standard classes another had been introduced that cut right across the policy of standardising the machinery of all GWR main-line locomotives. Churchward had built his first four-cylinder simple express engine, the *North Star*, and this remarkable prototype founded the parallel dynasty of four-cylinder 4—6—0 locomotives that is the subject of this monograph.

Before coming to the locomotives themselves it is extremely interesting and important to recall the events that led Churchward to diverge from the very simple policy he had laid down in 1901, and which could in actual fact have been completely adequate to meet all the motive power needs of the GWR up to the time of his retirement, at the end of 1921. In terms of tractive ability the two-cylinder express passenger 4—6—0s of the 'Saint' class could, until that time, have equalled anything achieved by the four-cylinder 'Stars'; but the development of the four-cylinder engine, from 1906 onwards, was yet another example of Churchward's breadth of vision, and it does not need much consideration to appreciate how difficult it would have been to enlarge the 'Saint' to the tractive capacity ultimately represented by the 'Kings' of 1927.

Two basic features of future Great Western practice had nevertheless been established before consideration was given to a four-cylinder engine. The beginnings of the great development in boilers have already been mentioned; the second basic feature was the evolution of the long-lap, long-travel piston valve. Both these features, in their earliest form, were incorporated in the first express passenger 4—6—0, No. 100, completed at Swindon in February 1902. In his own mind Churchward had established a yardstick of express locomotive performance that was to be a guide to Swindon design for many years, namely the ability to sustain a drawbar pull of 2 tons at 70 m.p.h. on level track. At the time this was considerably in advance

William Dean: Locomotive, Carriage and Wagon Superintendent from 1877 to 1902

G. J. Churchward: succeeded Dean in 1902. His title was changed to that of Chief Mechanical Engineer, in 1916

The first evidence of the Churchward boiler development. The 'Badminton' class of 1897, with raised Belpaire firebox

of anything demanded elsewhere in Great Britain, and in addition to developing a range of boilers that would steam freely Churchward set out to obtain greater efficiencies in the cylinders, and so to obtain greater power from a given volume of steam passing through.

A prolonged study of the characteristics of valves, supported by experimental work on a single-cylinder stationary engine, had taught Churchward that the admission of steam to a cylinder without excessive loss of pressure, and its subsequent release without excessive back-pressure on the piston, could only be attained by the use of large piston valves. These valves must have a lap and travel about 50 per cent larger than was customary in British locomotives. Furthermore, to give a high expansion ratio, the clearance volume at the end of the cylinder when the piston was at the end of its stroke must be as small as possible, and to reduce to a minimum the condensation of steam as it entered a comparatively cold cylinder the surfaces of the piston and of the ends of the cylinder must be flat, and the steam ports must be short and straight.

Engine No. 100 was no more than a first prototype, and it went into traffic at the time when Dean's days at Swindon were ending. He retired in June 1902, and Churchward, succeeding him at the relatively early age of 45, could expect to continue in office for 20 years at least. At that time the passenger traffic of the GWR did not immediately need much larger and more powerful locomotives.

A further development: 'Waterford' of the Badminton class, with domeless boiler, built at Swindon 1899

The flowing curves of the Dean era vanish in the 'Atbara' class of 1900. Engine No. 3373 'Atbara', built at Swindon, temporarily renamed 'Britannia' for a Royal Train working

There was no motive power crisis facing Churchward in 1902, such as faced George Whale on the London & North Western Railway, when he succeeded Webb in 1903. The Dean 7 ft. 8 in. 4—2—2s and the 'Atbaras' were entirely adequate for the job, and indeed while his 'big engine' policy was gradually evolved Churchward built more inside-cylinder 4—4—0s, in 1903. These engines, the 'City' class, significantly equipped with tapered boiler barrels, did such brilliant work in the years 1903 and 1904 that not a few experienced observers questioned the need for the large ten-wheeled express passenger engines that were emerging from Swindon in ones and twos in those years.

Nine months after Churchward became Chief his second 4—6—0 appeared—No. 98, later 2998 *Ernest Cunard*. In the year which had elapsed since the completion of No. 100, all the main features of the future Great Western outside-cylinder locomotive had been worked out. The boiler and the firebox had acquired tapers, and the cylinder layout and valve gear had reached the form which they were to retain until the construction of GWR locomotives ceased. There were refinements still to come—extended smokeboxes, superheating, topfeed, improved piston valves, and other details—but here was a locomotive which, with no change in its basic layout and proportions, was still to be engaged on express work fifty years later.

It has often been said that the principles under-lying the design of Churchward's locomotives were not revealed to his contemporaries. But for those who could combine a period of observation at Paddington with a study of such dimensions as were published in the technical press, and with the contributions made by Churchward to the discussions of the Institutions of Mechanical and Civil Engineers, there was little mystery. Furthermore, in the privacy of meetings of the Association of Railway Locomotive Engineers there emerged more detailed information than ever appeared in print. The reluctance of his contemporaries to adopt Churchward's ideas was not due to ignorance of the motives behind them, but to lack of conviction that there was justification for the complication and expense of the distinctive Churchward features.

It is interesting to follow the lines of Churchward's arguments as recorded by his own contributions to the proceedings of the engineering institutions. On 2 February 1906, Churchward read his only paper to one of these bodies—'Large Locomotive Boilers'—presented to the Institution of Mechanical Engineers. The opening words of this paper summarise the aims of his sequence of boiler experiments.

'The modern locomotive problem is principally a question of boiler. . . The higher temperatures incidental to the higher pressures have required . . . much more liberal water spaces and better provision for circulation.'

The pioneer GWR passenger 4—6—0 No. 100 as originally built 1902. Later named 'William Dean' and numbered 2900

He considered that the troubles which many engineers were having with large boilers were caused mainly by poor circulation between the inner and outer fireboxes, particularly adjacent to the rear tubeplate. As the 'main mass of the fire is nearer the tubeplate', it is here that the greatest circulation of water is required to absorb the heat. In many large boilers the water space for circulation round the inner firebox had not increased in proportion to the greater quantity of heat produced in the firebox, and this led to local overheating, damaged plates, and leaking stays and tubes. Insufficient water circulated around the front of the firebox for the water spaces at the sides of the firebox to be kept fully supplied, with consequent damage to the rear of the firebox.

Churchward discussed various methods for improving the circulation between the firebox itself and its outer casing, such as circulating pipes outside the boiler to bring the water to each side of the firebox, and the introduction of the feed water into the spaces between the inner and outer fireboxes. His own solution was to increase the space between the fireboxes where the need was greatest, that is,

at the front. At this section of the boiler he left a clear space between the tubes and the sides of the barrel equal to the combined area of the vertical spaces between the tubes, so ensuring that as water rose between the tubes and between the fireboxes an adequate down-flow was maintained to feed the water space in front of the throat plate. The effect of these proportions was to produce the tapered barrel and tapered firebox. Between the inner and outer fireboxes the water space increased in width from bottom to top, to allow for the greater volume of the water as bubbles of steam formed.

He had found that less trouble was experienced with the flat-topped firebox than with the round-topped. In a flat-topped firebox the surface area of the water is greater than in a round-topped, and there is thus more surface for the release of bubbles of steam. This had been found to reduce foaming, and had enabled him to take steam from the front of the firebox casing. He could then dispense with the dome—'always a source of weakness'. He had tried two identical boilers, one domed and the other domeless, and had found the domeless boiler 'decidedly freer from priming'. The 'liberal dimen-

The second express 4—6—0, No. 98, built 1903 in which all the standard features of the two-cylinder stud were incorporated

15

sion' of 2 ft. between the top of the firebox and the casing no doubt contributed to this.

Churchward's reasons for using high pressures were then given: 'Higher pressures have produced more efficient locomotives, both in respect of hauling power and coal consumption. The improvement was marked with every increment right up to 227 lb. per sq. in. By employing 225 lb. per sq. in. in the simple engine, and making the necessary improvements in the steam distribution, enabling higher [i.e. earlier] cut-offs to be used, corresponding improvements in efficiency and economy of fuel have been obtained. A great increase in drawbar pull has also resulted. Of course, a price for these improvements has to be paid in firebox repairs, but it is probably better to submit to this expense than to employ the very much heavier and more costly machines which would be necessary to give the same hauling power at high speeds' [that is, with lower pressures].

A sideline on the Churchward locomotives appeared in James Stirling's contribution to the discussion. He said: 'Many of the very interesting diagrams the author has shown are novel in shape and expensive in construction; they may be good, but they are certainly not "bonnie", to use a Scottish expression.'

In his reply, Churchward expressed his views on locomotive aesthetics: 'I feel really hurt that Mr. Stirling should have said that I have so disgracefully spoiled the appearance of the British locomotive. I know that I have been accused of spoiling the appearance of the British locomotive as much as any man in the country, but I take exception to the statement. In my opinion there is no canon of art in regard to the appearance of the locomotive as a machine except that which an engineer has set up for himself, by observing from time to time types of locomotive which he has been led from his nursery days upwards to admire.'

Which of the broad-gauge locomotives that Churchward must have seen in his native Devon had inspired the gaunt lines of No. 100 is not clear, but it is interesting to note that just a year after the reading of this paper 'Star' No. 4001 appeared with curved footplating at the front and rear. This simple change, the details of which were worked out by H. Holcroft, made a striking improvement in the appearance of Churchward's 4—6—0 locomotives, and was a standard feature of all subsequent Swindon 4—6—0s.

At a very early stage in his career it became evident that much of Churchward's genius lay in the ability to appreciate existing work, and to apply

The French-built four-cylinder compound 4—4—2 No. 102 'La France', introduced 1903; at Bristol, at the time when she was painted black

The Second French compound No. 103, after receiving the name 'President'; purchased 1905

it by adaptation and development to the needs of the GWR. He was not the isolationist inventor, working in the back room as it were with no heed of what was going on in the world at large; neither was he in the slightest degree a copyist. His development of the tapered boiler originated from his interest in American practice; but the final Swindon design, exemplified in the Standard No. 1 Boiler, and the progenitor of more than 2,000 boilers on the GWR, the LMS and the nationalised British Railways, was entirely his own. And from American ideas in the form of the so-called wagon-top boilers, bar frames and other detail features, he turned to France, where the four-cylinder compound 'Atlantics' of Alfred de Glehn's design were compelling the attention of all locomotive engineers, by their magnificent performances on the boat expresses running between Paris, Boulogne and Calais, and on other fast services of the Northern Railway.

Churchward's interest in these locomotives went to the extent of his obtaining permission to order one for trial in England. The French loading gauge was sufficiently near to that of the GWR for it to be possible to order a de Glehn compound 4—4—2 which was almost a replica of the Nord "2641" class. A few fittings were modified to suit Great Western requirements, notably the chimney, smokebox door, and brake equipment, and the rear end was made suitable for attaching to a standard tender. The locomotive was built by the Société Alsacienne des Constructions Mechaniques at Belfort in France, and was received by the GWR in October 1903. It was numbered 102 and named *La France*.

The design followed the normal lines of a de Glehn compound. The high-pressure cylinders were

outside, and drove the trailing coupled wheels, and the low-pressure cylinders drove the leading coupled wheels. The locomotive could be worked as a simple by allowing the exhaust from the high-pressure cylinders to pass to atmosphere, and by admitting boiler steam to the low-pressure cylinders through a reducing valve. There were separate sets of Walscheart's valve gear for the inside and outside cylinders, with provision for varying the cut-off in the two sets of cylinders independently or together. The firebox was 10 in. longer than that of the GWR 4—6—0s, giving a grate area of 29.5 sq. ft. instead of 27.1 sq. ft. The firebox heating surface was greater, and the use of Serve tubes made the tube heating surface greater despite a shorter barrel. The boiler pressure was 227 lb. per sq. in.

The fame of the de Glehn compounds came from their high power output at speed, and from their economy. In buying this locomotive Churchward intended to find by direct comparison whether or not the benefits of compounding could equal the improvements which he had made in the simple engine. His views on the experiment were expressed publicly in the discussion on a paper entitled 'Compound Locomotives' read on 18 March 1904 to the Institution of Mechanical Engineers by M. Edouard Sauvage, Chief Consulting Engineer to the Western Railway of France. The paper reviewed the development of the modern compound locomotive in France, and in his conclusions the author said that: '. . . by their use the French railways have been enabled to increase largely the weight and speed of their trains . . . without any large increase of coal consumption. . . . A complete solution of the problem would require proof that the same results might not be obtained in some other

17

B

way. Available data are not sufficient to give such a proof in an indisputable manner; still, it seems difficult to build an ordinary locomotive quite equal in every respect to the latest compounds.' It might have the same boiler, but 'with the ordinary valve gear of the locomotive, steam at such a high pressure cannot be as well utilised (in a simple locomotive) as by compounding'. The simple locomotive would require more steam for the same work.

These remarks gave Churchward the opportunity to outline the work which he had done to improve the performance of his locomotives, and at the same time to pay a tribute to his staff. After saying that the compound had been brought to a point of greater perfection in France than in any country—which explained his purchase of *La France*—he said that in his judgment 'no really fair and square tests between the advantages of compound and simple have ever been made'.

Some of the earliest trials had been between compounds working at 200 lb. per sq. in. and simple locomotives working at 175 lb. per sq. in. He then came to the crux of the matter: 'I shall no doubt be told that high pressures were used in the compound in the belief that it was impossible by any known valve gear to use the same pressures to advantage in a simple cylinder. I thought that that had yet to be proved, and I have had the courage to fit a simple engine with 18 in. by 30 in. cylinders, and with a boiler carrying 225 lb. per sq. in. I have done that with the deliberate idea of finding whether such improvements can be made in the valve gear, and consequent steam distribution, as to enable the simple cylinder to use steam of that pressure as efficiently as the compound engine.'

He had made the powers at high speed nearly equal. In the compound he used the recommended cut-offs of 55 per cent and 65 per cent in the h.p. and l.p. cylinders, and in the simple he used 20-25 per cent cut-off. He continued: 'It would seem no doubt ambitious to expect such power as was developed at 55 per cent and 65 per cent by the compound out of a cylinder cutting off at 20-25 per cent, but I am pleased to say that with the assistance of an efficient staff, a good deal of very hard work, and a determination to see what could be done with the valve gear, I believe such improvements have been made in the steam distribution that a satisfactory result can be ensured from as high a cut-off as 15-20 per cent.'

He had obtained a 2-ton drawbar pull at 70 m.p.h. both from *La France* and from his simple locomotive with 200 lb. per sq. in. working at 25 per cent cut-off. From the 225 lb. per sq. in. locomotive he expected to get 2 tons at 75 m.p.h.

on a shorter cut-off. Theoretically the steam consumption of the compound working at 55 per cent and 65 per cent was the same as that of the simple working at 25 per cent, so that he had the means for a more equal trial than ever before. He then said that although *La France* had not yet worked sufficient mileage to give reliable figures of coal consumption, it was doing 'very first class work indeed on the GWR', and had entirely fulfilled his expectations'.

Further remarks of Churchward's, later in the discussion, gave the first hint of his thoughts on four-cylinder locomotives. The author had stressed that the division of the drive between two axles on the de Glehn compounds reduced the loads on the coupling rods and axleboxes. Of this Churchward said: 'I am not sure that at present we have arrived at the point at which we must divide the engine, but we shall soon do so if the engine grows much bigger.' He further remarked that it had been suggested that a divided engine with four cylinders gave a more even torque, but he could not see this.

It is thus clear that in March 1903 Churchward was satisfied that his two-cylinder 4—6—0 was the equal of the French compound in power output at speed, and that as yet he saw no advantage to be derived from a four-cylinder locomotive. Tests soon showed that the fuel consumption of the compound was only slightly better than that of the GWR locomotives and there seemed to be no reason to expect that a departure from the two-cylinder locomotive would be deemed necessary in the foreseeable future—either for the possible fuel economy of a compound or for the mechanical advantages inherent in any four-cylinder locomotive with divided drive.

Churchward's remarks show that he believed that he had made a fair and square comparison of compound and simple working. The equality of his own locomotives with the compound came from the improvements which he had made in the valve gear and steam distribution compared with what he termed the 'old-fashioned simple engine'. It seems surprising that he did not incorporate these same improvements in a compound, to give an even fairer comparison with the simple. That he did not do so was not because he had finally rejected the compound from his plans, for two years later he ordered two more French compounds of another type. It can only be assumed that, as his own cylinder improvements were aimed at producing high power at short cut-offs, he did not expect them to produce a marked difference in a compound, which necessarily works at longer cut-offs than a simple engine giving the same power output.

For the tests against *La France,* Churchward had built a further 4—6—0, No. 171, later 2971 *Albion.* This differed from No. 98 in having the boiler pressure raised from 200 to 225 lb. per sq. in. This achieved the double effect of making the pressure almost equal to that of *La France,* and of making the nominal tractive effort of the two locomotives almost equal—23,710 lb. for *La France* and 23,090 for *Albion.* After the Frenchman had run for a year, the comparison was made even closer by the conversion of No. 171 to a 4—4—2. In retrospect this conversion seems surprising for, despite the easy gradients on many parts of the GWR, there were a number of stretches where the loss of adhesive weight would seriously prejudice the performance of the 'Atlantic'. Even more surprising was the construction of fourteen more 'Atlantics', thirteen with two cylinders and one with four. The two-cylinder engines appeared in 1905, and in the same year six more two-cylinder 4—6—0s were built. In later years these were all assimilated into the 'Saint' class, and it will be convenient to refer to them by that name.

In 1905 there also appeared the additional French compounds, Nos. 103 and 104. These locomotives were similar to the Paris-Orleans 3001 class, modified to suit the GWR loading gauge. They were larger than No. 102 in most of their leading dimensions, the most notable figure being the grate area of 33.4 sq. ft.

The trials of the new Frenchmen showed that there was again little difference in the fuel consumption from the Churchward locomotives; indeed, the larger Frenchmen were slightly inferior. The duplication of cylinders made their oil consumption greater. Against this it was expected that the division of drive between two axles, which reduced the loading on the axleboxes due to piston thrust, would enable the locomotives to run greater mileages between general repairs. The improved balance of the four-cylinder layout also made the riding better than that of the two-cylinder engines. The advantages of the Frenchmen were therefore mechanical rather than thermal, and Churchward finally abandoned any idea of compounding. The mechanical advantages, however, were not yet fully investigated.

But the French influence at Swindon was nevertheless profound. The compound 'Atlantics' ran with exceptional smoothness, and as mileage increased they were not subject to the roughness that develops almost inevitably in a locomotive with two outside cylinders. One can think of many other famous designs outside the GWR that were rough and uncomfortable to ride upon, such as 'King Arthurs' of the Southern, Stanier 'Black-Fives' and the whole range of British standard locomotives. The two-cylinder engine is ideal for general-purpose work; but in long-distance express passenger traffic, such as was being actively developed on the GWR in the early 1900s, the desire for a smooth-riding engine was more than a mere question of comfort on the footplate. To lessen vibration and knocking enginemen will work with longer cut-offs and partly-opened regulator; and this, in limiting the range of expansion of the steam would defeat the very object on which Churchward had so fixedly set his sights, in his adoption of high boiler pressure, and long-lap, long-travel valves.

Thus, by Frenchman out of *Albion* was born the first Great Western four-cylinder *simple* express passenger locomotive, the famous prototype, No. 40, *North Star,* built originally as an 'Atlantic' in 1906.

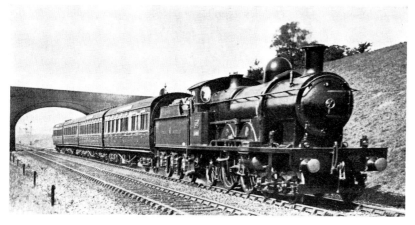

'La France', in standard GWR colours, working an up 2-hour Birmingham express near Denham

The third French compound, No. 104, as newly delivered, before the name 'Alliance' was added

By Frenchman out of Albion

'Albion' in later days, numbered 2971, and descending Dainton bank, near Newton Abbot, with the Penzance – Aberdeen express. The third and fourth coaches in the train are ex-North British Railway stock

CHAPTER 2

THE 'NORTH STAR'

CONSTRUCTION of the new and epoch-marking four-cylinder simple express locomotive was authorised by the Locomotive and Stores Committee of the Board on 19 July 1905, at an estimated cost of £3,600. This compared with £3,200 for the two-cylinder 'Atlantics' and £4,300 for the larger Frenchmen. The comparison of 4—4—2 and 4—6—0 locomotives had not yet convinced Churchward of the superiority of the 4—6—0, and as the inspiration of the four-cylinder design was the French 'Atlantic', the new design was therefore given this wheel arrangement. As on all the Churchward 4—4—2s, the trailing wheels were located in additional plate frames attached outside the main frames. The main frames had holes cut in them to reduce weight just where the trailing axle would fit if the engine were converted to a 4—6—0, but the holes were of such a size as to make it impracticable to use the same rear end of the frames in the conversion.

In less than two years from his statement that the time had not yet arrived at which 'we must divide the engine', Churchward had thus produced his first engine with divided drive, and in doing so

had evolved the prototype of 269 famous machines. It is clear that the move into four-cylinder engines was influenced not by any dissatisfaction with the existing two-cylinder engines, but by the new evidence produced by the experiences with the Frenchmen. This was the first sign of a decline in the American influence on Churchward, and of the rise of a French influence which was to affect a number of details of design in the coming years.

The design of No. 40, later named *North Star*, showed a marked regression from some of the extreme American influences apparent in Churchward's two-cylinder machines. The boiler was generally similar, and retained the working pressure of 225 lb. per sq. in. which had been introduced for comparison with the Frenchmen. The main difference in the boiler, and one which was quite noticeable, was that the taper of the barrel extended over its full length, whereas in the previous types of boiler on the ten-wheeled engines the taper extended along half the length only. The chassis showed marked differences from the two-cylinder types. Churchward considered that, for the full benefit to be derived from the improved balance

The 'North Star' as originally built, 1906, before receiving the name. Note the small holes below the valve rocker for access to the inside motion

21

The 'fountain head': the locomotive drawing office at Swindon in GWR days

of the divided drive, the inside and outside connecting rods must be of equal length. This could only be achieved by setting the outside cylinders as far back as possible, and the inside cylinders as far forward as possible. The outside cylinders were thus opposite the rear bogie wheels, a position which limited the size of cylinder which could be attained in later developments of the type. The inside cylinders projected beyond the smokebox, so that the inside slidebars and much of the valve gear were enclosed between the smokebox and the bogie, and were thus relatively inaccessible.

The wheelbase of the locomotive was 8 in. greater than that of the 'Saints'. Of the increase 6 in. was in the distance from the rear coupled axle to the trailing wheels, and the remaining 2 in. between the rear bogie axle and the leading coupled axle. The bogie was of the then-standard swing-link type, with the same wheelbase as those of the 'Saints'.

The arrangement of cylinders made the use of plate frames almost inevitable. The American type of cylinder and bar frame construction could not be adapted to a layout in which there were two pairs of cylinders out of line with one another. The alternate thrust on the front and back covers of an outside cylinder tends to 'rock' the cylinder on the frames, and if bending of the frames is to be avoided, there must be massive bracing of the frame opposite the cylinders. In the Churchward two-cylinder locomotives, the combined smokebox

saddle and cylinders form a rigid box well able to resist the thrust in the cylinders. The inside cylinders of the four-cylinder locomotives also formed a rigid box, as do any inside cylinders, but the outside cylinders presented a difficult problem. They were attached at a point where the frames were weakened by the cut-out required to allow translation of the rear bogie wheels. It was thus necessary to stiffen the frames by a massive bracket which impeded access to the inside cylinders from above, and made the use of a pit for working on the inside motion almost a necessity. The frames were stepped in, or 'joggled' opposite the inside cylinders to leave clearance for the translation of the front bogie wheels.

The position of the outside cylinders made it impossible to use the same type of slidebar as on the two-cylinder 4—4—2s. These latter had the motion bracket ahead of the coupled wheels, and the slidebars were supported at about the middle of their length. On the four-cylinder machine the only convenient place for the motion bracket was between the coupled wheels. The slidebars had therefore to be extended beyond their normal length to reach the motion bracket, and at their outer ends they had to be tapered outwards to give clearance for the connecting rod. This produced the very distinctive slidebars which were a conspicuous feature of all the Great Western four-cylinder locomotives.

22

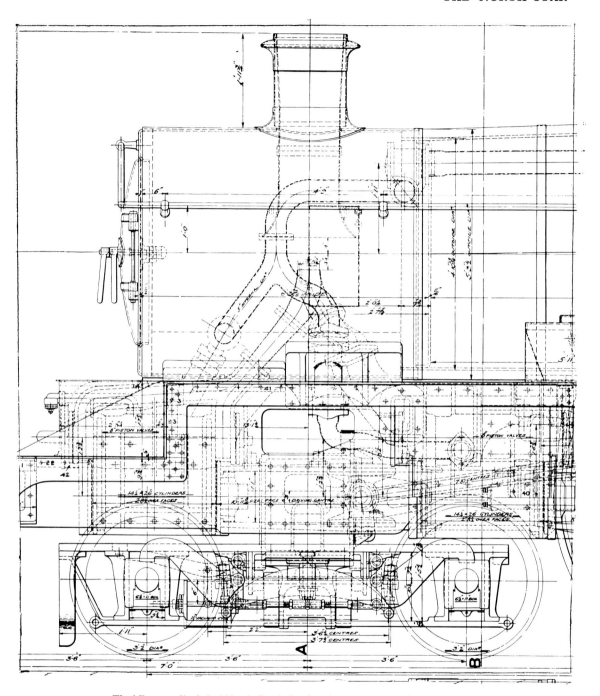

The 'Front end' of the 'North Star' showing the arrangement of steam pipes, the
two-framed bogie, and the bogie brake linkage

The use of inside cranks, combined with the generous size of axlebox and crankpin which Churchward employed, left insufficient room for inside Stephenson valve gear. Churchward was impressed by the Walschaert's gear of the Frenchmen, but he thought it very light, and described it as a 'watchmaker's job'. In his two-cylinder engines he had used a massive valve gear with generous bearing surfaces. This gear would not deflect under the heaviest loads, and would suffer little wear between general repairs; it ensured that the valve setting was maintained with little deterioration, in sharp contrast to the behaviour of the locomotives of some other railways. As Churchward proposed to use two valve gears for four valves, the valve gear of the four-cylinder engine must therefore be at least as massive as that of the two-cylinder machines and he considered that there was insufficient room within the loading gauge for an outside gear with links of the requisite size.

Yet another objection to an outside valve gear was that Churchward's outside connecting rods had solid-bush big ends, so that an outside valve gear would have had to be partly dismantled to allow the removal of a connecting rod (this in fact has to be done on thousands of locomotives on other railways). It was thought that, provided that the valve gear could be made as durable as that of the two-cylinder engines, the big end would need to be taken down more frequently than the valve gear.

With an outside gear behind the cylinder and a rocking lever ahead of it, some part of the valve gear would have had to be disconnected before an outside valve could have been removed. On top of all these technical objections was Churchward's aesthetic objection to any unnecessary outside fittings. Whatever the critics might dislike in his early locomotives, they must have agreed that only the bare essentials of the mechanism were visible.

A study of the characteristics of Stephenson and Walschaert's gears, designed with the same steam lap, port size, and valve travel, showed that at short cut-offs, although the maximum opening of the valve to steam was the same for both gears, the tendency of the valve with Walschaert's gear to 'dwell' at the end of its movement caused it to admit more steam to the cylinder whilst it was open. As it was expected that the four-cylinder engine would be capable of doing much of its work at 15 per cent cut-off, which gave the maximum possible expansion ratio in the cylinder, the Walschaert's gear offered an advantage.

W. H. Pearce, the draughtsman who had designed the Churchward Stephenson gear, began to sketch a Walschaert's gear for the four-cylinder engine, and hit on the idea of simplifying this gear further by eliminating eccentrics altogether. He proposed to use the crosshead of one inside cylinder to provide the equivalent of the eccentric of the other inside cylinder. In the Walschaert's gear the

The wooden model of the proposed 'scissors' valve gear made by
W. H. Pearce, in June 1905

24

final drive to the valve is compounded of two motions, one taken from the crosshead of the cylinder concerned, and the other from an eccentric or return crank at 90 deg. to the crank of the cylinder. This second component can alternatively be taken from the crosshead of the other cylinder, since the cranks of the two cylinders are at 90 deg. There is some geometrical complication in fitting two gears of this type between the two sets of slide-bars, but the arrangement eliminates eccentrics, and leaves the crank axle unencumbered. This gave two advantages: it reduced the unsprung weight on the crank axle, and it also removed a weakness of all gears in which a drive is taken from an eccentric or return crank—that in any position of the axle in which the eccentric rod is inclined to the horizontal, movement of the axle on its springs causes a small displacement of the valve.

Pearce made a wooden model of this gear in June 1905, and submitted it to Churchward, who ordered the gear to be fitted to the engine. The wooden model is still in existence. This same idea had previously occurred to a number of other engineers, both locomotive and marine, but Pearce was quite unaware of this when the idea came to him. R. M. Deeley is said to have designed a gear of this type when he was an assistant to S. W. Johnson on the Midland Railway at Derby. He showed the scheme to Johnson, who would have nothing to do with it; but when Deeley himself succeeded Johnson he revived the idea for his large 4—4—0 No. 990. On 11 August 1905 he applied for a patent for the gear, which was granted in June 1906. In the meantime No. 40 had appeared from Swindon fitted with Pearce's gear, which from the shape of the expansion link levers earned the name of 'scissors' gear.

It was said at Swindon that a strong letter arrived from Deeley accusing Churchward of using the Deeley gear without acknowledgement. There was no difficulty in establishing that the Swindon gear was designed before Deeley applied for his patent, and that Churchward had every right to use it. In its characteristics, the scissors gear was similar to Walschaert's, that is, the lead was constant at all positions of cut-off. The Stephenson gear, as used in the two-cylinder locomotives, has the characteristic that the lead decreases as cut-off is increased, and it therefore makes an engine better at starting, and on hill climbing at low speed.

The gear fitted to No. 40 had a disadvantage. If a defect developed in one cylinder, motion, or valve gear of a two-cylinder locomotive, involving dismantling of the connecting rod, the locomotive had a good prospect of moving itself off the running lines, or even of reaching a shed, on the surviving cylinder. With the cross-connected gear, the disconnection of one connecting rod automatically immobilised the valve gear of the other cylinder, and the locomotive could not move itself. For this reason the scissors gear was not used on subsequent four-cylinder engines, but it remained in No. 40 until 1929, when the engine was rebuilt as a 'Castle'. The valve gear of the subsequent Great Western four-cylinder locomotives incorporated a detail which made it easy to fasten one pair of valves in their mid-position in an emergency, so this requirement was evidently important to Churchward.

The rocking shaft for operating the outside valves was slightly cranked to allow for the angularity of the connecting rods. This design detail, which was due to Pearce, may be explained by mentioning that the inclination of the connecting rod causes the motion of the piston of a locomotive to be non-symmetrical, the piston being nearer to the rear of the cylinder at any instant (except at the dead-centres) than the position of the crank would suggest. The shorter the connecting rod in proportion to the throw of the crank, the greater is the inclination of the connecting rod. If the point of cut-off is to be the same at both ends of the cylinder, the movement of the valve must also be non-symmetrical to match the motion of the piston. In all well-designed valve gears there is a geometrical device for giving the valve the correct non-symmetrical motion. If, in a four-cylinder locomotive, the valve of one cylinder is driven by a rocker from the valve of another cylinder, the rocker has the correct motion for the valve from which it is driven, and this gives a 'correction' in the wrong direction to the valve which is driven by the rocker. The cranking of the rocker on the Great Western four-cylinder locomotives was cleverly arranged to cancel the correction given to the inside valves, and to apply the proper correction to the outside valves. Its success is proved by the clear, short beats which give no indication that two cylinders are exhausting simultaneously.

The gear contained another of Pearce's novel ideas. It was usual in Walschaert's gear of that time for the radius rod to be supported from the reversing crank by a vertical swinging link attached ahead of the expansion link. There was usually only a limited space above the valve gear for this swinging link, which had perforce to be short. The point of attachment to the radius rod therefore swung in a small arc, and there was significant rise and fall of the radius rod as it moved from one end of its travel to the other. This caused unnecessary slip of

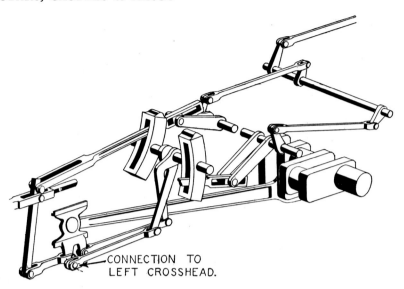

—CONNECTION TO
LEFT CROSSHEAD.

Pictorial drawing of the 'scissors' gear as applied to the 'North Star'

the die block in the expansion link, and consequent wear. With the long travel of the radius rod on the Great Western locomotives this slip would have been serious, and it was therefore reduced greatly by positioning the reversing crank behind the expansion link, and in line with the pivot of the link. The movement of the radius rod relative to the crank was accommodated by a die block working in a slot in the reversing crank. This die block introduced additional wearing surfaces, but slight wear at these surfaces does not affect the movement of the valve, whereas wear at the expansion link die block does. This method of supporting the radius rod was adopted by Gresley on his 2—6—0s, and later became a common arrangement.

One striking feature of the Churchward two-cylinder types was the use of 30 in. piston stroke. In a letter to Mr. A. V. Goodyear, dated 25 October 1909, Churchward wrote: 'It is correct that there are great advantages in the 30 in. stroke in the matter of expansive working. The long stroke in relation to the bore is the only way we know of making the simple engine equal in efficiency to the compound engine. You are correct in assuming that the adoption of the 4-cylinder design was not on account of any dissatisfaction with the 18 in. by 30 in. cylinders—the relation of stroke to bore is even greater in the 4-cylinder than in the 2-cylinder engines.'

The actual cylinder diameter was $14\frac{1}{4}$ in., an odd figure, but one which made the cylinder dimensions very close to those of the high-pressure cylinders of the larger Frenchmen ($14\frac{3}{16}$ in. by $25\frac{3}{16}$ in.). Whether this diameter was influenced by the

French figure, or whether it was reckoned to be the largest which would safely be used with the boiler, is not recorded. Certainly there is no evidence that it made the nominal tractive effort identical with any other engine. The reduction of the stroke to 26 in. made a useful contribution towards improving the balance of the four-cylinder locomotive, compared with the two-cylinder, by reducing the inertia forces of the reciprocating parts. Even in the four-cylinder design these forces produced couples tending to sway the engine, and as the whole justification for the complication of the four-cylinder arrangement was better balance, this further contribution was welcome.

The four-cylinder layout involved some other changes in detail from the two-cylinder machines, but these were kept to a minimum. In accordance with prevailing Swindon practice, bogie brakes were fitted. There were compensating beams between the springs of the coupled wheels. There was further evidence of French influence in the use of a forked big-end for the inside connecting rod. The arrangement of the exhaust pipes from the cylinders to the blast pipe was a problem on all the GWR four-cylinder types because of the considerable distances from the cylinders to the blast pipe. In No. 40 the four branch exhaust pipes were formed from copper plate, beaten to shape and brazed.

The coupling rods were of I-section, which allowed them to be of lighter weight than rectangular section rods designed to withstand the same maximum thrust. Unfortunately, No. 40 several times bent its coupling rods, and this trouble was cured by replacing the I-section rods by rectangular

'North Star' as an 'Atlantic' and as yet unnamed passing Old Oak Common with the down Cornish Riviera Express

ones. The explanation of this apparent anomaly is that rectangular rods designed to withstand the same thrust as I-section ones are less stiff laterally, that is, against bending in a horizontal plane. They can withstand a greater lateral deflection than the I-section rods before the metal reaches its 'elastic limit'. A similar trouble was encountered with the British Railways 'Britannia' Pacifics, and an investigation showed that the cranks of the two wheels on certain axles were not set at exactly 90 deg. As a result, at each revolution of the wheels, the coupling rods tried to lengthen and shorten, and were thus subjected to an alternating stress. The combination of this stress with the normal effect of the piston

thrust caused the rods to bend laterally. With the I-section rods this led to overstressing and ultimate failure, but when rectangular section rods were fitted the trouble was cured, as they could withstand the lateral deflection without distress.

Apart from two later experiments on small batches of engines with alloy steel rods, rectangular section coupling rods were used on all subsequent GWR ten-wheeled engines. It should be noted, however, that other railways used I-section rods without difficulty, and it is likely that with the high standards of accuracy which were later attained at Swindon they could have been used there also.

The general outline of the locomotive was in

The rear end of 'North Star,' showing back sanding gear and original brake gear

A later view of 'North Star' showing large diameter chimney, as later standardised

'North Star' as first rebuilt as a 4—6—0 in 1909 with half-cone superheated boiler, and de Glehn type bogie

accordance with the first phase of the Churchward 4—4—2s and 4—6—0s, that is, the footplating continued in an unbroken line under the cab, and there was a vertical rise in the footplating ahead of the cylinders. The external lines of the boiler were free from the various fittings which crept in over the next ten years. As already mentioned, the boiler had a taper extending over the full length of the barrel, but for the first time the length of the smokebox reached a figure of 6 ft. This increase in smokebox length was necessary to bring the smoke-box over part of the inside cylinders, so that the steam and exhaust pipes could be connected directly from the cylinder casting to the smokebox. The same length of smokebox was subsequently adopted as standard for the No. 1 Standard Boiler, and was thus used on the two-cylinder 4—6—0s also. The chimney was of smaller diameter than that which later became standard.

No. 40 was completed in April 1906, and in September of the same year was named *North Star*. This revived a famous broad-gauge name, and gave the name 'Stars' to a class that was eventually to include not only the celestial bodies, but also male and female royalty, the nobility, and finally some monastic buildings. The appearance of No. 40 aroused great interest amongst Great Western enthusiasts, and many of them must have made journeys behind the engine to record its performance. It is therefore surprising and disappointing to find no record in the contemporary press of any notable running by it. The loading of most of the main-line trains was still moderate, 300-ton trains being uncommon; and Churchward does not seem to have conducted any tests with heavy loads despite the fact that the four-cylinder design was contemplated only for the heaviest express work. The engine was not tested on the Swindon testing plant, because the capacity of the plant was then insufficient to produce any useful information about a locomotive of this size.

The only run by No. 40 recorded by C. Rous-Marten was on the down 'Cornish Riviera Express' with a tare load of 290 tons to Westbury, 255 tons to Taunton, 220 tons to Exeter, and 185 tons to Plymouth. The train made a net time of 92 minutes

No. 40 with the later standard full-cone boiler and top feed, at Laira shed

'North Star' in wartime austerity livery, numbered 4000

Another stage in the history of 'No. 40'; long cone boiler; small diameter chimney; no top feed. Shown passing Old Oak Common with the down Cornish Riviera Express in 1911

to Westbury, 142 minutes to Taunton, and 170 minutes to Exeter. The 32 miles from Reading to Savernake occupied 32 minutes. The maximum speed was 80 m.p.h. near Patney, and on Wellington bank speed fell to 45 m.p.h. before Whiteball and to 43 m.p.h. in the tunnel. The minimum on Dainton bank was 24 m.p.h. and on the climb to Rattery 25 m.p.h. Rous-Marten commented that this run was 'on the whole creditable, but there were indications that with heavier load, and less favourable weather, greater adhesion would be needed'. The performance was well within the capacity of a 'Saint'.

The later history of *North Star* can be summarised briefly here. In November 1909 it was rebuilt as a 4—6—0, with the wheelbase shortened by 6 in. to conform with the later 'Stars'. New frames were provided, but the footplate remained $2\frac{1}{2}$ in. higher than on the other 'Stars'. The casing over the inside cylinders was replaced by the more elegant pattern which had been introduced with No. 4021. By this time the exchange of boilers at general repairs had become normal, and *North Star* received one of the half-cone boilers originally fitted to 'Saints'. In June 1911 another long-cone boiler was fitted, and the engine ran in this condition—although not with the same boiler—for eighteen years. In November 1929 it emerged from its second rebuilding as a 'Castle'. This involved lengthening of the frames to take the larger firebox. The scissors gear was replaced by the normal Walschaert's gear of the four-cylinder engines. The footplating remained at its original height, so that *North Star*, which had been unique amongst 'Stars', now became a unique 'Castle'. In the partial renumbering of December 1912, which brought together engines of identical or similar type, *North Star* became No. 4000. It was withdrawn from service in May 1957.

CHAPTER 3

THE CELESTIAL 'STARS'

THE main attraction of the four-cylinder layout was that, by reducing the loads on axleboxes and motion bearings, it would enable the locomotive to run greater mileages between general repairs. It might therefore have been expected that a long period of trial running would have been necessary to produce evidence that the improvement in mileage would justify the additional cost of the four-cylinder express locomotive. The construction of a batch of ten 4—6—0s was authorised by the Locomotive Committee on 8 August 1906 at a cost of £3,700 each. Ten months only elapsed between the completion of *North Star* and the appearance of the first of the 4—6—0s—No. 4001 *Dog Star*. It is thus clear that Churchward had been impressed very quickly with the superior riding of the four-cylinder engine, and by its greater potentiality for future development as compared with the two-cylinder machine.

The most obvious change in the design of No. 4001 was the use of six coupled wheels. The verdict of the locomotive inspectors was that the two-cylinder 4—6—0s were more generally reliable in all weathers than the 'Atlantics', although the 'Atlantics' were freer running. At this distance in time it is a little difficult to appreciate why the *North Star* was ever built as a 4—4—2. Presumably the object was to make a closer comparison between its performance and that of the Frenchmen, and the 2-cylinder 'Atlantics'; but the decision to standardise upon 4—6—0s was evidently taken so soon after the completion of *North Star* as to raise doubts as to whether a comparison of 'Atlantics' of three kinds was the true reason.

The other important change in the design compared with *North Star* was in the valve gear, the scissors gear being replaced by Walschaert's. This was a notable step; Walschaert's gear between the frames has never been common in Britain, and in 1907 a well-laid-out Walschaert's gear was a novelty either inside or out. Like the scissors gear, the new gear was the work of W. H. Pearce. Following the pattern set by the development of the Churchward Stephenson gear, great care was taken in its design to ensure accurate compensation for the angularity of the connecting rods in a gear which gave, for its day, an exceptional valve travel.

The arrangement of the reversing gear linkage was similar to that used in No. 40, in that the reversing rod from the cab was connected to a reversing shaft extending across the locomotive. There was an individual auxiliary reversing shaft for each valve gear, connected by an auxiliary reversing rod and crank to the main reversing shaft. A short link was provided near each auxiliary reversing shaft by which the auxiliary reversing arm could be attached to a bracket on the engine frame if it was necessary to immobilise one cylinder. The auxiliary reversing shaft of the defective side was disconnected, leaving the other valve free to be operated by its own auxiliary reversing rod. This arrangement of the reversing gear made it a simple operation to put one side of the engine out of action in an emergency, but had the arrangement not been necessary in No. 40 for the scissors gear, a simpler arrangement might have been devised for the Walschaert's gear. The valves had a steam lap of $1\frac{5}{8}$ in., a lead of $\frac{1}{8}$ in., and a travel of $6\frac{7}{8}$ in. at the maximum cut-off of $76\frac{1}{2}$ per cent. A small but significant difference from No. 40 was an inspection hole in the framing opposite the inside slidebars. This gave a useful means of access to the slidebars and the front part of the valve gear, and mitigated the inaccessibility of the inside motion.

The exterior of No. 4001 was noticeably different from that of No. 40. The Churchward 'Atlantics' were ungainly engines; the closely-spaced driving wheels, combined with the large space under the

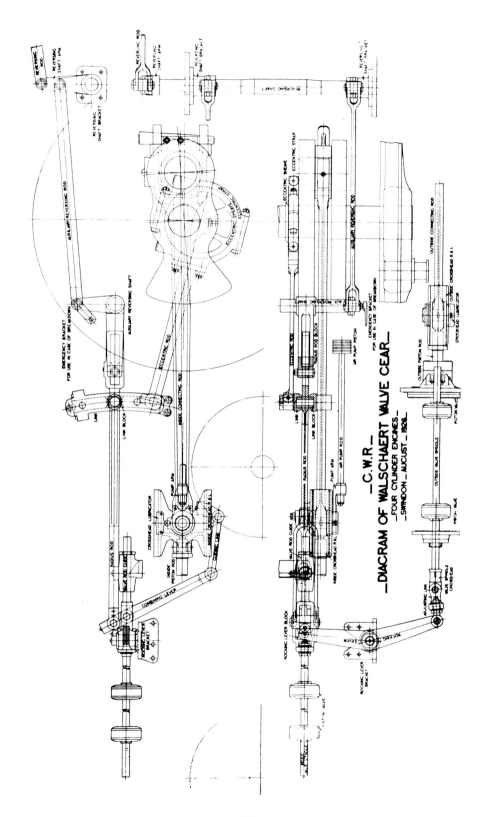

_C.W.R._

DIAGRAM OF WALSCHAERT VALVE GEAR

FOUR CYLINDER ENGINES

SWINDON — AUGUST — 1908

31

No. 4002 'Evening Star' as originally built in March 1907. The joggle in the main frame can be seen immediately behind the leading bogie wheel

firebox and cab, gave an impression that the boiler and chassis did not match. The additional driving wheels of the 4—6—0 dispelled that impression, and produced a much more pleasing blend of boiler with chassis. The rearward position of the outside cylinders of the four-cylinder engine seemed to make the improvement in the 4—6—0 more pronounced than in the two-cylinder design. The improvement apparent in No. 4001 was completed by the insertion of curved sections between the horizontal sections of the footplating, together with the lowering of the footplating under the cab. In its initial form the Churchward four-cylinder 4—6—0 attained what was, in the opinion of many people, its highest aesthetic level. The chimney was of smaller diameter and more graceful than that which was later adopted as standard, and the boiler was free from the fittings which later characterised it —top-feed, superheater fittings, and ejector.

The first batch of ten engines was built between February and May of 1907. They were numbered 4001-10, and were given the names of stars which had been carried by broad-gauge engines of 1839-41. The names were:

No.	Name
4001	*Dog Star*
4002	*Evening Star*
4003	*Lode Star*
4004	*Morning Star*
4005	*Polar Star*
4006	*Red Star*
4007	*Rising Star*
4008	*Royal Star*
4009	*Shooting Star*
4010	*Western Star*

Nos. 4001 and 4002 had a small but visible difference from the remainder of the class; whereas

No. 4008 'Royal Star' when running with front steps; the hindrance to access to the inside motion is apparent

the slidebars fitted to the later engines were of T-section those on 4001/2 were of I-section, that is, they appeared to have a slot cut in them. These slidebars were considered to be unsatisfactory. At a later date they were re-designed. The new pattern introduced the conspicuous tie-bar connecting the upper and lower bars, which had been seen first on the Frenchmen. It became a standard feature of all subsequent Swindon four-cylinder engines. Another visible difference which characterised 4002/8/9 for a time was the fitting of front steps, ahead of the outside cylinders. The last locomotive of the batch, No. 4101 *Western Star*, had a much more important variation—the fitting of a Cole super-heater.

The first experiment with a superheater on the GWR had begun a year before the appearance of No. 4010 with the fitting of a Schmidt superheater to engine No. 2901, *Lady Superior*. The object of a superheater is to raise the temperature of the steam above that at which it has been formed in the boiler, without any further increase in pressure. The steam thus becomes 'dry', and when it enters the cylinder it can withstand appreciable loss of heat to the comparatively cold cylinder walls before condensation occurs. Condensation is accompanied by a great reduction in volume, a loss of pressure, and a consequent reduction in the useful work done by the steam. Churchward studied closely the developments in locomotive design in other countries, and he was attracted by any device which offered the possibility of a saving in fuel. The Schmidt superheater was a proven appliance, and it was natural that this should be tried first.

Subsequent history of superheating at Swindon provides a classic example of the way Churchward took an established principle, and then developed the details to suit his own requirements. There were some features of the Schmidt apparatus that did not appeal to him. Furthermore, the adoption of

it in its entirety was at that time generally governed by conditions involving the use of other patent Schmidt devices, such as the well-known 'wide' piston valve ring. Churchward was the last man to be constrained by any circumstances of that kind, and one can imagine that his development in the first place stemmed from a desire to avoid the Schmidt patents as much as anything else. From the maintenance viewpoint those elements which were attached to the rearmost part of the header could not be removed unless the elements in front of them were removed. The elements themselves were bent at the header end, so that internal cleaning was difficult. Churchward therefore turned to the Cole superheater, an American design, in which the elements were straight. A superheater of this type was fitted to No. 4010 when built in May 1907. It incorporated elements of a special and complicated design, but it was sufficiently successful for the first Swindon superheater to be developed from it.

It is convenient at this point to complete the story of superheating in the 'Stars', although it involves anticipating the account of the later engines of the class. No. 4011 appeared in March 1908 fitted with the Swindon No. 1 superheater, and the same pattern was fitted to *The Great Bear*. The elements of this superheater could be removed more readily than could those of the Schmidt design, but there were still complications in the joints by which they were made steamtight. The second Swindon superheater, No. 2, differed from No. 1 mainly in that the complicated elements were replaced by simple ones. It was fitted only to 'Saint' No. 2922 in October 1908. The third Swindon design appeared in No. 4021 in June 1909. Whilst retaining some of the features of the No. 1 and No. 2 designs, it was a more radical development than the earlier patterns. A notable characteristic was that the elements were of smaller diameter

No. 4006 'Red Star' as originally built with full-cone non-superheated boiler

No. 4010 'Western Star' as originally built, May 1907, with Cole superheater

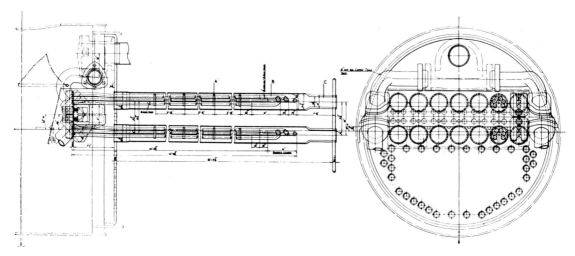

The standard Swindon No. 3 superheater

than in the earlier patterns, whilst the construction of the header was novel. Each flue tube contained a group of three pairs of elements (four pairs in boilers made between 1914 and 1919). The elements were expanded into a distribution box, or junction header, shaped like a hollow horseshoe, which was attached to the header by one stud and nut. The element group was released by the removal of this nut, and any group could be extracted independently. The weakness of the assembly was that a steamtight joint was maintained by one stud holding two flat surfaces together. Any steam which leaked from the joint blew across the ends of the tubes, with devastating effects upon the smokebox vacuum. In August 1909 the fitting of superheaters to the earlier 'Stars' began, and all engines of the class from No. 4031 of October 1910 were built with them. The conversion of the earlier engines was completed in May 1913.

The introduction of superheaters made it necessary to improve the lubrication of cylinders. The higher temperatures in the cylinders, and the absence of the lubricating action of particles of moisture, made it difficult to maintain adequate lubrication, and there was an increase in the wear of cylinder barrels. The problem of lubrication was greater in 1906 than in later years because less work had been put into the development of oils which could work at the temperature of superheated steam, and it is believed that Churchward's use of a lower superheat than was usual on other railways was influenced by the lack of suitable oils for use at higher temperatures. The additional wear of the cylinders was accentuated if the system of lubrication was such that the supply of oil was cut off

when the engine ran with steam shut off. The first Great Western superheated locomotives were fitted with mechanical lubricators but Churchward considered that a sight-feed lubricator emulsified the oil better than did a mechanical lubricator, and thus gave more uniform distribution of the oil over the walls of the steam chest and cylinder. Furthermore, the mechanical lubricator was an unnecessary complication, and took the control of lubrication out of the driver's hands.

An attempt was therefore made to devise a simpler arrangement by developing the sight-feed lubricator in the cab. With the adoption of the No. 3 superheater, with a lower temperature than in the Schmidt apparatus, a new system of hydrostatic lubrication was introduced. In this it was arranged that oil was supplied in atomised form to the steampipe between the superheater and the cylinders, the control of the steam supply to the lubricator being taken from the movement of the regulator handle. When the regulator was moved slightly from its closed position, a supply of oil, combined with a little steam, was fed to the cylinders. The regulator was put in this position when the engine was coasting, and a supply of oil was thus maintained to the cylinders, and sufficient pressure was maintained in the exhaust passages to discourage smokebox ashes from being sucked down the blastpipe.

In the early superheated engines both on the GWR and on other railways, dampers were fitted to cover the ends of the flues when steam was shut off. These were considered necessary to prevent the elements from overheating when they were not being cooled by steam passing through them. The

No. 4001 'Dog Star' after fitting with the de Glehn type bogie

dampers shut off the flow of gases through the flues. A common arrangement, and the one which was used on the GWR, was to have the dampers hinged, with a counterweight which normally held them shut. When the regulator was opened, steam was admitted to a small cylinder on the outside of the smokebox, and a piston thereby moved a lever to open the damper. The cylinder can be seen on the right-hand side of the smokebox of the early Great Western superheated engines. The first cylinders were kidney-shaped, but from 1910 a smaller and neater cylinder was introduced. Later it was found that the advantages to be derived from the use of dampers were not worth the additional expense, and between 1917 and 1924 they were removed. It may be mentioned that on other railways, using variants of the Schmidt superheater, the dampers were also discarded.

It has always been accepted that the Swindon superheater gives a lower degree of superheat than is obtained with the size of superheater used on most other British railways. There was ample evidence of this from Sir William Stanier's experiences on the LMSR and from the marked improvement in the performance of the 'Kings' when they were fitted with larger superheaters. It is therefore surprising to find that Churchward once denied that his superheaters gave a lower temperature. In January 1914, Sir Henry Fowler read a paper to the Institution of Civil Engineers on 'Superheating in Locomotives'. He had tried both Schmidt and Swindon superheaters in his No. 4 class 0—6—0s on the Midland Railway and had found that the Swindon apparatus gave 183 deg. of superheat (560 deg. Fah. steam temperature at 175 lb. per sq. in.),

whereas the Schmidt apparatus gave 250 deg. (620 deg. Fah. steam temperature at 160 lb. per sq. in.). Churchward said: 'The author must be labouring under some misapprehension. The position in which the pyrometer is placed—whether in the header or in the steamchest—makes a very considerable difference.'

After saying that he had not found pyrometers consistent over any series of tests, he added that from his own observation of the valves and pistons of other railways (that is, after running with superheated steam) he thought that the GWR superheat was higher than that commonly employed in England. After this evasive and inconclusive defence of his superheater, Churchward added that he had recorded steamchest temperatures of 550 deg. to 580 deg. at 225 lb. per sq. in., but this figure is higher than has been quoted by other people in contact with Swindon. In any case it was far lower than superheat temperatures regularly attained on the London & North Western Railway. Like Stirling's remarks on the appearance of Churchward's locomotives, Fowler's figures appear to have touched Churchward on the raw. But he then went on to say that it was incorrect to say that maximum superheat should be aimed at; anything could be got if desired. Any given engine required a certain degree of superheat for maximum economy and: 'Engines of modern design with small clearances showed less improvement by superheating than engines with longer and tortuous ports.'

Churchward said that the GWR had fitted superheaters for some years but 'he had not done much in the way of experiments'. In 12 months' working in 1913, 625 engines with superheaters had saved 60,000 tons of coal. He considered it better to save coal now than to go on with experiments. As Churchward had made as many experiments in superheating as any engineer in the country, his disclaimer was modest. His total of superheated engines at that time exceeded that of all the other British railways combined. The superheaters had been fitted economically, for Churchward had sought approval for the expenditure of only £90 per boiler rebuilt with a superheater.

An attraction of the superheater which Churchward considered as important as the saving in coal was the saving in water. Superheated steam is much less dense than saturated steam, and a smaller weight of steam is therefore used in a superheated engine than in a saturated engine working at the same speed and at the same cut-off. This reduced the amount of water passing through the boiler, and reduced maintenance costs. The introduction of superheating on the GWR may be summarised by saying that Churchward had less to gain by this development than had other engineers, yet he tackled the problem more energetically and originally than his contemporaries, and was rewarded with a rapid and significant saving in coal, and a reduction in boiler repairs.

After this digression on superheating, the early history of the 4001-10 series may be completed. In 1909 the Cole superheater in 4010 was replaced by the Swindon pattern. For two periods (in 1911 and 1914/5) this engine carried a half-cone boiler, and five others of the series carried this type of boiler for a period. After a period of running by this series, the locomotive inspectors reported that the four-cylinder locomotives were 'a coach better' than the 'Saints' on 12 to 14-coach expresses at about 60 m.p.h. The boilers of the 'Stars' and 'Saints' were identical; despite the slight advantage of the Walschaert's gear at short cut-off, there can have been little difference in cylinder efficiency. The reported improvement must therefore have been due largely to an increase in mechanical efficiency, helped by the greater comfort of riding of the four-cylinder engines when working hard at speed. On a normal run, in which the evidence was based on visual and physical impressions, and not on quantitative measurements, the 'Saints' gave an impression of working harder than the 'Stars'. The characteristics of the valve gear made it necessary to limit them to a minimum cut-off of 22 per cent to prevent excessive knocking, whereas the 'Stars' could be, and were regularly, worked at 15 per cent. Against the locomotive inspectors' views it must be recorded that there exist a few logs of runs by 'Saints' on heavy West of England trains which equal the best work done by the 'Stars'; but this is not to say that the 'Stars' did not show a slight superiority in day-in, day-out running.

When the Churchward ten-wheeled engines were first introduced, the work which they were given was within the capacity of the existing 4—4—0s; but the combination of accelerated schedules, heavier traffic, and more commodious rolling stock soon made the larger engines necessary. The three-hour trains between Paddington and Exeter were an example of a service which was based upon the capacity of the larger engines; but even those trains

No. 4006 'Red Star', fitted with a half-cone boiler in October 1909; non-superheated, but with regulator lubricator feed. Large diameter chimney: de Glehn bogie

in their early days were made up to loads which were later considered light for a 4—6—0. Details are tabulated of a run by a non-superheated 'Star' on the 3.30 p.m. from Paddington in 1909. Although by this time loads of 400 tons were being worked through to Exeter on the three-hour trains this run is representative of the loadings for which the schedules were originally prepared.

The 3.30 p.m. train slipped one coach at Westbury and another at Taunton. The interest of this particular run lies in the delays which were encountered. After a fast start from Paddington, speed was up to 75 m.p.h. by Slough, but a signal check at Taplow caused a loss of 3 min. Its effects had been almost wiped out by Reading. At this time the turnout to the old Berks and Hants line had not been re-aligned, and a slack to 20 m.p.h. was in force. After this *Morning Star* ran well to Savernake, and without being pressed in the later stages of the climb, had $2\frac{1}{2}$ min. in hand at that point. Unfortunately adverse signals approaching West-

bury made it necessary to stop to detach the slip coach. This caused a loss of $3\frac{1}{2}$ min., which had been reduced to $1\frac{1}{4}$ min. by Castle Cary; but the combination of the cautious running which was still customary over the new line, and a permanent way slack at Curry Rivel Junction, made the train still 2 min. late at Cogload Junction. All seemed set for a good climb to Whiteball, but another signal check made a second stop necessary, to detach the Taunton slip portion. Despite a smart climb to Whiteball, another permanent way slack made the arrival at Exeter $6\frac{3}{4}$ min. late, though the net time was only $171\frac{1}{2}$ min. In respect of the delay at Taunton it should be explained that until the rebuilding of the station in the 1930s there were only two running lines. If, as frequently happened in the holiday season, the down platform was occupied by another train, a non-stopping express would be diverted through the goods line to the east of the passenger station. This was sharply curved, and involved drastic reduction of speed at entry and exit of this by-pass.

A second table sets out details of three runs by saturated engines on the 11.50 a.m. from Paddington. These are from an extensive series recorded by A. V. Goodyear from 1909 to 1911. The train normally slipped portions at Westbury and Taunton. On the first run with *Royal Star* the load was 360 tons, which was normal at this period for the first part of the journey, but on this run there were no slip portions, so that after Westbury the load was above normal. The start was gentle, and speed did not reach 60 m.p.h. for the first 10 miles. Then there was a marked increase in effort, and for $16\frac{1}{2}$ miles from Slough speed averaged 66 m.p.h. After the recovery from the Reading slack, speed was maintained mainly between 61 and 63 m.p.h. on the rising gradients to Bedwyn, and for 27 miles did not fall below 58. On the final climb to Savernake there was a fall from 62 to 52 m.p.h. Savernake was passed half a minute early, and a fast descent, with a maximum of 84 m.p.h., brought the train through Westbury 3 min. early. The driver then ran easily for the next 45 miles, but despite two slight permanent way slacks was still 3 min. ahead of time at Taunton. However, the train was turned through the loop at that station, requiring a slack to 10 m.p.h., and so lost its momentum for the climb to Whiteball. The recovery was vigorous, speed reaching 53 m.p.h. before the main part of the climb; the minimum of 37 was good for this load. Whiteball was passed 1 min. late, and after a maximum of 80 m.p.h. Exeter would have been reached on time had not the train been brought almost to a stand twice by signals.

3.30 p.m. PADDINGTON TO EXETER

Date: 1909

Engine: 4004 *Morning Star* (saturated)

Load: To Westbury, 287 tons tare, 305 tons full
To Taunton, 262 tons tare, 277 tons full
To Exeter, 237 tons tare, 250 tons full

Dist. Miles		Sch. Min.	Actual m. s.	Speeds m.p.h.
0·0	PADDINGTON .	0	0 00	
9·1	Southall . .	12	11 32	67
18·5	Slough . .	21	19 20	75
—			sigs.	30
24·2	Maidenhead .	26	26 20	45
34·0	Milepost 34 .		36 07	69
36·0	READING .	38	38 10	20
44·8	Aldermaston .		48 17	64
53·1	NEWBURY .	57	55 50	66/63
58·5	Kintbury . .		60 53	68
61·5	Hungerford .		63 38	62
66·4	Bedwyn . .		68 13	66
70·1	Savernake . .	74	72 27	51
86·9	Lavington . .		86 47	73 (max.)
95·6	WESTBURY ⌠ arr.	97	96 44	
—	⌡ dep.		98 26	
101·3	FROME . .	104	107 18	30/55
108·5	Milepost 122¾ .	114	115 59	47/73
115·3	Castle Cary. .	121	122 14	62
125·7	Somerton . .		131 32	69 (max.)
—			p.w.s.	
137·9	Cogload Junction .	144	146 04	68 (max.)
142·9	TAUNTON ⌠ arr.	149	152 04	
—	⌡ dep.		153 12	
144·9	Norton Fitzwarren		156 52	46
150·0	Wellington . .		162 08	61
153·8	Whiteball Box .	161	166 42	41
158·8	Tiverton Junction		171 12	77
170·2	Stoke Canon .		180 54	
—			p.w.s.	30
173·7	EXETER . .	180	186 50	

Net time $171\frac{1}{2}$ min.

11.50 a.m. PADDINGTON—EXETER

Run No.			1	2	3
Engine	.		4008	4008	4001
Load: tons, tare/full					
To Westbury	. . . .		—/360	409/435	—/480
To Taunton .	. . . .		—/360	409/435	—/455
To Exeter	. . . .		—/360	345/370	—/315
Weather	. . . .		Fine	Strong S.W. wind	Slight W. wind, Wet

Dist. Miles		Sch. Min.	Actual m. s.	Actual m. s.	Actual m. s.
0·0	PADDINGTON . .	0	0 00	0 00	0 00
5·7	Ealing		8 58	8 59	9 45
9·1	Southall .	11	12 28	12 27	13 32
15·0	*Milepost 15* . .			18 23	19 32
18·5	SLOUGH . .	20	21 32	21 38 sigs.	22 45
31·0	Twyford . .		32 57	34 15	34 35
36·0	READING . .	37	37 38	39 18	39 31
37·8	*Southcote Junction* .		40 58	42 55	43 00
40·0	*Milepost 40* .		43 21	45 28	45 35
53·1	NEWBURY . .	56	56 12	59 44	59 55
66·4	Bedwyn . .		69 08	73 57	74 45
70·1	Savernake . .	73½	73 04	78 30	79 19
81·1	Patney . .		82 41	89 04	89 58
95·0	*Milepost 95* .		93 55	101 28	102 22
95·6	WESTBURY .	97½	94 31	102 16	103 10
101·3	FROME .		101 48	110 13	111 14
108·5	*Milepost 122¾* . .	113½	111 16	120 03	121 26
			p.w.s. 50 Bruton		
115·3	CASTLE CARY . .	120	117 18	126 00	127 45
			2 slight slacks	p.w.s. 30	p.w.s. 50 four times
137·9	*Cogload Junction* .	144	139 45	148 32	152 00
			10 m.p.h. on to loop	p.w.s. 40	
142·9	TAUNTON . .	149	146 05	153 32	156 50
145·8	*Milepost 166* .		151 19	156 39	159 55
150·0	Wellington .		156 36	161 35	164 14
153·8	*Whiteball Box* .	161	162 12	167 56	169 48
158·8	Tiverton Junction .		167 10	172 54	174 39
171·8	*Milepost 192* .		177 12	183 11	185 13
			sigs. 5 Cowley Br.		
173·7	EXETER . .	180	184 27	186 04	188 03
Net time, min.:			174	182	185½
Minimum at Savernake, m.p.h. . . .			52	41	41
Minimum at Brewham, m.p.h. . . .			45	41	41
Minimum at Whiteball, m.p.h. . . .			37	29	30
Maximum speed, m.p.h. . .			84	80	78½

On the second run, again with *Royal Star*, the load was 435 tons to Taunton, and in the face of a strong south-west wind the train did well to drop only 2 min. to Exeter. As in the first run, 60 m.p.h. was reached after 10 miles, and speed had risen to 64 when the train was checked by signals at Slough; the check cost 1¾ min. From Reading to Savernake speed ranged between 55 and 58 m.p.h., and fell to 41 at the summit, which was passed 5 min. late. The driver did not attempt to regain time before Westbury, and the maximum was only 70½ m.p.h. The minimum at Brewham was 41 m.p.h., and the train was then 6½ min. late. The descent from Brewham was more lively, speed reaching 78 before Castle Cary. Despite two permanent way slacks,

one to 30 and the other to 40 m.p.h., 2 min. had been recovered by Taunton. On the climb to Whiteball speed fell from 60 to 29 m.p.h., 2 min. being lost. The actual time to Exeter was 186 min. 4 sec. The combination of wind and older stock made the load equivalent to about 500 tons of modern stock in calm conditions, and the average power output was as high as was ever recorded with a saturated 'Star'.

The third run with engine No. 4001, *Dog Star*, was recorded at an August Bank Holiday weekend, when the train was made up to 15 vehicles, including two diners and nine heavy modern vehicles. The gross load from Paddington was 480 tons, but slips were shed at Westbury and Taunton, so that after Taunton the load was less than on the second run. The start was slower than in the previous runs, $2\frac{1}{2}$ min. being dropped on the optimistic 11 min. booking to Southall, instead of the more usual 1 min. Speed reached 60 m.p.h. at milepost 13, and 64 at Slough. From Slough to Reading the average was $63\frac{1}{2}$ m.p.h., and the time between these points was only 40 sec. longer than in the first run, but with 120 tons more of load. Between Reading and Bedwyn there was heavy rain, and the maximum speed was 56 m.p.h., falling to 41 at Savernake. Speed rose to $73\frac{1}{2}$ m.p.h. on the descent to Westbury, which was passed in 103 min. 10 sec., nearly $6\frac{3}{4}$ min. late, and the lateness had increased to 8 min. by milepost $122\frac{3}{4}$. The maximum after Frome was only 46 m.p.h., but to fall from 46 to 41 on Brewham bank with 455 tons was very good. Four permanent way slacks over the new line were observed scrupulously, but the timetable made allowance for easy running over this stretch, and no further time was lost to Taunton. The climb to Whiteball was below the standard of the first run in the table, speed being down to $34\frac{1}{2}$ m.p.h. before the tunnel, and averaging $30\frac{1}{2}$ through the tunnel. The actual time lost to Exeter was 8 min. 3 sec., but the net loss was $5\frac{1}{2}$ min.

From a study of runs 2 and 3 in this table it might be imagined that the losses in time indicated that the saturated 'Stars' were beyond their limit with loads of this magnitude. They were fine runs in themselves, but they were made in relatively early days of the class, and it is probable that neither the drivers nor the firemen had gained that experience that was necessary to extract the 'extra' needed to secure timekeeping in these conditions of exceptional loading. Nevertheless, from his long experience A. V. Goodyear was inclined to give the palm to the 'Saints' for heavy feats in non-super-heater days. Apart from such outside observations Swindon opinion was unanimously in favour of the four-cylinder engines.

The expectation of longer mileages between general repairs was fulfilled. It was found that the 'Stars' could run from 120,000 to 130,000 miles, compared with 70,000 to 80,000 for the 'Saints'. This difference in mileage was not maintained in later years, when different criteria were adopted for deciding when an engine should have a general repair, and when the practice of intermediate repairs had become established. In these later days overhauls were determined by the general condition of the engine, and this led to the four-cylinder engines being shopped at lower mileages than could have been reached on the condition of the axleboxes alone; but they were in better condition at overhaul than were the two-cylinder engines.

No. 4006 'Red Star', approaching Chippenham with the Royal Train, conveying King Edward VII on a visit to Lord Lansdown, at Bowood

No. 4003 'Lode Star' on down West of
England expresss near Southall

No. 4005 'Polar Star' during the interchange trials
with the LNWR in 1910, passing Kilburn

In the 1950s the balance in favour of the four-cylinder engines would have been thought insufficient to justify the greater capital cost and the greater shed labour required. Before World War I the economics of locomotive operation were less stringent, and it was decided that four-cylinder engines would be built for heavy long-distance work. Two-cylinder engines would continue to be built for shorter-distance work where the advantages of the four-cylinder engines were less, and where the variable lead of the Stephenson valve gear gave more advantage at starting. In the event, construction of 'Saints' continued until 1913, after which all GWR express engines had four cylinders.

'A' erecting shop, Swindon, showing left to right, engines 4022 (on the crane); a French
compound, 'City' No. 3708, 4035, and 2948

4—6—0 No. 4003 'Lode Star' in later standard condition, and as now preserved in the Railway Museum, Swindon

CELESTIAL 'STARS'
Scintillating and Austere

4—6—0 No. 4010 'Western Star' as painted plain green with brass beadings to the splashers removed

CHAPTER 4

'STARS', CHIVALROUS AND ROYAL

TEN months after the appearance of No. 4010, in March 1908, the next batch of 'Stars' appeared, the 'Knights'. The first of these, No. 4011, *Knight of the Garter,* was, as mentioned in the account of the development of the Swindon superheater, the first engine to be fitted with a superheater of Swindon design. The batch introduced another change, and one which was destined to be adopted widely on British railways. The bogies so far fitted to the Churchward 4—6—0s had been of American pattern, in which the loads were applied to the axleboxes by equalising bars. Two springs, parallel to the equalising bars, transmitted the load from the bogie frame to the bars, and the bogie was connected to the frame of the engine by swing links.

The swing links were troublesome, and various experiments were made to obtain more satisfactory wear from their pivots, and to reduce flange wear on the leading coupled wheels. The swing links allowed freedom of lateral movement at the front of the engine, but in doing so caused the leading coupled flanges to do a considerable part of the work of guiding the engine into curves.

The bogie used on the Frenchmen was of different construction, in that the weight of the engine was transmitted to the bogie through sliding flat surfaces. The lower surface was on the bogie frame, and the weight of the engine was applied to the upper surfaces by hemispherical cups, which allowed angular movement of the bogie relative to the engine frame. The bogie centre pin on the engine frame engaged a centre block on the bogie, but lateral movement of the block relative to the bogie frame could take place under the control of springs. Movement of the bogie relative to the engine frame applied a load through these springs

Engine No. 4016 'Knight of the Golden Fleece' as originally built, with non-superheated boiler, but having the de Glehn bogie from the outset

42

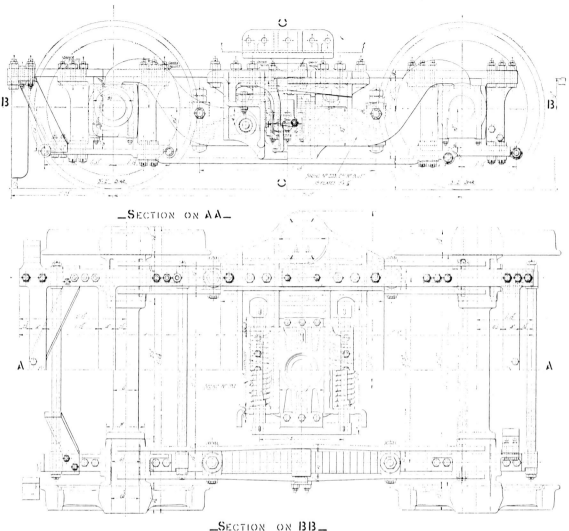

Section on AA

Section on BB

The de Glehn – Swindon bogie

which tended to lead the engine frame into the curve. Wear of the leading coupled wheel flanges would thus be reduced, at the expense of rather less increase in wear of the flanges of the bogie wheels and the trailing coupled or carrying wheels. A further benefit of the spring control was that it lessened the tendency for the front of the engine to develop lateral oscillations.

As Churchward gradually came to adopt practices brought over with the Frenchmen, he eventually tried the French type of bogie. The Swindon bogie was redesigned to incorporate the side control springs, and side bearers for transmitting the load. The equalising bar arrangement of wheel springing was retained. The modified bogie was soon accepted as an improvement on the old pattern, and was applied to the earlier ten-wheeled engines as they came in for repairs. It became widely established on other railways, either with the equalising bar springing or with individual axlebox springs. Its adoption by Thompson on the LNER 'B1' 4—6—0 was probably the last example of the adoption of a Swindon feature of design by another railway.

In the Swindon development initially an existing bogie was modified, and after successful trials the 4011 series of 'Stars' was built with the new bogie. The side-bearers of the modified bogie are clearly visible in photographs. The same type of bogie was fitted to other classes also. The larger diameter chimney, which was to be the standard pattern on the 'Stars' for many years, also appeared on this batch. The diameter of the parallel portion was

43

No. 4011 'Knight of the Garter', as originally built in 1908, superheated

1 ft. 8⅞ in., an increase of 2 in. on the earlier pattern. There were also slight variations in boiler dimensions. Nos. 4011-6/8 ran for a time with front footsteps.

THE 'KNIGHT' SERIES

No.	Name
4011	*Knight of the Garter*
4012	*Knight of the Thistle*
4013	*Knight of St. Patrick*
4014	*Knight of the Bath*
4015	*Knight of St. John*
4016	*Knight of the Golden Fleece*
4017	*Knight of the Black Eagle*★
4018	*Knight of the Grand Cross*
4019	*Knight Templar*
4020	*Knight Commander*

★ Renamed *Knight of Liege* in 1914

It is said that the grandeur of some of these names was not appreciated by all and sundry at Swindon, and some for a time had disrespectful nicknames. Engine No. 4014, for example, was known as 'Friday Night'!

Dynamometer car trials of a 'Star' were made in

April 1908 with No. 4013, *Knight of St. Patrick*. The locomotive developed a drawbar pull of 2.2 tons at 69 m.p.h., which was close to the figure of 2 tons at 70 m.p.h. which Churchward had taken as his target when developing the 'Saints'. The

12.5 p.m. EXETER TO PADDINGTON				
Dynamometer Car test run on 28 April 1908				
Engine: 4013 *Knight of St. Patrick*				
Load: 368 tons tare, 390 tons full				

Dist. Miles		Sch. min.	Actual m. s.	Speeds m.p.h.
0·0	EXETER . .	0	0 00	
3·5	Stoke Canon .		6 46	48
7·2	Silverton . .		10 58	57/56
12·6	Cullompton .		16 21	63
14·9	Tiverton Junction		18 40	56½/63
19·9	*Whiteball Box* .	25	23 57	47
23·7	Wellington . .		27 30	77½
—			sig.slight	
30·8	TAUNTON .	35	33 50	55½
35·8	Cogload Junction	40	38 55	62
42·7	*Curry Rivel Junc.*		46 05	59
46·8	*Milepost* 127			
	(in tunnel) .		50 21	50 (slip)
48·0	Somerton .		51 46	
49·8	*Milepost 124* .		53 38	63
51·3	Charlton Mackrell		55 05	59
55·8	*Milepost 118* .		59 17	71
58·4	CASTLE CARY .	64	61 40	64
63·0	*Milepost 125* .		66 22	52
64·0	*Milepost 124* .		67 33	51
64·5	*Milepost 123½* .		68 10	47
65·0	*Milepost 123* .		68 50	44
65·25	*Milepost 123¾* .	73½	69 11	41
72·0	*Milepost 116* .		75 50	68
72·4	FROME . .		76 24	slack 27
77·0	*Milepost 111* .		83 14	63
78·1	WESTBURY .	87½	84 45	slack 32
86·8	Lavington . .		95 13	61
92·6	Patney . .		101 50	
97·7	*Milepost 76* .		107 25	60
			p.w.s.	
98·4	Pewsey . .		108 33	9
103·6	Savernake . .	114	118 36	41
112·2	Hungerford .		126 52	69/66½
115·2	Kintbury .		129 29	71/66
120·6	NEWBURY .	130	134 10	70/67
124·1	Thatcham . .		137 16	70
127·0	Midgham . .		139 44	69/71
132·5	Theale . .		144 28	69
135·8	*Southcote Junction*		147 35	
136·7	*Milepost 37* .		149 08	slack 24
137·7	READING .	148	151 16	30
142·7	Twyford . .		157 56	58
149·5	Maidenhead .		164 15	68
155·2	SLOUGH .	166	169 15	69
157·5	Langley . .		171 16	68
160·5	West Drayton .		173 59	65½
164·6	SOUTHALL .	175	177 48	64½
168·0	Ealing Broadway .		180 52	66½
172·4	Westbourne Park		185 18	
—			sigs.	
173·7	PADDINGTON	185	189 58	

Net time 183 min.
Allowances: 5½ min. lost at Pewsey
1½ min. lost at Royal Oak

No. 4015 'Knight of St. John', as modified with super-heater, top feed, and experimental lubricator fittings below the damper cylinder

An early view of the stationary testing plant, at Swindon, with engine No. 190

accompanying table shows the log of the test run on the 12.5 p.m. from Exeter to Paddington, 'The Torquay Diner', on 28 April 1908. The load of 390 tons full was heavy for the period, and an examination of the drawbar pull recorded at various points in the journey shows that the resistance to motion of the older stock made the equivalent of about 450 tons of modern stock. The running throughout was good, and no better performance was recorded by a non-superheated 'Star' on an up West of England train. A severe permanent way slack at Pewsey

caused a loss of $5\frac{1}{2}$ min., and signal checks at Royal Oak cost a further $1\frac{1}{2}$ min. Arrival at Paddington was 5 min. late, but the net time was 2 min. less than the schedule of 185 min. The interest in the run lies in the fact that it is the most complete record of the work of a non-superheated 'Star' which has survived.

RECORDED VALUES OF DRAWBAR PULL, ENGINE No. 4013

Location (near)	Speed m.p.h.	Cut-off per cent	Pull tons
Tiverton Junction .	63	25	2·8
Langport . . .	56	20	2·4
Keinton Mandeville .	69	20	2·1
Milepost 122¾ .	41	25	4·3
Patney . . .	51	20	2·4

REGULATOR AND CUT-OFF CONDITIONS, ENGINE No. 4013

Location	Regulator position	Cut-off per cent
Milepost 192 to Whiteball .	Full	25
Whiteball to Curry Rivel Junc.	Part-open	12½
Curry Rivel Junc. to Bruton .	Full	20
Bruton to Milepost 122¾ .	Full	25
Milepost 122¾ to Milepost 116½	½	15
Recovering from Frome slack .	Full	20
Milepost 94½ to Milepost 76 .	Full	20
Recovering from Pewsey check .	Full	35
Milepost 74½ to Savernake .	Full	20
Savernake to Southcote Junc. .	Part-open	15
Reading to Milepost 3¾ .	Full	20

The Churchward dynamometer car as originally built

At this time the technique of driving the four-cylinder engines was not fully developed. The reverser was left in the same position for long periods, leading to uneven demands upon the boiler. Speed varied unnecessarily on some stretches and there were less vigorous accelerations and hill climbs than would have resulted had the cut-off been increased and decreased gradually. A further table shows the variations of regulator opening and cut-off, but there were some local variations not shown in this list, as some figures derived from this test include values of the drawbar pull at 11 per cent cut-off. Also tabulated are some values of drawbar pull recorded at various points. These figures are uncorrected for gradient and acceleration; an analysis of the drawbar characteristics of the engine based on corrected figures is included in Chapter 17 dealing with test results. The coal consumption was about $3\frac{1}{2}$ lb. per drawbar horse-power hour. Had Churchward seen fit to publish this figure, it would have shaken his contemporaries as severely as did the figure published in 1924 for the tests of *Caldicot Castle*.

It is interesting to compare the running of No. 4013 with the performance of superheated engine No. 4011 on the run on the up 'Cornish Riviera Express' which is tabulated herewith. With almost

1.45 p.m. EXETER TO PADDINGTON
Engine: 4011 *Knight of the Garter*
Load: 360 tons tare, 380 tons full

Dist. Miles		Sch. Min.	Actual m. s.	Speeds m.p.h.
0·0	Exeter . .	0	0 00	
3·5	Stoke Canon .		6 42	48
12·6	Cullompton .		17 05	56
14·9	Tiverton Junction		19 44	$48\frac{1}{2}$
16·9	*Milepost 177* .		21 55	$55\frac{1}{2}$
19·9	*Whiteball Box* .	23	25 44	$39\frac{1}{2}$
23·7	Wellington . .		29 13	82/78
28·8	Norton Fitzwarren		32 54	90
30·8	TAUNTON .	$32\frac{1}{2}$	34 17	84
35·8	*Cogload Junction* .	$37\frac{1}{2}$	38 18	60 slack
42·7	*Curry Rivel Junc.* . .		44 25	69
48·0	Somerton .		49 58	56
53·5	Keinton Mandeville		54 19	72
58·4	CASTLE CARY	$61\frac{1}{2}$	59 20	65
61·8	Bruton . .		63 02	50
65·2	*Milepost $122\frac{3}{4}$* .	$69\frac{1}{2}$	67 20	41
72·4	FROME . .		74 32	30 slack
78·1	WESTBURY .	$83\frac{1}{2}$	82 00	27 slack
86·8	Lavington . .		91 32	67
91·7	*Milepost 82* .		96 39	52
98·4	Pewsey . .		103 39	62
103·6	Savernake .		108 51	$57\frac{1}{2}$
107·3	Bedwyn .		112 05	75
—			sigs.	5
112·2	Hungerford .		117 20	
120·6	NEWBURY .	125	126 52	69
—			—	73 max.
137·7	READING .	143	143 28	30 slack
149·5	Maidenhead .	155	156 05	70
155·2	Slough .	$160\frac{1}{2}$	161 10	68
164·6	Southall .	$169\frac{1}{2}$	169 25	64
171·7	*Milepost 2* .		176 27 sig. stop	
173·7	PADDINGTON .	180	182 45	

Net time $176\frac{1}{2}$ min.

A detail of the rear-end of No. 4016 showing the first modified form of slide-bars

Engine No. 4022 'King William' as originally built, non-superheated

the same load as No. 4013, the superheated engine made very similar times over much of the journey. The start of No. 4011's run was slower, and despite the incentive of a late start of 7 min., nearly 3 min. was dropped to Whiteball. Then came a display of high speed so sudden as to suggest that the driver had left his controls unchanged from the positions used in climbing to Whiteball. After checking the speed from 82 to 78 m.p.h. at Wellington, he opened out again to reach the unusual maximum—for that time—of 90 m.p.h. at Norton Fitzwarren, and speed remained high until the slack at Cogload Junction. By Castle Cary the train was 2 min. within booked running time, and remained so until a bad signal check at Hungerford. Again time was recovered but a final signal stop before Paddington caused a total loss on running time of $2\frac{3}{4}$ min. The test run of No. 4013 was one of the best efforts recorded by a non-superheated 'Star', and it is therefore interesting to see a superheated engine making a very similar run in ordinary service at the same period.

In 1909 there appeared the third series of 'Stars', named after Kings of England. The first of the batch, No. 4021, *King Edward*, has already been

THE 'KING' SERIES

No.	Name
4021	*King Edward*
4022	*King William*
4023	*King George*
4024	*King James*
4025	*King Charles*
4026	*King Richard*
4027	*King Henry*
4028	*King John*
4029	*King Stephen*
4030	*King Harold*

mentioned as the first engine to be fitted with the Swindon No. 3 superheater. The remaining engines of the batch had saturated boilers with, as commonly happened in this period, slight variations in dimensions. Even these nine boilers were not identical. There was a small but significant change in the shape of the casing over the inside cylinders, the sides of which were given concave curvature. The effect was to make the casing less obtrusive, and to blend it more into the generally tapered front of the engine. This feature continued through the remainder of the 'Stars' and was also seen in the earlier 'Castles'. The names of this series were as shown in the previous column.

Whilst this batch was appearing, *The Engineer* published a series of articles on 'British Locomotive Practice of Today'. The articles invoked a long correspondence, including some letters from one correspondent which were highly critical of the GWR. It was pointed out that numerous types of ten-wheeled passenger engines had been built, which, to the writer, seemed to have made no difference to the 'revenue earning capacity of the locomotive'. The writer quoted from the half-yearly returns which railways made to the Board of Trade. These showed that on the GWR the expenditure on locomotive renewals and repairs for the half year ending in December 1908 were £175 per locomotive, which was quite the highest of any railway. For the Lancashire & Yorkshire the figure was £100, and other railways ranged up to £157, which applied to the Great Eastern and to the North Eastern. The total figure of locomotive expenditure for the GWR had increased half-year by half-year. The appearance of one particularly critical letter in a reputable technical journal could not escape the notice of the Directors of the GWR, and Churchward was asked to explain how it was

Engine No. 4021 'King Edward' decorated for hauling the funeral train of King Edward VII, carrying the standard GWR Royal Train headlamps, and with the side shield draped in purple

that the London & North Western could build three 4—6—0 locomotives for the cost of two of his. Churchward is said to have replied, rather tartly across the Board table: 'Because one of mine could pull two of their b—— things backwards!'

Although this incident had no bearing on future locomotive policy on the GWR, it is generally known to have been the inspiration of a locomotive exchange which was made with the London & North Western in 1910. Bowen-Cooke had arranged exchanges with other railways to assist him in formulating his ideas on future passenger engines, but there is evidence that the exchange of non-superheater 4—6—0 locomotives with the GWR was proposed by Churchward. As an exchange it was an uneven test, for there can have been little expectation that an 'Experiment' could equal the work of a 'Star'. That Bowen-Cooke was more interested in the work of the 'Star' on the London & North Western than in the work of his own Company's engine on the GWR is borne out by the fact that it was left to Camden shed to select the engine, and they were so little apprised of the importance of the trials that they sent the engine which they could most easily spare, that is, the one in the most run-down condition. As a result, whereas No. 4005 *Polar Star* went to the London & North Western in the pink of condition, No. 1471 *Worcestershire* was in a condition below that of an 'Experiment' at its best. *Worcestershire* found the work allotted to it on the GWR beyond its capacity, chiefly through water difficulties, and lost time badly. The circumstances so far as the LNWR engines were concerned are discussed fully in the Locomotive Monograph dealing with *The Precursor Family*. By contrast, *Polar Star* showed complete mastery

	L.N.W.R. 12.10 p.m. EUSTON—CREWE Engine: GWR 4-6-0 No. 4005 *Polar Star* Driver: J. Springthorpe (Old Oak Common) Load 388 tons tare, 410 tons full				
Dist. Miles		Sch. min.	Actual m. s.		Av. Speeds m.p.h.
0·0	EUSTON . .	0	0	00	
1·3	Chalk Farm		3	35	
2·4	Loudoun Road .		5	20	
5·4	WILLESDEN Jn.	9	9	15	46·0
11·4	Harrow . .		16	35	49·2
13·3	Pinner . .		19	05	45·6
17·5	WATFORD JN.	23	24	10	49·5
21·0	King's Langley .		27	55	56·0
28·0	Berkhamsted .		35	35	54·8
31·7	Tring . .	40	39	40	54·4
46·7	BLETCHLEY .	55	54	20	61·5
52·4	Wolverton . .		59	35	65·2
59·9	Roade . .	69	67	40	55·7
62·8	BLISWORTH .		71	05	50·9
—			p.w.s.		
69·7	Weedon . .		79	20	50·2
75·3	Welton . .		86	25	47·5
82·5	RUGBY . .	93	94	55	51·6
88·0	Brinklow . .		101	45	48·4
91·4	Shilton . .		105	15	56·5
93·5	Bulkington . .		107	45	52·8
97·1	NUNEATON .	109	111	15	61·7
102·3	Atherstone .		115	55	66·8
106·5	Polesworth .		119	35	68·7
110·0	TAMWORTH .	122	122	40	68·0
116·3	Lichfield . .		128	30	64·8
121·0	Armitage . .		133	45	53·7
—			sigs.		
124·3	Rugeley . .	137	138	40	40·3
			sigs.		
127·2	Colwich . .		145	15	26·4
133·6	STAFFORD .	147	155	15	38·4
138·9	Norton Bridge .	154	161	40	49·5
143·4	Standon Bridge .		166	50	52·4
147·6	Whitmore . .		171	15	53·0
150·1	Madeley . .		174	25	53·0
153·3	Betley Road .		177	25	64·0
158·0	CREWE . .	175	183	25	

over the work given to it on the North Western.

The exchange workings were between 15 and 27 August. In the first week *Polar Star* worked the 12.10 p.m. from Euston, allowed 175 min. for a non-stop run to Crewe, on Monday, Tuesday, and Wednesday. The load was 11 cars, including two twelve-wheeled dining cars, a gross load of about 370 tons. The engine returned each day on the 5.2 p.m. from Crewe, allowed 188 min. to Euston, including a stop of 5 min. at Rugby and one of 2 min. at Willesden. Thursday was shed day, and on Friday and Saturday the engine worked the 10 a.m. down Glasgow and Edinburgh express, and the 4.7 p.m. up from Crewe.

In the second week *Polar Star* worked the 10 a.m. down on Monday and Tuesday, had a shed day on Wednesday, and worked the 12.10 p.m. down on Thursday, Friday, and Saturday. The 'Experiment' *Herefordshire* worked the opposite turns each week.

A run was logged by Cecil J. Allen on the 5.2 p.m. up from Crewe, with a moderate load of 330 tons on which *Polar Star* kept time with ease, running the 75.5 miles from Crewe to Rugby in $84\frac{1}{2}$ min. start to stop, and continuing over the 77.1 miles to Willesden Junction in 84 min. 25 sec.—an aggregate gain of 2 min. on schedule. But a fully authenticated record exists of a run on the 12.10 p.m. down which shows the GWR engine in a less favourable light. The log of this run is tabulated herewith, and it would seem that the driver was definitely 'coal-dodging' rather than trying to run the train to time. The checks were severe, it is true; but little attempt was made to regain the lost time, and the arrival at Crewe was $8\frac{1}{2}$ min. late. The net time was certainly inside the scheduled allowance, but the driving lacked any particular enterprise and the running, particularly after the signal checks, was well below the standards established very shortly afterwards by the 'George the Fifth' class 4—4—0s over that section of line. The coal consumption of *Polar Star* was appreciably lower than that of the 'Experiment' class 4—6—0 *Herefordshire* against which it was tested.

For Churchward the exchange was a complete vindication; for Bowen-Cooke it was a spur to better things. For the GWR management the interchange with the London & North Western in August 1910 was very opportune, for in October of that year the direct route to Birmingham came into use, and two-hour trains were introduced in direct competition with the North Western. As the GWR had the more difficult route, the superiority of its engines was reassuring, even though the loads were at first so light that 4—4—0 engines could time the trains.

The fourth series of 'Stars' appeared in October

Royal Train on the Shrewsbury and Hereford Joint Line, hauled by engine No. 4033 'Queen Victoria'

Interior of Churchward's historic dynamometer car, as originally built

1910, Nos. 4031-40, named after Queens of England. They were fitted with No. 3 superheaters when built, but the boilers had the customary slight variations in dimensions from the previous series. For the interchange trials with the London & North Western, the tender of No. 4005 had its side fenders lengthened, and this change was incorporated as standard from engine No. 4031 onwards.

THE 'QUEEN' SERIES

4031	Queen Mary
4032	Queen Alexandra
4033	Queen Victoria
4034	Queen Adelaide
4035	Queen Charlotte
4036	Queen Elizabeth
4037	Queen Philippa
4038	Queen Berengaria
4039	Queen Matilda
4040	Queen Boadicea

These names were a much more satisfying lot than the 'Kings', for with all of them there was no mistaking which Royal Lady was intended. With the 'King', only the last three admitted of no ambiguity, though of course in the year 1909 *King Edward* would naturally have been associated with the reigning monarch, rather than with any of the six preceding Edwards, and after his death No. 4023 *King George* would obviously be similarly associated with King George V.

One of this series, No. 4039, *Queen Matilda*, was given a dynamometer-car trial on the 11 a.m. from Paddington to Bristol on 1 November 1911. The load was heavy for this train, 13 coaches weighing 400 tons full as far as Bath, and 12 coaches weighing 370 tons full after the shedding of the Bath slip. A log of the run is tabulated herewith, and the details include the dynamometer-car records of the conditions at which the engine was worked, and the drawbar pull at various locations. It is evident that the cut-off was changed from time to time to give readings at various combinations of speed and cut-off. For example, at milepost $40\frac{1}{2}$, with the train nearly 5 min. late, the cut-off was reduced from 23 per cent to 11 per cent. The readings shown are of interest in that speed variations were small for much of the journey, and the gradients easy, so that in many places the actual values of drawbar pull would differ little from the equivalent values at constant speed on the level.

The changes of cut-off for test purposes contri-buted to a loss of 2 min. on schedule, after allow-ing for two signal checks. Had the cut-off been sustained at 20 per cent as far as Wantage Road, this loss would probably have been avoided. Unfor-tunately no figures of coal consumption for this test have survived, for it would have been interesting to have seen the outcome of the working at short cut-off for much of the distance.

11 a.m. PADDINGTON—BRISTOL
Dynamometer Car Test Run on 1 November 1911
Engine: 4039 *Queen Matilda*
Load: To Bath, 13 cars, 378 tons empty, 400 tons full
To Bristol, 12 cars, 351 tons empty, 370 tons full

Dist. Miles		Sch. Min.	Actual m. s.	Speed m.p.h.	Reg. opening	Cut-off %	Drawbar pull, tons
0·0	PADDINGTON . .	0	0 00				
			sigs.				
1·3	Westbourne Park . .		3 42	23½			
2·5	*Milepost 2½* . . .		6 12	37	Full	22	2·9
5·7	Ealing Broadway . .		10 49	49	,,	22	2·6
7·4	Hanwell . . .		12 43	51	,,	20	2·2
9·1	Southall . . .	11	14 42	53	,,	20	2·2
13·2	West Drayton . .		19 10	59	,,	17½	1·85
16·2	Langley . . .		22 14	60½	,,	17½	
18·5	SLOUGH . . .	20	24 24	62	,,	15	1·6
—	Taplow . . .			57½	,,	20	2·1
24·2	Maidenhead . .		30 16	59	,,	20	
31·0	Twyford . . .		37 05	60	,,	20	2·2
34·0	*Milepost 34* . .		40 03	61	,,	19	1·9
36·0	READING . . .	37	41 58	63½	,,	19	1·9
38·7	Tilehurst . . .		44 29	64	,,	23	2·25
40·5	*Milepost 40½* . .		46 13	64½	,,	11	1·2
44·8	Goring . . .		50 30	57	,,	16	1·8
47·0	*Milepost 47* . .		52 49	58	,,	20	2·2
48·5	Cholsey . . .		54 22	59	,,	24	2·4
51·5	*Milepost 51½* . .		57 22	61	,,	24	2·4
53·1	DIDCOT . . .	53½	58 56	63	,,	19	
56·5	Steventon . . .		62 15	60½	,,	19	2·0
61·5	*Milepost 61½* . .			58	,,	20	
63·9	Challow . . .		69 48	57	,,	22	
71·5	Shrivenham . .		77 36	61	,,	23	
76·0	*Milepost 76* . .		81 57	61	,,	23	2·2
			sigs.		Shut		
77·3	SWINDON . . .	77	83 40	41	Full	30	3·3
78·0	*Milepost 78* . .			48½	,,	25	
80·0	*Milepost 80* . .		86 57	56	,,	19	2·0
82·9	Wootton Bassett . .		89 53	63	,,	19	1·9
83·3	*Milepost 83¼* . .			63	,,	16	1·7
87·7	Dauntsey . . .		94 07	76	,,	16	1·4
90·0	*Milepost 90* . .		95 57	74	,,	12	1·0
94·0	CHIPPENHAM . .	93½	99 24	62	,,	17½	1·85
96·1	*Thingley Junc.* . .		101 22	58	,,	20	
98·3	Corsham . . .		103 50	57	,,	20	2·1
99·0	*Milepost 99* . .				¼	20	
101·9	Box . . .		107 07	76	¼	20	
102·5	*Milepost 102½* . .			75	½	20	
104·6	Bathampton . .		109 17	73	½	20	1·45
105·8	*Milepost 105¾* . .			69½	Shut	38	
106·9	BATH . . .	107	111 55	36½	,,		
107·0	*Milepost 107* . .				Full	28	3·0
109·0	*Milepost 109* . .		114 16	55	,,	24	
113·8	Keynsham . . .		118 56	67	,,	24	1·85
116·7	St. Anne's Park . .		121 34	66	Shut	42	
118·4	BRISTOL (Temple Meads)	120	124 15				

Net time 122 min.

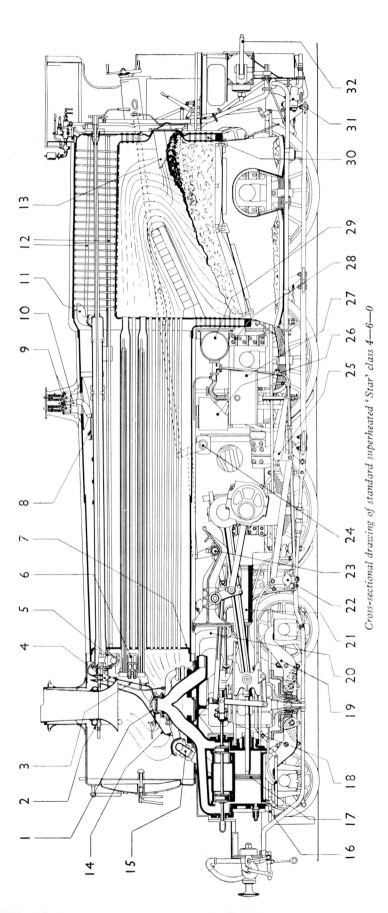

Cross-sectional drawing of standard superheated 'Star' class 4—6—0

KEY:

1. Jumper-top blast-pipe
2. Blower-ring
3. Spark-plate
4. Distributor for cylinder-oil
5. Regulator valve
6. Superheater header
7. Front tube-plate
8. Tray for feed-water
9. Safety valves
10. Delivery nozzle for feed water
11. Steam-collecting mouth
12. Longitudinal boiler stays
13. Fire-hole deflector-plate
14. Pipe discharging oil into steam passing to inside cylinder
15. Steam-pipe to inside cylinder
16. Top member of bogie frame
17. Piston
18. Rocking lever connecting inside and outside valve-spindles
19. Equalizing beam for bogie axle-loading
20. Steam-pipe to outside cylinder
21. Vacuum pump
22. Brake shaft
23. Reversing shaft
24. Intermediate reversing shaft
25. Intermediate brake-shaft
26. Sand-box
27. Brake cylinder
28. Horncheek
29. Vacuum brake reservoir
30. Fire-box water-space
31. Injector
32. Drawbar between engine and tender

As has been mentioned, Churchward's intention was to build 'Stars' for long non-stop runs and 'Saints' for runs with a number of intermediate stops. This policy continued until 1913, further batches of 'Saints' being built in 1907, 1911, and 1912. In 1913 a further batch of ten 'Saints' was ordered, but before the order was executed it was decided that in future only 'Stars' would be built. As a result, five 'Saints' only were built to this order, and the remainder of the batch appeared as 'Stars', Nos. 4041-5. This was the smallest batch of four-cylinder engines ordered at any time at Swindon. They were named after the five sons of King George V.

The 'Princes' incorporated the last major development in the Churchward boilers: top-feed. In the discussion on Churchward's paper on boilers, a speaker had suggested that the deleterious effect of introducing cold-feed water into a boiler could be mitigated by feeding the water into the steam space. Churchward replied that he was working on that question, and that he intended to pursue the plan until he had some success with it. Five years passed before the standard Swindon top-feed was perfected. Prior to its introduction the feed into the standard boilers was normally delivered at the bottom of the barrel immediately behind the smokebox. There was a hood which directed the water along the bottom of the barrel, where it promoted the general circulation. The release of air which had been trapped in the feed water led to pitting and corrosion of the barrel near the feed box.

The advantage of top feed is that the water is heated by contact with the steam before it makes contact with the metal of the boiler, and any entrapped air is released into the steam space. The air is then carried away with the steam. Deposits in the water, some of which result from water treatment, are left partly on the trays of the top-feed apparatus which can readily be removed for cleaning.

Top-feed had been tried in France in 1890, but had made no headway, and it seems that, although like many of Churchward's ideas it was not entirely original, the Swindon application was the first to be successful. The feed was delivered through clack boxes at the side of the safety valve on to sloping trays, which broke the feed into a fine spray and delivered it forwards over a wide area. The shape and slope of the trays was established by experiments in which a metered water supply was fed over trays standing in the yard at Swindon. After its adoption as standard in 1911, top-feed was soon fitted to all the Churchward boilers.

No. 4041 had cylinders 15 in. diameter, whereby

Nameplate of No. 4017, as altered in 1914

the nominal tractive effort was raised from 25,090 lb. to 27,800 lb. The main justification for this increase was the greater volume of steam which could be produced from the superheated boilers. The increase was not so great as might appear at first glance, as the cylinders of the earlier engines of the class had already been bored out at successive overhauls. A total increase in diameter of about $\frac{9}{16}$ in. was permissible on this type of cylinder. Cylinders of the 'Star' pattern but with a diameter when new of 15 in. had already been fitted to *The Great Bear*. The increase in diameter was considered successful and in due course all the 'Stars' had their cylinders increased to at least this size. The cylinders made new at that size would, in the course of time, increase beyond 15 in.

The continued growth of long-distance passenger traffic on the GWR, aided by successive improvements to the main lines, maintained a need for additional express engines, and in 1914 a further 15 'Stars' were built—Nos. 4045-60, named after Princesses. Externally they differed from the previous batch in having fluted coupling rods, this being one of the experiments with alloy steel rods previously mentioned. Some years later these rods were replaced by the normal pattern. On this batch also appeared the four-cone ejector.

Nameplate of No. 4056, the last 'Star' to remain in service

THE GWR STARS, CASTLES & KINGS

The standard GWR vacuum brake apparatus had incorporated a handle which served as an application valve, and which controlled also the single ejector cone. The vacuum was maintained during running by a vacuum pump driven from a crosshead, and the ejector was used to release the brakes after an application, and to hold them off when the train was standing. The increasing length of passenger trains made an enlargement of the ejector necessary, and a new ejector was therefore designed with four separate cones combined in one casing. The ejector was placed outside the firebox, with an exhaust pipe running along the boiler to the smokebox. In the earlier four-cone ejectors the steam to all four cones was controlled from one stop valve, but later two valves were fitted, one of which controlled one cone and the other the remaining three. The single cone could be used for maintaining the vacuum whilst the train was standing, and three or four cones could be used to release the brakes quickly. These ejectors were sometimes known as the 'three-one' pattern. The application of the brake was controlled by a separate handle. All the 'Stars' had been fitted with four-cone ejectors by 1919, and this feature was the last main development in the 'Stars', although many minor changes were made over the years. With the completion of the 'Princesses', construction of passenger engines ceased until 1922. The names of these 20 engines were:

THE 'PRINCE' AND 'PRINCESS' SERIES

No.	Name	No.	Name
4041	*Prince of Wales*	4051	*Princess Helena*
4042	*Prince Albert*	4052	*Princess Beatrice*
4043	*Prince Henry*	4053	*Princess Alexandra*
4044	*Prince George*	4054	*Princess Charlotte*
4045	*Prince John*	4055	*Princess Sophia*
4046	*Princess Mary*	4056	*Princess Margaret*
4047	*Princess Louise*	4057	*Princess Elizabeth*
4048	*Princess Victoria*	4058	*Princess Augusta*
4049	*Princess Maud*	4059	*Princess Patricia*
4050	*Princess Alice*	4060	*Princess Eugenie*

An exceptionally interesting photograph showing No. 4017 at the time it bore the original name of 'Knight of the Black Eagle'

CHAPTER 5

EARLY WORK OF THE 'STARS'

THE 'Stars' were built to work trains which made long non-stop runs, and were therefore used primarily on the West of England services in their early days. In due course the two-cylinder engines were gradually displaced from these workings, and for some time dominated the Bristol and Birmingham services. When the series from 4041 to 4060 were built, 'Stars' became more numerous on Bristol and Birmingham trains, but on the Birmingham line in particular there were few workings before World War I which taxed a 'Star' to its limit.

On the West of England services loads continued to grow, but the capacity of the 'Stars' also increased, partly by the increase in cylinder diameter in the later engines, and partly because the enginemen improved their techniques of handling the

engines. Firemen perfected the 'Haycock' fire, with a deep bed of coal on the horizontal section at the rear of the grate. Welsh coal gave excellent results with this method of firing, and there developed a tradition of rock-steady steaming, with the needle of the pressure gauge apparently fixed just below the blowing-off point. On other lines some engines might run for long periods with the boiler pressure well below the blowing-off point, the full pressure being used only for hill climbing or other extra efforts, but on the GWR a feather of steam from the safety valves became a sign that the engine was steaming normally. If the pressure fell by 20 lb. per sq. in. below the blowing-off point, the engine was considered to be steaming badly.

An important feature that assisted in the maintenance of 'rock-steady' steaming conditions was the

Up Birmingham and North express near Knowle; engine No. 4023 'King George'

continued use of Ramsbottom-type safety valves. The 'pop' type of valve was never used on GWR engines. With Ramsbottom valves the pressure could be kept at 'sizzling point', without full blowing off. There was no 'in-between' stage with 'pop' valves and full blowing off usually resulted in a drop of 5 or 10 lb. per sq. in. before the valves closed.

The ability to hold pressure near to blowing-off point for long periods depended not only on skilful firing but also upon the driver maintaining a fairly constant steam rate to the cylinders. On the long, gentle gradients of the Brunel routes this was easy, but on routes with rapidly-changing gradients frequent adjustments of the reverser were required. Over the years drivers developed the habit of

making the necessary adjustments to keep the steam rate as near as possible steady, and some intermediate passing times were regularly disobeyed because they made uneven demands upon the boiler. In later years, when the testing of engines at constant steaming rates was perfected, it was shown that the most important contribution to working an engine economically was a steam rate which remained as nearly constant as the gradients and speed restrictions allowed. Many GWR drivers had, by their own instinct and experience, long since arrived at very nearly the ideal conditions. The haycock fire was developed to suit the properties of Welsh coal, which burns most effectively on a thick and very hot firebed; but variations of the technique

THE DOWN 'CORNISH RIVIERA EXPRESS'

Run No.		1 Summer 1914	2 1916
Date		Summer 1914	1916
Engine		4045	4018
Engine name		*Prince John*	*Knight of the Grand Cross*
Load: cars, tons, tare/full			
To Westbury		13 441/470	14 457/490
To Taunton		13 441/470	11 373/400
To Exeter		13 441/470	9 301/320

Dist. Miles		Sch. Min.	Actual m. s.	Speed m.p.h.	Actual m. s.	Speed m.p.h.
0·0	PADDINGTON	0	0 00		0 00	
9·1	SOUTHALL		13 39		12 49	
16·2	Langley				19 53	64
					severe sig.	
18·5	SLOUGH	20	22 38	67 max.	22 41	
24·2	Maidenhead				30 32	
31·0	Twyford				37 24	64
35·0	*Milepost 35*		37 35			
36·0	READING	37	38 40		42 17	
44·8	Aldermaston				52 29	58
53·1	NEWBURY	56	57 41		61 21	
61·5	Hungerford				70 28	53/58
70·1	Savernake	73½	76 23	42½	80 20	44
81·1	Patney				90 38	71/66
82·0	*Milepost 82*		87 05			
91·4	Edington				98 42	83
94·0	*Milepost 94*		96 30	80½ max.		
95·6	WESTBURY	97½	98 17	slack	102 39	slack
101·3	FROME			slack	110 32	slack
106·6	Witham				117 26	
108·5	*Milepost 122¾*		116 23	39½		
115·3	CASTLE CARY	120	122 17	79½	125 42	80 max.
125·7	Somerton				134 17	
137·9	*Cogload Junction*	144	141 10		144 29	78 max.
142·9	TAUNTON	149	145 38	63·4†	149 14	
150·0	Wellington		153 03	51·0†		
150·8	*Milepost 171*		154 01	51·0†	157 33	
151·8	*Milepost 172*		155 26	42·5†	158 50	46·7†
152·8	*Milepost 173*		157 15	32·8†	160 19	40·5†
153·8	*Whiteball Box*		159 31	26·5†	161 54	37
158·8	Tiverton Junction				166 33	76 max.
166·5	Silverton				172 52	
173·7	EXETER	179*	177 41		179 29 slip	arrival

* 180 minutes on run No. 2
† Average over full mile.

Net time 175¼ min.

Cornish Riviera Express leaving Paddington, engine No. 4042 'Prince Albert'

proved equally effective with the hard coals from Staffordshire and North Wales which were supplied to the northern sheds of the GWR.

The growth of the West of England traffic was due largely to the popularity of the holiday resorts, and exceptional peaks of traffic at holiday periods were therefore inevitable. From about 1910 onwards train-loads of 500 tons were found at these periods. In the early years of World War I no further increases were made in train services, but the traffic continued to grow, and very heavy trains became more common. There were no general decelerations until January 1917, and the 'Stars' proved their ability to work the heaviest trains to pre-war schedules. Not all the heavy trains kept time, but sufficient records exist to show that the engines could reach Exeter in three hours with trains of up to 470 tons, although some of the intermediate times would not be observed with such a load. Five years earlier it seemed that 400 tons was the limit for timekeeping on these services.

The accompanying table shows two examples of heavy loads on the down 'Cornish Riviera Express'. Run No. 1 was unusual in that the full load of 470 tons was taken through to Exeter, and it is probably the finest down run recorded in the pre-war period. In the early days of the 3-hour bookings to Exeter, the passing times allowed for cautious running over the Somerton cut-off line where the earthworks were still consolidating. Subsequent alterations to the timetable never made the demands upon the locomotive even throughout the journey from Paddington to Exeter, and drivers could normally count on recovering some lost time between Castle Cary and Taunton. The driver of *Prince John* was thus able to drop nearly 3 min. in the first 70 miles to Savernake, in which there is little respite other than the Reading slack, and after passing milepost 122¾ 2¼ min. late, to be nearly 3½ min. early at Taunton, without attaining any unusually high speeds. The allowance of 24 min. for the 22.6 miles from Castle Cary to Cogload Junction was cut to 18 min. 53 sec., an average of 71.8 m.p.h. Speed was well maintained on the approaches to Wellington, suggesting that cut-off was being advanced progressively, and the train thus had sufficient momentum to cover the final mile from milepost 173 to Whiteball box at an average of 26.5 m.p.h. without excessive demands upon the engine. Time was dropped on the climb, but the driver had judged his running well, and he was through Exeter in 1¼ min. less than the allowance of 179 min.

On the second run in the table, made in 1916, coaches were slipped at Westbury and Taunton, as was normal for the 'Limited'. For a train of 490 tons the start was vigorous, with a time of 12 min. 49 sec. to Southall. Speed rose to 64 m.p.h. at Langley, but there was a bad signal check at Dolphin Junction, Slough. This cost at least 4 min. but the driver was not discouraged, and on the gentle rise to Twyford he worked up to 64 m.p.h. again. The train was 5¼ min. late through Reading, and a further 1½ min. were dropped to Savernake, despite a fine climb from Bedwyn, with a minimum

*West of England express near Twyford,
engine No. 4024 'King James'*

*Bristol express near Twyford: engine
No. 4021 'King Edward'*

of 44 m.p.h. On the falling gradients to Westbury time was soon recovered; a maximum of 83 m.p.h. was reached near Lavington, and the Westbury slip was detached less than 5 min. late. Even with the load reduced to 400 tons, the allowance of $22\frac{1}{2}$ min. for the 19.7 miles from Westbury to Castle Cary was not easy, including as it did the recovery from the slacks to 30 m.p.h. at Westbury and Frome, and the climb to milepost $122\frac{1}{4}$. On this stretch $\frac{1}{2}$ min. was dropped, but the recorder did not note the details of the climb. Between Castle Cary and Taunton the remaining lateness was wiped out. With the load reduced to 320 tons, there was no difficulty in reaching Exeter on time. For the passenger travelling to Exeter or beyond this was an excellently judged performance, but against this it must be noted that the Westbury passengers reached their destination 5 min. late, due nevertheless mainly to the signal check near Slough.

Many excellent runs must have escaped the attention of recorders, and the only record of them was in the guard's journal. Fortunately, on the publicity-minded GWR the details from the guards' journals of a number of notable runs were published from time to time, and the run tabulated herewith was revealed in this way. On 10 June 1916 the down 'Limited' loaded to 15 coaches from Paddington, and as the train was crammed with passengers the gross load must have been at least 535 tons. This was reduced by slipping at Westbury, Taunton and Exeter to about 435, 340 and 265 tons. Even if a variation of a minute either way is allowed in the guard's passing times, the performance remains outstanding. Four minutes were dropped to Reading, and a permanent-way slack between Reading and Newbury contributed to a further loss of $3\frac{1}{2}$ min. to Savernake; the Westbury

slip was detached $6\frac{1}{2}$ min. late. The running from Castle Cary to Taunton was slower than on the two previous runs described, but time recovery continued right to Exeter, a minute being recovered between Taunton and Whiteball and another minute by Exeter. The train was finally recorded as one minute early at Plymouth.

THE DOWN 'CORNISH RIVIERA EXPRESS'
Date: 10 June 1916
Engine: 4018 *Knight of the Grand Cross*
Load: To Westbury 15 cars, 494 tons tare, 535 tons full
To Taunton 12 cars, 402 tons tare, 435 tons full
To Exeter 9 cars, 314 tons tare, 340 tons full
To Plymouth 7 cars, 244 tons tare, 265 tons full

Dist. Miles		Sch. Min.	Actual Min.	Average speed m.p.h.
0·0	PADDINGTON.	0	0	
18·5	SLOUGH .	20	$23\frac{1}{2}$	47·3
36·0	READING .	37	41	60·0
			p.w.s.	
53·1	NEWBURY .	56	62	48·8
70·1	Savernake .	$73\frac{1}{2}$	81	53·7
95·6	WESTBURY .	$97\frac{1}{2}$	104	66·6
115·3	CASTLE CARY	120	127	51·4
137·9	*Cogload Junction* .	144	$146\frac{1}{2}$	69·5
142·9	TAUNTON .	149	151	66·7
153·8	*Whiteball Box* .	$161\frac{1}{2}$	$162\frac{1}{2}$	56·9
173·7	EXETER .	180	180	68·3
193·9	NEWTON ABB.	203	$202\frac{1}{2}$	53·8
202·5	Totnes .	$215\frac{1}{2}$	$214\frac{1}{2}$	43·0
209·4	Brent .	225	$227\frac{1}{2}$	31·9
225·7	PLYMOUTH .	247	246	52·9

The only run in the up direction with loading comparable to the down runs just described was recorded by Cecil J. Allen in the summer of 1913. The 3.27 p.m. from Exeter to Paddington loaded to 14 coaches, weighing 490 tons full, and with this load No. 4030 made a moderate run to Taunton, dropping $5\frac{1}{2}$ min., of which 3 min. could

58

be debited to a bridge repair slack. At Taunton a further coach was added, so that the total load increased to 520 tons. The delays which resulted from the crush of passengers, and from the addition of the extra coaches both at Exeter and Taunton, made the train half an hour late from Taunton, and inevitably signal checks were encountered. Nevertheless the driver made a determined effort, and without the checks might just have kept the booked time of 154 min. for the 142.9 miles to Paddington. On the level beyond Athelney a speed of $63\frac{1}{2}$ m.p.h.

Down West of England express near Acton, engine No. 4035 'Queen Charlotte'

4.11 p.m. TAUNTON TO PADDINGTON
Date: 1913
Engine: 4030 *King Harold*
Load: 15 cars, 473 tons tare, 520 tons full

Dist. Miles		Sch. Min.	Actual m. s.		Speed m.p.h.
0·0	TAUNTON	0	0	00	
5·0	Cogload Junction		7	55	51/63½
17·2	Somerton		21	05	48½
27·6	CASTLE CARY		32	20	61½
34·4	Milepost 122¾		41	40	30½/68
41·6	FROME		49	20	slack 67
47·3	WESTBURY		56	20	slack 60
56·0	Lavington		66	25	45 on 1 in 222
61·8	Patney		73	45	59
67·6	Pewsey		80	20	
72·8	Savernake		86	25	48
	Bedwyn				71½
81·4	Hungerford		94	15	74
89·8	NEWBURY		101	30	
—	Thatcham				70½
—	Aldermaston				68
101·7	Theale		111	55	67
	Reading West				long check
106·9	READING		119	20	severe check
111·9	Twyford		125	35	58
118·8	Maidenhead		132	10	62½
	Taplow				64
124·4	SLOUGH		137	30	67
133·8	SOUTHALL		146	35	62½
138·6	Acton		151	30	eased
142·9	PADDINGTON	154	160	20	

Net time: 154 min.

was reached and sustained, and the fall from $61\frac{1}{2}$ m.p.h. at Castle Cary to $30\frac{1}{2}$ at milepost $122\frac{3}{4}$ was good with this load. But an even better effort was made from Westbury to Savernake. On the level before Lavington speed rose to 60, and on the 1 in 222 to Patney it fell to a steady 45 m.p.h., requiring about 1,200 drawbar horsepower. There was a recovery to 59 before Pewsey, and the minimum at Savernake was 48 m.p.h. The average speed over the $16\frac{3}{4}$ miles of uphill running from Lavington to Savernake was 50.3 m.p.h. This is one of the most

notable uphill efforts recorded by a 'Star' in prewar years.

Between Savernake and Newbury speed ranged between 71 and 74 m.p.h., falling gradually to 68 to Theale, but with the train so much behind time it was not surprising that checks were encountered at Reading, costing about $2\frac{1}{2}$ min. After Reading there was a gradual recovery to 68 m.p.h. at Slough, and it was not until after Southall that the engine was eased. Final checks outside Paddington made the overall time 160 min. 20 sec., but the net time was about equal to the booking of 154 min.

In assessing the merits of the runs described in this chapter so far it must be noted that the trains were composed almost entirely of modern stock, whereas the trains hauled by saturated engines in the runs described in Chapter 3 consisted largely of older coaches, with a higher resistance per ton. Furthermore, a full assessment of a run requires a knowledge of the wind conditions, and these are not available in detail for the period up to and including the runs described in this chapter. On the assumption of a slight westerly wind, the runs by superheated engines in this chapter required a slightly smaller average horsepower than run No. 2 on page 38, which was noted to have been made against a strong south-west wind, and in which the train included some older stock.

Down express passing Old Oak Common engine No. 4026 'King Richard'

There are insufficient records of runs by 'Saints' on very heavy trains for a comparison to be made with the 'Stars', but A. V. Goodyear analysed a number of runs which he made between 1909 and 1913 to compare the uphill work of the two classes. An analysis of 18 up runs showed that for six trains hauled by 'Saints' the average time from milepost 88 to Savernake was 19 min. 40 sec., with an average load of 369 tons. For 12 trains hauled by 'Stars' the average time was 19 min. 32 sec. with an average load of 338 tons. This showed a slight advantage to the 'Saints'. The engines included saturated and superheated members of both classes. The best time was made by No. 4041, with 295 tons. The time over the 17.7 miles from milepost 88 to Savernake was 16 min. 51 sec., giving an average speed of 63.3 m.p.h. The initial speed on this stretch was 69, after six miles of 1 in 222 it fell to 59, and at Savernake was 59½ m.p.h. The best performance by a saturated engine equalled this in merit, when allowance is made for the greater load. Goodyear was on the footplate of No. 4013 on 29 July 1909 with Driver Springthorpe, who drove *Polar Star* on the London & North Western, and whose work appears again in Chapter 6. The train was the 12.5 p.m. from Exeter with a load of 310 tons. The time for the climb was 17 min. 3 sec., giving an average of 61.6 m.p.h. Speed was 66½ m.p.h. at milepost 88, fell to 55 on the 1 in 222, and rose to 63 at the summit.

The heaviest load worked by a 'Star' in this series was 455 tons behind No. 4002, by that time superheated. The time for the climb was 21 min. 40 sec., speed falling from 60 to 42 on the 1 in 222, and recovering to 48 m.p.h. at the summit. A similar comparison of 15 ascents from Exeter to Whiteball showed that eight 'Saints' took an average of 25 min. 41 sec. with 384 tons, and seven 'Stars' took an average of 25 min. 53 sec. with an average load of 360 tons.

A more detailed comparison of saturated engines of the 'Saint' and 'Star' classes is shown in the accompanying table. This shows the detailed times for two down runs between Frome and milepost 122¾. On the first run 'Saint' No. 2903 *Lady of Lyons* was hauling 360 tons, and on the second No. 4008 *Royal Star* had 350 tons. This second run is shown in full in column 1 on page 38. The times shown are from a point at Frome (evidently not the middle of the station, as the times to milepost 117 are insufficient). On both runs the trains had slowed to about 30 m.p.h. to observe the slack through the station. The 'Saint' made the more rapid recovery from the slack and the more rapid ascent. The average horsepower required between

Engine No. 4015 'Knight of St. John', as originally built in March 1908, standing in Paddington station

mileposts 117 and 122¾ was about 890 for No. 2903 and 760 for No. 4008. Too much importance should not be attached to these isolated runs, but as an experienced recorder had picked them out for detailed comparison he probably considered them representative of the two classes. They support the general impression which was formed by many observers of the superiority of the 'Saints' at starting and at hill climbing at moderate speeds.

By 1914 the 'Stars' were appearing on some of the Bristol 2-hour workings, and the accompanying table shows three runs on these trains. These were all behind superheated engines. On the first run No. 4005 encountered a signal check near the start, and was 2½ min. down on schedule by Southall. The passing time of 11 min. to Southall

COMPARISON OF THE UPHILL WORK OF 'SAINT' AND 'STAR' CLASS LOCOMOTIVES ON THE CLIMB FROM FROME TO MILEPOST 122¾

The times shown are from an unspecified point in Frome station, which was passed at about 30 m.p.h. on both runs. The milepost distances are from Paddington via Chippenham. The average gradient is 1 in 310.

Engine Load, tons		2903 360		4008 350	
Location	m. s.		Speed m.p.h.	m. s.	Speed m.p.h.
FROME	0 00			0 00	
Milepost 117	1 59		48½	2 09	43
Milepost 118	3 10		50	3 27	46
Milepost 118½	3 43		54½	4 06	46
Milepost 119	4 16		54½	4 43	48½
Milepost 119½	4 49		54½	5 21	47½
Milepost 120	5 23		53	5 58	48½
Milepost 120½	5 55		56	6 35	48½
Milepost 121½	7 00		55	7 50	48
Milepost 122	7 32		56	8 28	47½
Milepost 122½	8 05		54½	9 08	45
Milepost 122¾	8 23		50	9 28	45

PADDINGTON TO BATH

Run No.		Sch. Min.	1			2			3	
Date			1916			1915			1914	
Train			11.5			11.5			11.0	
Engine No.			4005			4019			4017	
Engine Name			*Polar Star*			*Knight Templar*			*Knight of the Black Eagle*	
Load: cars, tons, tare/full			11 358/380			13 398/420			— /505	
Dist. Miles		**Sch. Min.**	**Actual** m. s.	**Average Speed** m.p.h.		**Actual** m. s.	**Speed** m.p.h.		**Actual** m. s.	
0·0	PADDINGTON	0	0 00			0 00			0 00	
—	Westbourne Park		sigs.							
—	Ealing					p.w.s.				
9·1	SOUTHALL	11	13 30			14 05			13 30	
18·5	SLOUGH	20	22 24	63·4		23 15	69		23 00	
24·2	Maidenhead		27 34	66·3						
31·0	Twyford		33 40	66·8						
36·0	READING	37	38 10	66·7		39 05	69		40 15	
44·8	Goring		45 43	70·0		46 50	69			
53·1	DIDCOT	53½	53 00	68·3		54 20	64		57 00	
60·4	Wantage Road		59 38	66·0		61 05	64/62½			
66·5	Uffington		65 22	63·7		66 55	64			
71·5	Shrivenham		70 06	64·5						
77·3	SWINDON	77	75 30	63·3		76 50	65		80 45	
82·9	Wootton Bassett		80 46	63·9		82 05	66			
87·7	Dauntsey		84 45	72·1		86 15	76			
						sigs.				
94·0	CHIPPENHAM	93	89 41	76·5					95 15	
98·3	Corsham		93 41	64·5						
101·9	Box		97 04	63·9						
102·0	*Milepost 102*									
104·6	Bathampton		99 29	67·0					105 00	
106·9	BATH	105	101 53	57·5		108 15			107 45★	

Maximum and minimum speeds, run No. 1:

Uffington 63 m.p.h.
Dauntsey 82 „
Corsham 61 „
Box 69 „

★ Arrival of slip portion, schedule 107 min.

made an undue demand upon an engine at the beginning of a long run, before the fire was fully burned through, and it was normal to drop time on this section in the knowledge that it could be recovered later. Despite this check even time was attained by Didcot, and over the 53.1 miles from Maidenhead to Swindon the average was 66.5 m.p.h. The steady speed over the easier gradients to Didcot, followed by a gradual fall to Swindon, showed that the steaming rate remained steady during this period. By Swindon the train was 1½ min. early, and despite easier running from there onwards, the gain had increased to 3 min. by Bath. The overall time to Bristol was 116 min. 35 sec.

The second run, with a load of 420 tons, was only slightly slower, until spoiled by signal checks from Chippenham onwards. From Slough to Swindon the time was only 19 sec. slower than in the previous run, and the variation in speed was between 62½ and 69 m.p.h. The train evidently included some older coaches, so that the resistance would be slightly greater than the increase in weight alone would suggest.

The third run was made with a load of 505 tons, but the recorder did not note the composition, nor, unfortunately, did he record more than the barest details of the run. There is, however, sufficient evidence to show that it was a notable performance. The time of 40 min. 15 sec. to Reading was an improvement on the times recorded earlier in this chapter for West of England trains (which would, however, have slowed in anticipation of the slack for Reading West Junction). The average speed from Slough to Didcot was 61.2 m.p.h., which was good, but even better was the maintenance of the same average from Didcot to Swindon. The 97.7 miles from Southall to Bath were covered in 94¼ min., which was 1¾ min. under a scheduled time which had been laid down for loads of 100 tons less than on this run.

Engine No. 4004, 'Morning Star', as fitted with the forward-chimney smokebox in 1927. This photograph was taken at the same time as that on page 121, *at Old Oak Common*

On another run by the 11 a.m. down express, No. 4028 had a load of 530 tons. In the early stages the work was as good as that of No. 4017, the times to Southall and Slough being 13 min. 25 sec. and 23 min. 15 sec. Between Slough and Reading speed varied between 56 and 58 m.p.h. and reached a maximum of 60 at Tilehurst. From Slough onwards the times were greater than for No. 4017, and by Swindon the difference between the runs was 4 min. 10 sec. (84 min. 55 sec. from Paddington by No. 4028). On this day the train was booked to call at Bath, and as this would increase the steam consumption in the long gap between Goring troughs and Fox's Wood troughs, the driver was anxious to conserve water, and this was reflected in the easier running after Swindon. The time to the Bath stop was 115 min. 5 sec.

Records of up runs by 'Stars' on Bristol trains do not show any efforts comparable with those given above for down runs, but one run is interesting in pointing the way to the later schedule of the 'Bristolian'. A run by No. 4020 with 230 tons on the 12 noon from Bristol is tabulated. As far as Swindon the train observed the pre-1939 schedule of the 'Bristolian'. The load was the same as that of the 'Bristolian' in its early days, and the passing times as far as Didcot differ by no more than 9 sec. from those recorded on a typical unchecked 'Bristolian' run with the same load. After Swindon the running was less vigorous, although the speed of 75 m.p.h. at Wantage Road was unusual for the

period. Signal checks were encountered approaching Reading, and after a recovery to 72 m.p.h. at

	12 noon BRISTOL TO PADDINGTON Date: 1911 Engine: 4020 *Knight Commander* Load: 230 tons full			
Dist. Miles		Sch. Min.	Actual m. s.	Speed m.p.h.
0·0	BRISTOL . .	0	0 00	
4·8	Filton Junction .		8 45	
13·0	Chipping Sodbury		18 00	
17·6	Badminton .		22 30	62 before tunnel
27·9	Little Somerford.		31 00	83
34·7	Wootton Bassett .		36 55	
40·3	SWINDON .		42 40	
51·1	Uffington . .		52 20	
57·2	Wantage Road .		57 30	75
64·5	DIDCOT . .		63 45	
72·9	Goring . .		71 00	
—			sigs. Reading West Junction	
81·6	READING .		79 30	
—	Taplow . .			72—eased
93·4	Maidenhead .		90 50	
99·1	SLOUGH .		95 45	
108·5	SOUTHALL .		103 45	
			sigs. Acton	
116·3	Westbourne Park .		114 00	sigs.
			sig. Royal Oak	
117·6	PADDINGTON.	120	117 30	

Net time 113 minutes.
Average speed, Chipping Sodbury to Badminton 61 m.p.h.
Average speed, Swindon to Didcot 69 m.p.h.

	11.5 a.m. PADDINGTON TO BIRMINGHAM					
Run No.			1		2	
Date			August 1915		pre-1914	
Engine			4048		4023	
Engine name			*Princess Victoria*		*King George*	
Load: cars, tons, tare/full						
To Leamington			12 348/370		14 /435	
To Birmingham			10 297/315		12 /375	

Dist. Miles		Sch. Min.	Actual m. s.	Speed m.p.h.	Actual m. s.	Speed m.p.h.
0·0	PADDINGTON	0	0 00		0 00	
3·3	*Old Oak Common West*	7	6 10	35	6 18	
7·8	Greenford	(11)	11 28	59	12 15	
10·3	*Northolt Junction*	15½	14 05	60		
14·1	*Milepost 3¾*				19 12	
14·8	Denham		18 30	60		
21·1	*Milepost 10¾*				28 00	45
21·7	Beaconsfield		26 15	51½	28 55	
26·5	HIGH WYCOMBE	32	slight sig.		33 55	slack
		(30)	31 20	35		
28·8	West Wycombe				37 12	
31·5	Saunderton		37 50	47		
33·0	*Milepost 22¾*			45	43 54	37
34·7	PRINCES RISBOROUGH	42	41 30	62	46 00	
		(40)				
40·1	Haddenham		45 40	82		
44·1	*Ashendon Junction*	(50)	48 12	slack	54 03	slack
50·4	Blackthorn		54 30	73		
51·6	*Milepost 7½*				61 13	
53·4	BICESTER	(60)	57 10	65	63 05	
57·1	*Milepost 13*				67 41	46
57·2	Ardley		61 14	51½		
62·4	*Aynho Junction*	69	66 25	60	73 15	
67·5	BANBURY	74	71 30	63½	78 25	
73·4	*Milepost 92*				84 52	
76·3	Fenny Compton		80 52	55/70½		
81·2	Southam Road		85 15	69/72½		
87·3	LEAMINGTON	93	90 50	40	98 05	
89·2	Warwick		93 00			
93·5	Hatton		99 58			35
100·2	Knowle		106 55		sigs.	
103·6	Solihull		110 25			
107·4	Tyseley		114 02			
109·5	Bordesley		116 50	sig. 50		
110·6	BIRMINGHAM	120	119 05	p.w.s. 35		

Net time 117½ min.

The schedule times in brackets apply to run No. 2, where different from run No. 1.

Taplow the engine was eased. Further signal checks from Acton onwards made the total time 117 min. 30 sec. but the net time, based on the standard of running displayed, was about 113 min. Had the energy of the early stages been maintained, a net time of 105 min. would have been possible, and 110 min. could have been attained easily.

Loads on the Birmingham 2-hour trains were at first light, and of many runs recorded on these trains by A. V. Goodyear, few had loads in excess of 300 tons south of Banbury. These loads were well within the capacity of the 'Stars' and 'Saints',

but interest in the running of up trains was heightened by the extensive improvements which were made to track layouts and stations in the Birmingham area in the years before 1914. Up trains often had the incentive of late starts caused by delays in the Birmingham area, whereas down trains booked to call at Leamington could not prepare for these delays by gaining time in the early stages of a run.

Two runs are tabulated relating to the 11.5 a.m. from Paddington. This train slipped coaches at Leamington, and the driver could therefore attempt

Up Torquay and Kingswear express on the sea wall near Teignmouth:
engine No. 4060 'Princess Eugenie'

to gain some time to allow for the slacks near Birmingham. On the first run No. 4048 was driven by Bill Brooks of Wolverhampton, one of the best enginemen of his day on this route. The load was 12 coaches, weighing 370 tons gross, and reduced to 10 coaches at Leamington. There was a steady gain of time all the way. The run was made in August 1915, and the passing times are those which applied at that date. The additional figures in brackets show where the booked times in force before 1914 (which apply to run No. 2) differ from those in force in 1915. It will be seen that the times to High Wycombe and Princes Risborough had each been eased by 2 min., and the times made by No. 4048 show the wisdom of this change. On a run on which the driver was clearly making a continual effort to gain time, he failed to observe the old passing times, although he was well within the new ones. Of the GWR routes from London, the Birmingham road is the least amenable to uniform steaming. If a driver had time in hand, it would pay him not to force his engine on the principal gradients, as each of them was followed by a downhill stretch on which high speeds were possible. On this run the minima at the summits were not abnormally high, but there was fast run-

ning on the easier stretches. A fast start gave a gain of 1½ min. to Northolt Junction, but this had been reduced to 40 sec. by High Wycombe as a result of a slight check approaching that station. Exact time was kept from High Wycombe to Princes Risborough, with a minimum of 45 m.p.h. at Saunderton. Fast running to Bicester, and a good climb to Ardley, brought the train 2½ min. ahead of schedule, and this gain was maintained until reduced by a signal check to 50 m.p.h. near Bordesley, and a permanent-way slack to 35 m.p.h. after that station. Snow Hill was reached 1 min. early, and the net time was 117½ min.

The second run was made with two additional coaches, giving a gross load of 435 tons from Paddington. With this load timekeeping proved impossible, and the impression is given that 400 tons was about the limit for timekeeping in all weathers. On this run there was a side wind, and it is just possible that without it time might have been kept. The minima at the various summits compare favourably with the previous run. Lateness reached a maximum of 6 min. at Princes Risborough and had been reduced to 3 min. at Bicester, the average from Princes Risborough to Bicester being 65.6 m.p.h. Signals were encountered so severely from Knowle onwards that the recorder did not note the remainder of the times.

The last table shows a run on the 2.5 p.m. 2-hour train from Birmingham to Paddington. This train attached a coach at Leamington and slipped others at Banbury. On 29 May 1914 it had 13 coaches from Birmingham, a gross load of 370 tons, increased to 400 tons by the addition of a coach at Leamington, and reduced to 300 tons by the slipping of four coaches at Banbury. Severe signal checks had delayed the train between Hatton and Leamington, so Driver Moore had every encouragement to gain time. On the 1 in 187 past Fosse Road a steady speed of 44 m.p.h. was maintained, increasing to 58 in the dip before Fenny Compton, and falling only to 54 m.p.h. at the summit beyond that station. Speed reached 73 m.p.h. below Cropredy, and the time of 24 min. 16 sec. to Banbury was good with this load. A further rise to 78 m.p.h. by King's Sutton gave useful momentum for the climb to Ardley, on which the minimum was 53 m.p.h. The average from Bicester to Princes Risborough was 68½ m.p.h., with a maximum of 80. A further fast sprint from Beaconsfield gave a maximum of 82 m.p.h., and the train made even time by Northolt. Despite signal checks at Royal Oak, including a stop for ¼ min., the train gained 28 sec. on the schedule of 91 min. from Leamington, but the net time was only 88½ min. for 87.3 miles.

At this stage a pause can be made to reflect upon the results achieved so far, in the great development work on the four-cylinder simple engines of Swindon design, pioneered by Churchward. The close of the year 1916 rang down the curtain upon the first phase of high-speed express running. The development of the design had taken seven years, in moving from the 'Atlantic' No. 40 to the first of the 15 in. engines, No. 4041. Runs like those of *Prince John* and *Knight of the Grand Cross* on the down Limited showed clearly the potentialities of these engines; but the loadings were exceptional, and everyday demands were not so severe. No 'Star' had yet produced a dynamometer-car record of power output to equal, let alone surpass, the maximum achieved up to that time at Crewe. But the quality was there, and what was more, the design was capable of very considerable enlargement. Four lean years were nevertheless to follow before the 'Stars' began really to sparkle once again.

2.34 p.m. LEAMINGTON TO PADDINGTON
Date: 29/5/14
Engine: 4036 *Queen Elizabeth*
Load: cars, tons, tare/full To Leamington 13 349/370
To Banbury 14 378/400
To Paddington 10 276/300
Driver: Moore
Weather: Wet

Dist. Miles		Sch. Min.	Actual m. s.	Speed m.p.h.
0·0	LEAMINGTON	0	0 00	
—				44 steady
6·1	Southam Road .		10 15	48/58
11·0	Fenny Compton .		15 56	54
16·2	Cropredy . .		21 20	71
19·8	BANBURY .		24 16	73/78
24·9	*Aynho Junction* .		28 25	
30·1	Ardley . .		33 30	53 min.
33·9	BICESTER .		36 48	80
36·9	Blackthorn . .		39 02	
39·9	Brill . . .		41 25	70
43·2	*Ashendon Junction*		44 25	60 slack
47·2	Haddenham .		48 11	68/60
52·6	PRINCES RISBOROUGH		53 12	62
55·1	*Milepost 22* .		55 53	52
58·5	West Wycombe .		59 12	
60·8	HIGH WYCOMBE .		61 55	slack
65·6	Beaconsfield .		67 28	56
69·9	Gerrards Cross .		71 18	77
72·5	Denham . .		73 15	82
77·0	*Northolt Junction* .		76 40	78
79·5	Greenford . .		78 38	78
84·0	*Old Oak Common West Junction* .		83 10	
—	Royal Oak . .		signal stop	¼ min.
87·3	PADDINGTON .	91	90 32	

Net time 88½ min.

Up Torquay express, running on the relief line at Twyford East:
engine No. 4019 'Knight Templar'

65

CHAPTER 6

AUSTERITY AND RESURGENCE

THE first two years of the war brought little change in locomotive practice or train working on the GWR. There were less extra trains at peak periods, with consequent overloading of regular trains, but the 'Stars' had already shown their ability to work trains of 450-500 tons on existing schedules. From January 1917 austerity set in; restaurant cars were withdrawn and schedules eased. At Swindon there were signs of austerity also. Copper caps on chimneys were painted over, safety-valve bonnets were painted green, and all lining was omitted. In 1915 Swindon had adopted a sandy shade of khaki for the upper parts of engines, but this was replaced in 1917 with unvarnished green. The brass beading was removed from the edges of splashers of the 'Stars', never to be replaced except on engines which were rebuilt as 'Castles'. New chimneys were made with steel caps. There was a plan to fit all engines with plain cast-iron chimneys, but these never appeared on the 'Stars'. Instead, in common

A wartime holiday express leaving Paddington, for Falmouth and Newquay: engine No. 4060 'Princess Eugenie'

Engine No. 4061 'Glastonbury Abbey' as built at Swindon, 1922

with other ten-wheeled passenger engines, they were fitted for a time with smaller chimneys reminiscent of the Dean type.

In 1919 a tapered cast-iron chimney was introduced for use on all types except some small tank engines, and these were duly fitted to 20 'Stars' in the period 1919-24.* With the introduction of the 'Castles', the fitting of copper caps to chimneys was renewed, and in due course all the 'Stars' again received chimneys of this type.

In 1920, No. 4060 appeared with an experimental smokebox, with the chimney further forward than usual. The aim of this experiment was to get a more uniform distribution of draught over the tubes, but it produced no apparent difference. The boiler was removed from 4060 in 1923, and appeared on 4043 in 1925 and on 4004 in 1927, after which it disappeared. A further sign of austerity introduced during World War I and continued afterwards was the use of snap-head rivets, of which the head is visible, in place of countersunk rivets, which cannot be seen when properly painted. Snap-head rivets are stronger and cheaper, and can be removed much more easily. They were used on smokeboxes, cabs, and tenders, where previously countersunk rivets had been used.

On 1 January 1922, Mr. Churchward was succeeded as Chief Mechanical Engineer by C. B. Collett, who had been Deputy CME since 1919. The title of the office had been changed from Locomotive Carriage and Wagon Superintendent in 1916. Unlike the arrival of a new C.M.E. on some railways, Collett's succession made little change in locomotive practice on the GWR and Churchward can have had nothing but satisfaction at seeing his work continued so ably by his successor.

At the time of Churchward's retirement there

were already on order twelve more 'Stars', Nos. 4061-72. These appeared between May 1922 and February 1923. Although they were ordered under the same 'Lot' number, there was a gap of six months between the second and third engines of the batch. Externally they showed all the signs of post-war austerity—cast-iron chimneys, no beading or lining, and snap-head rivets. Internally they had a small change in that the crank axles had the webs extended on the opposite side of the crank to form balance weights for the rotating parts of that axle. The crank pins were of heat-treated steel, and it was soon found that the heat treatment did not penetrate to the centre of the crank pin. The crank pins were therefore drilled hollow to give better penetration of the heat treatment. The series were named after Abbeys as follows:

THE 'ABBEY' SERIES

No.	Name
4061	*Glastonbury Abbey*
4062	*Malmesbury Abbey*
4063	*Bath Abbey*
4064	*Reading Abbey*
4065	*Evesham Abbey*
4066	*Malvern Abbey*
4067	*Tintern Abbey*
4068	*Llanthony Abbey*
4069	*Margam Abbey**
4070	*Neath Abbey*
4071	*Cleeve Abbey*
4072	*Tresco Abbey*

* Renamed *Westminster Abbey* in 1923

Nos. 4061/2/7-72 had I-section coupling rods. Lining-out of 'Stars' began again in 1923. Nos. 4021 and 4038 retained cast-iron chimneys for a time after receiving lining, but otherwise copper-capped chimneys were restored with the new livery.

*Nos. 4000/1/8/10/3/7/8/21/2/4/8/35/8/44/7/51/4/5/ 7/60

A scene near the end of the austerity period: engine No. 4018 'Knight of the Grand Cross' in plain green, but with most of the coaches in chocolate and cream

The GWR had for long prided itself in its braking system, and a characteristic of all the Churchward locomotives was the fitting of brakes to the bogie wheels. This contributed to the high figure of 70 per cent of the total weight available for braking. The vacuum brake cylinder for the bogie was originally 11 in. in diameter, but this was later increased to 13 in. to allow of a redesign of the brake levers. With the smaller cylinders the leverage was so great that very little wear of the blocks was needed to bring the brake piston to the end of its travel. With the larger cylinders, a smaller leverage sufficed, and more wear could be allowed before adjustments to the brake rigging were needed. Despite this improvement, bogie brakes remained a doubtful asset, causing more trouble than they were worth. Churchward, however, would not agree to their removal, but shortly after Collett's succession their use was discontinued. Tests were made with and without the bogie brake in use, and no perceptible difference in braking was found. From November 1923 they were gradually removed from all engines. Small footsteps were then fitted to the bogie frames to assist drivers in oiling the inside motion.

Nos. 4000/3/6 were reported as fitted with automatic train control in 1908 when the system was installed on the main line between Reading and Slough. From 1923 the apparatus was fitted generally to the class.

Engine No. 4063 'Bath Abbey', as built

Engine No. 4070 'Neath Abbey' on Birmingham express at Kensal Green

Boiler changes were made between the various classes carrying the No. 1 standard boiler, and this resulted in 'half-cone' boilers appearing on a total of 24 'Stars' at various times between 1909 and 1921. These boilers had originally been fitted to 'Saints', but were in due course modernised with superheaters and top-feed. All the 'Stars' were built with 'long-cone' boilers. From 1925 to 1927, with pre-war lining restored, and all boiler and other modifications incorporated, the appearance of the class was fairly uniform, but in 1927 further external modifications began to appear. During this period the fitting of whistle shields began. These were inclined plates between the whistle and the cab to discourage steam from the whistle from drifting across the cab windows. In 1927 variations of tender also began to appear, and boilers with the more modern short safety valve bonnets were fitted. These bonnets were first required when one of the Frenchmen was fitted with a Great Western boiler, and they were also used on *The Great Bear* and the 47XX 2—8—0s. After the first 'Castles' had been fitted with them, they came into general use. There were two variants, one being intermediate in height between the original and final forms.

Experience with the 'Castles' soon showed that the cost of maintenance was less than that of 'Stars' employed on similar work (the difference was later estimated at one penny per mile). The reason for this was that on the heaviest work the 'Star' boilers were steamed very hard, whereas the 'Castle' boilers were less extended at the same steam rate. The 'Castle' boilers therefore suffered less wear than those of the 'Stars'. It was therefore decided to rebuild a number of 'Stars' into 'Castles', and in 1925-6 four engines which were in need of new cylinders were converted. The work was financed out of the annual allocation for repairs, and Lot numbers were not therefore issued, nor did the conversions appear in the list of withdrawals from, or additions to, stock. The rate of rebuilding was determined partly by the rate at which 'Castle' boilers became available, and few of them could be spared. By 1927, with sufficient 'Castles' and 'Kings' now available to cover the heaviest duties, there was less case for the conversions.

The first renaming of a 'Star' was made necessary by the outbreak of World War I in August 1914. No. 4017 had been *Knight of the Black Eagle,* but it was renamed *Knight of Liège.* The accent on the 'e' of Liège was later altered from grave to acute, and this apparent correction led, according to *Locomotives of the GWR,* to 'a great deal of unexpected and rather erudite correspondence, with the resultant conclusion that whereas the grave

No. 4026 'King Richard', on down 2-hour Bristol express, near Old Oak Common

accent is correct in French, the acute accent is correct in Belgium for certain words of Flemish origin with a different shade of pronunciation'. The accent remained acute. Fortunately subsequent re-namings of 'Stars' were not attended by such complications. In 1927, when the 'King' class appeared, Nos. 4021-30 were renamed after monarchs, in the form *The British Monarch.* A few months later the names were again altered by the omission of 'The' (*Italian Monarch* was renamed later than the others and missed the intermediate stage). There were a few other changes of name, which will be listed in the tables in Part 2.

From the time of the deceleration of the main-line trains in 1917 until 1921 there was little of note in GWR locomotive performance. On occasional runs in which time was recovered there was some vestige of pre-war standards, but those standards had been so high that nothing short of the restoration of pre-war schedules could revive them. This revival came sooner than many people had

No. 4054 'Princess Charlotte' on the Birkenhead – Bournemouth express (LSWR stock)

expected. Marked accelerations were planned for the summer services of 1921, but these had to be postponed for two months because of labour troubles in the coal industry. Despite this setback further accelerations followed in October 1921, when full pre-war speeds were restored on the principal main-line services of the GWR. It was soon clear that Swindon had done its work well, for the deterioration in the condition of the engines during the war had been made good, and the 'Stars' were ready to perform even better work than before 1917. This was timely, for it was soon apparent that loads of 500 tons were to become more common on West of England trains.

Cecil J. Allen travelled from Paddington to Penzance and back on the 'Cornish Riviera Express' soon after the restoration of the old schedule. On the down journey, J. Springthorpe was driving No. 4003, *Lode Star,* with loads of 406/425 tons to Westbury, 341/355 tons to Taunton, 282/295 tons to Exeter, and 249/260 tons to Plymouth. Four permanent-way slacks were in force, and a rather slow recovery from one of them caused the engine to lose 1 min. 50 sec. to Westbury. From there Springthorpe made a determined recovery, and by Plymouth had gained $12\frac{1}{2}$ min. in actual running time, and $16\frac{3}{4}$ min. net. Deducting the loss by the engine before Westbury left a clear gain to the engine of 15 min. From Brewham to Exeter the average speed was 68.9 m.p.h., and 113.2 miles from Brewham to Plympton were covered in 111 min. 50 sec.

The accompanying table shows three runs on down West of England expresses, the first two on the 'Cornish Riviera Express' and the third on the 12 noon from Paddington. On the first run, No. 4018 with 460 tons made a good start, dropping only $1\frac{1}{2}$ min. on the optimistic allowance of 11 min. to Southall. Speed reached 61 m.p.h., but then came the first of four signal checks. This reduced speed to 42 m.p.h., but there was a recovery to 68 by Twyford. The second check came at Reading and the third approaching Patney. Up the Kennet Valley speed ranged between 57 and 60 m.p.h., and the minimum at Savernake was 45 m.p.h. After the Patney check there was a quick recovery to 74 m.p.h., and despite the checks the train passed Westbury only $2\frac{1}{4}$ min. late. With the load reduced to 385 tons there was now some fast running. The fall from $51\frac{1}{2}$ to $47\frac{1}{2}$ on the climb to milepost $122\frac{3}{4}$ was good, and the allowance of 28 min. from Castle Cary to Taunton was cut to $23\frac{1}{2}$ min., with a maximum of 74 m.p.h. A signal check to 45 after Taunton hindered the climb to Whiteball. There was a permanent-way slack near the summit, but

this had little effect as speed had already fallen almost to the required 30 m.p.h. Exeter was passed a minute early in $174\frac{1}{2}$ min. net.

On the second run No. 4020 had a load of 485 tons from Paddington, and dropped $2\frac{1}{4}$ min. to Reading, partly because of a slow start. A permanent-way slack at Southcote Junction spurred Driver Cresswell to greater efforts, and the allowance of $41\frac{1}{2}$ min. from Newbury to Westbury was cut to 40 min. 12 sec., with an unusual maximum of $85\frac{1}{2}$ m.p.h. at Lavington. Despite a further permanent-way slack between Westbury and Frome, recovery of time continued, and the train was almost on time at Cogload Junction. Unfortunately Cogload troughs were under repair, and in addition to the permanent-way slack for this work, a stop was needed at Taunton for water. This cost fully 8 min., and a brisk run brought the train to Exeter $7\frac{3}{4}$ min. late, but in a net time of 176 min. Beyond Exeter, with the load reduced to 260 tons, there was more fast running; the allowance of 68 min. for the last 52 miles of the journey was cut to $59\frac{1}{4}$ min., and the train reached Plymouth a minute early.

The third run was made on the last Friday before the introduction of the summer service in 1925. The full load of thirteen 70-foot coaches was taken through to Exeter. This run may be compared with the one shown on page 56, in which a load of 470 tons was taken through to Exeter on an unchecked run. The difficulties which developed in run No. 3 of the accompanying table make the performance even more meritorious. In the early stages the run was normal for the load, 2 min. being dropped to Reading. A permanent-way slack at Kintbury was followed by a signal stop at Hungerford. A vigorous start from Hungerford brought speed to 48 m.p.h. at Bedwyn, and it fell only to 41 at the summit, where the train was $10\frac{3}{4}$ min. late. After Westbury the run was of greater interest, as the load was above normal for this part of the route. Another hard acceleration gave a maximum of 55 m.p.h. between Westbury and Frome, and the fall from $50\frac{1}{2}$ to $44\frac{1}{2}$ m.p.h. on Brewham bank was very good.

The allowance of $22\frac{1}{2}$ min. from Westbury to Castle Cary was tight, including as it did the climb to Brewham, for which little momentum could be attained. To observe this allowance with 500 tons of train was notable. Fast running from Castle Cary to Taunton recovered a further minute, despite a permanent-way slack at Keinton Mandeville. With this load the driver would have been fully justified in stopping at Taunton for a banker, but given a clear road through Taunton he proceeded without

PADDINGTON TO EXETER

Run No.		Sch. Min.	1 10.30 a.m.		2 10.30 a.m.		3 12 noon 7/25	
Train								
Date			—		—			
Engine			4018		4020		4042	
Engine name			*Knight of the Grand Cross*		*Knight Commander*		*Prince Albert*	
Load: cars, tons, tare/full								
To Westbury			— 429/460		— 459/485		13 469/500	
To Taunton			— 359/385		— 387/410		13 469/500	
To Exeter			— 359/385		— 324/345		13 469/500	
Driver			—		Cresswell		Perry	

Dist. Miles		Sch. Min.	Actual m. s.	Speed m.p.h.	Actual m. s.	Speed m.p.h.	Actual m. s.	Speed m.p.h.
0·0	PADDINGTON	0	0 00		0 00		0 00	
1·3	Westbourne Park		3 04		3 22		3 05	
5·7	Ealing		9 02		9 53	51½	9 20	50
9·1	Southall	11	12 38	61	13 51	56	13 10	55
			sig.	42				
18·5	SLOUGH	20	22 30	56	22 58	66½	22 25	65
24·2	Maidenhead		28 18	65	28 15	65	27 45	63½
31·0	Twyford		34 35	68	34 30	64	34 15	61½
36·0	READING	37	38 55	slack	39 43	slack	39 05	slack 45
			sig.	20	p.w.s.			
37·9	*Southcote Junction*		41 54		43 47		41 40	
46·7	Midgham		51 51	59	54 02	56	51 00	59
53·1	NEWBURY	56	58 17	60	60 38	58	57 50	56
							p.w.s.	
61·5	Hungerford		66 44	57	69 30	53	69 00	signal
							70 05	stop
66·4	Bedwyn		71 46	57½	74 50	58	79 15	48
70·1	Savernake	73½	76 05	45	79 06	43	84 15	41
75·3	Pewsey		81 18	65½			89 45	69/64½
			sig.					
81·1	Patney			45	89 28		94 55	68
86·9	Lavington		92 10	74	93 51	85½	99 40	80½
91·4	Edington		95 55	70½	97 09		103 10	74
95·6	WESTBURY	97½	99 50	slack 30	100 50	slack 30	107 00	slack 30
				54½	p.w.s.			55
101·3	FROME		106 48	slack 30	108 07	slack 30	114 00	slack 30
	Blatchbridge			51½		50½		50½
108·5	*Milepost 122¾*		115 53	47½/72½	117 22	47½	123 15	44½/75
115·3	CASTLE CARY	120	121 30	65/74	123 28		129 25	69
							p.w.s.	
125·7	Somerton		130 22		132 23		140 30	
137·9	*Cogload Junction*	143	141 15	slack 55	143 21		151 55	60/62½
				65	p.w.s.			
142·9	TAUNTON	148	146 00	60	151 16	water	156 50	55½/57½
			sig.	45	154 06	stop		
150·0	Wellington		153 42	46	163 48	50½	164 55	47½
			p.w.s.					
153·8	*Whiteball Box*		160 08	30	169 41	32	171 45	25½
158·8	Tiverton Junction		165 15	73½	174 28		176 55	74
170·2	Stoke Canon		174 48	72	183 45		186 05	76½
173·7	EXETER	179	177 55	pass	186 44	pass	190 10	stop
	Net time, min.:		174½		176		180	

assistance. Speed was only 55½ m.p.h. at that station, so that it required complete confidence in his engine for the driver to tackle the climb of 11 miles with a train so much in excess of what the regulations required. The last quarter of a mile before Whiteball tunnel was covered at 30 m.p.h.

to the accompaniment of a truly thunderous exhaust as I vividly recall, having timed the run. In the last mile speed fell to 25½ m.p.h., and the engine then made the fastest time on any of the three runs from Tiverton Junction to Stoke Canon. The net time was just the three hours allowed to

71

No. 4034 'Queen Adelaide' on up Cornish Riviera Express near Reading

Exeter. From the Hungerford stop to Exeter the net time was 117½ min., giving an average speed of 57 m.p.h., which with this load was outstanding, even by 'Star' standards. It is also notable that the run was made two years after the introduction of the 'Castles', when the driver might reasonably have felt that he was entitled to have one of the larger engines for such an assignment.

The working of up trains at this period is well illustrated by the run of the 6.28 p.m. from Taunton to Paddington which is shown in a second table; this also I clocked personally. The further addition of three coaches at Taunton to a 13-coach train brought the total load to 550 tons, reduced to 515 tons at Newbury by the slipping of a coach. This is the heaviest load behind a 'Star' of which records have remained, and the work was of the highest standard. A signal stop shortly after leaving Taunton would have discouraged many drivers, but not Walter Springthorpe, a son of James Springthorpe, who drove *Polar Star* on the London & North Western in 1910. At the first timing point, Cogload Junction, the train was 6 min. down on

No. 4016 'Knight of the Golden Fleece', in plain green livery

6.28 p.m. TAUNTON TO PADDINGTON

Date: July 1925
Engine: 4026 *King Richard*
Load: To Newbury   16 cars, 514 tons tare, 550 tons full
        To Paddington   15 cars, 480 tons tare, 515 tons full
Driver: W. Springthorpe (Old Oak Common)
Weather: Hot and still

Dist. Miles		Sch. Min.	Actual m. s.	Speeds m.p.h.
0·0	TAUNTON .	0	0 00	
—			sig. stop	
2·4	*Creech Junction*		7 40	
5·0	*Cogload Junction* .	6	11 00	50
8·0	Athelney .		14 15	58½
11·9	*Curry Rivel Junc.* .		18 15	61
15·0	Long Sutton		21 40	50
17·2	Somerton . .		24 15	48
				58½
20·5	Charlton Mackerell		27 45	55
22·7	Keinton Mandeville		30 05	60
25·5	Alford Halt. .		32 45	64½
27·6	CASTLE CARY	30	34 45	58½
31·1	Bruton .		38 35	45
34·4	*Milepost 122¾* .		44 40	24
36·3	Witham .		47 05	66
41·6	Frome .	.	52 30	slack
—	*Fairwood Troughs*			62½
47·3	WESTBURY .	53	59 40	slack
51·5	Edington . .		65 00	53
56·0	Lavington . .		69 35	61½
—	*Milepost 82* .			48
61·8	Patney . .		76 20	
67·6	Pewsey . .		82 35	60
72·8	Savernake .		88 10	53
76·5	Bedwyn .	82	91 50	66
81·4	Hungerford .		96 00	72½
84·4	Kintbury . .		98 30	75
89·8	NEWBURY (Slip Coach) . .	94	102 55	74
93·3	Thatcham . .		105 50	72½
96·2	Midgham . .		108 15	72
98·1	Aldermaston .		109 50	72
101·7	Theale . .		112 50	72
105·0	*Southcote Junction*		115 55	
106·9	READING .	112	118 20	40
108·8	*Sonning Box* .		120 45	50
111·9	Twyford . .	117	124 15	57
118·7	Maidenhead .	124	130 45	65
121·9	Burnham Beeches		133 40	68
124·4	SLOUGH . .	130	135 50	69½
126·7	Langley . .		137 50	68
129·7	West Drayton .		140 30	67
133·8	SOUTHALL .	140	144 25	62½
137·2	Ealing . .		147 35	64½
138·6	Acton . .		148 55	
—			sig.	
141·6	Westbourne Park		154 40	
—			sigs.	
142·9	PADDINGTON.	152	158 00	

Net time, 152 min.

booked running time. A further 5 min. was dropped on the uphill stretches, but on the downhill and level sections 6½ min. were recovered, so that by Southall the engine had made a net gain of 1½ min. from Cogload. But for signal checks in the later stages of the run the recovery would have been greater. The net time just equalled the booked

The Torbay Express near Twyford: engine No. 4070 'Neath Abbey', fully lined out and with large chimney

time of 152 min. The most notable uphill work was from Lavington to Savernake. The speed of 61½ m.p.h. on the level at Lavington was good with a load of 550 tons, and the 1 in 222 to Patney brought it down only to 48. There was a good recovery to 60 m.p.h. at Pewsey, and Savernake was passed at 53. After Savernake there was no restraint. A speed of 72 to 75 m.p.h. down the Kennet Valley was followed by a steady acceleration from the Reading slack, culminating in the surprising maximum, with this load, of 69½ m.p.h. at Slough. This run, like the third one in the table on page 71, was made two years after the introduction of the 'Castles', and would have been a highly creditable performance for a 'Castle'. Indeed less than a fortnight later one of the new engines, with nearly 100 tons *less* load, barely kept time on this same train.

On another journey of the down 'Limited',

recorded only in the guard's journal, No. 4042 had loads, on the four sections of the journey, of 525, 450, 385 and 310 tons full, and was at no point in the journey more than 2½ min. behind booked passing time. The journey ended 3 min. early at Plymouth. With lighter loads there was some fast running on the 'Limited'. On an up run No. 4008, with 370 tons, converted a lateness of nearly 8 min. at Savernake into an arrival at Paddington 2 min. early, covering 70.1 miles in 61 min. 16 sec.; 36.0 miles from Reading to Paddington occupied 32 min. 43 sec. On another run No. 4060, also with 370 tons, having been stopped by signals at Reading, passed Southall at 71½ m.p.h., and ran from Ealing to milepost 4 at 75 m.p.h. These runs are a great tribute not only to the engines and those who maintained them, but also to the enginemen, who made such determined efforts to keep time with loads with which they could justifiably have

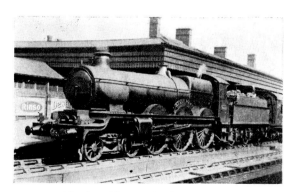

No. 4031 'Queen Mary' at Shrewsbury

French compound No. 104 in final condition with standard No. 1 boiler, at Oxford September 1927

dropped several minutes. It must not, however, be inferred that all heavy loads were handled with such competence by the 'Stars', for it is only fair to note that observers did from time to time express disappointment at the running of West of England trains. But this disappointment came only from the knowledge of what had been achieved on runs such as those described above.

The Paddington to Birmingham expresses were almost certainly documented more thoroughly than any other British services in the inter-war years. The considerable collection of logs by A. V. Goodyear and his friends were sufficient to give an excellent picture of the work of the 'Stars', 'Castles' and 'Kings', but it was overshadowed by the massive contribution of G. P. Antrobus, who logged

1,412 runs on the 6.10 p.m. from Paddington alone, mostly behind 'Kings'. As has been mentioned several times above, the Birmingham trains rarely taxed the 'Stars' before World War I; but after the restoration of the 2-hour schedules in 1921 the traffic grew rapidly, and within ten years the workings fully justified the use of 'Kings'.

Although a single journey on a Birmingham train was only half the length of the West of England workings to Plymouth, the task of the enginemen was no easier. There was less opportunity for the recovery of lost time, and the combination of more frequent changes of gradient and numerous speed restrictions made an intimate knowledge of the road essential if no time was to be lost. The majority of the trains on the service were worked by Stafford

			1	2	3	
Run No.			1928	4/10/24	1925	
Date			4071	4050	4067	
Engine No.			*Cleeve Abbey*	*Princess Alice*	*Tintern Abbey*	
Engine name						
Load: cars, tons, tare/full						
To Bicester			— 353/385	13 396/425	11 340/365	
To Banbury			— 353/385	12 367/390	10 313/335	
To Leamington			— 353/385	11 334/355	9 285/305	
Driver			—	W. Brooks	J. Williams	
Weather			fine	calm	—	

6.10 p.m. PADDINGTON TO BIRMINGHAM

Dist. Miles		Sch. Min.	Actual m. s.	Actual m. s.	Actual m. s.	Speed m.p.h.
0·0	PADDINGTON	0	0 00	0 00	0 00	
3·3	*Old Oak West Junction*		6 05	6 08	6 45	slack 25
7·8	Greenford		11 40	11 33	p.w.s. 15 00	
			p.w.s.		sig.	30
10·3	Northolt	15½	14 40	14 10	19 35	
14·8	Denham		19 30	18 32	24 50	61½
17·4	Gerrards Cross		22 25	21 15	27 30	
21·7	Beaconsfield		27 20	25 58	31 50	58½/79
26·5	HIGH WYCOMBE	32	32 05	31 00	36 05	slack 35
31·5	Saunderton		38 30	37 10	42 30	55
34·7	PRINCES RISBOROUGH	41	42 10	40 48	45 40	74
40·1	Haddenham		46 20	45 15	49 30	90
44·1	*Ashendon Junction*	49	49 25	48 39	52 25	slack
47·4	Brill		52 45	52 05	55 25	64
50·4	Blackthorn		55 15	54 38	57 50	80½
53·4	BICESTER	58	57 50	57 10	61 10	
57·2	Ardley		61 55	60 58	6 45	48½
62·4	*Aynho Junction*	67	66 50	65 49	11 40	slack 62
67·5	BANBURY	72	71 45	70 32	17 20	
71·1	Cropredy		75 10	73 55	5 40	
			p.w.s.	sig.		
76·3	Fenny Compton		80 40	80 22	10 30	
81·2	Southam Road		85 05	84 51	14 10	82/92
				sig.		
87·3	LEAMINGTON	91	90 30	91 38	19 40	
Net times, minutes:			89½	89½	83	
Average speeds:						
Gerrards Cross—Beaconsfield			52·5	54·8	59·6	
Haddenham—Ashendon Junction			77·8	70·7	82·3	

Road engines and men, and the engines normally made a return trip between Wolverhampton and Paddington without re-coaling; this limited the coal consumption to about 50 lb. per mile. Under normal conditions of loading and of weather this was ample, but when loads were heavy or the wind adverse there was little to spare.

A further table shows the logs of three runs on the 6.10 p.m. from Paddington. On each run the net time from Paddington to Leamington was less than the allowance of 91 min. The runs were timed by myself, A. V. Goodyear and Cecil J. Allen respectively.

Run No. 1 was recorded at a holiday period, when the train was divided, and the full load of 385 tons was taken through to Birmingham. After a permanent-way slack near Greenford, speed recovered to $61\frac{1}{2}$ m.p.h. at Denham, and fell to 50 at Gerrards Cross. After a minimum of 44 m.p.h. at Saunderton there was some fast running, with speeds of 85 m.p.h. at Haddenham, 75 at Blackthorn, 51 at Ardley, and 69 before Aynho. Despite a further permanent-way slack between Cropredy and Fenny Compton the arrival at Leamington was $\frac{1}{2}$ min. early.

On the second run No. 4050 was driven by W. Brooks, and slip portions were detached at Bicester and Banbury. The load from Paddington was 13 cars totalling 425 tons, reduced by one coach each at Bicester and Banbury. The climb to Beaconsfield was excellent, with an average of 54.8 m.p.h. from Gerrards Cross to Beaconsfield. Downhill speeds were not unusually high, but with a load of 390 tons the climb to Ardley was also very good, the average speed over the last 4 miles being 60 m.p.h. Signals before Leamington made the arrival $\frac{1}{2}$ min. late, but the net time was $89\frac{1}{2}$ min. On another run with No. 4034 on 14 coaches weighing 440 tons full, reduced to 410 and 350 tons at Bicester and Banbury, Driver A. Taylor made a net time of 89 min., but his average speeds on the uphill stretches were lower than in the run just described—48.7

No. 4025, when named 'Italian Monarch', at Shrewsbury

m.p.h. from Gerrards Cross to Beaconsfield and 55.0 on Bicester bank. The improvement on run No. 2 of the table came from higher downhill speeds.

Run No. 3 was probably the fastest ever recorded on this route with a train of more than 300 tons; the loads on the three sections were 365, 335 and 305 tons. No slip coaches had been provided in the rake, and stops were therefore needed at Bicester and Banbury. The engine was No. 4067 and the driver J. Williams. A very severe permanent-way slack at Greenford, and a signal check later, gave additional incentive, and Williams responded fully. Up the 1 in 175-264 gradients to Beaconsfield speed was between $58\frac{1}{2}$ and 59 m.p.h., and there followed a quick acceleration to 79 before High Wycombe. Slacks were observed scrupulously, and from a speed of 50 m.p.h. at West Wycombe there was a gradual recovery to 55 at Saunderton summit, a fine ascent. This was followed by a very fast descent at Ashendon Junction, with an average of 84.4 m.p.h. from Princes Risborough to Ashendon, and a maximum of 90. After the Banbury stop even faster running followed, even time being made between Banbury and Leamington, including the climb to Fenny Compton. The distance of 10.2 miles from Fenny Compton to milepost 105 was covered in 7 min. 20 sec. at an average of 83.5 m.p.h., and the exciting maximum speed of 92 m.p.h. was reached and sustained for three-quarters of a mile. This equalled the highest speed recorded by a 'Star'. Allowing $4\frac{3}{4}$ min. for the Greenford and Northolt checks, $5\frac{1}{4}$ min. for the stop at Bicester and 5 min. for Banbury, gives an equivalent non-stop run of 83 min. 10 sec. for the 87.3 miles from Paddington to Leamington, a remarkable achievement with these loads.

The runs quoted above were all of great merit, but with the heavier trains timekeeping was not always possible. A. V. Goodyear commented that on the evidence of about 50 down runs by 'Stars' with loads of 330 to 427 tons, mainly on the 6.10

No. 4026, when named 'The Japanese Monarch'

p.m. from Paddington, he had found that time was usually kept to Leamington with tare loads up to 360 or 370 tons. Beyond that load the main influence on timekeeping was the quality of the coal. Beyond Leamington the 6.10 p.m. down was allowed 26 min. for the remaining 23.3 miles to Birmingham, but this part of the schedule was difficult to maintain with loads in excess of the official maximum of 320 tons. No. 4067, on the run described above, cut this time to 24 min. 20 sec. with a fall from 57 to 49½ m.p.h. on Hatton bank, and a maximum of 76½ m.p.h. at Tyseley, but this was as exceptional as the earlier part of the run.

In 1924, Cecil J. Allen published details of a series of four runs on the down Birmingham 2-hour trains with loads which ranged between 190 and 290 tons to Bicester, and between 190 and 235 tons from Leamington to Birmingham. The minimum station-to-station times of these runs combined to give an equivalent non-stop run to Birmingham in 105 min. 55 sec., showing a generous recovery margin on the prevailing schedules. The growth of train loads ruled out any possibility of an acceleration below the 2-hour timing. Even the introduction of larger engines, combined with the incentive of a cut to 1 hour 55 min. of the principal trains from Euston to Birmingham, never persuaded the GWR to improve upon the 2-hour schedule.

Up running on the Birmingham line was equally good. The up 2-hour trains were the only trains in the country at this period which commonly reached speeds of 80 m.p.h. at four separate locations on one journey—on Hatton bank, and near Cropredy, Bicester and Denham. The fastest snippet recorded by a 'Star' on an up train was timed by C. Mannison on 29 August 1925. No. 4029, *King Stephen*, driven by Thomas, with a 7-coach train weighing 225 tons on the 9 a.m. from Birmingham,

Oxford and Worcester Express passing Reading West Junction; engine No. 4066 'Malvern Abbey'

Date: 29/8/25
Engine: 4063 *Bath Abbey*
Load: 14 cars, 418 tons tare, 445 tons full
Driver: Field (Old Oak Common)
Weather: Fine and calm

Dist. Miles		Sch. Min.	Actual m. s.	Speed m.p.h.
0·0	LEAMINGTON	0	0 00	
1·1	Milepost 105		3 04	
4·1	Milepost 102		7 00	48½
6·1	Southam Road		9 38	46½
11·0	Fenny Compton		14 52	60
13·1	Milepost 93		16 53	57½
16·2	Cropredy		19 49	70
18·6	Banbury Junction		21 57	70½
19·8	BANBURY	24	23 49	
3·5	Kings Sutton		5 49	55½
5·1	Aynho Junction	6	7 22	62
10·3	Ardley		13 07	52
14·1	BICESTER		16 19	75
17·1	Blackthorn		18 32	83½
20·1	Brill		20 52	70
—				66½/70½
23·4	Ashendon Junction	23	23 53	slack 55
27·4	Haddenham		27 29	70
32·8	PRINCES RISBOROUGH	33	32 28	61
36·0	Saunderton		35 48	50½
38·7	West Wycombe		38 14	68
41·0	HIGH W'COMBE	42	40 41	slack 45
—	Tylers Green			58½
45·8	Beaconsfield		46 00	56
50·1	Gerrards Cross		49 54	71
52·7	Denham		51 52	84
55·4	Ruislip		53 51	80
57·2	Northolt Junction	58	55 13	78½
59·7	Greenford	60	57 04	84½
62·9	Park Royal		59 30	73½
64·2	Old Oak Common West Junction	65	61 02	
66·2	Westbourne Park		64 10	
—			sig.	
67·5	PADDINGTON	70	67 24	

covered the 17.2 miles from Beaconsfield to Park Royal in 12 min. 30 sec. at an average speed of 82.7 m.p.h., with a maximum of 92 m.p.h. at Denham, and a further maximum of 90 at Greenford.

As with the down trains, the loads of up trains gradually increased, and interest centres mainly on the runs by heavy trains. Of many runs recorded by A. V. Goodyear and his friends, the one shown in the table on this page stands out above all others. This run was also recorded by C. Manison on 29 August 1925. The second part of the 3 p.m. from Birmingham loaded to 14 coaches, weighing 445 tons full, and was hauled by No. 4063, *Bath Abbey*. This train was worked by Old Oak men, and the driver on this occasion was Field. Delays

Cornish Riviera Express leaving Paddington, engine No. 4050 'Princess Alice'

were encountered soon after leaving Snow Hill, but from Leamington the run was unchecked until the approaches to Paddington. The start from Leamington set the standard for the remainder of the run, with an acceleration to $48\frac{1}{2}$ m.p.h., followed by a fall only to $46\frac{1}{2}$ m.p.h. on the 1 in 187 gradient after Fosse Road. A quick recovery to 59 m.p.h. after Southam Road and a minimum of $57\frac{1}{2}$ m.p.h. after Fenny Compton completed an excellent climb. Speed reached $70\frac{1}{2}$ m.p.h. at Cropredy, and after a slow run into Banbury the stop was made in 23 min. 49 sec. for the distance of 19.8 miles. After

Banbury the acceleration was again good for such a load, although time was dropped as far as Ashendon Junction. *Bath Abbey* reached 62 m.p.h. at Aynho Junction, and fell to 52 at Ardley. After a maximum of $83\frac{1}{2}$ m.p.h. at Blackthorn, the Ashendon Junction slack was observed carefully. On gradients which are on the average slightly unfavourable, speed recovered from 55 at Ashendon to 70 m.p.h. at Haddenham, and another excellent climb brought the train over Saunderton summit at a minimum of $50\frac{1}{2}$ m.p.h. A smart acceleration from the High Wycombe slack was followed by a fast descent from

3.54 p.m. BANBURY TO PADDINGTON

Engine No.	Name			Load tons tare	Actual time m. s.	Net time min.	Max. speed m.p.h.
4065	Evesham Abbey	.	.	323	68 52	$68\frac{3}{4}$	82
4023	King George	.	.	358	70 17	$69\frac{3}{4}$	87
4058	Princess Augusta	.	.	363	69 46	$69\frac{1}{4}$	82
4033	Queen Victoria	.	.	362	72 00	69	81
4030	King Harold	.	.	377	70 10	$69\frac{1}{2}$	$85\frac{1}{2}$
4067	Tintern Abbey	.	.	409	74 16	$68\frac{3}{4}$	$86\frac{1}{2}$
4045	Prince John	.	.	453	75 17	$72\frac{1}{2}$	79

Engine No. 4040 'Queen Boadicea,' with outside steam pipes

Engine No. 4043 'Prince Henry', with large 4000 gallon tender

Beaconsfield, with an average of 80.3 m.p.h. from Gerrards Cross to Park Royal, and maxima of 84 m.p.h. at Denham and 84½ at Greenford. Despite a loss of about ½ min. by a check outside Paddington, the terminus was reached in less than even time—67 min. 24 sec. for 67.5 miles. This was in every way a magnificent performance.

A table, p.77, shows a summary of seven other runs on the 3.54 p.m. from Banbury to Paddington. Only on one of these, when No. 4045 had a load of 453 tons tare, and about 500 tons full, was the net time greater than the allowance of 70 min.

The post-war running so far described was made by trains which were working to schedules which had been originally introduced before the war. The first post-war accelerations of note came in 1923, when the 2.30 p.m. from Cheltenham to Paddington was accelerated to cover the 77.3 miles from Swindon to Paddington in 75 min. The average speed of 61.8 m.p.h. was the first advance on the North Eastern Railway's old-established booking of 43 min. for the 44.1 miles from Darlington to York, and the distinction thus conferred on the train was emphasised by its receiving the nickname 'Cheltenham Flyer'. At first it was worked by 'Saints', but soon the 'Star' class took over, and the

3.45 p.m. SWINDON TO PADDINGTON 'THE CHELTENHAM FLYER'									
Run No.		1			2			3	
Engine No.		4059			4017			4072	
Engine name		*Princess Patricia*			*Knight of Liege*			*Tresco Abbey*	
Load: cars, tons, empty/full		7 212/235			8 239/260			8 251/265	
Dist. Miles		Sch. Min.	Actual m. s.	Average speed m.p.h.	Actual m. s.	Average speed m.p.h.	Sch. Min.	Actual m. s.	Speed m.p.h.
0·0	SWINDON	0	0 00		0 00		0	0 00	
5·8	Shrivenham		7 15					7 06	
10·8	Uffington		11 12	76·2	11 27			11 07	
13·4	Challow		13 12	79·6				13 09	
16·9	Wantage Road		15 50	79·7	16 16	76·7		15 47	
20·8	Steventon		18 40	82·3	19 02	84·0	19	18 40	83½
24·2	DIDCOT	24	21 12	80·7	21 23	86·8	22	21 13	sig. *70
28·8	Cholsey		24 45	78·9	24 45	83·1		24 58	76½
32·5	Goring		27 38	77·3	27 26	83·0		27 58	72½
35·8	Pangbourne		30 10	76·2	29 49	80·9		30 36	
38·6	Tilehurst		32 28	75·7				32 52	
41·3	READING	40	34 35	75·3	33 56	81·7	36½	34 54	79
46·3	Twyford		38 45	71·3	37 45	78·0		38 49	75
53·1	Maidenhead	50½	44 20	73·0	42 45	81·3		43 54	82
58·8	SLOUGH	55½	49 15	70·7			51	48 09	
64·1	West Drayton		53 35	72·3				52 08	
68·2	SOUTHALL	64	57 05	71·2			59	55 25	
71·6	Ealing		59 52	71·0	56 51	78·8		58 00 sigs.	80†
76·0	Westbourne Park		63 40	70·2				61 59	
77·3	PADDINGTON	75	66 12				70	64 24	

Net time 63½ min.
*Foxhall Jc.
†Acton

train remained the preserve of four-cylinder engines until it lost its distinction once and for all in the 1939 wartime decelerations.

Successive accelerations eventually brought the time from Swindon to Paddington down to 65 min., and the early days of the 65-minute booking brought the most spectacular displays of high speed running which had ever been seen in Britain. By that time the 'Castles' were responsible for the working and, apart from one run by No. 4072 when the schedule was 70 min., there are no records of the train being worked by a 'Star' after the schedule was cut below 75 min. However, some performances of the 'Stars' when the schedule was 75 min. show that these engines were quite capable of observing the 65-minute schedule with 8 coaches, which was the most that the 'Castles' were required to do except at holiday times. Two notable runs by 'Stars' on this train are tabulated. The second of these was included in a summary of 27 runs on the train recorded by J. P. Pearson, which was published in *The Railway Magazine* in December 1924 by Cecil J. Allen. The summary showed the minimum times between each successive pair of stations

on any of the 27 runs, and gave a cumulative time for the whole journey of 60 min. 55 sec. Although most of the best times were made by 'Castles', No. 4072, *Tresco Abbey*, had the best time from Ealing to Acton, but more strikingly No. 4017, *Knight of Liége*, had the best times over five of the 25 sections of the journey, and had the longest continuous stretch at an average of 80 m.p.h. of any of the runs. The distance of 60.8 miles from Uffington to Ealing was covered in 45 min. 14 sec. at an average of 80.7 m.p.h. Unfortunately the full details of this run were not published, and column No. 2 of the table shows as much of the log as was recorded. This was the fastest sustained running recorded by a 'Star', and was comparable with contemporary 'Castle' running. With a clear run into the terminus Paddington could have been reached in 63 min.

Run No. 1 in the table shows a performance of No. 4059 in more detail. With a coach less than No. 4017, No. 4059 made a better start, and continued to gain as far as Wantage Road; but thereafter its level of speed fell. Even so, time was gained progressively, and the total time of 66 min. 12 sec. was 9 min. less than schedule.

Up Worcester and Hereford express entering Evesham:
engine No. 4066 'Malvern Abbey'

CHAPTER 7

'THE GREAT BEAR'

STRICTLY speaking, this huge 'Pacific' engine does not fall within the scope of this monograph; but it was so closely associated with the 'Star' class in its machinery, and could, both in design and name be considered a development of them that it is certainly appropriate to include it. Eventually, of course, in its conversion to a 4—6—0 it became a member of the 'Castle' class. Nevertheless to all who have studied the work of Churchward in any detail the reasons behind the building of this engine have always been a matter of conjecture. One thing can now be said for certain; the conception was entirely due to Churchward, and not to outside influences that pressed the project upon him. In his classic paper, 'Large Locomotive Boilers', to which reference has already been made, he opened with these significant words: 'The modern locomotive problem is principally a question of boiler.' In that paper he illustrated, in drawings beautifully executed by F. W. Hawksworth, the relative proportions of many British, French and American locomotive boilers, and the latter included several examples of wide fireboxes.

At that time Churchward was very attracted to American practice, and had already included some of its features in his standard Swindon designs;

and although he had not adopted compounding as a standard on the GWR his interest in current French practice remained strong. The later French compound 'Atlantics' imported were of Paris-Orleans design, and it so happened that the first European 'Pacific' was also put to work on that line. His interest in the development of large boilers, together with current events in both America and France, without much doubt inspired the idea of a Swindon 'Pacific'. The suggestion of a 'super' locomotive was accepted by the Board and on 30 January 1907 a sum of £4,400 was voted for the construction of it, while a subsequent vote of £860 was made to cover additional expenditure on the project. Churchward had already shown himself one of the most far-sighted of British locomotive engineers, and such was the upward surge in traffic resulting from the enterprising new services put into operation since 1906 that he foresaw the time when his 4-cylinder 4—6—0s would be extended to their limit. It was not his nature to allow himself to be overtaken by circumstances, and the building of the 'Pacific' was a step toward the provision of still greater power.

It is remarkable that he should have turned to the 'Pacific' type as early as the year 1907. In this

'The Great Bear', as originally built

A front view of 'The Great Bear'

Cab layout, showing reverser extended back, as on early 'Stars'

he was followed by Gresley 15 years later, and Stanier on the LMSR in 1933. The senior draughtsman responsible for the boiler design was W. L. Watson, and at his drawing-board Churchward spent much time. The American boilers with wide fireboxes illustrated in his paper to the Institution of Mechanical Engineers were mostly designed for using low-grade coals and had grate areas varying between 44 up to no less than 72 sq. ft., even at that time in history. Churchward himself was mindful of some of the disadvantages of using a very large grate, because in that same paper he wrote: 'The wide firebox evidently requires a higher standard of skill in the fireman, for unless the grate is kept well and evenly covered, there is a tendency to have an excess of air, reducing efficiency and increasing tube trouble.' On *The Great Bear* he used a grate area of 41.9 sq. ft. This was a very big step forward from the 27 sq. ft. of the standard No. 1 boiler, and in practice it took a good deal of getting used to.

Before considering the boiler in detail reference must be made to the 'engine'. The front end lay-out was the same as that of the 'Stars', but with the cylinders increased to the maximum diameter permissible using the standard GWR tyre width of $5\frac{3}{4}$ in. This was wider than usual on other British railways, and a narrowing of this to the more customary $5\frac{1}{4}$ in. would have permitted larger cylinders

to be used, and still give adequate clearance for the rear bogie wheels. But Churchward would not consider changing the existing GWR standard tyre width, and the cylinders were made to 15 in. diameter. The drawing on page 82 shows a longitudinal section at the front end, and illustrates the layout of the smokebox, blastpipe and superheater. A further drawing relates to the trailing end. Unlike the trailing truck, an existing piece is used here.

So we come to the boiler. None of the American wide-firebox boilers which Churchward had studied so carefully had combustion chambers extending forward into the boiler barrel, as became common in later years. But that practice involved some very intricate press-work, and flanging of the firebox front and tubeplate, and at that time in the development of high-pressure boilers at Swindon it was enough to perfect a firebox with a relatively simple shape. Having decided that point, and at the same time maintaining the same dimensional relations as on the 'Star' for the smokebox tubeplate in relation to the cylinders, the length of the boiler barrel was determined by the wheel spacing. On *The Great Bear* the spacing between the centre and the rear pair of driving wheels was made 7 ft., as with the leading pair and centre pair. But even with this slight reduction the boiler barrel came out at 23 ft. By comparison with British 'Pacifics' of much later years this dimension could be criticised as exces-

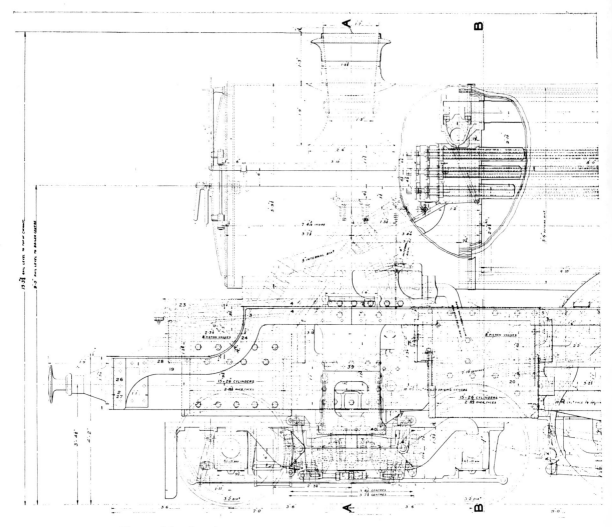

Front end drawing of No. 111, from the original drawing made by F. W. Hawksworth

sive, but it was the subject of very careful consideration in the design stage, and the tube size was increased from 2 in. diameter on the 'Stars' to $2\frac{1}{2}$ in. In his paper of 1906 to the Institution of Mechanical Engineers, Churchward said:

'The ratio of diameter to length of the tube undoubtedly has a most important bearing upon the steaming qualities of the boiler and upon the efficiency of the heat absorption. This is more particularly noticeable when the boilers are being worked to the limit of their capacity. If 2 in. tubes, say, are employed in barrels 11 to 12 feet long, when the boiler is being forced the length is not sufficient to absorb the heat from the amount of gases that a 2-inch tube will pass, and overheating and waste result.'

While the ratio of diameter to length of tube was less on *The Great Bear* than on the 'Stars', the reputation that the engine earned at first for being an indifferent steamer was almost certainly due to the difficulty firemen experienced in feeding a grate that was so unlike those already in use on the Great Western Railway. This has occurred time and again with new locomotive designs, when engineers from the drawing office have had to ride the locomotives for weeks on end, fire themselves, and find by hard experience the correct technique to use. One has known firemen almost break their hearts, and their backs (!), shovelling for dear life, when a much simpler and less fatiguing method would have produced far better results. This was certainly the case on the first Stanier 'Pacifics' on the LMSR, the

Rear end of No. 111, showing the firebox arrangement, and the radial guides for the trailing axle mounting

'The Great Bear' in No. 1 platform Paddington

boiler proportions of which have many points of similarity to those of *The Great Bear*. In later years the engine steamed well. I came to know some of the men who worked regularly on her, and they had nothing but praise for her general working, and beautiful riding.

Like the Gresley 'Pacifics', however, good riding was not obtained from the start. The springing of the trailing truck was subject to some modification. The engine had the characteristic short cab, though at first a move to provide more top shelter was made by extending the roof rearwards beyond the side-sheets. It is extraordinary how enginemen of the 'old school' seemed to rebel against any attempt to close them in on the footplate. On 'The Bear', a fireman unused to having a roof above the fall-plate managed to get a fire-iron so jammed between that roof and the floor that three men were needed to

'The Great Bear' on the 6.30 p.m. Plymouth express at Paddington

dislodge it. After, the roof was cut back somewhat. The tender was something of a curiosity. In capacity it was no larger than the rather small 6-wheeled standard type at first attached to the 'Stars', carrying 3,500 gallons of water and 6 tons of coal. It was nevertheless built as an 8-wheeler, to match more appropriately the impressive appearance of the engine. It was adapted, after construction had already begun, and to the end of its days it carried a patch covering the hole where the water scoop would have been on a 6-wheeler. The bogies were of standard locomotive type but with shorter wheelbase.

The water pick-up was in the middle, and a questionable feature was the siting of the manhole for filling in the dome covering the top end of the duct from the water-scoop. This did not last long. One day someone either forgot to fasten the manhole cover, or did not fasten it down securely, and at the first water troughs the strong upward rush of water burst it open, and surged with such force over the back of the tender as to burst open the gangway door of the leading coach, and flood that coach throughout to a depth of some 18 in. !

The engine had its first trial trip on 4 February 1908. As with many large engines of new design there were minor clearance troubles. When 'The Bear' went to Paddington for the first time the leading step, opposite the smokebox, scraped a platform, and was later removed. At the time of its construction the civil engineer would not accept the engine on any route except between Paddington and Bristol, because of its axle-loading. But while this would have given adequate scope for the development of the design to perfection, in the haulage of heavy loads at high speed over a level track that could be very trying in adverse weather conditions, it so happened that the engine took the road at the time of the celebrated feud between many senior officers of the GWR, led by Churchward, and the General Manager, Sir James Inglis. A new organisational 'tree' of responsibility had been proposed by Inglis, and was being strenuously resisted. Churchward had to walk warily so far as track loading was concerned, and so it came about that the full capacity of the engine was never really determined.

How far development work would ultimately have been carried out on the engine it is not possible to say. The 1913 modifications had scarcely begun to show their effect when war broke out, and any further experimenting with a prototype locomotive had inevitably to stop. Nevertheless, although there had never seemed to be any occasion for proving the full capacity of the engine, either

A later view of No. 111, after fitting of top-feed apparatus

on a special dynamometer-car test, or in regular service, in many ways, both officially and by railway enthusiasts, it continued to be regarded as the 'flag-ship' of the fleet, and it occupied the principal position in published material and internal documents. In 1919, when the GWR published its shilling booklet, containing the names, numbers, types and classes of its locomotives, while all other classes were illustrated by no more than a broadside official photograph 'The Bear' had in addition a weight diagram, and she was the only engine of the entire stud for which full details of the heating surfaces, boiler and firebox dimensions, and even steam and exhaust port sizes, were quoted.

In her earlier days 'The Bear' had worked on the Bristol expresses, and a regular turn was the down evening dining-car train, non-stop to Bath. After the war, however, still stationed at Old Oak Common, she was in a link of four engines which included the first 5 ft. 8 in. 2—8—0 No. 4700 and two 4—6—0s. This was before the '47XX' class

had grown beyond the pioneer engine, and No. 4700 was in some ways an isolated engine, as much as *The Great Bear* was. It was during the years 1919 to 1923 that the engine became most familiar to travellers and to the limited number of railway enthusiasts then existing. Although working, as always, on the Paddington-Bristol route it was, however, not used on the fastest and hardest trains. There were, from the autumn of 1921, four expresses running non-stop between Paddington and Bristol in the even two hours. Three of these, the 11.45 a.m. and 5.15 p.m. up, and the 1.15 p.m. down, were Bristol turns, and were thus worked by 'Saint' class engines. The remaining train was the 11.15 a.m. down, worked by Old Oak and Laira sheds on alternate days as part of a double home duty between Paddington and Plymouth. *The Great Bear* worked on such unexciting duties as the 10.45 a.m. down, and it was on this train that it became frequently photographed in those years.

A very interesting record of the engine's work,

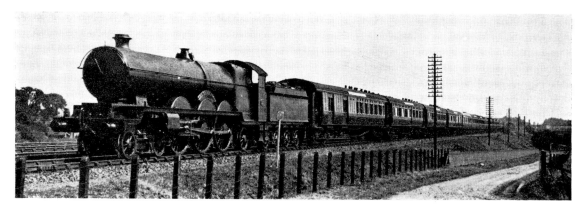

No. 111, in austerity style on the 10.45 a.m. ex Paddington near Twyford

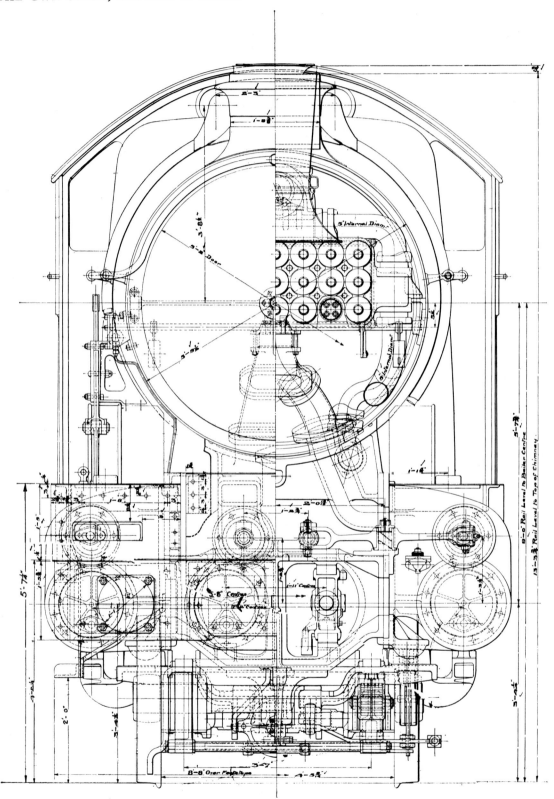

Front end cross-section of No. 111, showing the engine as fitted with top feed

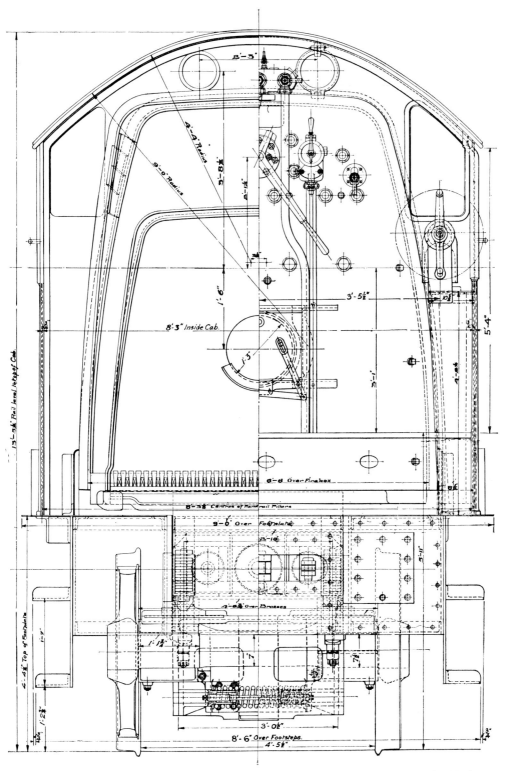

Cab and firebox cross-sections. The dotted line indicating the turning circle of the reverser handle shows why it was necessary to mount it so far back

'The Great Bear' on the 10.45 a.m. down passing Twyford East Box

which relates to the 6.40 p.m. from Paddington to Bath on 5 February 1913, has been put at our disposal by Mr. E. L. Bell, and is detailed in the accompanying log. The load of 310 tons was not heavy; but the engine started briskly from Paddington, and after a leisurely acceleration after Ealing ran well until the slight check nearing Reading hindered progress. The recovery was good, with speeds ranging round 66-68 m.p.h. on to Didcot. But there was a sudden falling off afterwards, presumably because the train was by then well on time. The average speeds after Wootton Bassett indicate a maximum of over 70 m.p.h. on Dauntsey bank, and despite very easy running after Chippenham the train would have been comfortably on time at Bath—112-minute schedule—but for the final check.

Over the years several modifications were made to *The Great Bear*. It was in shops from June to December 1913, when the Swindon No. 1 superheater was replaced by the No. 3 pattern. The superheating surface was reduced from 545 sq. ft. to 506 sq. ft. This was a special form of No. 3 superheater with four pairs of elements in each flue. In about 1920 the normal pattern of No. 3 superheater, with three pairs of elements per flue, was fitted, making the superheating surface 399 sq. ft. Each of the superheater modifications made a slight increase in the free area through the tubes, and thus made some small improvement to the steaming. At this same period a cast-iron chimney, four-cone injector, and a steel cab roof were fitted.

6.40 p.m. PADDINGTON—BATH

Load: 310 tons (less 25 tons slipped at Chippenham)
Engine: 4—6—2 No. 111 *The Great Bear*

Dist. Miles			Actual m. s.		Av. Speed m.p.h.
0·0	PADDINGTON	.	0	00	
1·3	Westbourne Park	.	3	28	
5·7	Ealing	.	9	25	44·3
9·1	Southall	.	12	59	57·2
13·2	West Drayton	.	17	14	57·8
16·2	Langley	.	20	09	61·8
18·5	SLOUGH	.	22	17	64·3
22·5	Taplow	.	26	06	63·0
24·2	Maidenhead	.	27	48	60·0
31·0	Twyford	.	34	22	62·2
—			sigs.		
36·0	READING	.	40	22	50·0
38·8	Tilehurst	.	43	07	58·8
41·5	Pangbourne	.	46	01	
44·8	Goring	.	49	03	65·2
48·5	Cholsey	.	52	26	66·5
53·1	DIDCOT	.	56	42	64·8
56·5	Steventon	.	60	05	60·3
60·4	Wantage Road	.	64	07	58·8
63·9	Challow	.	67	48	57·1
66·5	Uffington	.	70	42	53·8
71·5	Shrivenham	.	76	09	55·0
77·3	SWINDON	.	82	12	57·5
82·9	Wootton Bassett	.	87	33	62·8
87·7	Dauntsey	.	91	46	68·3
94·0	CHIPPENHAM	.	97	15	69·0
98·3	Corsham	.	101	57	54·9
101·9	Box	.	105	45	56·8
—			sigs.		
106·9	BATH	.	113	38	

Cost of checks: Reading 1½ min.
Bathampton 2 min.
Net time: 110 min.

A broadside view of No. 111 in her final condition (at Old Oak Common)

Modifications were also made to the springing, and a number of adjustments were made to the weight distribution. In 1916 the total adhesive weight was given as 61 tons 6 cwt, and Ahrons quoted 61 tons 7 cwt, the distribution between axles being different in the two cases.

In his own last years of office, from the end of the war till December 1921, Churchward apparently took no further steps to develop the 'Pacific', and instead sought to increase the steaming capacity of his larger tender engines by the fitting of larger boilers to the 'Saints', 'Stars' and 28XX 2—8—0s. This proposal was coupled with the design of the 47XX 2—8—0. A drawing dated May 1919 showed the estimated weights for these types fitted with a larger boiler; but the Civil Engineer could not accept the increase in axle load of the 4—6—0s. In the event, the 47XX was the only one of these types to receive the larger boiler, and the first of that type ran for some time with a No. 1 boiler. Although officially allowed only between Paddington and Bristol, it is recorded that the 'Pacific' made at least one appearance each at Newton Abbot and Wolverhampton.

After Churchward's retirement at the end of 1921, his successor resumed work on the design of a larger passenger engine, and found that by careful design a worthwhile increase in size could be attained in a 4—6—0 which met the requirements of the Civil Engineer. The introduction of this class, the 'Castle', in 1923 was the occasion for a big publicity campaign, proclaiming the 'Castle' as the most powerful passenger engine in Britain (based on a dubious criterion of tractive effort). *The Great Bear* then ceased to have any publicity value; indeed it became an embarrassment in the

A striking view of the great engine inside Old Oak Common shed

Engine No. 111 rebuilt as a 'Castle' and named 'Viscount Churchill': the 8-wheeled tender attached

presence of the 'Castles'. In 1924 it required heavy repairs, and it was therefore dismantled, work beginning on 7 January 1924. Parts of the engine were used in the production of a 'Castle' carrying the same number but a different name. Despite the removal of the need of *The Great Bear* for publicity purposes, there is said to have been indignation in some quarters at Paddington when news was received of its decease, and Churchward is known to have been very upset.

Under the 1919 scheme, No. 111 was classified as 'Special Red', indicated by a black plus sign on a red disc. The total mileage of the engine as a 'Pacific' was 527,272. The bogie tender, No. 1755, survived the 'Pacific' by twelve years. Between 1924

and 1936 it ran behind the following engines, in order: 'Counties' 3804/2/16, 'Saints' 2914/6/2, 'Stars' 4045/22. It was then condemned, but is believed to have been used as a water carrier for some time afterwards. There is no doubt Churchward had a deep affection for the engine, as one could have for a child on which much care and attention had been lavished in early youth, but who had not come up to expectations. Affection or not, even Churchward came to regard the engine more as a 'white elephant' rather than 'a great bear', and when he heard of the construction of the first Gresley 'Pacific' for the Great Northern he remarked jocularly: 'What did that young man want to *build* it for? We could have sold him ours!'

The first 4-cylinder 4—6—0, No. 4001 'Dog Star', in plain green, with small chimney, as fitted to the 'Abbeys'

'STARS' IN AUSTERITY

No. 4064 'Reading Abbey' as originally built, in full austerity style

CHAPTER 8

THE 'CASTLES'

IN the previous chapter it was mentioned that Churchward had a scheme in 1919 for fitting larger boilers to the 'Stars' and 'Saints', a proposal which was vetoed by the Civil Engineer on account of weight. The restoration of pre-war speeds on the GWR main lines in 1921, together with the continued increase in traffic to the West Country resorts, made the need for a larger passenger engine even greater in 1922 than it had seemed in 1919. Little increase in weight beyond the 'Star' could be accepted without reduction of route availability. Collett therefore compromised by making the greatest increase in boiler size which was possible consistent with retaining the full 'Red' route classification. This resulted in a boiler which was significantly better than the No. 1 boiler, but was lighter than the No. 7 boiler proposed in 1919.

In basic dimensions the 'Castle' showed remarkably little difference from the 'Star' other than in the boiler. The wheelbase of the engine was the same, but 1 ft. was added to the rear of the frame. This helped to accommodate a longer firebox, but it also allowed the fitting of a larger cab. By reducing tyres and clearances, it was found possible to increase the cylinder diameter to 16 in. As the same size of valve was used as in the 'Star', the valve and port size in relation to cylinder diameter was less favourable than in the 'Stars'. The design of the cylinders was so similar to that of the 'Star' that the initial drawing for issue to the works was made by altering in red certain dimensions on a copy of the cylinder drawing of the 'Star'. The pattern for the inside cylinders had a loose section which provided the smokebox saddle, and could be changed to allow the manufacture of cylinders for both 'Star' and 'Castle' boilers. There was a minor change in the valve setting in that the lead was $\frac{3}{16}$ in., in place of $\frac{1}{8}$ in. in the 'Stars'. The layout of the motion and chassis was almost identical with the 'Stars'. Changes in the dimensions of the motion parts were made, where necessary, by alterations to a 'Star' drawing.

In the boiler, the main increase was an addition of 1 ft. to the length of the firebox, making it 10 ft. To give a further increase to the grate area the water space above the foundation ring was

Engine No. 4073 'Caerphilly Castle' as originally built—in photographic grey

*C. B. Collett, Chief Mechanical Engineer
1922–1941*

reduced below the normal Churchward figure of $3\frac{1}{2}$ in. to 3 in. The grate area was thus 30.3 sq. ft. This was an increase of 12 per cent on the 'Stars', which closely matched the increase of 14 per cent in the nominal tractive effort. The barrel was 3 in. greater in diameter throughout than in the No. 1 boiler, but 3 in. less than in the No. 7. The back of the firebox was sloped slightly outwards, so that the increase in length was less at the top than at the bottom. The back of the firebox in the No. 1 boiler was vertical. The general proportions of the boiler followed normal Churchward lines, except for the reduction in the water space.

Outwardly the changes in the locomotive were more spectacular than the internal changes. The outside steam pipes were an innovation for the GWR. This change brought several benefits. The joints of the steam pipes for the outside cylinder were removed from an inaccessible position at the rear of the smokebox to the outside. The 'Star' steam pipes emerged from the bottom of the rear of the smokebox, and then turned through two right angles to reach the cylinders. Their removal from this position not only made a useful clearance in the congested space between the frames, but also removed an obstruction from the lower smoke tubes, which had previously made access to those tubes difficult. The new pattern of steam pipe was more flexible than the old one, and was therefore less affected by those movements of the cylinders on the frames, and flexing of the frames themselves, which were euphemistically described as 'breathing'.

The other notable change from Churchward

practice was the longer cab, with side windows. It is said that Churchward's apparent lack of interest in the comfort of his enginemen stemmed from complaints which were made about the side-window cab of the 4—4—0 *Earl Cawdor*. Whether that is true or not, it is a fact that Churchward's cabs were meagre, even by the standards of the early twentieth century. There were no seats, and there was rarely a position in which the enginemen could stand comfortably, whilst the combination of high footplate and low tender made them very exposed. Some men, however, say that older cabs were less draughty than the later ones, although more exposed to side and following winds. The Frenchmen had introduced a more commodious cab to the GWR, but it was not until the 47XX 2—8—0 of 1919 that any attempt was made to improve the lot of the enginemen (and then not a very successful one). It remained for Collett to produce a cab of which it could at least be said that it was no worse than was being fitted on two of the other three groups. The roof was extended over the fall plate, giving much better shelter, and the cut-out of the side plates made it possible for the enginemen to lean out without losing all protection from the roof. Cab seats were fitted, but these were not upholstered. Even forty years later many drivers found it more comfortable to stand in a GWR cab. The first engine had an inclined gutter on the cab roof, but this was soon removed.

The appearance of the 'Castle', with its higher boiler, larger cab, and outside steampipes, was automatically more impressive than that of the 'Star', but the effect was clinched by the restoration of the embellishments which had characterised Swindon engines in pre-war days—copper-capped chimney, brass beading on the splashers, and fully-lined livery. The only weakness in the effect was

*No. 4082 'Windsor Castle', hauling the
LNWR Royal Train*

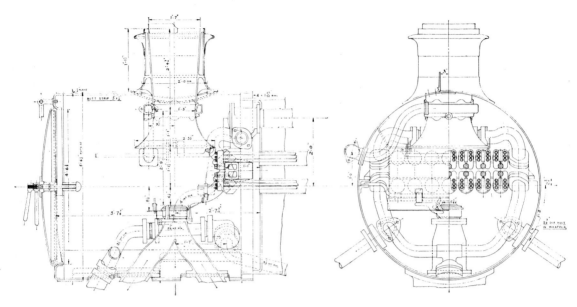

Smokebox layout of the 'Castle' 4—6—0

the continuation of the small 3,500-gallon tender. The increase of 12-14 per cent in potential output was achieved for an increase of 6 per cent in the weight. This permitted a total increase of 5 tons 9 cwt on the coupled wheels. For this small increase in weight, a significant improvement was made in the most outstanding British type of the pre-war period; adherence to existing standards made manufacture simple and cheap, and the engine was able to go straight into main-line service.

The tractive effort of the 'Stars' had been unsurpassed in British passenger engines until the introduction of the Hughes four-cylinder 4—6—0 in 1921; but from 1922 there had also been the Gresley and Raven 'Pacifics' to surpass them. The 'Castles' restored the lead to the GWR, and this was seized upon by the Publicity Department. A book was published under the name of the first locomotive—*Caerphilly Castle*—in which the engine was described as a 'super-locomotive' and the 'most powerful passenger train engine in the Kingdom'. The validity of this claim, based upon nominal tractive effort, was dubious, but it emerged two years later, in the locomotive exchanges with the London & North Eastern, that the claim had been nearer the mark than the authors could have supposed in 1923. The first edition was of 10,000 copies of the book, but within a month a further 30,000 copies were required. This was publicity on a grand scale, and the large crowds at the end of the old No. 1 platform at Paddington showed its effectiveness.

The names of the first ten of these engines were:

No.	Name
4073	*Caerphilly Castle*
4074	*Caldicot Castle*
4075	*Cardiff Castle*
4076	*Carmarthen Castle*
4077	*Chepstow Castle*
4078	*Pembroke Castle*
4079	*Pendennis Castle*
4080	*Powderham Castle*
4081	*Warwick Castle*
4082	*Windsor Castle*

No. 4073, *Caerphilly Castle*, appeared in August 1923, and was followed, between December 1923 and April 1924, by nine more. The first six were named after Welsh castles, but the series ended with *Windsor Castle*. The publicity which had attended the introduction of the class was further developed with this last engine. On 28 April 1924, Their Majesties King George V and Queen Mary visited Swindon works. The Royal Train was worked by *Windsor Castle*; at the end of the visit, on the return journey from the works yard to the station, the King and Queen rode on the engine, and the King drove. Brass plates were later fitted to the cab sides bearing the remarkable inscription set out on the following page. From that time, for many years, *Windsor Castle* became the recognised GWR Royal engine.

All concerned had cause to thank Collett for providing a more roomy cab; a gathering of this size on a 'Star' would have been too matey for a Royal party.

G   R

This engine

No. 4082 "Windsor Castle" was built at Swindon in April 1924 and was driven from the works to the station by

His Majesty King George V accompanied by Queen Mary on the occasion of the visit by their Majesties to the Great Western Railway Works at Swindon on April 28th 1924

With Their Majesties on the footplate were

Viscount Churchill	Chairman
Sir Felix Pole	General Manager
Mr. C. B. Collett	Chief Mechanical Engineer
Locomotive Inspector	G. H. Flewellyn
Engine Driver	E. R. B. Rowe
Fireman	A. W. Cook

In March 1924, No. 4074, *Caldicot Castle*, was given a thorough series of tests between Swindon and Plymouth. The test trains were made up to the maximum tonnage allowed to an unassisted engine over each section of the line. These limits were as follows:

Down line:

Swindon to Taunton	485 tons
Taunton to Newton Abbot	390 tons
Newton Abbot to Plymouth	288 tons

Up line:

| Plymouth to Newton Abbot | 288 tons |
| Newton Abbot to Swindon | 485 tons |

The logs of the three down journeys, as between Swindon and Taunton, are tabulated herewith. Weather conditions varied between the runs, the effect of west winds being very apparent on the exposed stretch of line over the marshes south of Bridgwater. Before Badminton the passing times were fairly uniform, and a further table shows the variations in cut-off which contributed to this uniformity.

No high speeds were attempted down to Stoke Gifford, and it was beyond Pylle Hill Junction that the running became energetic again. On each run 25 per cent cut-off was used as far as the summit at Flax Bourton, and on the first run this cut-off was maintained to Uphill. On the dead level between Yatton and Puxton speed was between $73\frac{1}{2}$ and 75 m.p.h., with a drawbar pull of 2.3 to 2.4 tons and full boiler pressure. At Uphill cut-off was reduced to 22 per cent, and speed fell away gradually to 62 m.p.h. south of Bridgwater.

On the second run cut-off was reduced to 21 per cent at Flax Bourton, and speed fell to $62\frac{1}{2}$ m.p.h. at Uphill, but it then varied by no more than 2 m.p.h. over the next 18 miles. On the third run conditions were more favourable, and a cut-off of 20 per cent from Flax Bourton gave a steady speed of 68 for 14 miles from Brent Knoll. The effect of the wind was also marked on the return trips; on 15 March a drawbar pull of 2.25 tons sufficed for a speed of 64 on the level, but on 20 March 2.75 tons was needed for 56 m.p.h.

The handling of the engine on the climb to Whiteball was interesting. Cut-off was fixed at 30 per cent once the train was under way from Taunton, and was left in this position to the summit. By this date it was more usual for cut-off to be advanced progressively on a climb such as this. A further table shows the log of one of the runs between Taunton and Exeter.

Although these were full-dress trials, the per-

Engine No. 4074 'Caldicot Castle', with dynamometer car, ready for the 1924 trial runs

DYNAMOMETER CAR TRIALS—MARCH 1924
Engine: 4074 *Caldicot Castle*
Load: 14 cars + dynamometer car, 484 tons tare

Run No. Date		1 March 14		2 March 19		3 March 25	
Dist. Miles		Actual m. s.	Speed m.p.h.	Actual m. s.	Speed m.p.h.	Actual m. s.	Speed m.p.h.
0·0	*Milepost 78*	0 00		0 00		0 00	
2·0	*Milepost 80*	5 55		5 06		4 55	
		check		check			
4·9	Wootton Bassett	9 43		9 20		8 36	
9·0	*Milepost 87*	15 12		13 53		12 56	
11·0	*Milepost 89*	17 07	63½	15 47	65	14 43	69
16·0	*Milepost 94*	22 15	52	20 57	53	19 37	53
18·0	*Milepost 96*	24 34	51½	23 16	50½	21 54	52
20·0	*Milepost 98*	26 55	51½	25 36	51½	24 14	50½
21·0	*Milepost 99*	28 07	50	26 46	51½	25 24	51½
22·0	Badminton	29 19	50	27 56	51½	26 36	50
		check		check		check	
26·6	Chipping Sodbury	34 12		33 00		31 24	
31·9	Winterbourne	40 51	65	39 19	66	37 48	66
34·8	Filton Junction	44 46		43 18		41 35	
38·0	Stapleton Road	50 26		49 06		47 08	
				sigs.			
40·3	*Pylle Hill Junction*	55 14		55 43		52 49	
41·6	*Milepost 120*	58 11		57 43		54 53	
44·6	*Milepost 123*	62 18	45	61 51	44	58 51	45
45·9	Flax Bourton	63 51		63 26		60 09	
50·6	*Milepost 129*	68 00	75	67 44	71	64 37	73
55·2	Puxton	72 05	73½	72 04	68	68 47	72
59·6	*Milepost 138*	75 23		75 37		72 12	
60·2	Uphill	75 57	70½	76 14	66½	72 48	69
64·1	Brent Knoll	79 23	65½	79 47	66½	76 13	68
66·9	HIGHBRIDGE	81 57	63	82 17	64½	78 39	68
70·7	Dunball	85 35	62	85 49	65½	82 02	68
73·2	BRIDGWATER	87 55	63	88 03	65½	84 12	68
77·6	*Milepost 156*	92 05	62	92 04	65½	88 05	68
						sigs.	
79 6	*Milepost 158*	94 12	55½	93 59	61	90 03	
81·6	*Milepost 160*	96 14	60	95 53	64½	sigs.	
83·6	*Milepost 162*	98 15		97 46		sig.	
84·7	TAUNTON	100 30		100 15		stop	
	Average speeds:						
	Milepost 129 to 138	73·2		68·5		71·3	
	Mileposts 138 to 156	64·7		65·7		68·0	

formance of the engine was in accordance with everyday running. This was demonstrated very clearly by a run that I recorded myself with the same engine in 1953 on the 8.55 a.m. from Paddington, with 14 coaches loading to 495 tons. The train experienced a check at Wootton Bassett similar to the first two test runs, and the cut-off was set at 25 per cent for the climb to Badminton, as on 14 March 1924. Between Hullavington and Badminton the difference in speeds between the 1924 and 1953 runs was no more than 1 m.p.h.

In 1924 there was held in London the First World Power Conference. A number of papers was read on railway electrification, and the only one on steam locomotives was by Collett on 'Testing of Locomotives on the Great Western Railway'. The paper gave an account of testing methods on the GWR—itself the most detailed account of that part of Swindon's work which had yet been published—but later in the paper came the great surprise. Churchward's reticence about details of performance went by the board, for there appeared the results of a series of tests made with No. 4074, *Caldicot Castle*. The figures were more detailed than had ever before been published about a British locomotive, and they included one which shook many British locomotive engineers—the coal per unit of work done. As mentioned in Chapter 4, the figure obtained from tests of a saturated 'Star' was 3½ lb. per drawbar horsepower hour. By 1923

DYNAMOMETER CAR TEST RUN, MARCH 1924
Engine: 4074 *Caldicot Castle*
Load: Dynamometer car+11 cars, 385 tons tare
Driver: Rowe

Location		Actual m. s.	Av. speed m.p.h.	Cut-off %	Reg. opening
Milepost 163¼ (Taunton yard) . . .		0 00		45	Full
,, 163¾				35	,,
,, 164		1 57		35	,,
,, 164½				30	,,
,, 165		3 23	41·9	,,	,,
,, 166		4 34	50·6	,,	,,
,, 167		5 42	52·9	,,	,,
,, 168		6 51	52·2	,,	,,
,, 169		7 59	52·9	,,	,,
,, 170		9 08	52·2	,,	,,
,, 171		10 15	53·7	,,	,,
,, 172		11 29	48·6	,,	,,
,, 173		13 00	39·6	,,	,,
,, 174 (Whiteball) . . .		14 48	33·3	18	⅛
,, 177		18 03	55·4	,,	,,
,, 179 (Tiverton Junction) . .		19 42	72·7	,,	,,
,, 180		20 34	69·2	,,	,,
,, 182		22 13	72·7	,,	,,
,, 185		24 45	71·0	,,	,,
,, 187		26 27	70·6	,,	Full
,, 189		28 03	75·0	,,	,,
,, 191		29 40	74·3	,,	⅛
,, 192		31 29	73·5	,,	Shut
,, 193½		32 08	54·6	,,	,,
EXETER (193·9 miles) . . .		32 50		25	Full
Milepost 194 . . . PASS		32 59	35·3	,,	,,

there were few British locomotives off the GWR which could better 4 lb., and many famous types were using 4½ to 6 lb. The figure for No. 4074 was 2.83 lb. To make this figure a true basis for comparing engines burning different grades of coal, allowance must be made for the heat content, or calorific value, of the coal. For Northern hard coals the figure equivalent to this would be about 3.0 lb., but no allowance for calorific value could make this other than a remarkable result. More than one engineer came to the conclusion that it just could not be true; E. S. Cox has told how this opinion was reached at Horwich after a detailed comparison had been made of the 'Castle' and of the Hughes 4—6—0 to see if any difference in design could be found which would account for the difference between the 2.83 lb. of the 'Castle' and the 5 lb. of the Lancashire & Yorkshire engine.

In fairness it should be said that, although this figure came from the average of several trials, in later years, when the standard of testing at Swindon had been raised still higher, more confirmation of figures between road and plant tests would have been demanded before a published claim was made. At this time the testing plant at Swindon could not absorb the power of a large locomotive so road tests were the only means of obtaining the information.

The years 1924 and 1925 provided further opportunities for the publicity value of the 'Castles' to be exploited. In those years there was staged the Empire Exhibition at Wembley the greatest exhibition seen in Britain. In the Palace of Engineering were displayed, end to end, No. 4073 *Caerphilly Castle* and London & North Eastern No. 4472 *Flying Scotsman*. Both engines glistened in the highest finish which their respective works could achieve, the brass beading and copper chimney cap of the 'Castle' being matched by the fittings of the 'Pacific' which were made from an alloy devised at Doncaster to look more like gold than normal brass. To the casual observer there can have been little doubt about the capacities of the engines. With its extra wheels, higher boiler and vast firebox, the 'Pacific' almost dwarfed the 'Castle', and the comparison was accentuated by the eight-wheeled tender of the 'Pacific'. What then of the board displayed before the 'Castle' proclaiming it to be the most powerful passenger engine in Britain?

Fortunately for later LNER locomotive history, the idea of putting the claim to the test occurred to other people than the exhibition visitors and the amateur railway fraternity. The suggestion for an exchange of locomotives seems to have been made by Sir Felix Pole, the General Manager of the

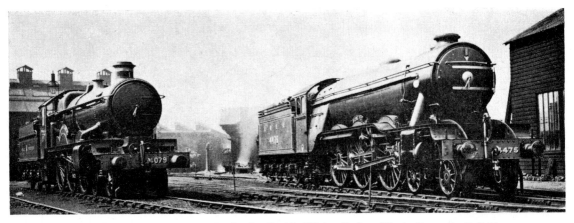

'Pendennis Castle', alongside the Gresley Pacific 'Flying Fox' at King's Cross, April 1925

GWR, to his opposite number on the LNER; when asked about this at a later date Pole was reticent, but this may have been because he regretted the ill-feeling which was later caused by the exchange. Gresley is said to have been unenthusiastic as he was not yet fully satisfied with the performance of his 'Pacifics', but to those close to him he gave the impression of welcoming an opportunity for an interchange of technical information.

The proposal was accepted by the Boards and managements of the two companies, and it was arranged that a 'Castle' should work on the LNER for a week, and a Gresley 'Pacific' on the GWR. Coal and water consumptions would be measured but, unfortunately, although both railways had dynamometer cars they were not used.

On the GWR the test engines worked the up and down 'Cornish Riviera Express'; on the LNER they worked on alternate days on the 10.10 a.m. from King's Cross to Grantham and the 1.30 p.m. from King's Cross to Doncaster, returning on the 3.7 p.m. and 6.21 p.m. trains from those towns. On the GWR, loads in the down direction decreased gradually from 530 tons on leaving Paddington to 310 tons from Exeter to Plymouth. In the up direction they varied from 310 tons from Plymouth to Exeter to 345-380 tons from Exeter to Paddington. On the LNER 475-485-ton loads were normal. The exchange was held between 27 April and 2 May 1925, and was preceded by a week of preparatory running for the visiting drivers and firemen to learn the roads. On the GWR, No. 4474 was tested against *Caldicot Castle*. On the LNER, No. 4079 *Pendennis Castle* was compared with No. 2545.

The general running of *Pendennis Castle* on the Great Northern main line equalled anything which had been recorded at that time by the Gresley 'Pacifics' with similar loads, and it included a

number of sectional times which were without precedent. The first five minutes of the first down journey revealed one of the most notable characteristics of the engine—its ability to make clean

LNER 1.30 p.m. KING'S CROSS TO DONCASTER
Date: 30/4/25
Engine: 4079 *Pendennis Castle*
Load: 16 cars, 453 tons tare, 475 tons full
Driver: Young (Old Oak Common)
Fireman: Pearce (Old Oak Common)

Dist. Miles		Sch. Min.	Actual m. s.	Speeds m.p.h.
0·0	KING'S CROSS .	0	0 00	
2·6	Finsbury Park .		5 45	40
5·0	Wood Green .		8 50	56¼
9·2	New Barnet .		13 50	49
12·7	Potters Bar .		18 20	48
17·7	HATFIELD .	25	23 25	70
22·0	Welwyn North .		27 25	
25·0	Knebworth .		30 45	52
28·6	Stevenage . .		34 15	
31·9	HITCHIN .	39	37 15	
35·7	Three Counties .		40 20	77½
41·1	Biggleswade .		45 00	eased
44·1	Sandy . .		47 40	
47·5	Tempsford .		50 50	
51·7	St. Neots . .		55 05	53
56·0	Offord . .		59 30	
58·9	HUNTINGDON	64	62 35	57
62·0	*Leys Box* .		66 25	44
69·4	Holme . .		73 15	79
72·6	Yaxley . .		75 55	70½
75·0	*Fletton Junction* .		78 00	65
76·4	PETERBORO' .	83	80 05	
3·1	*Werrington Junc.* .		5 55	57½
8·4	Tallington . .		11 20	65
12·2	Essendine .		15 00	60
15·8	Little Bytham .		18 40	54
20·7	Corby . .		24 30	48
23·7	*Stoke Box* .		28 25	44½
29·1	GRANTHAM .		33 55	eased
43·7	NEWARK . .		47 40	
62·2	RETFORD .		67 45	
79·6	DONCASTER .	88	86 20	

'Pendennis Castle', ready to leave King's Cross with the 1.30 p.m. Leeds express

starts through the notoriously difficult Gas Works and Copenhagen tunnels. On every run Finsbury Park was passed in less than six minutes, and on the five successive runs in the test week proper the time to Finsbury Park varied between no greater limits than 5 min. 42 sec. and 5 min. 57 sec. These times were about a minute less than was normal with 'Pacifics' hauling similar loads, and were achieved with only the slightest trace of slipping on one run. Experienced observers had in mind the greater proneness of 'Pacifics' to slipping than 4—6—0s having the same adhesive weight; *Pendennis Castle* demonstrated this advantage clearly. The impression made on sceptical LNER officials on King's Cross platforms was profound.

LNER 3.7 p.m. ex-GRANTHAM—KING'S CROSS
Date: 1/5/25
Engine: GWR No. 4079 *Pendennis Castle*
Load: 463 tons tare, 485 tons full
Driver: W. Young (Old Oak Common)

Dist. Miles		Actual m. s.	Speed m.p.h.
0·0	PETERBOROUGH .	0 00	
1·4	*Fletton Junction* . .	3 09	
3·8	Yaxley . . .	6 03	
7·0	Holme . . .	9 04	69
12·9	Abbots Ripton . .	14 28	56½
14·4	*Milepost 62* . .	16 04	
17·5	HUNTINGDON . .	18 54	77
20·4	Offord . . .	21 13	
24·7	St. Neots . . .	24 50	66½
28·9	Tempsford . .	28 36	70½
32·3	Sandy . . .	31 33	
35·3	Biggleswade . .	34 18	57
39·4	Arlesey . . .	38 24	62
40·7	Three Counties .	39 41	
44·5	HITCHIN . .	43 37	56½
47·8	Stevenage . .	48 02	43
51·4	Knebworth . .	52 18	
54·4	Welwyn North . .	55 33	
58·7	HATFIELD . .	59 18	70½
63·7	Potters Bar . .	64 14	56½
67·2	New Barnet . .	67 45	
		p.w.s.	
71·4	Wood Green . .	72 15	
73·8	FINSBURY PARK . .	74 38	
76·4	KING'S CROSS . .	78 58	

The uniformity of the ascents to Finsbury Park was representative of the work of Driver Young on the LNER. The variation between runs was slight, and points of particular note were spread throughout the runs. The log of the down run of 30 April is tabulated. Of the four runs made with the full load of 475-480 tons, this had the best time to Arlesey, but the greatest variation between any of the runs on this section was only 80 sec., and by Tempsford the variation was only 35 sec. Thereafter the engine was eased by varying amounts as it was ahead of schedule. One run ended with a fast entry into Peterborough, and the overall time was 78 min. 30 sec.; for the other runs it was 80 min. 5 sec., 80 min. 37 sec. and 80 min. 45 sec. The maximum speed on any run was 83½ m.p.h., sustained for 1½ miles near Three Counties. The fastest sustained speed was an average of 71.2 m.p.h. from Hitchin to Huntingdon, 22 min. 45 sec. for 27.0 miles.

On the second stage of the down journey the interest lay in the climb to Stoke. The run tabulated gave the best time on this section, with a maximum of 65 m.p.h. at Tallington, and minima of 48 before Corby and 44½ at Stoke summit. On another run the minimum at Stoke was 46, and the lowest minimum on any run was 43 m.p.h. After Stoke the engine was eased to avoid excessive gaining of time.

On the up runs *Pendennis Castle* had little in hand as far as Grantham, and actually dropped ½ min. on one run, but again it was the uniformity of running under strange conditions which stood out, rather than the small differences. The best time from Doncaster to Grantham, on 2 May, was 55 min. 51 sec., but full details of the speeds on this run were not recorded.

Of the final stages of the up journeys one run, that on 1 May, stood out above the others, mainly because of a very vigorous start from Peterborough. The log of this run is also shown. On Abbots Ripton bank speed fell from 69 to 56½ m.p.h., and a maximum of 77 at Huntingdon contributed to even time being reached by St. Neots, and maintained from there to Hitchin. On 28 April the train was stopped for three minutes by signals at Tempsford, and after a moderate start speed rose to 63 m.p.h. at Three Counties. The minimum at Stevenage was 45, followed by 60 at Langley, 54 at Woolmer Green, 73 at Hatfield, and $57\frac{1}{2}$ at Potters Bar. The load was 475 tons.

Cecil J. Allen was able to quote runs recorded by 'Pacifics' at other times which in parts equalled those of *Pendennis Castle*; but as mentioned above, some of the times recorded were without precedent. During the actual test running the 'Pacifics' fell below their usual form, possibly encouraged by the drivers' attempts to restrain the coal consumption. If this was so, it availed little, for both on the LNER and on the GWR the 'Castle' showed a significant saving. On the round trips to Grantham, the 'Castle' burned 55.7, 55.9 and 59.2 lb. per mile (on the third trip there was a severe gale), and the 'Pacific' burned 59.6, 58.1 and 59.2. On the longer Doncaster runs the 'Castle' averaged 49.8 and the 'Pacific' 55.3 lb. per mile. These figures not only showed the greater thermal efficiency of the 'Castle' but also dispelled the theory that Swindon engines could only show a superiority over other engines when burning Welsh coal. On the GWR, No. 4474 burned 50.0, 48.8 and 52.4 lb. per mile on successive down runs (the gale mentioned above affected the third run), and *Caldicot Castle* burned 44.1, 45.6 and 46.8 lb. per mile (the rise on the third day was explained by the exceptional effort made on that run). On the up runs, No. 4474's figures were 50.9, 45.2 and 40.2, and *Caldicot Castle's* were 40.6, 36.8 and 37.9 lb. per mile. Overall therefore the 'Castle' bettered the 'Pacific' by $12\frac{1}{2}$ per cent on the GWR with Welsh coal, and by $6\frac{1}{2}$ per cent on the LNER with Yorkshire coal. The performance of the 'Castle' on its own line is discussed in Chapter 9.

There is little doubt that the LNER management regarded the results of the tests as information private to the two companies, but in the *Great Western Railway Magazine* of June 1925 there appeared an account of the trials, presented more like the results of an international sporting contest than of a friendly exchange of technical information. The figures showed that on both lines the 'Castle' had a clear lead over the 'Pacific' in coal consumption. The GWR account of the trials emphasised the time which had been lost by the 'Pacifics', but did not mention that some of the lateness of arrival ascribed to the engine had been incurred before the test engine took over the train. The publication of the account, with its element of unfairness towards the LNER engine, brought a letter of complaint from the LNER to the GWR General Manager; but he replied that as Cecil J. Allen, an LNER employee, had broadcast an account of the trials which, it was claimed, showed partiality towards the LNER, the GWR felt justified in presenting its side of the story. However the results were interpreted, they were a complete triumph for the GWR. As if to rub salt into the wounds, the GWR sent *Pendennis Castle* to stand next to *Flying Scotsman* at the second Wembley Exhibition from May to October 1925.

One of the first 'Stars' rebuilt as a 'Castle' No. 4009 'Shooting Star', with tall safety valve bonnet and large tender

No. 4000 'North Star' rebuilt as a 'Castle', hauling a Weymouth express near Southcote Junction

In May 1925 there appeared the second batch of 'Castles', Nos. 4083-92. These differed from the first batch in the omission of bogie brakes. The saving in weight by their omission has never been recorded on the official engine diagrams.

The names of this batch were:

No.	Name
4083	Abbotsbury Castle
4084	Aberystwyth Castle
4085	Berkeley Castle
4086	Builth Castle
4087	Cardigan Castle
4088	Dartmouth Castle
4089	Donnington Castle
4090	Dorchester Castle
4091	Dudley Castle
4092	Dunraven Castle

The rebuilding of 'Stars' to 'Castles' began in April 1925, with the conversion of No. 4009. Three more were rebuilt between then and June 1926, after which the only further conversion until 1937 was the odd engine, No. 4000, which was dealt with in November 1929. These were all true 'rebuilds' in that the original frames were retained, with an extension of 1 ft. at the back. As previously mentioned, No. 4000 lost its 'scissors' valve gear, but retained its non-standard footplating. New cylinders and cabs were fitted which, with the boiler, constituted the main differences between the 'Stars' and 'Castles'. In September 1924 another rebuild had produced a 'Castle' from *The Great Bear*. Here also the original frames were retained, but with more modifications at the rear. A new section was fitted from behind the middle coupled wheels.

The third batch of 'Castles' appeared from May 1926. In accordance with Great Western practice of using the second digit of the number to indicate the wheel arrangement or some other characteristic of a type, the numbers followed on from 4099 to 5000. Their names are given on page 102.

This batch introduced a change in a detail of construction which had been a visible characteristic of all the GWR four-cylinder locomotives so far. The position of the inside cylinders opposite the

No.	Name
4093	*Dunster Castle*
4094	*Dynevor Castle*
4095	*Harlech Castle*
4096	*Highclere Castle*
4097	*Kenilworth Castle*
4098	*Kidwelly Castle*
4099	*Kilgerran Castle*
5000	*Launceston Castle*
5001	*Llandovery Castle*
5002	*Ludlow Castle*

leading bogie wheels made it necessary to provide clearance for the movement of these wheels. This was done by setting the frames in, or 'joggling' them, from a section just to the rear of the leading bogie wheels. This reduced the distance between the frames from 4 ft. 1 in. to 3 ft. 5½ in. by curves of 6 in. radius. The vertical fold or joggle in the frame was clearly visible in a three-quarter view of the locomotives. From No. 4093 the frames were continued straight to the buffer beam, with a hollow 'dished' in the frame to allow of the translation of the bogie wheels. The effect of the change was that the cylinder casting was made wider, and the greater width was apparent. The line of rivets by which the buffer beam was attached to the frames by an angle iron was nearer to the buffers. The omission of the joggle remedied a weakness in the frames; the reaction of the thrust in the inside cylinders was transmitted through this part of the framing, and this thrust imposed an alternating bending action on the curves of the joggle. The greater piston thrust of the 'Castle' compared with the 'Star' was causing fatigue cracks to appear at the joggle, on account of the alternating stress. The elimination of the joggle also simplified construction, as the accurate fitting of joggled frames to the

No. 4037 'Queen Philippa' converted to 'Castle' class, and fitted with experimental A.T.C. pick-up

inside cylinder casting had always been a difficult operation.

As the alteration in the frames did not affect the leading dimensions as shown on the standard GWR engine diagram, it was not acknowledged by the issue of a new diagram. The straight frames were fitted to all subsequent new four-cylinder locomotives, and one 'Star' conversion, No. 4037, later acquired them. In the later years of the 'Castles' they were fitted to a number of earlier engines of the class, when the front section of the frames was renewed.

In 1926 there appeared a small number of enlarged tenders. These could be distinguished, when attached to 'Castles', by the bottom edge of the flared top being in line with the bottom of the cab windows. On the original tenders this edge was well below the cab windows. These tenders were a step towards the introduction of a much improved design with the water capacity increased from 3,500 gallons to 4,000 gallons. The tanks of the new tenders were entirely above the footplating and frames, whereas in the 3,500-gallon tenders a portion of the tank had been in a well between the frames. The new tanks were thus simpler to construct and to maintain, and some improvements in the framing were possible. The coal space was given a sloping floor, so that the coal tended to feed

No. 4082 'Windsor Castle,' hauling the GWR Royal Train at the Railway Centenary celebrations 1925

No. 5000 'Launceston Castle' entering Euston during the 1926 trials on the LMSR

locomotives, and by 1930 the 'Castles' originally fitted with small tenders had acquired the larger pattern. It may be mentioned here, out of chronological order, that an experimental eight-wheeled tender with a rigid frame was built in 1931. It weighed 49 tons 3 cwt., and ran behind a number of 'Halls', Stars' and 'Castles'.

The earlier 'Castles' were fitted with Automatic Train Control, but Nos. 4096-9, 5000-2 ran for a time without it. All later engines received it when built, and the omission from these engines was soon remedied. Engines from No. 5000 were built with whistle deflector shields; Nos. 4082-5 had received them earlier, and by 1936 all the earlier engines had received them.

Early in its life, No. 5000 took part in the last of the loans to other railways, when it worked for five weeks on the West Coast main line of the LMSR, being stationed at Crewe North shed. The exact administrative procedure by which the loan was effected has never been fully explained, but it originated in the division of responsibility for LMSR motive power between the Chief Mechanical Engineer, who designed, built and overhauled the engines, and the Operating Department, who, through the Superintendents of Motive Power, operated and serviced them. Midland influences predominated on the operating side and, in accordance with the Midland 'small engine' policy, large numbers of Midland compound 4—4—0s were ordered. By 1925, when Sir Henry Fowler succeeded George Hughes as Chief Mechanical Engineer, he realised that a larger engine than a 4—4—0 would be needed sooner or later. It was therefore natural to propose a 4—6—0 version of the compound. Before this design had proceeded far, Fowler was attracted by the work of the compound 'Pacifics' in France. The 4—6—0 was therefore dropped in favour of a four-cylinder compound

towards the front; this made the tender almost self-trimming, and eliminated much of the need to rake the coal forward. There were improvements in the springing; straight leaf springs were used for the first time on the GWR, and the spring hangers were supported from the framing by rocking washers instead of pins. In the earlier 4,000-gallon tenders the spring hangers were long, and the rocking washers were just below the level of the tender frame. In later tenders the hangers were shorter, and the force between the hanger and frame was transmitted through a rubber block.

The new tenders weighed 46 tons 14 cwt. loaded against 40 tons for the smaller tenders. The first appeared behind No. 5000 *Launceston Castle* in September 1926, and 4093 soon acquired one; 5002-3 were supplied with them new, after which 5004-12 appeared with small ones. Thereafter only the larger tenders were fitted to four-cylinder

A very rare picture showing No. 5000 entering Crewe from the south, and passing an unidentified LNWR 2—4—0 'Jumbo' on the left

'Pacific', and work proceeded as far as the casting of some cylinders, and in the experimental conversion of a Hughes 4—6—0 to compound working. The Operating Department saw no attractions in this proposal; some memories of the Webb compounds still remained on the LNW section; there was opposition to the use of a 4—6—2 if a 4—6—0 would suffice, and to the use of four cylinders if three would suffice.

Such was the disagreement between the ideas of the Operating Department and those of the C.M.E. that the Operating Department persuaded the management to borrow a 'Castle'. This was known to be a first-class specimen of the wheel arrangement (unlike any of the existing LMSR engines), and it was hoped to establish that a 4—6—0 would do all that was required on the West Coast main line, and do it economically without the complications of compounding. As on the LNER in 1925, the 'Castle' showed itself a master of all that it was given to do. The tests began on Monday 25 October with a series of runs from Crewe to Euston returning on alternate days. No. 5000 was driven by Young, of Old Oak Common shed, who had worked 4079 on the LNER, and he made a good start on the first day by gaining at least 14 min. on a 175-minute schedule from Crewe to Euston with 410 tons. Over the two weeks of this series of trials the load was progressively increased to 510 tons, but the 'Castle' kept time every day. After a week's rest, a second series of trials was run between Crewe and Carlisle, on Anglo-Scottish expresses which left Euston and Glasgow respectively at 10 a.m. Over the two weeks the loads were progressively increased from 300 tons to 450 tons, and with this maximum load Shap had to be climbed one day in a gale of wind and rain.

The accompanying tables show the logs of two of the runs. The first one is the final up run from Crewe, with a 17-coach train of 489 tons tare, and 510 tons full. The start from Crewe was leisurely, and after a fall to $37\frac{1}{2}$ m.p.h. on Madeley bank, Whitmore was passed $3\frac{1}{2}$ min. late. Recovery of time began at once, and without exceeding 72 m.p.h. Young had time comfortably in hand when he was stopped by signals at Rugby No. 7. Recovery of the time lost by this check was more energetic, and after a minimum of 57 at Roade, speed reached 75 m.p.h. at Castlethorpe. After a fall to $63\frac{1}{2}$ between Wolverton and Bletchley, speed rose to 68. There was then a gradual fall to 60 at Cheddington, and the climb to Tring ended with a minimum of $52\frac{1}{2}$ m.p.h. Continued fast running brought the train through Watford $3\frac{1}{2}$ min. early, and there was ample reserve to allow for a permanent-way slack

	LMSR 10.30 a.m. CREWE—EUSTON			

Date: 27/10/26
Engine: GWR No. 5000 *Launceston Castle*
Load: 17 cars, 489 tons tare, 510 tons full
Driver: Young (Old Oak Common)

Dist. Miles		Sch. Min.	Actual m. s.	Speed m.p.h.
0·0	CREWE	0	0 00	
4·7	Betley Road .		10 00	$40\frac{1}{2}$
7·9	Madeley .		14 55	$37\frac{1}{2}$
10·4	Whitmore . .	15	18 25	
14·6	Standon Bridge .		22 45	$64\frac{1}{2}$
19·1	Norton Bridge .	24	26 55	$70\frac{1}{2}$
24·4	STAFFORD .	30	31 45	slack 40
28·6	Milford . .		37 00	$55\frac{1}{2}$
33·7	Rugeley .	40	42 20	65
37·0	Armitage .		45 25	59
41·7	LICHFIELD .	48	50 05	
48·0	TAMWORTH .	55	55 35	72
51·5	Polesworth .		58 55	$58\frac{1}{2}$
55·7	Atherstone .		63 15	55
60·9	NUNEATON .	69	68 40	62
64·5	Bulkington .		72 40	$52\frac{1}{2}$
70·0	Brinklow .		78 20	$63\frac{1}{2}$
			sig. stop	0
75·5	RUGBY .	85	87 10	
77·7	*Hillmorton* .		90 45	45
82·7	Welton .		97 05	
88·3	Weedon .		102 25	$72\frac{1}{2}$
95·2	BLISWORTH .	107	108 40	
98·1	ROADE .	110	111 40	57
103·2	Castlethorpe .		116 20	75
105·6	Wolverton .		118 20	$63\frac{1}{2}$ min. after
111·3	BLETCHLEY .	124	123 40	68
117·8	Leighton Buzzard .		129 50	62
121·9	Cheddington .		133 55	60
126·3	TRING .	141	138 50	$52\frac{1}{2}$
130·0	Berkhamsted .		142 40	68
133·5	Hemel Hempstead .		145 40	72
137·0	King's Langley .		148 35	$76\frac{1}{2}$
140·5	WATFORD JN. .	155	151 30	$72\frac{1}{2}$
155·7	Hatch End .		155 10	68
146·6	Harrow .		156 50	72
149·9	Wembley .		159 35	$77\frac{1}{2}$ p.w.s. 35
152·6	WILLESDEN JUNCTION .	167	163 45	slack 25/70
156·9	*Camden No. 1* .		169 25	
158·0	EUSTON . .	175	173 25	

Net time: $166\frac{1}{2}$ min.				

to 35 m.p.h. between Wembley and Willesden, together with the slack to 25 m.p.h. through Willesden Junction station, which was imposed throughout the trials because of limited cylinder clearance. The time to the arrival at Euston was 173 min. 25 sec., a gain of $1\frac{1}{2}$ min. on schedule. The net time was $166\frac{1}{2}$ min.

A second table shows the run of 16 November when, with a gross load of 415 tons, No. 5000 gained 8 min. on the 167-minute schedule from Crewe to Carlisle, despite a loss of $2\frac{1}{2}$ min. by two permanent-way slacks. The climb to Coppull summit was good, with minima of 46 m.p.h. at Boar's Head, and $47\frac{1}{2}$ at milepost $11\frac{1}{2}$. The running from Garstang to Carnforth was fast, with speed not falling below 65 m.p.h., and reaching $71\frac{1}{2}$ at Hest bank. With nearly $6\frac{1}{2}$ min. in hand there was no call for a vigorous climb to Shap, but with minima of $26\frac{1}{2}$ m.p.h. at Grayrigg and 20 at Shap summit, with a recovery to 66 m.p.h. at Tebay, running time was just kept from Carnforth to Shap summit. On the return journey on the following day with the same load time was gained more rapidly. A speed of 36 m.p.h. was maintained both on the 1 in 131 from Carlisle to Wreay and on the long 1 in 125 to Shap station. This gave a gain of

No. 5000 'Launceston Castle' at Durran Hill shed (former Midland Railway) Carlisle in 1926

$7\frac{1}{2}$ min. to Shap summit. The descent was lively, with speeds of $86\frac{1}{2}$ m.p.h. at Scout Green, and $80\frac{1}{2}$ at Hay Fell. By Oxenholme the train was 11 min. ahead of schedule, and despite signal checks at Burton and Lancaster, the gain had increased to 14 min. by Wigan. Signal stops at Bamfurlong and Winsford reduced the gain to $7\frac{3}{4}$ min., and the actual time to Crewe was 168 min. 15 sec.; the net time was 157 min., the same as the actual time on the northbound run.

With 450 tons on the following day, Young had the added difficulty of a westerly gale and heavy rain. On exposed stretches of line north of Preston the engine began to slip, and the gravity sand gear could not force the sand under the wheels before it was swept away by the gale. Some time was lost between Preston and Tebay, but on Shap itself less trouble was experienced, and time would have been bettered by Carlisle but for a signal stop at Penrith. This run was a severe test for the engine and its crew, but Young and his fireman Pearce had already proved their ability to master a strange road, and were to survive an even more severe test in America in the following year.

The times achieved in these runs were good, but not unprecedented; what was revealing was, in E. S. Cox's words, the way the 'engine performed with quiet mastery all the work on which the "Claughtons" . . . made the welkin ring with their reverberating exhaust'. Furthermore, the coal consumption per drawbar horsepower hour was less than had been recorded with any LMSR engine, although greater than had been recorded in the 1924 'Castle' tests. The trials made a profound impression, and the Operating Department was able to prevail upon the management. Work on the compound 'Pacific' was stopped, and it was decided

LMSR 1.10 p.m. CREWE TO CARLISLE (10 a.m. EUSTON TO GLASGOW)

Date: 16/11/26
Engine: GWR 5000 *Launceston Castle*
Load: 57 axles, 400 tons tare, 415 tons full
Driver: W. Young (Old Oak Common)

Dist. Miles		Sch. Min.	Actual m. s.	Speeds m.p.h.
0·0	CREWE . .	0	0 00	
4·8	Minshull Vernon		8 20	$58\frac{1}{2}$
8·7	*Winsford Junction*	10	12 00	$71\frac{1}{2}$
14·4	Acton Bridge .		16 50	$72\frac{1}{2}$
16·2	Weaver Junction .	18	18 25	65★
21·2	Moore . .		22 50	74
22·3	*Acton Grange Junc.*		23 50	$64\frac{1}{2}$
—			p.w.s.	25★
24·0	WARRINGTON	28	26 25	48/$55\frac{1}{2}$
29·8	*Golborne Junction* .		33 10	$50\frac{1}{2}$
33·2	Bamfurlong .		36 45	64
35·8	WIGAN . .	41	39 15	$57\frac{1}{2}$
38·0	Boar's Head .		41 50	46
39·1	Standish . .	45	43 10	50
41·6	Coppull . .		46 15	$47\frac{1}{2}$/$71\frac{1}{2}$
45·5	*Euxton Junction* .	53	49 40	65★/ 67
50·9	PRESTON .	61	55 35	25★
52·2	*Oxheys Box* .	64	58 20	35
55·7	Barton . .		62 50	$55\frac{1}{2}$
60·4	Garstang .	72	67 30	65
67·6	Galgate . .		74 10	67
70·8	*Lancaster No. 1 Box*		77 10	65
71·9	LANCASTER .	84	78 10	68
75·0	Hest Bank .		80 50	$71\frac{1}{2}$
78·2	CARNFORTH .	90	83 40	65
82·7	Burton . .		88 20	$50\frac{1}{2}$
85·5	Milnthorpe .		91 00	59
91·0	OXENHOLME .	104	97 30	$43\frac{1}{2}$
94·5	*Hay Fell Box* .		103 00	$34\frac{1}{2}$
98·1	Grayrigg . .		110 00	$26\frac{1}{2}$
104·1	TEBAY . .	122	116 40	66
107·1	*Scout Green Box* .		120 20	32
109·6	*Shap Summit* .	133	126 40	20
118·9	Clifton . .		135 55	79
123·1	PENRITH .	147	139 40	57★
133·6	Southwaite .		149 20	$70\frac{1}{2}$
136·1	Wreay . .		151 35	64★
—			p.w.s.	
141·0	CARLISLE .	165	157 00	

★Speed reduced by brakes.
Net time: $154\frac{1}{2}$ min.

that the new engine should be a 4—6—0. The Operating Department, despite its inclination towards three cylinders, was so impressed that it would have accepted the 'Castle' design as it stood, and an approach was actually made to the GWR, by way of a 'feeler', to find whether Swindon would build 50 'Castles' for the LMSR. Somewhat naturally this request was declined, as was also the subsequent request for a set of drawings. The LMS in its extremity then looked elsewhere.

Although not a strict part of Great Western locomotive history, it may be mentioned that in 1923 and 1924 the Chief Mechanical Engineer of the Southern Railway was faced with the problem of designing a passenger engine capable of working 500-ton trains at average speeds of 55 m.p.h. over the principal routes of the system. A 'Pacific' and a 4—6—0 were considered, but before a decision was reached J. Clayton, Personal Assistant to the C.M.E. of the Southern, made a footplate trip on No. 4076 on the down 'Cornish Riviera Express' on 1 October 1924. Ten days later he made a trip on a Gresley 'Pacific'. He was thereby confirmed in his opinion that a 4—6—0 would do the job, and the Lord Nelson was the outcome. The design of the Lord Nelson owed much to the association of Maunsell's assistant, James Clayton, with Churchward during the latter part of World War I, when proposals for new standard locomotive designs were being worked out by certain prominent members of the Association of Railway Locomotive Engineers. As Clayton came to realise the genius that lay behind Churchward's practice on the GWR he became a most fervent admirer of it, and it influenced all his subsequent design work on the Southern Railway. This was a continuation of the Swindon influence that had commenced at Ashford in 1914, when Maunsell had recruited some of his new staff on the SECR from former Great Western men. For the GWR, the important point about the Lord Nelson when it appeared in 1926 was that the tractive effort of 33,500 lb. was nearly 2,000 lb. in excess of that of the 'Castle'. As the GWR had chosen to equate tractive effort with power in its publicity, it could not complain when the Southern claimed to have Britain's most powerful passenger engine.

Reverting to the story of the 1926 trials with Launceston Castle, when the Chief Mechanical Engineer of the LMSR had been instructed to get 50 powerful 4—6—0s built ready for the summer traffic of 1927, after the failure to obtain drawings of the 'Castle' the Southern Railway was approached, and a set of drawings of the Lord Nelson sent to Glasgow for helping the North British

'Pendennis Castle', with intermediate type tender, hauling an up mail train circa 1926

Locomotive Company who had been awarded the contract for building the new engines. Swindon influence, not only through Launceston Castle but also through the Lord Nelson, was thus brought to bear in the design of the 'Royal Scots'. It is interesting to recall that in all the earlier LMS correspondence about these engines they were referred to as 'Improved Castle type' !

For three successive years the month of May saw the appearance of a new batch of 'Castles'; in 1927 it was the fourth series, Nos. 5003-12. These were:

No.	Name
5003	Lulworth Castle
5004	Llanstephan Castle
5005	Manorbier Castle
5006	Tregenna Castle
5007	Rougemont Castle
5008	Raglan Castle
5009	Shrewsbury Castle
5010	Restormel Castle
5011	Tintagel Castle
5012	Berry Pomeroy Castle

As has been mentioned, No. 5003 had a 4,000-gallon tender when new, but the others ran for up to three years with 3,500-gallon tenders. Before the completion of No. 5012, the first 'King' had been completed; a heavier axle loading had been accepted, an engine larger than the 'Improved Star'

No. 4086 'Berkeley Castle' on down stopping train near Twyford

The Cornish Riviera Express (530-ton load) passing Twyford East hauled by engine No. 4086
'Builth Castle'

of 1919 had materialised, and the 'compromise' appeared to have completed its role. In fact, only a quarter of the 'Castles' had yet been built, and five years later construction was to be resumed.

Engine No. 5001 of the 1926 batch of 'Castles' was the subject of an experiment in connection with the design of the 'Kings'. From December 1926 to March 1928 it ran with a set of driving wheels turned down to 6 ft. 6 in. After a period it was reported that there was no significant difference in its performance, but this was scarcely surprising as the normal 'Castles' wheels of 6 ft. $8\frac{1}{2}$ in. dia. could be turned down a total of nearly 4 in. overall, and the minimum diameter before the tyres were scrapped was 6 ft. $4\frac{7}{8}$ in.

The first 40 'Castles' were originally allocated to Old Oak Common, Newton Abbot and Laira thus:

Old Oak Common	4073-83/9-94/7-9
	5000-2/5/6/10
Newton Abbot	5003/11/2
Laira	4084-8/95/6, 5004/7-9

These are the original allocations; by the time 5012 had appeared, some of the others had changed sheds. In the late nineteen-twenties, after the building of the 'Kings', the 'Castles' were dispersed over the system, and in 1932, before construction was resumed, the 40 pure 'Castles' and six conversions were distributed as follows:

Old Oak Common 19, Bristol 2, Exeter 1, Newton Abbot 8, Laira 6, Wolverhampton 2, Cardiff 6, Chester 2.

Engine No. 4079 'Pendennis Castle', photographed at Old Oak Common soon after construction

'CASTLES' NOW PRESERVED

'Caerphilly Castle', at Old Oak Common in 1923, during the first running trials

CHAPTER 9

PERFORMANCE OF THE 'CASTLES'

In the previous chapter, dealing with the inception of the 'Castle' class locomotives, and the remarkable results of certain dynamometer-car test runs that were communicated to the World Power Conference of 1924 in a paper by C. B. Collett, the influence of the design on other railways was also described, and the fine runs made during the respective Interchange Trials commented upon. These were inevitably special occasions, when the locomotives concerned were in first-class condition, and supplied with good coal. They were also handled by specially chosen enginemen. To judge the performance of the 'Castles' in their early days by these runs alone would be to gain a misleading impression. It is important to recall also that the 'Castles' held the position of premier passenger locomotive class of the Great Western Railway for barely four years. *Caerphilly Castle* was turned out in the summer of 1923, and *King George V* followed in 1927. Furthermore, in that period came the General Strike of 1926, followed by the prolonged coal strike, during which latter the railways of this country had to rely on large quantities of imported coal.

My own first experiences of these engines were in 1925 and 1926 and were anything but impressive, time being lost by engines on the 5.42 p.m. Exeter to Paddington; on the 4.15 p.m. Paddington to Swindon, and on the 3.30 p.m. Paddington to Exeter. The last two runs were made in 1926 and both showed all the symptoms of poor steaming; but the first of the three was in the summer of 1925, when performance on the West of England service was at a remarkably high level generally. This to some extent is anticipating, because the first really comprehensive account of 'Castle' performance was published by Cecil J. Allen in *The Railway Magazine* for December 1924, when full details of three runs on the 'Cornish Riviera Express', with maximum winter load, were tabulated. On one of the runs Allen rode on the footplate, with Chief Locomotive Inspector George Flewellyn keeping a close watch on all the proceedings. The engine was the celebrated No. 4079 *Pendennis Castle*, and the fully-documented record of this run provides a most valuable example of current standards of maximum performance. The booked point-to-point times were carefully observed, except where certain anomalies in the timings had remained unchanged over many years; but while the performance was impeccable in this respect it is important to realise that it was not always so.

No. 4074 'Caldicot Castle', with large tender, at Shrewsbury

One of the later 'Castles', No. 5070 'Sir Daniel Gooch' at Swindon

THE DOWN 'CORNISH RIVIERA EXPRESS'

	1	2
Run No.	1	2
Date	13/10/24	2/5/25
Engine	4079	4074
Load: cars, tons tare/full		
To Westbury	14 495/530	14 498/530
To Taunton	12 423/455	12 426/455
To Exeter	10 360/390	10 363/390
To Plymouth	7 255/275	8 292/310
Driver	W. Young	E. Rowe
Fireman	Chellingworth	H. Cook

Dist. Miles		Sch. Min.	Actual m. s.	Speed m.p.h.	Reg. opening	Cut-off %	Actual m. s.	Speed m.p.h.
0·0	PADDINGTON	0	0 00		½	75	0 00	
1·3	Westbourne Park		3 15		¾		3 15	42
5·7	Ealing		9 20		,,	30	9 08	
9·1	SOUTHALL	11	13 00	61	,,	26	12 42	59
13·2	West Drayton		17 00	65	,,	,,	16 44	65½
18·5	SLOUGH	20	21 45	69	,,	,,	21 26	68
24·2	Maidenhead	25½	26 55	65	,,	,,	26 36	66½/65
36·0	READING	37	37 50	slack 45	,,	,,	37 25	slack
44·8	Aldermaston		47 05	62½	,,	,,	46 20	62
53·1	NEWBURY	56	55 45	57½	,,	,,	54 38	60
58·5	Kintbury		61 05	61	,,	27	60 05	60½
61·5	Hungerford		64 10	57	,,	,,	63 12	55½/60½
66·4	Bedwyn	69½	69 15	60	,,	29/30	68 17	57
70·1	Savernake		73 25	48	,,	20	72 25	46
75·3	Pewsey		78 30	74	small port	20	77 26	72
81·1	Patney		83 20	71½	,,	17	82 16	70
86·9	Lavington		88 05	80½	,,	,,	87 00	77½
95·6	WESTBURY	97½	95 35	slack 35	¾	25	94 40	slack
98·5	*Milepost 112¾*		99 10		,,	,,	98 13	52
101·3	FROME		103 00	slack 35	,,	22	101 40	slack/51½
106·6	Witham		109 50	48½	,,	23	108 03	50
108·5	*Milepost 122¾*		112 30	39½	small port	17	110 24	46
111·9	Bruton		115 55	74	,,	,,	113 25	72½/76
115·3	CASTLE CARY	120	118 55	slack 64	,,	,,	116 18	75
120·2	Keinton Mandeville		123 15	70½/64	,,	,,	120 26	72½
125·7	Somerton		128 25	68	,,	,,	125 28	64
127·9	Long Sutton		130 35	60	,,	,,	127 30	
131·0	*Curry Rivel Jc.*		133 20	71½	,,	,,	130 09	72
137·9	*Cogload Junction*	143	139 35	65	¾	20	136 06	68
142·9	TAUNTON	148	144 25	60	,,	,,	140 30	64
144·9	Norton Fitzwarren		146 25	60	,,	,,	142 22	67
150·0	Wellington		152 10	50½	,,	30	147 17	58
151·8	*Milepost 172*		154 30	40½	,,	35	149 19	41
152·8	*Milepost 173*		156 15	31	,,	35	150 42	41
	Whiteball Tunnel		p.w.s.	25	,,			40
153·8	*Whiteball Box*		158 28		small port	17	152 12	45
158·8	Tiverton Junction		163 35	75	,,	15	156 46	75
161·1	Cullompton		165 35	69	,,	,,	158 38	76½
170·2	Stoke Canon		173 10	76½	,,	,,	166 00	72/74
173·7	EXETER	179	176 30	slack 30	½	,,	169 10	
178·4	Exminster		182 10	65	,,	,,	174 40	
188·7	Teignmouth		193 15	57½	small port	,,	184 54	
			p.w.s.	10				
193·9	NEWTON ABBOT	203	200 30		full	20	190 25	
195·0	*Aller Junction*		202 00	50	,,	,,	192 25	p.w.s.
196·7	*Milepost 217*		204 15	35	,,	42 max.		
197·7	*Dainton Box*	209½	206 25	24½	shut	15	197 40	
202·5	Totnes	215½	211 55	57½	full	41	203 00	
205·3	*Tigley Box*		215 50	27	,,	33	206 55	30
207·1	*Rattery Box*	223	219 20	33	,,	25	210 25	35
209·4	Brent	225	222 40	49	,,	22	213 28	56
211·6	Wrangaton		225 25	50	small port	15	215 40	
219·0	*Hemerdon Box*	237	233 40	53	shut	,,	223 10	
221·7	Plympton		236 35	64½ max.	,,	,,	226 55	72
			p.w.s.	25			p.w.s.	
224·2	*Lipson Junction*	245	240 20	23	,,	25		
225·7	PLYMOUTH	247	244 00				231 58	

The three runs just mentioned all conveyed gross loads of 515 to 525 tons behind the tender from Paddington to Westbury, and of 440 to 450 tons from Westbury to Taunton. At that time the scheduled allowance over the 95.6 miles from Paddington to Westbury was 97½ min. and the three engines took 103 min. 10 sec., 99 min. 54 sec. and 95 min. 35 sec. The second train, which was hauled by engine No. 4077 *Chepstow Castle*, had lost about 2 min. through a permanent-way check; but the first run, on which nearly 5¾ min. were lost, was unchecked, as was the third run with *Pendennis Castle*. Despite some fast subsequent running with the reduced load, the first run did not recover all the lost time by Exeter, which was passed ¾ min. late. Furthermore, on Cecil J. Allen's return run from Plymouth on the following day, with the same engine and crew, the performance had little of the sparkle that had so distinguished it on the down journey. But as an example of 'Castle' working at its best, that down journey is worthy of special study. The times and speeds, together with the regulator openings and cut-offs, are shown in the accompanying table.

The details of engine working, which were the first ever to be published regarding GWR locomotives in *The Railway Magazine*, created almost as great an impression as Collett's paper to the World Power Conference had done some eight months earlier. At that time the idea of a 4—6—0 locomotive hauling a train of 525 tons at 69 m.p.h. on level track and working in 26 per cent cut-off was unheard of, among followers of Allen's monthly articles. Actually, by GWR standards it was very hard work. On ordinary express passenger duties the usual working for the four-cylinder locomotives was in 17 or 18 per cent, and rarely as much as 20 per cent for fast work on the level. It depended upon whether the drivers worked with an absolutely full regulator opening or, as on Allen's footplate trip, had the regulator open only about ¾ full. This was preferred by many of the men. The driver of *Pendennis Castle* was William Young of Old Oak Common shed, who later became one of the most widely experienced express drivers in Great Britain. He had the distinction of working *Pendennis Castle* between King's Cross and Doncaster; *Launceston Castle* between Euston and Carlisle; and then, in 1927, he was selected to take the *King George V* to the U.S.A. and drive it on test over the Baltimore and Ohio Railroad.

Careful analysis of the performance of *Pendennis Castle* on this 1924 run on the 'Cornish Riviera Express' indicated that the engine was being steamed at approximately 24,000 lb. per hour be-

No. 4078 'Pembroke Castle' on up express near Reading

tween Paddington and Savernake, and that the coal rate was somewhat over 3,000 lb. per hour. In his account of the trip Allen laid emphasis on his impression that between Paddington and Westbury there had been nothing to suggest that the engine was being thrashed. Actually this was very far from being the case. When scientific train timing methods were introduced by the nationalised British Railways, and point-to-point timings were closely reconciled with the capacity of the locomotives, a firing rate of 3,000 lb. per hour was fixed as the very maximum that could be expected on a hand-fired locomotive for any length of time; so that on this run of *Pendennis Castle* in 1924, even if the boiler was not steamed to its absolute limit, the engine was being worked almost to the limit of the fireman. This provides ample explanation why performance of the standard put up on this journey was not consistently achieved in the working of the down 'Cornish Riviera Express'. Drivers preferred to drop a little time to Westbury, and get it back afterwards where the point-to-point timings did not make such severe demands.

On Allen's run, having passed Westbury 2 min. early, the subsequent proceedings were a 'cake-walk' by comparison—at any rate until Newton Abbot was reached. For example, No. 4075 *Cardiff Castle*, which had lost 5¾ min. to Westbury, gained 4 min. on *Pendennis* between there and Stoke Canon. The accompanying log reveals the very easy steam under which *Pendennis* was worked for most of the way between Westbury and Taunton. It is significant that on the last day of the 1925 Interchange Trial with the London & North Eastern, when Driver Rowe, on No. 4074 *Caldicot Castle*, was given instructions to make the fastest time he could, that in the early stages the only appreciable advantage he gained on *Pendennis Castle*, as shown in the log adjoining, was by a liberal interpretation of the speed restrictions at Reading. The engine was again being steamed up

Up Ocean Mail special in Sonning cutting: engine No. 4094 'Dynevor Castle'

to the limit of the fireman's capacity, as far as Savernake. *Caldicot Castle* began to draw ahead when *Pendennis Castle* was being run easily.

On the journey recorded by Cecil J. Allen, some interesting details were published of the engine working on the difficult stretch of line between Newton Abbot and Plymouth. It was only here, on climbing the steep gradients, that an absolutely full opening of the regulator was used. On Dainton bank from a maximum speed of 50 m.p.h. at Aller Junction cut-off was gradually increased from 20 per cent up to a maximum of 42; and this took the train over Dainton summit at a minimum speed of $24\frac{1}{2}$ m.p.h. On Rattery bank full regulator was again used throughout from Totnes, and the maximum cut-off employed was 41 per cent. The speed fell from $57\frac{1}{2}$ m.p.h. through Totnes to 27 at Tigley Box, which point marks the end of the steepest part of the bank. Although there was a permanent-way slack to 25 m.p.h. between Tavistock Junction and Laira Junction, the arrival in Plymouth was 3 min. early. The net times were $175\frac{1}{2}$ min. to passing Exeter, and 239 min. to Plymouth.

On this occasion the load conveyed beyond Exeter was one of seven coaches, whereas the 'Castles' were permitted to take eight on the fastest schedules over the South Devon line; but the run showed a comfortable margin in hand on every stage of the journey after Westbury and emphasises the uneven nature of the booking, which required inordinately hard work over the first 70 miles from Paddington to Savernake. The inspector estimated that $3\frac{1}{2}$ tons of coal had been burned, giving an average of 35 lb. per mile, but in the early stages the consumption was nearer 50 lb. per mile. By the tender gauge there were 3,250 gallons of water in the tank at Paddington, and this was supplemented by 1,500 gallons at Aldermaston troughs, by 1,700 at Westbury, 900 at Cogload, and 1,100 gallons at Starcross. The total water consumption was about 6,900 gallons, or 30 gallons per mile. Both these figures for consumption were very good, the coal figure being particularly notable as there was appreciable slack in the coal. No figures of boiler pressure are shown in the table, for Allen observed that only twice did the pressure fall perceptibly below 225 lb. per sq. in. For two short periods, when slack in the coal was causing trouble, it fell to 215 lb. per sq. in.

On the very fast run made by engine No. 4074, on the last day of the Interchange Trials in 1925, the general running beyond Newton Abbot was well above that of No. 4079, despite the extra coach. This sustained effort near to the end of a four-hour journey was notable, though the broad indications are that the steaming rate of the engine was considerably less throughout from Savernake than the effort sustained in that first 70 miles. Time was also gained first at Reading and then by a liberal interpretation of the speed restrictions along the coastal section from Starcross to Teignmouth. Permanent-way checks impeded the running at Aller Junction and again near Plympton, but the train nevertheless reached Plymouth in 231¾ min. giving an arrival a little over 15 min. early. Although this was the fastest run on record with a 'Castle' hauling the full load of the down 'Cornish Riviera Express'—an appreciably faster run than the earlier runs of the test series—the coal consumption was only slightly greater than on the earlier runs, on which 44.1 and 45.6 lb. per mile had been consumed. On the very fast run made on the last day the consumption was 46.8 lb. per mile and the very substantial advance over the estimated consumption on Cecil J. Allen's trip namely 35 lb. a mile, is a clear indication of the extra effort being put forth on this notable occasion. It might be added that despite the very hard effort put forward the coal consumption on this trip was less than on any of the rival LNER 'Pacific' journeys, when the overall time from Paddington to Plymouth was about a quarter of an hour longer.

In general, the working of the up 'Cornish Riviera Express' was a much easier task. The load was unchanged between Exeter and Paddington, and as only the Cornish resorts and Plymouth were provided for the tonnages were generally lighter than the gargantuan down train. The normal load of the up service was usually about 350 tons; but holiday workings could provide more interesting occasions, and two of these are set out in the accompanying table. They display the work of the same two drivers whose work has just been discussed on the down train—E. Rowe and W. Young. The first of these two runs was made on the first day of the Interchange Trials 1925, when by obvious arrangement with the Traffic Department, the 'Cornish Riviera Express' was run very much harder than the schedule required and arrived in Paddington 15 min. early. As a piece of stage management in a publicity campaign it was superb; as a piece of

Down West of England express at Twyford: engine No. 4090 'Dorchester Castle'

locomotive running it was extremely good though, of course, no traffic man could honestly commend the idea of a train arriving at its destination a quarter of an hour ahead of time. So far as the performance of the 'Castle' class engines was concerned, however, the run provides an extremely interesting and important piece of data, because it is probably the fastest time ever actually recorded between Exeter and Paddington. There was a steady gain of time throughout the journey; but perhaps the finest individual feat was the acceleration, after Westbury slack, to 69 m.p.h. on the level before Lavington and the subsequent minimum speed to 61 m.p.h. up 4 miles of 1 in 222 gradient. Time was gained by speed somewhat in excess of the limits through Reading, and the finish was very fast. Despite the hard work throughout, coal consumption was only 40.6 per mile.

The companion run with engine No. 4077 *Chepstow Castle*, driven by W. Young, was particularly interesting because it was made in the summer of the long coal strike, with the engine burning low-grade imported fuel. In the circumstances it was no mean task to have to haul a load

Engine No. 4032 'Queen Alexandra' rebuilt as a 'Castle'

THE UP 'CORNISH RIVIERA EXPRESS'

			1		2	
Run No.			27/4/25		19/8/26	
Date			4074		4077	
Engine						
Load: cars, tons, tare/full			10 358/380		12 431/465	
Driver			E. Rowe		Manning	
Fireman			H. Cook		unknown	

Dist. Miles		Sch. Min.	Actual m. s.	Speed m.p.h.	Actual m. s.	Speed m.p.h.
0·0	EXETER . . .	0	0 00		0 00	
3·5	Stoke Canon . . .		6 14		6 11	50
7·2	Silverton . . .				10 32	52
12·6	Cullompton . . .		15 33		16 35	53½
14·9	Tiverton Junction . .				19 43	44/51
19·9	*Whiteball Box* . .		23 31	47½	26 10	37½
23·7	Wellington . . .		26 54		29 52	80
28·8	Norton Fitzwarren . .				33 32	88
30·8	TAUNTON . . .	33	32 12		34 58	80
35·8	*Cogload Junction* . .	38	36 30		38 58	slack 55
43·8	Langport . . .				46 30	60
48·0	Somerton . . .				50 57	55
53·5	Keinton Mandeville .				56 22	62
58·4	CASTLE CARY . .	61	56 10		60 55	62
61·9	Bruton . . .		59 11		64 35	50½
65·2	*Milepost 122¾* .		63 09	46	69 10	34½/72
72·4	FROME . . .		70 00	slack	76 35	slack 30
78·1	WESTBURY . .	83	76 14	slack	83 25	slack 30
82·3	Edington . . .		81 00	61		
86·8	Lavington . . .		85 21	69/61	93 13	61
91·7	*Milepost 82* . .		p.w.s.		98 48	50
92·6	Patney . . .		92 10			
94·9	Woodborough . .		94 34	57		
98·4	Pewsey . . .		98 00	64/65	105 50	59
103·6	Savernake . . .		102 57	62	111 22	55
107·3	Bedwyn . . .	112			114 55	66
112·2	Hungerford . . .				118 58	72
120·6	NEWBURY . .	124	117 19		125 55	72
127·0	Midgham . . .				131 16	70
135·8	*Southcote Junction* .		129 59		139 10	
137·7	READING . . .	142	132 10	slack	141 35	slack 50
142·7	Twyford . . .		136 58		147 23	64
149·5	Maidenhead . . .	153½			153 35	68
155·2	SLOUGH . . .	159	147 09		158 45	67½
164·6	SOUTHALL . .	168	155 01		167 45	65
168·0	Ealing . . .				170 54	
172·4	Westbourne Park . .		161 27		175 12	56
					sigs.	
173·7	PADDINGTON . .	179	164 01		179 05	

	Net times, min.:		162		178¼	

of 460 tons from Exeter to Paddington in 179 min., particularly as at that time the by-pass lines at Frome and Westbury had not been constructed, and severe speed restrictions to 30 m.p.h. were in force at both places. The engine was being very skilfully handled, so as to avoid having to steam the boiler hard on any section. Throughout the journey time was lost on uphill stages and regained by very free running downhill. A maximum speed of 88 m.p.h. at Norton Fitzwarren will be particularly noted.

The impression one gains is that on the heaviest trains of the West of England service the 'Castles'

were overloaded. When all conditions were favourable they could handle maximum load trains to time; but they could not be relied upon in all circumstances. This became even more apparent on the Birmingham route, although these engines never came into general use on the line in the same way as the 'Stars' had done previously, and the 'Kings' did subsequently. All the 'Castles' of the first batch were stationed at Old Oak Common, and consequently it was at first only on the one London single-home turn—the 9.10 a.m. down, and the 2.35 p.m. up from Wolverhampton—that one sometimes found a 'Castle'. A few engines of later batches were stationed at Stafford Road, but the finest work recorded by 'Castles' on the Birmingham service came, curiously enough, after the introduction of the 'Kings', when the smaller engines were deputising for the larger ones on the very difficult 6.10 p.m. down. For a time in 1930 engine No. 4088 *Dartmouth Castle* was at Wolverhampton and she was on the most difficult turn of the day for weeks on end. This turn was of course the 11.35 a.m. up (12 noon from Birmingham) and the 6.10 p.m. down.

During this period, which included the Whitsun holiday, I was able to travel by the train when the first portion was loaded to 14 coaches. The slip coaches were carried on the second part, so that the gross tonnage of 475 had to be conveyed through to Wolverhampton. A very dependable driver was on the job, A. Taylor of Stafford Road shed; the running throughout was of a very high standard, and Leamington was reached in a net time of 89¼ min. A slight signal check after Westbourne Park caused a loss of half a minute, making the train exceed the allowance of 7 min. to Old Oak Common West Junction by 20 sec. From that junction the adherence to point-to-point times was remarkable, the only further loss being between High Wycombe and Princes Risborough. The fall by only 1½ m.p.h., from 52½ to 51 m.p.h. in the 4.3 miles from Gerrards Cross to Beaconsfield, including 3½ miles at 1 in 254, was outstanding. The climb to Saunderton was aided by a speed of 50 m.p.h. through High Wycombe, where the limit is 35 m.p.h., but even so the minimum speed of 42 at milepost 22 was excellent with this load. The high standard of work was maintained to Leamington. Between Leamington and Birmingham timekeeping was impossible with such a load, and the net time, after allowing for a permanent-way slack approaching Snow Hill, was nearly 3 min. over the booking.

Nameplate of No. 4037 (rebuilt from Star) after renaming, from 'Queen Philippa'

The ascent of Hatton bank is tackled less than a mile from the Leamington start, and despite half a mile of 1 in 109 down, there is little chance to gain momentum. No. 4088 did well to reach 45 m.p.h. before Warwick, and in passing Hatton without falling below 32 m.p.h. had equalled the best hill climbing by 'Castles' in the West of England. On the continuation of this run to Wolverhampton, Taylor actually cut the booking of 20 min. to 18¼ min., with speeds of 35½ m.p.h. on the climb to Handsworth Junction and an unusual maximum of 64 m.p.h. before the Wednesbury slack. That time should be gained with an abnormally heavy train on this very difficult section of the route was an indication of the crew's determination and skill.

6.10 p.m. PADDINGTON—BIRMINGHAM
Load: 14 coaches, 440 tons tare, 475 tons full
Engine: 4088 *Dartmouth Castle*
Driver: A. Taylor (Stafford Road)

Dist. Miles		Sch. Min.	Actual m. s.	Speed m.p.h.
0·0	PADDINGTON	0	0 00	
1·3	Westbourne Park	3	3 55	
			sigs.	
3·3	*Old Oak Common West Junction*	7	7 20	slack
7·8	Greenford		12 55	57½
10·3	Northolt Junction	15½	15 35	54½
14·3	Denham		20 05	63½
17·4	Gerrards Cross		22 55	52½
21·7	Beaconsfield		27 50	51
24·2	*Tylers Green*		30 05	70½
26·5	HIGH WYCOMBE	32	32 15	slack 50
28·8	West Wycombe		35 05	47
31·5	Saunderton		38 45	
32·3	*Milepost 22*		39 45	42
34·7	PRINCES RISBOROUGH	41	42 30	70½
40·1	Haddenham		46 40	83½
44·1	*Ashendon Junction*	49	49 40	slack 58
47·4	Brill		52 55	
50·4	Blackthorn		55 35	70½
53·4	BICESTER	58	58 15	62
57·2	Ardley		62 15	52½/69
62·4	*Aynho Junction*	67	67 15	slack 64½
64·0	King's Sutton		68 45	65½
67·5	BANBURY	72	71 55	67
71·1	Cropredy		75 15	57½
76·3	Fenny Compton		80 15	76½
81·2	Southam Road		84 15	74/78
87·3	LEAMINGTON	91	89 50	
2·0	Warwick		3 45	45
6·2	Hatton		10 15	32
10·4	Lapworth		15 20	58
12·9	Knowle		18 05	54½
16·3	Solihull		21 40	60½
20·1	Tyseley		25 00	68
			p.w.s.	
22·2	Bordesley		27 10	
23·3	BIRMINGHAM	26	29 30	

Net times, min.: Paddington—Leamington 89¼
Leamington—Birmingham 28¾

One of the later 'Castles', No. 5046 'Earl Cawdor', originally 'Clifford Castle'

By the year 1928, with the introduction of the 'Kings', sufficient 'Castles' were available at Old Oak Common for them to be drafted on to duties additional to the West of England, and the one Wolverhampton 'single-home' job. They were, for example, put on to some of the South Wales trains. But those worked by Old Oak shed were not normally the heaviest on the service and the trains which were loaded most heavily were still 'Saint' workings. Amongst trains which were 'Castle' turns was the 3.55 p.m. down. This train was allowed 140 min. for the 133.4 miles to Newport, including a conditional stop at Badminton, which was usually made. A series of runs published in *The Railway Magazine* on this train gave, on one run, a net time of 92¾ min. for the 100.0 miles to Badminton, with 325 tons, and on another run a net time of 99 min. with 385 tons. There were a number of other runs of little less merit than these. The observer who timed these runs remarked that on undelayed runs some drivers seemed to saunter out of Paddington as if they had all day before them; but when hindered by enforced slowings they 'stirred their engines to mighty feats of acceleration'. Enforced slowings were common, particularly on the congested line through the Severn Tunnel and amidst the coal traffic of South Wales.

On the run which achieved the net time of 92¾ min., the engine was No. 4090 *Dorchester Castle*. Even time was reached by Reading, which was passed at 74½ m.p.h.; Didcot, 53.1 miles out, was passed in 50 min. 20 sec. at 75½ m.p.h., speed having fallen in between to 70 at Goring. A distance of 43 miles had been covered at an average of 71½ m.p.h. when a signal check to 43 m.p.h. at Wantage

Road cut progress short. After a slow recovery to Swindon the driver opened his engine out, and from a speed of 76 m.p.h. at Little Somerford he stopped at Badminton, 10.3 miles away, in 9 min. 45 sec. Up the long gradient at a nominal 1 in 300 speed fell to 66 m.p.h. and then recovered to 68, and was still rising when steam was shut off for the Badminton stop. The actual time to Badminton was 96 min. 20 sec. As the train was ahead of schedule, signal checks followed, and there was a permanent-way slack before Newport, but Newport was reached a minute early.

The second run mentioned above was unchecked and the actual time to Badminton was 99 min. 5 sec. The start was leisurely, and nearly 4 min. were dropped to Slough, but running then became more lively. Speed reached 70 m.p.h. at Maidenhead and 74 at Goring, on the level. The minimum at Uffington was 66 m.p.h. and there was an increase to 69 at Shrivenham. For 36 miles the average was 70 m.p.h. High speeds down to the Severn Tunnel were uncommon, and the maximum in the tunnel itself was usually 60-65 m.p.h., with a fall to 30-32 m.p.h. on the 1 in 90 climb to Severn Tunnel Junction. On one run, however, No. 4083, with 385 tons, was allowed to reach 80 m.p.h. in the tunnel, and surmounted the 3 miles of 1 in 90 at a minimum of 45 m.p.h. The distance of 5.5 miles from Severn Tunnel East Box to Severn Tunnel Junction were covered in the unusual time of 5 min. 15 sec.

The last service on which the work of the 'Castles' at this period is worthy of record was the 3.45 p.m. from Swindon, the 'Cheltenham Flyer'. In 1929 the schedule was cut to 70 min., a figure

Torquay – Bradford express on the sea wall near Teignmouth: engine No. 4098 'Kidwelly Castle'

which had already been shown to leave a sufficient margin for out-of-course delays. The work of the 'Castles' on the new schedule soon showed that further acceleration was possible, but the most spectacular run during the period of the 70-minute booking was made by a 'Star', as recounted in Chapter 6. Two good 'Castle' runs that I logged personally are shown in the accompanying table. In both of these the start was, by 'Flyer' standards, leisurely. No. 5003 *Lulworth Castle*, with an eight-coach train, had a slight signal check after Shrivenham, and the driver then extended his engine to

The Cheltenham Flyer near Uffington: engine No. 5043 then named 'Banbury Castle', but later 'Earl of Mount Edgcumbe'

117

			'THE CHELTENHAM FLYER'		
Run No.			1		2
Date			1929		1930
Engine			5003		4090
Load: tons, tare/full			254/275		265/280
Dist. Miles		Sch. Min.	Actual m. s.		Actual m. s.
0·0	SWINDON	0	0 00		0 00
5·8	Shrivenham		7 40		7 38
			sigs.		
10·8	Uffington		11 55		11 50
13·4	Challow		14 00		13 55
16·9	Wantage Road		16 35		16 37
20·8	Steventon	19	19 25		19 34
24·2	DIDCOT	22	21 50		22 09
28·8	Cholsey		25 05		25 46
32·6	Goring		27 45		28 45
35·8	Pangbourne		30 00		31 22
38·7	Tilehurst		32 05		33 40
41·3	READING	36½	34 00		35 45
46·3	Twyford		37 55		39 48
53·1	Maidenhead		43 10		45 00
58·8	SLOUGH	51	47 35		49 25
64·1	West Drayton		52 05		53 30
68·2	SOUTHALL	59	55 35		56 50
71·6	Ealing		58 20		59 31
			sigs.		
76·0	Westbourne Park		63 15		63 18
			sigs.		
77·3	PADDINGTON	70	67 15		65 38
	Net time, min.:		64¼		65⅝

good effect. Speed crossed the 'eighty' line near Challow, and reached 86½ m.p.h. at Didcot. From there to Reading it was held between the limits of 83½ and 86½ m.p.h. After Reading there was a decided easing of the engine, but nevertheless the net time was only 64¼ min. On the second run No. 4090 *Dorchester Castle*, with a nine-coach train of somewhat lighter stock, encountered no checks. and with no station-to-station average reaching 80 m.p.h., stopped in Paddington 4¼ min. early. These runs showed that a further cut in the schedule would be quite practicable if the condition of the engine and the quality of fuel could be assured. However, the publicity value of the 'Flyer' was clearly established, and the early 1930s were to see an astonishing demonstration of the capacity of the 'Castle' for high-speed running on track which was little better than level.

Engine No. 5010 'Restormel Castle', as originally built with small tender

118

Foretaste of the 1930s: No. 5016 'Montgomery Castle', with special headboard. The engine in the background is the 'North Star'

Nameplate of engine No. 5069, destined to achieve the all-time steam record for an Ocean Mail special from Plymouth to Paddington

CHAPTER 10

INTRODUCTION OF THE 'KINGS'

IN 1919 Churchward proposed to fit to the 'Star' chassis a boiler of maximum diameter 6 ft. and with a firebox of length 10 ft., giving a grate area of 30.3 sq. ft. This design of boiler fitted later to the 47XX 2—8—0 resulted in a 4—6—0 of 82½ tons, with a maximum axle load of 20½ tons. The civil engineer could not accept this, and the resultant compromise, four years later, was the 'Castle', with a boiler of maximum diameter 5 ft. 9 in., but with the same size of grate as had been proposed in the 1919 scheme. The reduction in the size of boiler held the total engine weight to 79 tons 17 cwt, and the axle loading to 19 tons 14 cwt.

Whether or not the 1919 proposal would have given a locomotive significantly better than the 'Castle' is doubtful, as the grate area would have been the same. It is, however, unlikely that its introduction would have eliminated the need for a still larger engine as soon as a relaxation of Civil Engineering limitations allowed an increase in axle loads. In 1926 Stanier, then Principal Assistant to the C.M.E., had the idea of a compound version of the 'Castle' and got F. W. Hawksworth to have this interesting proposition sketched out in outline. Compared with the simple 'Castle', the most conspicuous difference in the compound would have been that the outside high-pressure cylinders, with a diameter of 17 in., would have been ahead of the trailing bogie wheels. The wheelbase of the bogie was increased by 1 ft. to 8 ft. and the bogie centre was moved forward by 1 ft. 10 in. This would have placed the leading bogie wheels ahead of the inside cylinders, which could thus have had a diameter of 25 in. The inside cylinders would have been slightly inclined, a proposal which Churchward would never have countenanced. The starting tractive

No. 6000 'King George V' as originally built, in photographic grey

*After the triumphant return from the U.S.A. No. 6000 posed alongside Nos. 5010
and 4004 at Old Oak Common*

effort would have been 35,700 lb. The engine would have had greater cylinder volumes than the larger Frenchmen, but a smaller grate.

The outcome was vividly described to me by Hawksworth himself. The scheme had progressed far enough for Stanier to suggest it was time to show it to Collett. They went in to see him, and as Hawksworth put it: 'In about five minutes we were out again!' So much for compounds in the post-war era on the GWR.

In 1919 the Government set up a committee to investigate the stressing of railway bridges. The committee was to review the methods of calculating the stresses in bridges, with particular reference to the allowance to be made for impact loading, that is, the effect of a locomotive and train running on

'A' shop at Swindon, during the building of the 'Kings'

to a bridge at speed. An important influence on the impact loading is the method of balancing the reciprocating parts of the locomotive. The inertia effect of the reciprocating parts (that is, the piston, crosshead, part of the weight of the connecting rod, and, with Walschaert's valve gear, parts of the valve gear) tends to produce fore-and-aft forces on the locomotive, which may be transmitted through the drawbar to the train. The only completely satisfactory way of balancing these effects is by equal and opposite reciprocating parts. The effects can, however, be partially offset by adding additional balance weights to the driving wheels, in such positions that the centrifugal forces which they apply to the axles are directly opposite to the inertia forces of the reciprocating parts when these forces are at their greatest values (that is, approximately, when the balance weights are at the same height above the rails as the axles). These additional balance weights, over and above what is required to balance the rotating parts, are commonly called 'overbalance'. Unfortunately, at each revolution of the wheels the centrifugal forces which these balance weights produce tend to lift the axles and then to press them harder on the rails. This varying vertical force on the rails is called 'hammer-blow' or 'dynamic augment', and in some two-cylinder locomotives as conventionally balanced it exceeded 10 tons. It thus effectively increased the maximum axle load by this amount.

In a four-cylinder engine with the cranks equally spaced the hammer-blow can be eliminated entirely if all four cylinders drive on to one axle, as in the LNWR 'Claughtons'; but if the drive is on two axles, as in the GWR 'Stars' and 'Castles', other factors have to be taken into account. The Bridge Stress Committee tested a total of 39 types of locomotive on 42 bridges in many parts of the country, and certain of the results were unexpected, to say the least of it. It was shown, for example, that a four-cylinder engine is not inherently better than a two-cylinder, and it was with Churchward's locomotives that this was demonstrated. Until that time on the 'Stars' it was the practice at Swindon to balance a proportion of the reciprocating parts separately for the inside and outside cylinders, in the leading and middle pairs of coupled wheels respectively. Although the balance applied to the leading coupled axle was opposed to that of the middle one, and the total engine hammer-blow was relatively small, the hammer-blow from each of the individual axles actually exceeded that of the two-cylinder 'Saint' class! During the course of the Bridge Stress Committee's work the method of balancing was revised, and the

relative figures for the 'Saint', 'Star' and 'Castle' classes were then as follows:

Engine Class	Max. Axle Load	Speed at 6 r.p.s.	Hammer-blow at 6 r.p.s.		Max. Combined load at 6 r.p.s.
			Whole engine	Axle	
	tons	m.p.h.	tons	tons	tons
'Saint'	18.4	86	17.9	6.9	25.3
'Star'	18.6	86	3.7	3.7	21.5
'Castle'	19.7	86	3.5	3.5	23.1

Until the work of the Bridge Stress Committee civil engineers had not made any concession in the maximum axle load limits imposed. The limits had been based on dead weight. The classic case had been that of the LNWR 'Claughtons', on which restriction was placed on the size of the boiler, to avoid increasing the axle-load, whereas the maximum combined load imposed upon the track at 6 r.p.s. was only 19¾ tons, compared with 33¼ tons of the 4—4—0 'George the Fifth' class.

Two major factors, and an incidental one, helped to hasten the course of events on the GWR. Taking the incidental one first, the scrapping of *The Great Bear* caused a considerable stir at Paddington. Sir Felix Pole, so it is said, was surprised to learn how the workings of the 'Pacific' engine had been restricted by its axle-loading; but a matter of more serious concern was that the 'Castles', despite their inherent excellence, had very little in reserve on maximum West of England loadings, and the period of the Coal Strike in 1926 had shown how quickly that reserve could be used up when fuel conditions were not ideal. Within the limit of a 20-ton axle-load, however, there was little that could be done about it, and then, of course, the second major factor intervened—the construction of the Southern Railway 'Lord Nelson' class 4—6—0 with a nominal tractive effort of 33,500 lb. The publicity folks at Waterloo immediately proclaimed, by poster and other means, that their new engine was the most powerful in Great Britain—which it was on the basis of nominal tractive effort—and the Great Western, which had taken immense pride in possessing that distinction up to that time, in the 'Castle', had cause for much concern. The deliberations of the Locomotive Committee of the directors under the enthusiastic and well-informed chairmanship of Sir Aubrey Brocklebank made a strong plea for the relaxation of the 20-ton axle-loading and as the strength of bridges imposed the limitation on axle load, the Civil Engineer should prepare diagrams to show what each bridge could carry. The

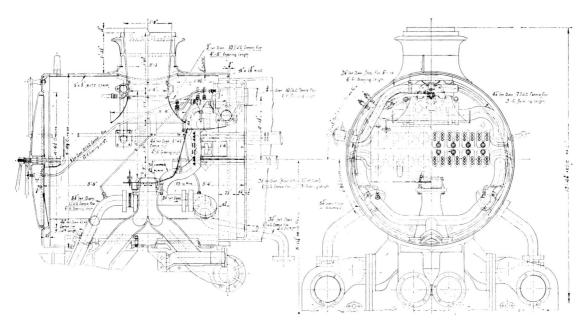

Smokebox arrangements on the 'King' Class

Civil Engineer, J. C. Lloyd, was called in, and he agreed to produce the information. He was also asked what axle load was now provided for in new bridges, and he replied that for 22 years all new bridges had been designed for a nominal axle load of 22 tons. Because of the hammer-blow in GWR two-cylinder engines, the static axle load had been limited to $19\frac{1}{2}$ tons; but in the light of the Bridge Stress Committee's work he could now agree to a static axle load of 22 tons for four-cylinder engines on bridges which had been rebuilt to these standards.

This increase in bridge strength had been agreed between the then Civil Engineer, J. C. Inglis, and the Civil Engineering Committee of the Board. Such, however, was the narrow departmentalism of the GWR in the early years of the twentieth century that, although Inglis later became General Manager, neither his successors as General Manager, nor the Chief Mechanical Engineer, knew of the development. Lloyd was then asked if he could allow a further concession to $22\frac{1}{2}$ tons for four-cylinder engines, and to this he agreed.

Pole then instructed Collett to prepare the design of a locomotive with $22\frac{1}{2}$ tons axle load, and to have the first engine ready for the summer traffic of 1927. The Civil Engineer was instructed to have the Paddington-Plymouth route ready for the increased axle loading, and it was found that only four bridges remained to be strengthened. In commissioning this new design, Pole was as much concerned with prestige as with meeting traffic requirements, for the introduction of the *Lord Nelson,* with a tractive effort of 33,500 lb., had enabled the Southern Railway to publicise it as the most powerful passenger engine in the country. As the GWR had seen fit to equate tractive effort with power in its publicity, the only answer which it could make to this claim was the introduction of an engine with a still higher tractive effort. The 1926 exchange had shown that a larger passenger engine could be expected on the LMS, and Collett was therefore instructed to get the tractive effort up to 40,000 lb., a figure which was unlikely to be exceeded on other railways for some time.

The importance which Pole attached to this numerical distinction was shown by a statement which he made in the *GWR Magazine,* beginning: 'Not only GWR employees, but a wide circle of well-wishers and enthusiasts, have anxiously enquired whether the GWR Company would surrender the honour of possessing the most powerful passenger locomotive in the country. . .'

Each dimensional factor contributing to the tractive effort formula was considered:

(a) diameter and stroke of cylinders
(b) coupled wheel diameter
(c) boiler pressure

In the event each one of the four was altered from the 'Castle' figures, and it is interesting to see how much each change contributed to the increase in nominal tractive effort from the 31,625 lb. of the

'Castle' to the 40,300 lb. of the new engine proposed.

Dimension	'Castle'	'Super-Castle'	Increases in Nom. T.E. lb.
Cyl. dia. in.	16	16¼	990
Cyl. stroke in.	26	28	2560
Boiler pressure p.s.i.	225	250	3980
coupled wheel dia. ft. in.	6—8½	6—6	1145

Of these, on the engines as first built the increase in cylinder diameter was no more than nominal. Only the first six engines were built new with 16¼ in. cylinders. The rest were bored to 16 in., but of course they would be increased with successive reborings on overhaul, and the dimension of 16¼ in. was regarded as the official figure for purposes of calculating the nominal tractive effort. The two major factors contributing to the enhancement of power were the increase in cylinder volume, and the raising of the boiler pressure. One gathers that Collett would have been satisfied to use the standard diameter of coupled wheels, and avoid the cost of making new patterns, and of subsequent design changes that were occasioned at the front end. With 6 ft. 8½ in. wheels the nominal tractive effort of the new engine would have been 39,100 lb. But Sir Felix Pole was most anxious to have at least 40,000 lb. and so 6 ft. 6 in. coupled wheels were adopted, with the attendant problems they introduced. Many years later that celebrated model engineer, the late J. C. Crebbin, who was a most intimate friend of Sir Felix, told me how Pole had once confided to him the very high capital cost of introducing the new engines, in patterns, tools and special machinery. Crebbin added that a good deal of this cost would have been avoided if insistence had not been placed upon topping the 40,000 lb. mark.

Set out like this, it is relatively easy to lay down basic dimensions contributing to nominal tractive effort, but those basic dimensions had to be backed up by a boiler that would make the 'nominal' figure a reality. The detail design of the new engine was due to F. W. Hawksworth, who was then Chief Draughtsman, and a remarkable piece of design work it was, to build a locomotive of such tractive capacity, with an overall weight of no more than 89 tons.

The boiler was to be longer than that of the 'Castle', and this, together with the greater weight, called for an increase in wheelbase. The spacing of the coupled wheels was increased by 1 ft. 6 in. and the bogie wheelbase by 8 in., the distance from the rear bogie wheels to the leading coupled wheels remaining unchanged. Except for changes resulting from these increases in length, the motion remained unchanged from the previous four-cylinder locomotives. Adhering to Churchward's insistence on horizontal inside cylinders meant that the use of smaller driving wheels reduced the clearance under the inside cylinders. This could have been met by adopting Churchward's early practice of having the cylinder centre line offset from the centre of the driving axle, but in fact the wheel diameter of the bogie was reduced from the previous standard figure of 3 ft. 2 in. to 3 ft., and the bogie was redesigned.

At about this period there were a number of failures of Churchward bogies through rivets breaking, and it was felt that a plate-framed bogie would be stronger. The late A. W. J. Dymond was given the job of designing such a bogie, and he soon

The first five 'Kings', lined up at Old Oak Common shed

124

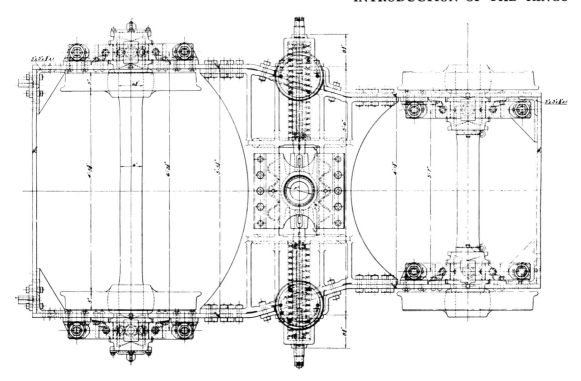

Plan view of the bogie, 'King' class locomotives

found that it was very difficult to fit inside plate frames under the inside cylinders, consistent with making the frame of adequate depth. He therefore arrived at a design in which the frame abreast of the leading bogie axle was outside the wheels, and the rear part of the frame inside the wheels. This curious arrangement was submitted to Collett who, to the designer's surprise, immediately accepted it.

Later investigation showed that the weakness of the Churchward bogie lay not in the strength of its frames, but in inadequacy of diagonal bracing. A proposal to fit plate-framed bogies to the 'Halls' was therefore abandoned in favour of inserting additional diagonal bracing in the standard bogie. Had this decision been reached a little earlier, the 'Kings' would probably have had a standard Churchward bogie.

The equalising bar arrangement was abandoned, and the new bogie had individually-sprung axles. At first the only springing for the axleboxes was short laminated springs with rigid hangers. To mitigate the effects of the longer engine wheelbase, the trailing coupled axleboxes were given one inch of lateral play under the control of inclined slides, like the Cartazzi slides of the standard GWR pony truck. The trailing section of the coupling rods had spherical bushes to accommodate the translation of the trailing axle.

The boiler, designated Standard No. 12, was the largest narrow-firebox boiler in Britain, but its design followed closely on previous Swindon practice. Before the boiler was designed, the locomotive inspectors were asked which type of boiler was the most dependable steamer, and they all replied that it was the No. 1 boiler. As the new boiler was not hampered by the restrictions which were imposed on the 'Castle' boiler, it was possible to make the main ratios much nearer to those of the No. 1 boiler than were those of the 'Castle'. It was thus said that the 'King' boiler was a true enlargement of the Standard No. 1. Some boiler ratios for the 'Star', 'Castle' and 'King' are shown in the following table:

COMPARISON OF BOILER RATIOS

Ratio	Star	Castle	King
Firebox heating surface/grate area	5·72	5·42	5·66
Total evaporative heating surface/grate area . . .	6·45	6·78	6·45
Superheating surface/grate area	9·69	8·66	9·14

The maximum diameter was 6 ft., as in the No. 7 boiler, and the firebox length 11 ft. 6 in. The barrel

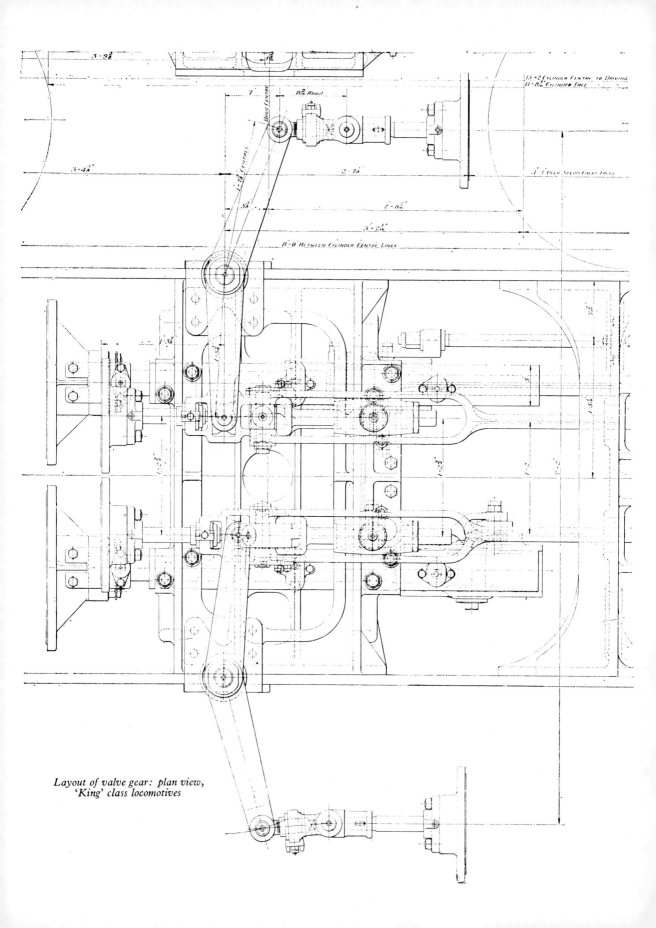

Layout of valve gear: plan view,
'King' class locomotives

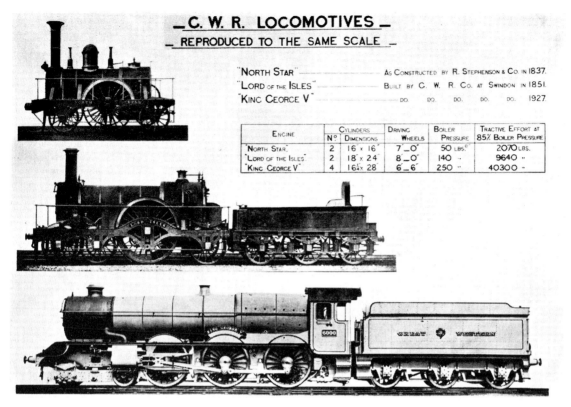

C. W. R. LOCOMOTIVES

REPRODUCED TO THE SAME SCALE

"NORTH STAR" — As CONSTRUCTED BY R. STEPHENSON & CO. IN 1837.
"LORD OF THE ISLES" — BUILT BY C. W. R. CO. AT SWINDON IN 1851.
"KING GEORGE V" — DO. DO. DO. DO. DO. 1927.

| ENGINE | CYLINDERS | | DRIVING | BOILER | TRACTIVE EFFORT AT |
	Nº	DIMENSIONS	WHEELS	PRESSURE	85% BOILER PRESSURE
"NORTH STAR"	2	16 × 16"	7'_0"	50 LBS.	2070 LBS.
"LORD OF THE ISLES"	2	18" × 24"	8'_0"	140 "	9640 "
"KING GEORGE V"	4	16¼ × 28"	6'_6"	250 "	40300 "

Development of GWR locomotive power: 1837 to 1927

length was 16 ft., an increase of 1 ft. 2 in. on the No. 1 boiler. The grate area was 34.3 sq. ft., an increase of 16½ per cent on the 'Castle'. This was balanced by an increase of 18 per cent in the firebox heating surface, and of 19 per cent in the superheating surface. To distribute the weight of the boiler evenly over the rear section of the engine frame, flat leaf springs about 8 in. long were fitted in grooves in the boiler carrying brackets beneath the firebox.

The increase of 27 per cent in the nominal tractive effort was not fully matched by the increase in the size of boiler, and thus, even more so than in the previous four-cylinder engines, short cut-off working would be required.

Collett's part in the day-to-day design work was less than Churchward's had been, and the detailed design work owed much to the fine team of senior draughtsmen working under the direction of F. W. Hawksworth.

The class was initially dubbed a 'Super-Castle', and it was rumoured that the engines were to be named after cathedrals. The plan to send the first engine to America led to the choice of a more striking name, and the decision to name them after Kings of England was taken before the first engine

had been completed. Unlike the 4021-30 series of 'Stars', which omitted the numbers of individual monarchs, the 'Kings' were named after individual Kings of England, starting with King George V and running in reverse order to King Stephen. Whether this arrangement was of greater assistance to railway enthusiasts in teaching them the order of the English Kings, or in helping them to remember the numbers of the 'King' class engines, is not recorded.

The striking appearance of the 'Kings' came from a combination of their generally massive size and specific details of the design. The chimney was shorter and of larger diameter than those of the 'Castles'; the outside bearings of the bogie and the conspicuous front stretcher of the bogie frame implied solidity, and the straight diagonal top line of the main frames adjoining the inside cylinder, together with the box-like steam chest cover, gave a more thrusting appearance ahead of the smokebox than in the 'Stars' and 'Castles'.

The measure of improvement in train loading which the 'Kings' brought to the West of England services is shown by the following summary of the maximum loadings with which an unassisted engine was expected to keep time.

	Paddington to Taunton	Taunton to Plymouth
Saint	392 tons	252 tons
Star	420	288
Castle	455	315
King	500	360

The most important gain was the additional 45 tons from Taunton to Plymouth, which enabled much double-heading to be avoided between Newton Abbot and Plymouth with the summer loading of the West of England expresses. Furthermore, even with the increased loading, it was possible to reduce the time of the 'Cornish Riviera Express' from its long-standing 247 min. to an even 4 hours from Paddington to Plymouth. The 'Kings' were allowed initially to work only between Paddington and Plymouth, and between Paddington and Wolverhampton via Bicester. This restriction was indicated on the engine route map as 'hatched red', and was indicated on the engine by two red discs. No power classification was given to them in GWR days.

No. 6000 appeared in June 1927 and, after some trial running, it reappeared from Swindon fitted with Westinghouse brake. It was soon revealed that this did not presage a brake revolution on the GWR but was in preparation for a visit to America. The idea of the visit originated in 1925. Daniel Willard, the President of the Baltimore & Ohio Railroad, was already considering how his Company would celebrate its centenary in 1927. He therefore commissioned an eminent railway enthusiast, Edward Hungerford, to attend the centenary celebrations of the Stockton & Darlington Railway, and to report his observations. During his stay in England,

Hungerford met Pole, and from their conversation emerged the idea that an English engine (that is, for Pole, a GWR engine) should take part in the celebrations. When the decision to build the new engine was taken, it was clear that this was the engine which must go to America, though at first this was not appreciated in Swindon Works. K. J. Cook, then Assistant Locomotive Works Manager, has told how the general outline of the new class was known, but that very few drawings had yet reached them. Then one day he was called into his chief's office; Stanier was there, and Cook began to explain how he was planning to have the first engine of the new class completed by the end of September. But Stanier cut him short by saying, 'Young man, she's got to be in the USA by August!' The task was achieved with sufficient margin for the engine both to complete the necessary trial trips, and to be exhibited at a number of stations in aid of the GWR 'Helping Hand' fund, which aided members of the staff in time of need. At Paddington, on 1 July, nearly 3,000 people inspected the engine, and many were turned away disappointed. On 20 July the engine worked the down 'Limited' for the first time, and made an excellent run.

The expedition to the U.S.A. was in the personal charge of Mr. W. A. Stanier, as he was then, in his capacity of Principal Assistant to the Chief Mechanical Engineer. The engine arrived at Roath Dock, Cardiff, on 2 August 1927, and was loaded on the S.S. *Chicago City* on the following day. It was accompanied by the replica broad-gauge engine *North Star*. The boiler was loaded separately from the chassis on the deck of the ship, no crane capable of lifting the locomotive in one piece being available. It reached Locust Point, Baltimore, on

The two locomotives that visited the U.S.A. in 1927: 'King George V' and the replica 'North Star'

Engine No. 6000, ready for the American visit fitted with Westinghouse brake

21 August, and was taken thence to the Mount Clare shops of the Baltimore & Ohio. The fineness of its detailed work compared with contemporary American locomotives immediately attracted attention.

The exhibition was open from 24 September to 15 October, and was visited by a quarter of a million people. No. 6000, handled by Driver W. Young and Fireman Pearce of Old Oak Common, led the procession each day, and attracted great interest. An oval track had been laid in the exhibition grounds, and a procession of locomotives paraded round the track past the viewing stands. There was a gentle slope approaching the grandstand, and Young allowed No. 6000 to coast down it. The engine moved past the stand in complete silence, whereas the American engines, even new ones, groaned, squeaked and clanked. Never was the excellence of Swindon workmanship shown up more strikingly. Amongst the visitors who were allowed to ride on the engine was Henry Ford I, who took many photographs, and announced his intention of making a model of the engine.

Two days after the close of the exhibition, No. 6000 was given a test run on the Baltimore & Ohio railroad. Starting from Baltimore, the engine ran to Washington (36 miles), and then made a trip to Philadelphia (132½ miles); finally it returned to Baltimore. The load comprised a dynamometer car and six coaches which, in the heavyweight American stock of the day, weighed 544 tons tare. The task set Driver Young and Fireman Pearce was thus formidable. The load was as great as was handled on the West of England trains, but instead of the progressive shedding of load by the 'Limited' on its four-hour journey, this load was to be hauled over 272 miles, with a total running time for the day of seven hours. Instead of the familiar soft Welsh coal, the engine was burning hard gas coal, which formed large quantities of clinker, and was better suited to grates of twice the size of that of *King George V*. Added to this was the Westinghouse brake, a strange road, the different feel of the roadbed, the need for additional vigilance on a railway without fencing, and the general unfamiliarity of all the lineside equipment. And to crown all, the work of the engine was being studied in the dynamometer car by senior officers of three American railroads.

A 'Star' and two 'Castles' had previously maintained the honour of the Great Western when tested on two 'foreign' lines in England. Now, under much more severe conditions, *King George V* and its crew ably maintained the honour not only of Swindon but of British locomotive engineering generally. Pearce's contribution was notable; despite the difficult fuel, pressure was never below 205 lb. per sq. in., and on the last leg of the test

Front end of No. 6000, with 'Britannia' (Miss Bruhl) showing also the original bogie springing

station, speed rose to 23 m.p.h., and the drawbar pull was nearly 9 tons at one point. The equivalent drawbar pull, corrected for gradient, was nearly 60 per cent of the nominal tractive effort. The cut-off was recorded as 55 per cent; in the 1953 tests of No. 6001 this tractive effort at 23 m.p.h. required a steam flow of 28,000 lb./hour and a cut-off of 50 per cent.

Although the Baltimore & Ohio had water troughs, the water level was lower than on the GWR and No. 6000's scoop was ineffective. Two stops were thus needed for water, one at Camden station, Baltimore, and the other at Elks Mills. The start from Elks Mills was on a 1 in 115 gradient, and it was here that the drawbar pull of 5 tons at

was maintained at 235–245 lb. per sq. in. There was an almost complete absence of black smoke from the chimney, in contrast to the American engines both at the exhibition and in ordinary service. At the request of the railroad officials speed did not exceed 74 m.p.h., and for much of the test was limited to 65, but the general running was up to the standards maintained on the home railway. The gradients varied down to 1 in 79. Amongst notable figures recorded was a drawbar pull of 5 tons sustained at 48 m.p.h. on a gradient of 1 in 115; the equivalent drawbar horsepower was nearly 1,700.

The accompanying table shows the log of the second leg of the journey, from Washington to Philadelphia. It was on the early stages of this run that the worst trouble with fuel was experienced. Cut-off was 25 per cent up the bank towards Muirkirk, 20 per cent on the undulating section to Camp Meade Junction, and 15 per cent on the falling gradients towards Halethorpe, where a maximum speed of 73 m.p.h. was reached. On the 1 in 79 gradient, which extends for 2½ miles out of Camden

BALTIMORE AND OHIO RAILROAD,
WASHINGTON—PHILADELPHIA
Date: 17/10/27
Engine: GWR No. 6000, *King George V*
Load: Dynamometer car + 6 cars, 544 tons tare
Driver: W. Young (Old Oak Common)

Dist. Miles		Actual m. s.		Av. speed m.p.h.
0·00	NEW YORK AVENUE	0	00	
0·57	'F' Tower . . .	2	30	13·6
4·68	Alexandria Junction .	8	20	42·4
7·49	Berwyn . . .	12	00	46·0
12·83	Muirkirk . . .	17	55	54·0
16·45	Laurel . . .	21	45	56·5
19·87	Camp Meade Junction	25	00	63·4
24·37	Dorsey . . .	29	10	66·4
28·79	Relay . . .	33	30	61·4
30·54	Halethorpe . .	35	50	44·9
34·42	Carroll . . .	40	55	45·6
36·00	CAMDEN . .	44	55	
0·00		0	00	
1.44	Mount Royal . .	5	10	16·7
2·47	Huntington Avenue .	8	25	18·3
3·40	Waverley . . .	10	50	23·2
6·79	Bay View . . .	15	40	41·8
13·14	Poplar . . .	22	40	54·6
15·67	Cowenton . . .	25	10	57·9
19·69	Bradshaw . . .	30	15	47·3
21·34	C.N. Tower . .	32	40	41·3
23·62	Van Bibber . .	35	10	54·3
27·33	Belcamp . . .	38	50	60·7
32·23	Aberdeen . . .	43	50	58·8
36·93	Havre de Grace .	48	50	57·6
39·35	Aiken . . .	53	40	30·1
47·80	Leslie . . .	63	10	53·5
52·56	Childs . . .	69	05	48·3
	Elks Mills: water stop 6 min. 40 sec.			
59·36	Newark . . .	85	55	
65·34	Stanton . . .	92	40	53·2
67·69	W. J. Tower . .	96	05	41·5
68·51	Wilsmer . . .	97	50	28·1
69·63	Elsmere . . .	98	55	62·0
71·48	Wilmington . .	102	05	35·1
76·12	Silverside . . .	108	20	44·5
82·42	Feltonville . .	114	40	59·7
95·02	East Side . . .	133	15	
96·51	PHILADELPHIA (Chestnut St.) .	137	45	

The pageant of locomotives at the Baltimore and Ohio centenary celebrations

48 m.p.h. was recorded. The American officials were very impressed with the riding of the engine, but, as is recorded later, the engine might well have given a different impression. The engine was fitted with a bell for its trial run, and retained this for the remainder of its life. It bears an inscription: 'Presented to the locomotive *King George V* by the Baltimore and Ohio Railroad in commemoration of its centenary celebrations, September 24—October 15, 1927.' Two medals were also fixed to the cab sides. The clean lines of the engine created a great impression in the United States, and a number of express engines on the Baltimore & Ohio and other railroads appeared with cleaner external lines and, in some cases, with copper-capped chimneys.

The first twenty 'Kings' were ordered on the same Lot number, but they appeared in two batches, the first six by July 1927, and the remaining fourteen between February and June 1928. Soon after the first engines entered traffic, reports were received of rough riding, and as wear developed in the axleboxes, the engines developed alarming motions, nosing at the front and lurching from side to side at the rear. On 10 August 1927, the bogie of No. 6003 was partially derailed whilst travelling at speed near Midgham on straight track. Fortunately the derailment did not spread to the train, and the results were not serious. They were, however, alarming, not only because there was no obvious reason why this derailment should have occurred on good track, but also because No. 6000 was about to be tested in America, where the track might be well below GWR standards.

There is a story, possibly apocryphal, that Collett visited the scene of the derailment, and poking his umbrella into several sleepers, found that the metal

The two plaques presented to the GWR in commemoration of the American visit, affixed to the cab sides of engine No. 6000

View of bogie and front end 'King' class locomotive, showing finalised arrangement of bogie springing

tip penetrated. He therefore blamed the Civil Engineer for the derailment, on the grounds that the track was defective.

Nevertheless, an immediate investigation was made into the riding of the 'Kings' and, as suspicion fell on the bogie springs, a section was cut from the head of a rail on the weighbridge at Swindon. This allowed one wheel to drop, and it was found that a drop of $1\frac{1}{2}$ in. relieved the wheel of all load. There was thus little margin for defects in the track consistent with the wheel loads remaining sufficiently great to ensure adequate flange control. Coil

springs were therefore introduced into the spring hangers to soften the springing. Plates were also inserted in the trailing axleboxes to reduce the lateral clearance to $\frac{1}{16}$ in., in place of 1 in., and the inclined slides were later removed. From the seventh engine onwards the slides were omitted, but the spherical bushes were fitted to all the engines of the class. It was not until the mid-fifties that it was realised that these were no longer required, and they were then replaced by cylindrical bushes.

These changes eliminated the rolling of the

Engine No. 6004 'King George III' with intermediate arrangement of bogie springing

No. 6021 'King Richard II' on West of England express near Reading

The Cornish Riviera Express near Shaldon bridge, Teignmouth: engine No. 6012 'King Edward VI'

engines, but fracturing of bogie springs continued, and after some months the trailing coupled wheel springs were redesigned to make them softer (33 plates at $\frac{3}{8}$ in. and one at $\frac{1}{2}$ in., in place of 21 at $\frac{7}{16}$ in. and one at $\frac{1}{2}$ in.). This cured the trouble, and the 'Kings' then gained the reputation of being amongst the best-riding engines in Britain.

After the Midgham derailment, Stanier received a cable from Collett telling him that No. 6000 was not to be run on a main line until permission was received from Swindon. When the modifications to the bogie springing had been agreed, details were sent to Stanier, and he was able to arrange with the Baltimore & Ohio Company for the necessary work to be done in their shops. Fortunately the engine was not troubled by the rolling which affected other members of the class at this time. The 'Kings' soon established themselves as powerful engines, and they showed mastery over the West of England workings. Their introduction was heralded by the usual blaze of publicity, including the publication of a book entitled *The King of Railway Locomotives*. The high tractive effort was exploited to the full, as Pole intended.

A further batch of ten 'Kings' was built in 1930 and appeared between May and August. They displayed a few visible changes from the earlier engines. In September 1930, No. 6029 travelled to Manchester for the centenary celebrations of the Liverpool & Manchester Railway, and was serviced at Agecroft shed on the former L & YR. This was the furthest north ever reached by a 'King'.

The Midgham incident: the Cornish Riviera Express halted, with the bogie of engine No. 6003 derailed

CHAPTER 11

THE 'KINGS' AT WORK

SIR Felix Pole's promise that the first engine of this new class should be exhibited and run during the centenary celebrations of the Baltimore & Ohio Railroad in August 1927 set the target for production of the 'King' class, and the pioneer engine was completed at Swindon in June of that year, followed by five more in July. It was essential that No. 6000 should be fully run-in before leaving England, because it was not only to be exhibited but also run out on the line. The ordinary running-in turns were successfully performed and on 20 July 1927, No. 6000 worked the down 'Limited' non-stop from Paddington to Plymouth. The day was a Wednesday, and at mid-week in the period of the summer service the load was no more than moderate, namely 425 tons gross as far as Westbury

and 350 tons beyond. But the particular point of interest was that for the first time ever a load of 338 tons was taken from Newton Abbot to Plymouth without assistance.

The tare load for the new engines was later fixed at 360 tons, but initially bank engines were taken for lighter loads. Two days after the inaugural run, engine No. 6001 *King Edward VII* was put on to the train with a load one coach heavier throughout, and crowded with passengers. The skeleton log opposite shows an excellent performance, particularly as it included two stops: one to attach the bank engine at Newton Abbot and one to put it off at Brent. This second log was compiled by Mr A. V. Goodyear.

The potential of the 'Kings' was exploited

Engine No. 6003 on down West of England express near Reading, a week before the Midgham derailment

quickly; in the winter timetable of 1927, 7 min. were cut from the schedule of the down 'Limited'. But despite the publicity that accompanied the introduction of the 'Kings', and the magnificent appearance of the new engines, there was definitely something about them that left the more thoughtful of outside observers slightly unimpressed. By the year 1927 the slight recession in Great Western locomotive performance that had followed the Coal Strike of 1926 had largely disappeared, and both 'Stars' and 'Castles'—not to mention the trusty old 'Saints'—were back on top form. And when vast new locomotives were introduced to do work that the older engines had done so brilliantly, when conditions were favourable, the need for so great an advance was questioned. The publicity was inclined to be regarded purely as publicity. After all, it was argued, if *Knight of the Grand Cross* could take 530 tons out of Paddington on the down 'Limited', and with appropriate reductions of load at Westbury, Taunton and Exeter bring the train into North Road 3 min. early, was there really a need for locomotives of 40,300 lb. tractive effort, in order to cut a mere 7 min. off the schedule? In any case the Interchange Trial of 1925 had shown that a 'Castle' could cut 15 min. off that schedule!

The inaugural runs of engines Nos. 6000 and 6001 on the 'Cornish Riviera Express' included nothing that was really significant in the way of performance. If the 'Stars' had taken 288 tons over the South Devon line, on the proportions of tractive

effort to load the 'Kings' ought to have had 410 tons, not 360. It only needed news of the derailment at Midgham to give a slightly jaundiced view of the new locomotives. Neither was the first detailed account of their working any more reassuring. Following his very successful footplate run from Paddington to Plymouth on a 'Castle' in the autumn of 1924, Cecil J. Allen was accorded a similar privilege on a 'King' in October 1927, with results that led to a good deal of controversy in the columns of *The Railway Magazine*! All the arguments that had centred around the differences in boiler design between Swindon and Doncaster practice were revived, and the instances of bad steaming of GWR engines during the period of the 1926 Coal Strike were recalled.

The engine was No. 6005, and the loads on the four successive stages of the journey were much the same as on Allen's footplate run with *Pendennis Castle*, three years earlier, namely 525, 450, 380 and 270 tons gross behind the tender. The tender had been loaded with indifferent coal, however, and although having a nominal tractive effort vastly greater than that of a 'Castle' the engine was never master of the schedule until the load was reduced to 7 coaches at Exeter. By Slough 1 min. 40 sec. had been dropped, and speed was only $62\frac{1}{2}$ m.p.h. A permanent-way slack to 40 m.p.h. caused further delay, and the lateness rose to $3\frac{1}{2}$ min. There was a further permanent-way slack at Aldermaston, and speed did not rise above $57\frac{1}{2}$ m.p.h. until Savernake

CORNISH RIVIERA EXPRESS

Date			20/7/27	22/7/27
Engine No.			6000	6001
Engine Name			*King George V*	*King Edward VII*
Load: tons E/F				
To Westbury			410/425	447/480
To Plymouth			338/350	375/400

Dist. Miles		Sch. Min.	Actual m. s.	Actual m. s.
0·0	Paddington	0	0 00	0 00
—			p.w.s.	p.w.s.
9·1	Southall	11	16 19	13 03
18·5	Slough	20	24 53	21 15
36·0	Reading	37	41 57	36 55
53·1	Newbury	56	59 18	55 25
66·4	Bedwyn	69½	72 18	68 35
95·6	Westbury	97½	98 58	95 55
101·3	Frome		105 44	103 32
115·3	Castle Cary	120	120 11	118 45
142·9	Taunton	148	146 20	143 30
153·8	*Whiteball Box*		159 04	157 28
173·7	Exeter	179	176 43	176 15
225·7	Plymouth	247	242 26	246 59

Engine No. 6005 'King George II' with indicator shelters ready for dynamometer car trial runs

had been passed 6 min. late. There was a gradual recovery, and by Taunton lateness was under 2 min., but with only 380 tons a further minute was lost by Exeter. However, there was no difficulty in recovering this loss after Exeter, and Plymouth was reached in 237 min. 50 sec., or 233½ min. net. Much work with the pricker had been needed, and the interest of the run lay in the fireman's efforts to combat difficulties which at that time were not frequent on the GWR. The publication of this run, in very extended detail, caused something of a sensation among students of locomotive performance, and there were some, with no particular partisan feelings, who were inclined to the view that Swindon design practice, in enlarging the 'Star' to the proportions of the 'King', had overreached itself, and that for locomotives of 40,000 lb. tractive effort the large boiler and wide firebox favoured by Doncaster was preferable.

In any event, Allen was offered another trip, and at the second try he was favoured with an immaculate performance from the locomotive point of view, though the incidence of no fewer than *eight* permanent-way checks prevented the end-to-end schedule being maintained. The steaming was as near perfect as made no matter, and there appeared

in print for the first time details of a run on the GWR when the working cut-offs for fast, high output running on level track were less than 20 per cent. Between Paddington and Reading, where *Pendennis Castle* had needed 26 per cent cut-offs, *King James I* was doing equal or slightly faster work on 18 per cent. Of course cut-offs of this order were nothing new on the Great Western. They had been a commonplace for many years on 'Stars' and 'Castles' when those engines were working under optimum conditions. It was only in the haulage of 500-ton trains on the 'Limited' and similar duties when so loaded that the driving had to be much harder. Complete details of this run are given in the accompanying table.

It must nevertheless be emphasised that although the 'King' class engines, in good working conditions, were completely master of any task the traffic department liked to put to them, their ultimate capacity, like that of the 'Castles', was the ability of the fireman to shovel coal. On that day in May 1925, when *Caldicot Castle* brought the 'Limited' into Plymouth 15 min. ahead of time, neither the front-end limit nor the grate limit of the engine had been reached. Whether the engine was a 'King' or a 'Castle' the same amount of steam had to be

No. 6000, with presentation bell, on up Bristol express near Swindon

No. 6018 'King Henry VI' on up West of England express

THE DOWN 'CORNISH RIVIERA EXPRESS'

Load to Westbury 14 cars 492/525 tons   to Exeter 10 cars 337/380 tons
to Taunton 12 cars 421/450 tons   to Plymouth 7 cars 253/270 tons
Engine: No. 6011 *King James I*
Driver: Wright: Fireman: Hounslow

Dist. Miles		Sch. Min.	Actual m. s.	Speed m.p.h.	Regulator Opening	Cut-off %	Boiler pressure lb./sq. in.
0·0	PADDINGTON . .	0	0 00		$\frac{1}{2}$	75	230
1·3	Westbourne Park . .		3 05		$\frac{3}{4}$	23	240
5·7	Ealing . . .		9 10		$\frac{3}{4}$	20	240
9·1	SOUTHALL . . .	11	12 45	59	full	18	245
13·2	West Drayton . .		16 55	65	,,	18	245
18·5	SLOUGH . . .	20	21 35	70½	,,	18	245
24·2	Maidenhead . .	25½	26 40	66	,,	18	245
36·0	READING . . .	37	37 30	slack 40			245
44·8	Aldermaston . .		46 55	65	,,	20	245
53·1	NEWBURY . . .	55½	54 55	61	,,	18	240/235
58·5	Kintbury . . .		60 10	62½	,,	18	240
61·5	Hungerford . .		63 15	57½/61½	,,	20	240
66·4	Bedwyn . . .	68½	68 15	58½	,,	20	230
68·6	*Grafton Curve Junction* .		70 50	p.w.s. 20	,,	30	240
70·1	Savernake . . .		73 55		,,	18	240
75·3	Pewsey . . .		79 05	71½	,,	18	225
81·1	Patney . . .		83 50	77½/80½	$\frac{1}{2}$	16	235
86·9	Lavington . . .		88 35	p.w.s. 20	full	20	240
95·6	WESTBURY . . .	96	98 35	slack 35	,,	20	240
98·5	*Milepost 112¾* . .		102 05	54	,,	20	245
101·3	FROME . . .		105 30	slack 35	,,	20	250
106·6	Witham . . .		112 00	53½	,,	20	245
108·5	*Milepost 122¾* . .		114 15	50½	$\frac{1}{2}$	16	240
111·9	Bruton . . .		117 15	77½/83½	1st port	16	245
115·3	CASTLE CARY . .	118	120 00	slack 50	$\frac{1}{2}$—$\frac{3}{4}$	16	245
120·2	Keinton Mandeville .		124 55	67	$\frac{3}{4}$	16	245
125·7	Somerton . . .		129 45	75	full	16	240
131·0	*Curry Rivell Junction* .		134 05	79	$\frac{1}{2}$	16	240
137·9	*Cogload Junction* . .	140	140 55	p.w.s. 10	full	20	245
142·9	TAUNTON . . .	144½	147 45	58½	,,	20	240
144·9	Norton Fitzwarren .		149 45	62½	,,	20	240
147·5	*Milepost 167¾* . .		152 10	64	,,	20	240
150·0	Wellington . . .		154 40	58½	,,	25	240
152·8	*Milepost 173* . .		157 55	42½	,,	30	235
153·8	*Whiteball Box* . .		159 25	44	full ½	16	230
158·8	Tiverton Junction .		164 05	76½	$\frac{1}{2}$	16	240
161·1	Cullompton . . .		165 55	80½	$\frac{1}{2}$	16	240
170·2	Stoke Canon . .		173 05	76½	1st port	16	240
173·7	EXETER . . .	174½	175 55	70	full	16	240
178·4	Exminster . . .		179 40	82	shut	20	240
				p.w.s. 10	$\frac{1}{2}$	20	245
188·7	Teignmouth . . .		195 25	slack 40/65	$\frac{1}{2}$	20	245
193·9	NEWTON ABBOT . .	198½	201 25	slack 25	full	20	245
195·7	*Milepost 216* . .		204 13	50½	,,	25	245
197·7	*Dainton Box* . .	204½	207 50	24½/60	shut	35 (max.)	240
202·5	Totnes . . .	210½	213 35	53	full	20	245
204·7	*Milepost 225* . .		216 49	31½	,,	30	245
205·3	*Tigley Box* . .		217 50	29	,,	35	245
207·1	*Rattery Box* . .		221 15	36	,,	25	245
209·4	Brent . . .	219½	224 10	54	,,	25	245
211·6	Wrangaton . . .		226 40	p.w.s. 25	shut	20	245
219·0	*Hemerdon Box* . .	231	235 55	60/68	$\frac{1}{2}$	20	240
221·7	Plympton . . .		238 30	50	$\frac{1}{2}$	20	235
225·4	Mutley . . .		sigs.			20	
225·7	PLYMOUTH . . .	240	245 35			20	

Net times, Paddington to Exeter   167¾ min.
Paddington to Plymouth   228 min.

137

The down Cornish Riviera Express: a photograph taken near Reading West showing the full 14-coach load: engine No. 6000 'King George V'

put through the cylinders. The 'Kings' did not represent any advance in locomotive design technique or practice. They were, rather, a very ingenious enlargement of the 'Star', and embodying all the principles established by Churchward in years before World War I.

Nevertheless, as the engine crews became thoroughly used to the workings of these great machines, and learned the art of exploiting the vast tractive power without causing an undue drain upon the boiler, the standards of performance on the West of England line positively soared, and the reputation of the 'Kings' as the really great locomotives they were became established. Their tractive effort was no mere paper figure, because they enjoyed that immunity from slipping that was characteristic of all Great Western 4—6—0s, and that tractive effort could be used with confidence for lifting heavy loads smartly away from rest or climbing steep gradients.

Three exceptionally fine runs of the 1929-30 period are clearly shown in the accompanying table—all on the 'Cornish Riviera Express', after some adjustments had been made in the intermediate timing. Allen had remarked that an allowance of 37 min. to Reading seemed unnecessarily severe; but the new time was 36 min., and runs 1 and 2 show that it was quite practicable with trains of 500 tons gross. Exeter was booked to be passed in $171\frac{1}{2}$ min., an allowance which was at that time one of the fastest bookings in the world over such

a distance, if not the fastest.

Run No. 1 shows a good all-round performance by No. 6000 in July 1929, when only the Weymouth slip portion was carried. By Slough the train was almost on time, and even time was reached by Twyford. The time of 35 min. 15 sec. to Reading was notable, but the slack was evidently treated lightly. Up the Kennet Valley more time was gained, and Savernake was passed in 68 min. for 70.1 miles. A permanent-way slack to 15 m.p.h. at Woodborough spoiled the descent, but there was a recovery to 82 m.p.h. at Edington, and the time to Westbury was 92 min. 40 sec. Running beyond Frome was similar to that of No. 6011, except that Castle Cary was passed at the full 60 m.p.h. which was allowed. Despite signal checks before and after Cogload, Taunton was passed at 57 m.p.h. in 139 min. 51 sec., and speed fell to 26 m.ph. at Whiteball Box. The train was a minute early at Exeter. The continuation of this run is shown in a separate table and is discussed later.

The second run was notable for the very quick start, probably the fastest ever recorded with so great a load. To be within 36 sec. of the Southall booking and 18 sec. ahead of the Slough booking was remarkable for a 500-ton train, and showed the advantages to the operating authorities of the tractive effort of the 'Kings'. A speed of $76\frac{1}{2}$ m.p.h. at Slough was also notable with this load. The passing time at Reading was thus 1 min. 45 sec. inside the new booking, and running of a similar

THE DOWN 'CORNISH RIVIERA EXPRESS'

Run No.		1		2		3	
Date		7/29		1930		1/9/30	
Engine No.		6000		6020		6013	
Load: cars, tons, tare/full							
To Westbury		14 479/510		14 — /505		16 543/580	
To Taunton		11 378/405		12 — /430		13 443/475	
To Exeter		11 378/405				13 443/475	

Dist. Miles		Sch. Min.	Actual m. s.	Speed m.p.h.	Actual m. s.	Speed m.p.h.	Actual m. s.	Speed m.p.h.
0·0	PADDINGTON	0	0 00		0 00		0 00	
1·3	Westbourne Park		2 55		2 37		3 40	
5·7	Ealing				8 13		10 10	52½
9·1	SOUTHALL	11	12 00	60	11 36	63	13 55	59
18·5	SLOUGH	20	20 20	73	19 42	76½	22 35	71½
24·2	Maidenhead	25	25 00	72	24 28	71½	27 35	68
31·0	Twyford	30½	30 50	69	30 03	74	33 30	73
36·0	READING	36	35 15	slack	34 15	slack 45	37 55	slack 50
37·8	*Southcote Junction*		37 20	56			39 50	
44·8	Aldermaston				43 25	68	46 50	61
53·1	NEWBURY	54	51 35	62	50 58	62½	55 10	58½
58·5	Kintbury				55 58	67	60 45	
61·5	Hungerford				58 54	61	63 55	58½
66·4	Bedwyn	67	64 05	64	63 31	65	68 45	59
70·1	Savernake		68 00	52	67 19	53	73 05	45½
75·3	Pewsey		72 55	75	72 03	77½	78 10	72½
78·8	Woodborough		76 10	p.w.s. 15				
81·1	Patney		80 05	55	76 42	70½	82 55	75
86·9	Lavington				81 13	79	87 35	83½
91·4	Edington		89 00	82			91 10	74
95·6	WESTBURY	94	92 40	slack	89 24	slack	95 00	slack 40
101·3	FROME		99 30	slack	p.w.s.		102 00	slack 40
106·6	Witham					51	108 15	49½
108·5	*Milepost 122¾*		108 45	50/82	108 26	49	110 40	45
111·9	Bruton				111 38	82	113 50	82
115·4	CASTLE CARY	116	114 35	slack 60	114 29	slack 60	116 35	slack 69
120·2	Keinton Mandeville				118 57			
125·7	Somerton		124 00	72 max.	123 54	65	125 40	64½
129·9	Langport		127 39		127 39	77½	129 20	75
			sigs.					
137·9	*Cogload Junction*	137	134 45	55	134 41	70½	136 15	65
			sigs.					
142·9	TAUNTON	142	139 55	57	140 57★		140 55	60
144·9	Norton Fitzwarren						143 00	63½
150·0	Wellington		147 25	54			148 25	
153·8	*Whiteball Box*		153 20	26			154 35	28
158·8	Tiverton Junction		158 25	72			159 30	74
161·1	Cullompton						161 35	76½/79
							sigs.	
170·2	Stoke Canon		167 30	81 max.			169 25	
							sigs.	
173·7	EXETER pass	171½	170 20	slack 60			173 10	

Net time, min.:								
To Taunton					138★			
To Exeter			166				172½	

★Arrival of slip coach

standard to that of the previous run, but unimpeded by checks, brought the train through Westbury in 89 min. 24 sec., 5½ min. early. The Taunton slip portion came to rest in 140 min. 57 sec., or 138 min. net.

On the third run No. 6013 had a formidable load of 16 coaches, 543 tons tare, and 580 tons full, reduced only to 475 tons by the slipping of three coaches at Westbury. The new booking proved to be too severe for this loading in the earlier stages, but with 43 tons over the full load for standard timekeeping, Driver Wimhurst was quite entitled

Down Cornish Riviera Express near Twyford: engine No. 6004 'King George III'

to a few extra minutes. Nevertheless, he was ahead of time by Cogload Junction, and it was only signal checks before Stoke Canon and Exeter that prevented him from passing Exeter on time. Speed passed the seventy line twice before Reading, with $71\frac{1}{2}$ m.p.h. at Slough and 73 at Twyford. Up the Kennet Valley No. 6013 managed to reach 61

m.p.h. at Aldermaston, and the fall from 59 m.p.h. at Bedwyn to $45\frac{1}{2}$ at Savernake was creditable with this load. This run gave the highest speed on the descent to Westbury of any of the 'King' runs so far described, with $83\frac{1}{2}$ m.p.h. at Lavington. Another fine climb followed after Frome, with a fall from $49\frac{1}{2}$ m.p.h. at Witham to 45 at the sum-

A scene in Sonning Cutting, with No. 6011 'King James I' overtaking No. 4085 'Berkeley Castle'
on a stopping train

Up Cornish Riviera Express near Reading: engine No. 6002 'King William IV'

mit. As the train was ahead of time at Taunton, Whiteball could be taken gently, and speed fell from $63\frac{1}{2}$ at Taunton to 28 m.p.h. at the summit. A brisk run down to Exeter, with a maximum of 79 m.p.h. after Cullompton, was interrupted by the signal checks mentioned previously.

A separate table herewith shows the continuation to Plymouth of the run by No. 6000 shown on page 139. With 18 tons more than the maximum unassisted load, the driver carried on to Plymouth without assistance, and cut 50 sec. from the allowance from Exeter to Plymouth. Along the coastal stretch 3 min. were gained, and this allowed for some loss of time on the banks. On Dainton there was a fall from 45 to 20 m.p.h.; but the climb to Rattery was excellent for a load of 405 tons. The speed at Totnes was only 52 m.p.h., but Tigley was passed at 25 m.p.h. and there was a good recovery to 32 m.p.h. at Rattery. A clear run into Plymouth gave an arrival 3 min. early.

The debut of the 'Kings' on the Birmingham line was not auspicious. Engines 6017, 6018 and 6019 were sent new to Wolverhampton in the summer of 1928, and a run clocked by myself on the 6.10

THE DOWN 'CORNISH RIVIERA EXPRESS'

Date: July 1929
Engine: 6000 *King George V*
Load: 11 cars, 378 tons tare, 405 tons full
All distances and times are measured from Paddington

Dist. Miles		Sch. Min.	Actual m. s.	Speed m.p.h.
173·7	EXETER . pass	$171\frac{1}{2}$	170 20	slack 60
178·4	Exminster . .		174 45	68
188·7	Teignmouth .		185 30	slack 47
193·9	NEWTON ABB.	$195\frac{1}{2}$	191 20	slack
195·7	*Milepost 216* .		194 10	45
196·7	*Milepost 217* .		195 55	32
197·7	*Dainton Box* .		198 25	20
202·5	Totnes . .		204 40	52 max.
205·3	*Tigley Box* .		210 20	25
207·1	*Rattery Box* .		214 05	32
209·4	Brent . .	218	217 35	45
219·0	*Hemerdon Box* .	230	228 30	60
223·8	*Laira Junction* .		233 20	68/48
225·7	PLYMOUTH .	240	237 00	

Net time: Paddington to Plymouth $232\frac{1}{2}$ min.

p.m. from Paddington on 3 August, with No. 6019 *King Henry V*, showed a net loss of 3 min. on

Engine No. 6013 'King Henry VIII' at Old Oak Common

sign that things were going well on the footplate, that speed restrictions were scrupulously observed. There was no need to snatch the odd seconds by 'cutting' the limits, and at Ashendon Junction speed was reduced to 52 m.p.h. The recovery from this slack was immediate and vigorous. Blackthorn was passed at 75 m.p.h., but after detaching the Bicester slip portion one minute early and being relieved of 55 tons of load the engine was justifiably

schedule from Paddington to Leamington. The load was 480 tons gross to Bicester, 450 tons to Banbury and 385 tons onwards. Generally it can be said that the uphill work was poor, and despite very fast downhill speeds the lost time could not be recovered. This run indicated that the 'Kings' required getting used to, because the Wolverhampton top link of that period included some of the most capable enginemen that have ever served the GWR, and in later years, indeed they did wonderful work with the 'Kings'. Another journey that I made at Whitsun 1929 on the same train, also with engine No. 6019, was much better, as a net time of 90 min. from Paddington to Leamington was made with a load of 475 tons. The train was divided and no slips were included in the first portion. But taken all round, this run was completely eclipsed by the experience I enjoyed on the same train at Whitsun 1930, when a 'Castle' was used instead of a 'King'. The remarkable performance of *Dartmouth Castle* on that later occasion is detailed in Chapter 9.

A much finer run with a 'King' on the Birmingham line was that set out in the accompanying table, with engine No. 6008. The start was inclined to be slow, with an unusually leisurely exit from Paddington itself, and speed not rising above 58 m.p.h. at Greenford. But after a maximum of 63 m.p.h. at Denham, some magnificent performance developed. Up the 1 in 175 to Gerrard's Cross speed did not fall below 54½ m.p.h. and it recovered to 59 m.p.h. on the 1 in 254 to Beaconsfield. There was no more than a slight excess over the speed limit of 35 m.p.h. through High Wycombe, and then the hill climbing to Saunderton was very fine with a minimum speed of 50 m.p.h. at the summit.

From the subsequent work it is evident that these strenuous uphill efforts had been achieved without any mortgaging of the boiler. Fast work followed to Ashendon Junction, with a top speed of 83½ m.p.h. at Haddenham, and it was a sure

2.10 p.m. PADDINGTON–BIRMINGHAM

Engine: 6008 *King James II*

Load: To Banbury: 14 cars, 457 tons tare, 490 tons full
To Leamington: 12 cars, 405 tons tare, 435 tons full
To Birmingham: 10 cars, 370 tons tare, 400 tons full

Driver: Brunsdon (Stafford Road)

Dist. Miles		Sch. Min.	Actual m. s.	Speed m.p.h.
0·0	PADDINGTON .	0	0 00	
1·3	Westbourne Park .		4 02	
3·3	*Old Oak Common*			
	West Junction .	7	7 33	slack 40
4·6	Park Royal .		9 17	
7·8	Greenford .		13 03	58
10·3	Northolt Junction .	15½	15 37	58
14·8	Denham .		20 05	63
17·4	Gerrard's Cross .		22 45	54½
21·7	Beaconsfield .		27 27	59
24·2	*Tylers Greene* .			69
26·5	HIGH WYCOMBE .	32	31 50	slack 42
28·8	West Wycombe .		34 45	
31·5	Saunderton .		37 58	50½
32·2	*Milepost 22* .		38 46	50
34·7	PRINCES			
	RISBOROUGH .	41	41 18	70
40·1	Haddenham .		45 27	83½
44·1	Ashendon Junction .	49	48 36	52
47·4	Brill .		52 02	69
50·4	Blackthorn .		54 30	75
53·4	BICESTER .	58	56 55	67½
57·2	Ardley .		60 32	59½/68
62·4	*Aynho Junction* .	67	65 20	slack 60
64·0	King's Sutton .		66 55	
67·0	*Milepost 85¾* .		70 27	sig. stop
67·5	BANBURY .	72	77 00	stop
71·1	Cropredy .		6 20	51
76·3	Fenny Compton .		11 35	73½
81·2	Southam Road .		15 40	81
86·3	*Milepost 105* .		19 35	
87·3	LEAMINGTON .	91	21 28	
2·0	Warwick .		3 20	54½
6·2	Hatton .		8 12	46
10·2	Lapworth .		12 24	64
12·9	Knowle .		14 51	63
16·3	Solihull .		17 57	68
20·1	Tyseley .		20 58	75
22·2	Bordesley .		22 40	
23·3	BIRMINGHAM .	26	24 35	

Net times, min.: Paddington—Leamington   87¾
Leamington—Birmingham   24½

Cornish Riviera Express, with Centenary Riviera stock (1935) in Sonning Cutting: engine No. 6020 'King Henry IV'

cased a little, and speed fell off to $50\frac{1}{2}$ m.p.h. at Ardley summit. Unfortunately the driver was denied a clear run through Banbury, and a lengthy signal stop outside made it necessary to stop in the station in order to detach the slip portion.

A very smart run was made onwards to Leamington, and then after shedding another coach and continuing with a load of 405 tons, a very hard run followed into Birmingham. The usual very rapid start was made out of Leamington, with no more than 3 min. 20 sec. taken for the first 2 miles, to Warwick. Then on the $3\frac{1}{2}$ miles of 1 in 104 to

Hatton speed fell only from $54\frac{1}{2}$ to 46 m.p.h., giving the fast time of 8 min. 12 sec. to Hatton station. Thereafter speed ruled high, and one can note particularly the almost precipitate entrance into Birmingham, with no more than 3 min. 37 sec. for the last 3.2 miles from Tyseley to the stop in Snow Hill station. This, however, was not peculiar to this run. It was quite typical of the way the Wolverhampton drivers used to run in. With a good track, a clear road, and a very long platform in the station itself there was no risk involved in these very rapid approaches.

A 16-coach summer holiday load near Somerton (Somerset)

CHAPTER 12

SOME TECHNICAL DETAILS

THE general proportions of the Churchward standard boilers were settled by 1903 when 4—6—0 No. 98 appeared. Various small changes were made subsequently in the dimensions of the fireboxes, but the only notable change was the extension of the coning of the barrel. As previously mentioned, the first coned barrels had the taper on the second ring only, whereas the boiler fitted to No. 40 had the taper extending over the full length of the barrel. The drawing opposite shows the boiler fitted to 4—6—0 No. 100 in 1902 and that fitted to No. 98 in 1903. These diagrams show clearly the tapering water spaces between the inner and outer firebox in the later boiler, together with the slope of the crown of the firebox. It also shows the outline of the No. 1 boiler as it appeared on a drawing dated July 1904. Apart from the first two boilers built in 1903, the main dimensions of the No. 1 boiler did not vary by more than $\frac{3}{16}$ in., although there were numerous small changes in the number of firetubes and, later, in the length of the superheater elements. These changes affected the areas of heating surface commonly published.

Two dimensions remained standard throughout the development of the Churchward boiler. There was a clear space of 2 ft between the crown of the inner firebox and the crown of the firebox casing. This provided a large space for the collection of steam, and the steam at the top of the space was sufficiently dry for there to be no advantage in fitting a dome. In the first Churchward boilers, with parallel barrels, the crown of the firebox casing was 9 in. above the top of the barrel; this dimension remained in the taper boilers, although it then referred to the front of the barrel only.

The boilers in the upper two illustrations opposite show the position of the feed as originally arranged, at the bottom of the barrel. At a later date top feed was adopted as standard as described in Chapter 4.

The tapered form of the barrel and firebox resulted from increasing the width of the water space at the cross-section of the boiler where the rate of heat release was greatest, that is, at the front of the firebox. It ensured adequate circulation of the water at that section. It gave a further advantage in that, compared with a boiler of equal volume but without taper, there was less change of level of water over the inner firebox when the engine breasted a steep gradient, or when the brakes were applied fully. The slope of the firebox roof from front to rear was introduced to minimise the change of water level under these conditions.

All corners of the firebox had large radii to minimise the stresses set up when the boiler distorted under pressure and heat. For the same reason, stays were not brought to the edges of the firebox plates; this allowed flexibility at the corners. All stays were as nearly as possible at right angles to the surfaces which they connected; this meant, that while stays on the sides of the firebox were almost at right angles to both barrel and firebox plates, some top stays were sharply inclined through the barrel.

A total of 924 No. 1 boilers were built between 1903 and 1944. Of these, 132 were originally saturated, but, apart from a few early ones, these were all fitted later with superheaters. Between 1914 and 1919, 108 boilers were fitted with superheaters having four element groups per flue, but apart from these and the experimental superheaters mentioned later in this chapter, all the boilers of this group were built or rebuilt with the standard Swindon No. 3 superheater, with three element groups per flue. The boilers with three-row superheaters which appeared from 1944 onwards were not fitted to 'Stars', but boilers of the other variations could be, and were, used on the class. For use on the 'Stars' the boilers required the special smokebox, which, although of the same dimensions

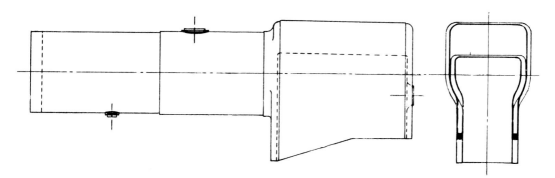

Std. Boiler No. 1 February 1902

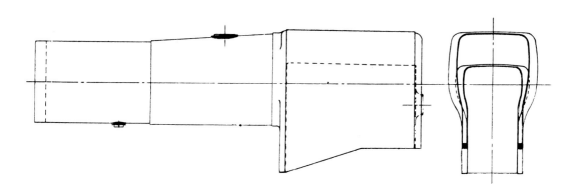

Std. Boiler No. 1 February 1903

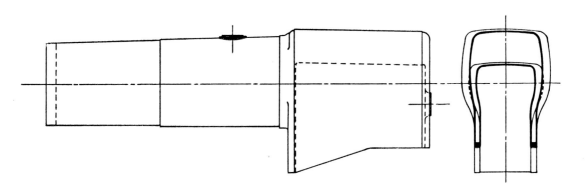

Std. Boiler No. 1 July 1904

Development of the No. 1 standard boiler

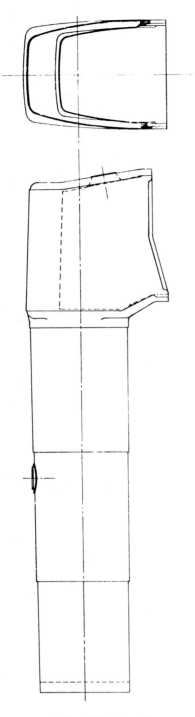

Boiler of The Great Bear

as the one used on the two-cylinder engines, was not interchangeable. Changes of smokebox were, however, made at overhaul, and boilers originally fitted to two-cylinder engines could at a later date appear on 'Stars'. By this means some short-cone boilers originally fitted to 'Saints' were fitted to 'Stars' between 1909 and 1920.

The boilers of the 'Castles' and 'Kings' were not, of course, fitted to any other classes. A total of 60 No. 8 boilers were made between 1923 and 1927 with the original large grates. These met the needs of the first 46 'Castles'. For the 'Kings' 34 boilers were made to the original design.

The diagram immediately below shows the automatic 'jumper' blastpipe top—another Swindon speciality. With heavy loads, and the corresponding admission of a maximum amount of steam to the cylinders, excessive back pressure can occur if the capacity of the blastpipe is designed to give a free exhaust in normal conditions. By automatically increasing the capacity of the blastpipe, by the rising of the jumper ring, a free exhaust is obtained in both normal and maximum working conditions.

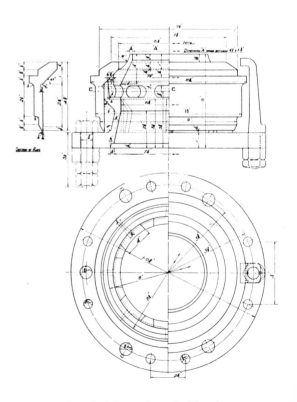

Detail of 'Jumper' top for blastpipe

1. DAMPER CONTROLS.
2. COAL WATERING COCK.
3. EXHAUST INJECTOR CONTROL.
4. FLAP PLATE.
5. FIREHOLE DOORS.
6. WATER GAUGE.
7. STEAM HEATING PRESSURE GAUGE.
8. " " VALVE
9. BOILER STEAM PRESSURE GAUGE.
10. EXHAUST INJECTOR LIVE STEAM VALVE.
11. RIGHT HAND " " " "
12. VACUUM GAUGE.

13. EJECTOR STEAM VALVE
14. " AIR "
15. BLOWER VALVE.
16. REGULATOR HANDLE.
17. LUBRICATOR.
18. REVERSING HANDLE.
19. TIP-UP SEAT.
20. SANDING GEAR LEVERS
21. AUDIBLE SIGNALLING APPARATUS.
22. CYLINDER COCK LEVER.

Cab-layout, 'King' class engines

THE GWR STARS, CASTLES & KINGS

The standard pattern of exhaust for the blower and ejector adopted by Churchward consisted of a ring inserted between the base of the chimney and the petticoat. The ring had two annular passages, to the lower of which the blower exhaust was led, and to the upper the ejector exhaust. The steam was exhausted from the annular passages into the chimney by inclined holes. This arrangement of 'blower ring' was later adopted by the LMS and SR.

The regulator valve of the GWR locomotives was a slide valve designed to give very gradual opening to steam. Movement of the valve through half its travel gave an area of opening to steam of one-eighth of the full opening. The use of a smokebox regulator and a small superheater made GWR engines much more sensitive to changes of regulator opening than engines with dome regulators and large superheaters, because there was less steam contained between the regulator valve and the cylinder. This was of importance at starting, for it resulted in slipping of the wheels being checked very quickly when the regulator was shut. It was found that the 'Kings' were more prone to slipping at starting after they had been fitted with larger superheaters, for there was a greater volume of steam to be drawn from the superheater before pressure in the steamchest dropped sufficiently for a slip to be checked.

GWR cabs were notable for the height of the footplate from rail level, and for the nearness of the firehole door to the cab floor. The main firehole door consisted of two sliding plates, operated by a single handle and links. There was also a hinged flap, attached below the main door, which could be raised by a chain to cover most of the door. The common technique for firing the engine was for the flap to be lowered before each shovelful was fired, and to be raised again immediately afterwards. This reduced the ingress of cold air to the minimum, but it was a complicated operation, and could well have been assisted by arranging a balance weight and treadle, so that the fireman could operate the flap by light foot pressure.

A single water gauge was provided, with test cocks for use in case of failure of the gauge. Two whistles were provided, one for normal and one for emergency use.

There were no cab doors, and this, combined with the height of the footplate, made the cabs exposed. Some enginemen maintain that the short Churchward cabs, in conjunction with the low tender, were less draughty than the side-window cabs with high tenders.

Cab and tender, showing exposed layout on early Churchward engines. The early 'Stars' were like this

The exposed sides of a 'Castle' footplate, even after introduction of the large tenders

VALVES

Churchward realised at an early stage that the cylinder performance at which he was aiming could be attained only by the use of piston valves. Slide valves could not give the areas of port opening, unless they were of such a size that friction losses would be prohibitive. In 1903 he said: '. . . they [piston valves] are undoubtedly one of the most troublesome pieces of mechanism with which anyone can have to deal. I have set before myself the task of curing the defects, if possible. . .'

His first piston valves, used on the 2—4—2Ts, were of the solid plug type; that is, they were solid discs with three narrow grooves round the periphery. Theoretically, these valves produced no friction, for they were smaller than the bore of the valve liner, and should have made no contact, but in fact distortion of the valve liner due to heat caused binding, wear and excessive leakage. An American valve with L-shaped spring rings, and a flat 'bull' ring clamped between them, was then tried. This did not prove entirely satisfactory, but when another American design, known as the 'semi-plug' valve, appeared Churchward acquired the manufacturing rights, and soon adopted it as his standard pattern.

The construction of the valve is shown alongside. The main seal is provided by a side serrated ring, which is split and normally closes up so that it does not touch the valve liner. When steam is admitted to the steam chest, it enters the valve head through holes, and acts on the inside surface of the serrated ring, thus pressing it tightly against the valve liner. The serrated ring is held by the exhaust snap rings, which are also split, and have cover plates over the splits to seal them. Inside the valve head is a wedge ring, which, by pressing against two other wedge-shaped rings (the wall rings) presses the exhaust snap rings tightly against the outer lips of the valve head. The whole assembly is locked solid whilst steam is on; when steam is shut off, the pressure inside the valve head falls, and all the split rings close up, allowing the valve to float freely in the valve liner.

The construction of the valve is complicated, and when it was first produced at Swindon considerable hand fitting was needed. Gradually the accuracy of the machining processes was improved, and the production of the valves was established as a mass-production process. All work on the valves was done at Swindon; running sheds changed complete valve heads. The performance of the valves was very good, steam leakage being small, but the development of solid valve heads with from four to

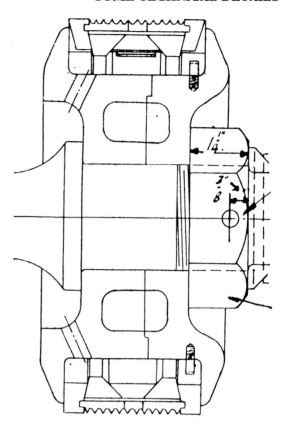

GWR standard piston valve arrangement, as applied on the 'Castle' class from the '5000' series onwards

six narrow rings provided a cheaper and equally satisfactory valve, and Stanier did not include the semi-plug valve amongst the 'Wiltshire wisdom' which he conferred on Derby.

The passage of the steam through the valve was controlled by the outer edges of the snap rings. On modern narrow-ring valves, with the outermost ring set well in from the edge of the valve head, the body of the valve forms a restriction when the valve first opens. In the GWR valves the body of the valve was well clear of the steam edge of the snap rings, and offered no restriction. This was a good feature. It was the unrestricted flow at the instant of opening which gave the GWR engines their characteristic bark at starting, and the machine-gun crack of the exhaust when working hard at speed. It also explains why, when some GWR engines were fitted with BR valves, it was found necessary to work them at a longer nominal cut-off than usual.

A locomotive valve gear must allow for the effect of the angularity of the connecting rod. With the

A set of Walschaert's valve gear set out for inspection in Swindon Works

crank in its mid-position, the crosshead is 0.7 in. to the rear of its mid-position, because of the inclination or angularity of the connecting rod. Thus when the piston is moving backwards, it is at $53\frac{1}{2}$ per cent of its stroke and when the piston is moving forwards, it is at $46\frac{1}{2}$ per cent of its stroke. The piston thus has a 'bias' towards the rear of the cylinder, and its motion is not symmetrical. If steam is to be cut off at the same position of the piston at each end of the cylinder, the valve must be given a similar non-symmetrical motion: otherwise the cut-off at the rear of the cylinder will be less than that at the front.

In a Walschaert's gear the non-symmetrical motion of the valve is produced partly by the inclination of the eccentric rod, and partly from the point of attachment of the eccentric rod to the expansion link being to the rear of the centre line of the link. As with the piston, the effect of the correction is to give the motion of the valve a 'bias' to the rear. If a straight rocker is used to drive the outside valve of the four-cylinder engine from the inside, the 'bias' is reversed by the rocker, and the outside valve thus has a bias towards the front of the steam chest, whereas the outside piston has a bias towards the rear of the cylinder. With the figures given above, if the inside valve is given the necessary bias to produce equal cut-off of 50 per cent at both ends of the cylinder, the outside

valve will be displaced in the wrong direction, and the error in the outside cut-off is doubled, that is, the cut-off at the front will be about 57 per cent and that at the rear about 43 per cent. This error is partially corrected in the Swindon valve gear by the cranking of the rocker lever.

The correction of the outside valve events by this method was a compromise; if the outside cut-offs were made exactly equal, the points of release to exhaust at the front and back of the cylinders would not be exactly equal. Great importance was attached at Swindon to synchronisation of the exhaust openings, as this was considered to contribute to the good steaming of the engine by maintaining an even blast. The setting of the outside valves was therefore arranged to favour the points of release more than the points of cut-off. The only published figures of actual valve setting of the GWR four-cylinder engine (a 'Castle') are given in Phillipson's *Locomotive Design: Data and Formulae*. When the front and back cut-offs for the right inside cylinder were 20.8 per cent and 20.4 per cent, the figures for the right outside cylinder were 26.9 per cent and 19.1 per cent. The points of release were 70.9 per cent and 68.5 per cent for the inside cylinder and 72.3 per cent and 67.6 per cent for the outside cylinder. The differences in release for the four valve heads were thus less than the differences in cut-off.

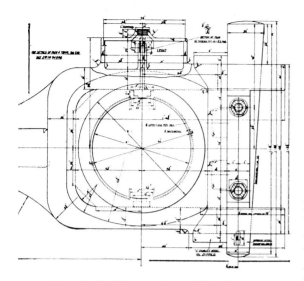

Big-end of inside connecting rod French type

classes, and trouble with what had been the 'Achilles heel' of those famous engines was virtually eliminated.

No less important and successful was the Swindon design of driving axlebox. The version of this used on the 'Castle' class is shown in the accompanying drawing. Its outstanding feature is the use of a cast-steel body, with a relatively thin gunmetal bearing having a thin, continuous white-metal lining. The effectiveness of Great Western practice in axlebox design became widely appreciated after Stanier went to the LMSR. On that line the 'Royal Scots', with driving axleboxes of standard Midland design, had a bad record with heating troubles. They were of solid manganese bronze, with three gunmetal inserts between which the white-metal was applied. In the relatively light working conditions that had been traditional on the Midland Railway this type of axlebox had given reasonable service; but in heavy express duty, and long non-stop runs such as were required from the

From the time of Churchward, Great Western locomotives have been noted for their freedom from heating troubles, and this has been due in large measure to the highly-developed designs of connecting rods and axleboxes used. With outside cylinder engines it had been the practice to make the connecting rod big-ends adjustable, so that allowance could be made in erection and maintenance for slight inaccuracies in the engine itself. But Churchward, by insisting on greater precision and uniformity in the building of his engines, was able to adopt solid big-ends for the outside cylinders, with far greater simplicity in design, and a relatively trouble-free job in service. But, of course, a solid big-end cannot be used for inside cylinders, and as became well known in more recent times the inside big-end could be a source of weakness in a locomotive developing high power outputs. No such trouble beset the Great Western Railway. The inside big-ends on the four-cylinder engines followed very closely upon the de Glehn design incorporated in the three French compounds. The forked end arrangement can be seen from the accompanying reproduction of the Swindon working drawing. It was adopted, with only slight detail changes on the Stanier 'Pacifics' of the LMSR, and a later and most interesting application was due to K. J. Cook when he was Chief Mechanical and Electrical Engineer of the Eastern and North Eastern Region of British Railways. What could be termed the 'de Glehn-Swindon' big-end was substituted for the original Doncaster design on the inside connecting rods of the Gresley 'Pacifics' of both 'A3' and 'A4'

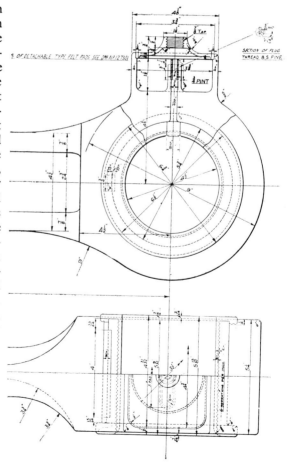

Outside connecting rod solid big-end

'Royal Scots', the inserts tended to work loose, and there were many failures. The substitution of the Swindon type of axlebox made a vast difference.

Associated with the design of bearings in maintaining the excellent reputation of Great Western locomotives for freedom from heating troubles was the design of the lubrication system. Swindon Works, like Crewe, designed most of their own fittings, and the various parts of the lubrication system were all 'home made'. A sight-feed lubricator of high capacity was mounted on the firebox backplate, within easy reach of the driver, as can be seen from the illustration on page 148. While the driver could regulate the amount of feed the supply of oil to the cylinders was initiated automatically by the opening of the regulator. The cam and linking arrangement which opened the oil feed valve can be seen above the quadrant plate of the regulator itself.

The first steam to reach the cylinders on starting the locomotive comes through an auxiliary steam pipe and brings with it a supply of oil. The shape of the cam slot in the link is such that the lubricator controlling the oil feed valve is not opened until the regulator has moved about $\frac{3}{4}$ in. from the 'shut' stop. The 'jockey' valve of the regulator does not admit steam to the cylinders until the handle has been moved about $\frac{3}{4}$ in. from

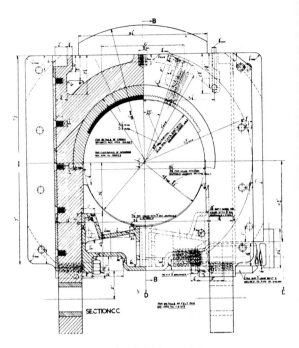

Detail of driving axlebox

the stop, but it is arranged that the oil feed valve is opened just before the jockey valve of the steam regulator opens.

ENGINE LOADINGS

The following note appeared in the GWR Service Timetable before the tables of loading of trains:

The loads given in the tables represent the capacity of the engine if the standard point-to-point timing is to be maintained. On sections where gradients will permit, these loads may be exceeded with a suitable increase in the point-to-point timing, but in sections where there are steep rising gradients it will be necessary to provide an assistant engine.

The following figures were current in the early 1930s.

	King	Castle	Star
Paddington—Westbury—Wellington	500	455	420
Wellington to Whiteball	455	420	392
Whiteball to Newton Abbot	500	455	420
Newton Abbot to Rattery or Brent (with a clear run through Aller Junction)	360	315	288
Rattery or Brent to Plymouth	455	420	392
Plymouth to Hemerdon (with a clear run through Plympton) .	360	315	288
Hemerdon to Newton Abbot	385	350	315
Newton Abbot to Paddington	500	455	420
Reading—Bristol—Taunton (up and down) . . .	500	455	420
Paddington to Cardiff (up and down)	—	455	420
Paddington to Wolverhampton (up and down) . . .	500	455	420
Paddington to Birmingham (special loading for 2-hour trains, up and down)	400	355	320

CHAPTER 13

'CHELTENHAM FLYER' RECORDS

AT the opening of the third decade of the twentieth century the Great Western Railway still had an impressively long lead over the other British railway companies in locomotive practice and achievement. It is true that important changes in detail design had greatly improved the Gresley Pacifics of the LNER, but on the LMS the 'Royal Scots', although potentially good engines, were unduly prone to casualties, and the much publicised 'Lord Nelsons' of the Southern fell a long way short of the high hopes expected of them. Against these the 'Stars', 'Castles' and 'Kings' were in superb form. Well designed, immaculately maintained, supplied with good coal and both driven and fired by men who were enthusiasts as well as experts, each class was incomparable in its particular category of loading.

It was this very supremacy that led to each one of them being outclassed before that momentous decade was out. In 1930 the Great Western Railway had locomotives that were supremely master of all tasks envisaged for some time. The year was one of mounting depression on a world-wide scale, and by the summer of 1931 the economic whirlwind had struck Great Britain. With such tools at its disposal there was no need for the Great Western Railway to incur expense in designing new express passenger locomotives. Even Sir Felix Pole, with all his enthusiasm, had been rather shocked at the capital cost of the new patterns and tooling incurred in the production of the 'Kings'. From 1930 to the outbreak of war in 1939 it was not a case of Swindon resting on its laurels, and, in a spirit of complacency,

Up two-hour Bristol - Paddington express near Stoke Gifford : engine No 4016
'Knight of the Golden Fleece', rebuilt as 'Castle'

153

splendid isolation, or whatever other derogatory term one likes to apply, allowing others to go ahead; there was then no economic nor engineering justification for doing otherwise.

And yet that decade was extremely fruitful and significant, in more subtle if less spectacular ways. I am referring to the science and practice of locomotive engineering, rather than of achievement on the road. There was certainly no subtlety about Great Western locomotive performance in those early years of the decade, when the 'Castles' established their reputation as world beaters. Before passing on to the developments in practice that were eventually to have effects influencing the very last years of steam on main lines far distant from the confines of the Great Western itself, it is pleasant to recall the brilliant saga of the 'Cheltenham Flyer' in those otherwise depressing years 1931 and 1932. The critics may well argue that the 'Cheltenham Flyer' was not representative of everyday Great Western passenger train service; that it was a 'stunt'

train, having little commercial value. These criticisms may be justified; but as a means of displaying the capacity of Great Western locomotives it was ideal, and the results achieved over the years are of great importance in the history of the 'Castle' class locomotives.

In the winter of 1929 I had my first experience of running on the 70-min schedule that then prevailed. It was a remarkable trip with engine No 5003 *Lulworth Castle*, and that most expert of drivers, Wasley of Old Oak Common. With a load of 275 tons we made an average speed of 84·5 mph over the 20·5 miles from Steventon to Reading, after which the engine had necessarily to be eased down. But the very fast running on level track, up to a maximum of 86·5 mph, was something of an eye-opener to us all. In September 1931 a modest 3 min was cut from the schedule, and despite the prevailing industrial depression the Great Western Railway made the inauguration of this accelerated timing a positively gala occasion. On the first three

'Holiday Haunts' special excursion near Reading West : engine No 6025 'King Henry III'

154

Up two-hour Bristol express topping Filton bank : engine No 4033 'Queen Victoria'

days, 14, 15 and 16 September, the engine crews were encouraged to 'have a go'. *Launceston Castle* was the engine on each run, with different crews, and on the three successive days the overall start-to-stop times over the 77·3 miles from Swindon to Paddington were 59 min 36 sec, 58½ min by the guard's journal, and a fully authenticated world record of 58 min 20 sec. After this astonishing inception of the new schedule, drivers were instructed to avoid further running ahead of time. Nevertheless the 'Cheltenham Flyer', with its booked average

speed of 69·2 mph, was then indisputably the 'world's fastest train', and for some time it carried a special headboard advertising the fact.

The Great Western authorities were nevertheless not content with the record achievements of September 1931. The run made on 16 September, with its average speed of 79·5 mph, surpassed by too slender a margin the previous world record made in the USA on the Reading Railroad, when the 55½ miles from Camden, Philadelphia, to Atlantic City were covered in 42 min 33 sec, an average

Engine No 5010 'Restormel Castle showing the modified style of painting on tender

speed of 78·3 mph. So, in June 1932 a deliberate attempt to make a 'record of records' was organised. In doing this the Great Western people were mindful of the assertion that the route of the 'Cheltenham Flyer' was 'all downhill'—which of course it is far from being!—and a very fast run was projected by the corresponding down express on the same day. Arrangements were made to have the two runs logged in the most minute detail, and Mr Cecil J. Allen and Mr Humphrey Baker of Bath were invited to collaborate in this task. To emphasise the special nature of the day's proceedings the 5 pm down Cheltenham Spa Express, which normally made its first stop at Kemble, was stopped specially at Swindon to set the recorders down. More than this, the 5.15 pm up 2-hour Bristol express, normally non-stop from Temple Meads to Paddington, was stopped at Swindon to take up Messrs Allen and Baker and get them back to London in quick time.

The record of 16 September 1931 was certainly beaten, reducing the overall time from 58 min 20 sec

to 56 min 47 sec and yielding an average speed of 81·7 mph start to stop, but it is most important to appreciate that this. was not an absolutely all-out effort, in which everything was to such a degree at concert pitch that it would be unlikely to be repeated again, and certainly not in ordinary conditions. It is true that the engine was a picked one, and all the running circumstances were favourable, including the limitation of the load to six coaches; but to remove any suggestion of abnormality about the run of 6 June 1932 I must take the story briefly forward five years, to 30 June 1937. Then the blaze of railway publicity had shifted to the northern lines. On the previous day the LMSR 'Coronation Scot' had made her somewhat hectic Press Trip, with its maximum of 114 mph a little too near Crewe to be comfortable; and on 30 June itself the LNER 'Coronation' made her *début*, with a fast run from Kings Cross to the Barkston triangle and back. On that day one of the most celebrated Old Oak drivers was on the 'Cheltenham Flyer' and quite unofficially he set out to show that the northern

THE 'CHELTENHAM FLYER' Three Record Runs							
Date		16/9/31		6/6/32		30/6/37	
Engine No . . .		5000		5006		5039	
Engine name . . .		*Launceston Castle*		*Tregenna Castle*		*Rhuddlan Castle*	
Load: cars . . .		6		6		7	
tons E/F . .		184/195		186/195		223/235	
Dist miles		Actual m s	Speeds mph	Actual m s	Speeds mph	Actual m s	Speeds mph
0·0	SWINDON . .	0 00	—	0 00	—	0 00	—
2·3	*Milepost 75* . .	—	—	3 28½	64	3 43	59
5·7	Shrivenham . .	6 15	80	6 15	81	6 35	80·5
10·8	Uffington . .	9 55	85	9 51	85·5	10 10	90
13·4	Challow . .	11 45	85	11 42	87	11 57	90
16·9	Wantage Road . .	14 10	87	14 05	89	14 12	94
20·8	Steventon . .	16 50	90	16 40	90	16 45	95
24·2	DIDCOT . .	19 05	88	18 55	91	18 57	90·5
28·8	Cholsey . .	22 15	87	21 59	91	21 58	91
32·6	Goring . .	24 55	82	24 25	92	24 25	88
35·8	Pangbourne . .	27 10	85	26 33	90	26 40	86·5
38·7	Tilehurst . .	29 15	84	28 28	92	28 40	90
41·3	READING . .	31 05	85	30 12	91	30 27	86·5
46·3	Twyford . .	34 35	86	33 31	89	33 50	90
53·1	Maidenhead . .	39 15	88	38 08	87	38 17	93
58·8	SLOUGH . .	43 15	85	42 10	87	42 08	90·5
64·1	West Drayton . .	46 55	85	45 51	84	45 47	84
68·2	Southall . .	49 55	84	48 51	81·5	48 46	82
71·6	Ealing Broadway .	52 20	84·5	51 17	84·5	51 40	eased
76·0	Westbourne Park .	56 00	—	54 40	—	57 40	—
77·3	PADDINGTON .	58 20		56 47		61 07	
Average speeds: mph							
Uffington - Cholsey . . .		87·8		89·0		91·6	
Cholsey - Reading . . .		85·2		91·4		88·5	
Twyford - Slough . . .		86·5		86·7		90·5	

Royal Train (LNWR stock) on the Westbury avoiding line : engine No 4082 'Windsor Castle'

companies should not have it all their own way. Fortunately a very experienced recorder in the person of the Rev J. E. T. Phillips was a passenger, and his log shows that the time of the 'record of records' was beaten by 5 sec to passing Southall; more important still is the fact that over the 62·5 miles from Shrivenham to Southall the time on 30 June 1937 was 42 min 11 sec, against 42 min 36 sec on 6 June 1932. Still greater significance is attached to the later run in that the gross load behind the tender was 235 tons, against 195 tons in 1932.

The detailed logs of the fastest of the September 1931 trilogy, the 'record of records', and the run of 1937 deserve the closest study. It shows that *Tregenna Castle* did not begin to draw seriously away from *Launceston Castle* until after Didcot, and then that the improvement was due to some exceptionally fast running on the winding stretch of line beside the Thames from Goring to Reading. By this time the 1932 record-breaker was roughly a minute ahead. After that the times between Twyford and Ealing were almost identical. Then *Tregenna Castle* gained considerably by an exceptionally rapid approach to Paddington. But her rather sensational 2 min 7 sec over the final 1·3 miles in from Westbourne Park was mild compared with the 1 min 45 sec of the record-breaking 'Ocean Mail' of 9 May 1904, with the 4—2—2 engine No 3065 *Duke of Connaught*. As a locomotive performance, however, as distinct from a display of enginemanship the improvement of *Tregenna Castle* over *Launceston Castle* can be considered as little more than marginal, seeing how much pre-preparation was made for the 1932 run. Details of the engine working with *Tregenna Castle* were subsequently published, and showed that the

regulator was gradually opened to the fullest extent by Shrivenham, and that the cut-offs were:

    17 per cent Shrivenham to Goring
    18 per cent Goring to Maidenhead
    17 per cent Maidenhead to Southall
    18 per cent Southall to Milepost 2

No details were given of any fluctuations in boiler pressure, but east of Reading it would seem there must have been some fall, or easing of the regulator, because the speed fell slightly on what is normally one of the fastest stretches of all, between Twyford and Maidenhead. It will be seen that *Launceston Castle* was accelerating here from 86 to 88 mph whereas *Tregenna Castle* fell from 89 to 87 mph even though continuing with the 18 per cent cut-off which had produced 92 mph on the level at Tilehurst. The easing of the cut-off at Maidenhead from 18 to 17 per cent may well have been to help rally the boiler.

We then come to the astounding performance of *Rhuddlan Castle* on 30 June 1937. With the extra coach the start was understandably slower, but then some magnificent speed was developed, rising to a maximum of 95 mph at Steventon. Somewhat easier running was made along the riverside section, though I certainly use the word 'easier' in no more than a relative sense. Then after Reading there came another display of tremendous speed, with a maximum of 93 mph at Maidenhead. By this, despite the heavier load, slower start, and easier running between Goring and Reading, *Rhuddlan Castle* took the lead from *Tregenna* from Slough onwards to Southall. The importance of this run is that it was a quite unrehearsed and unofficial effort: the combination of an expert driver and fireman, and a superb engine. It so happens that there *was* a representative of the Chief Mechanical Engineer's

157

Bristol - Paddington express near Sonning : engine No 4080 'Powderham Castle'

department on the footplate, a young engineer whose duty it was to check the working of the speedometers then being fitted as a standard item of equipment to all the 'Castle' class engines. The driver did not have any instruction to run specially fast for the purpose of this test. The engineer who was riding was Geoffrey Tee, now Carriage Works Manager at Wolverton, and he confessed to me many years later that he was taken completely by surprise at the speeds developed. This run shows clearly, however, that the 'record of records' could have been appreciably lowered, if necessary. The summary of fastest times in the table on page 156 gives an overall of 56 min 1 sec, by taking the times of *Tregenna Castle* from Swindon to Shrivenham, Cholsey to Twyford, and Ealing to Paddington; *Rhuddlan Castle* from Shrivenham to Cholsey, and Twyford to Southall; and *Launceston Castle* from Southall to Ealing. Collectively, this average of 82.8 mph is a resounding tribute to the high-speed prowess of the 'Castle' class engines.

Reverting to the events of 6 June 1932, the honour must certainly be shared between *Tregenna Castle* and No 5005 *Manorbier Castle*, which made the running on the 5 pm down express shown in the accompanying log. As Cecil J. Allen expressed it at the time, it was a pity about the odd second—60 min 1 sec start-to-stop from Paddington to Swindon—but in the interests of pure accuracy it had to be! The actual logs of Messrs Allen and

Baker gave this remarkable summary on that memorable afternoon:

Swindon	dep	3.48 pm
Paddington	arr	4.44¾ pm
,,	dep	5 pm
Swindon	arr	6 pm
,,	dep	6.6 pm
Paddington	arr	7.12½ pm

Between Southall and Shrivenham, by which points

5 pm PADDINGTON—SWINDON
Load: 6 cars, 199 tons tare, 210 tons full
Engine: 5005 *Manorbier Castle*

Dist miles			Actual m s		Speeds mph
0·0	PADDINGTON	.	0	00	—
1·3	Westbourne Park	.	2	34	—
5·7	Ealing	. .	6	52	74·5
9·1	Southall	.	9	25	81
13·2	West Drayton	.	12	26	85·5
18·5	SLOUGH .	.	16	03	86·5
24·2	Maidenhead	.	20	14	82·5
31·0	Twyford	.	25	17	79
36·0	READING	.	29	01	81·5
41·5	Pangbourne	.	33	03	83
48·5	Cholsey	.	38	03	84
53·1	DIDCOT .	.	41	23	85·5
56·5	Steventon	.	43	47	83·5
60·4	Wantage Road	.	46	35	81·5
63·9	Challow	.	49	13	80
66·5	Uffington	.	51	13	78·5
71·6	Shrivenham	.	53	05	81·5
76·0	*Milepost 76*	.	58	15	83·5
77·3	SWINDON	.	60	01	

practically full speed had been attained on both down and up runs, the difference in altitude is approximately 200 ft, representing an average inclination of 1 in 1650. On 6 June 1932, the average speeds over this 62·5 miles were 88 mph up and 82·5 mph down. Taking modern figures for train resistance, which one could reasonably expect to apply to coaching stock in first-class condition used on the 'Cheltenham Flyer', the resistance in lbs per ton can be taken at 14·2 and 12·7 respectively. Using these values the average equivalent drawbar horsepower work out at 550 by *Tregenna Castle* and 675 by *Manorbier Castle*. On the latter engine the cut-offs used were:

20 per cent Southall to Slough
19 per cent Slough to Reading
20 per cent Reading to Goring
19 per cent Goring to Didcot
20 per cent Didcot to Uffington
21 per cent Uffington to Highworth Jc

So far as engine performance is concerned the honours rest with *Manorbier Castle*, and the continuous working at 19 to 21 per cent cut-off with full regulator at 82·5 mph must be regarded as something very near the maximum steaming capacity at such speeds. Using the same basis of calcula-

tions, the running of *Rhuddlan Castle* at 93 mph on the falling gradient of 1 in 1320 between Twyford and Maidenhead indicates an equivalent drawbar horsepower of about 650. This output, which probably represents about the optimum with a standard 'Castle' of pre-war vintage, should be borne in mind for reference to achievements of the modified engines from 1951 onwards. It is perhaps not without significance that *Rhuddlan Castle* belongs to one of the later pre-war batches when constructional methods at Swindon had improved the accuracy of erection, with probable improvements in the free-running qualities of the engines concerned. This point is dealt with in Chapter 14 of this book.

So far as the achievements of 6 June 1932 are concerned, sentiments that were felt by all of us at the time were aptly summed up by Cecil J. Allen in *The Railway Magazine*. He wrote:

> The remembrances of the day still leave me breathless, but at the same time happy to have been a personal witness of all that transpired, and proud of the fact that British railways, and locomotives, and men were exclusively responsible. For a record of this character is not merely the private possession of one single railway and its staff; it is a national triumph, and a national asset.

Down West of England express leaving Bristol : engine No 6025 'King Henry III'

CHAPTER 14

THE 'CASTLES' : PHASE TWO

THE express passenger locomotive situation on the Great Western Railway at the end of 1930 could have been interpreted by an outsider in various ways. Apart from the rebuilding of the original four-cylinder simple engine *North Star* in 1929, no additions to the 'Castle' class had been made since July 1927 and the relative strengths of the three classes of four-cylinder 4—6—0 were: 'Stars' 67, 'Castles' 46, and 'Kings' 30. The last ten 'Kings' were built just three years after the then-last batch of 'Castles' numbered 5003 to 5012. It was representatives of this latter batch that were chosen for the record-breaking runs of June 1932. When a new batch of 'Castles' was turned out in that same year there were certain outside observers who jumped to the conclusion that because a reversion had been made to the older and smaller design of four-cylinder 4—6—0 that the 'Kings' were unsatisfac-

tory. In the restless times of the early 1930s, when signs of development and modernisation were looked for on all hands as a means of climbing out of the depression, to fall back upon a locomotive design of 1923, however well it had served its purpose, seemed to the neophytes a little retrograde.

From a traffic-working point of view the 'Castle' was an ideal engine. It had a high route availability, and could be used on many services where the 'Kings' were precluded on account of weight. Furthermore, quite a high proportion of the fast express trains were lightly loaded, and even if their route availability had permitted it, use of 'Kings' would not have been economical. Those engines, in their original form with low-degree superheat, were at their most efficient when being heavily worked, as on the West of England and Wolverhampton trains. The 'Castles' of the 1932, 1934 and 1935

Engine No 4082 'Windsor Castle', draped and decorated for the funeral journey of King George V, in January 1936

Up South Wales express climbing to Patchway : engine No 4089 'Donnington Castle'

batches were built as replacements for older 4—6—0 express locomotives that were withdrawn at roughly the same time. In the prevailing conditions of financial stringency it might be questioned as to whether it was really necessary to make such replacements when the duties that were subsequently worked by 'Castles' were being quite satisfactorily handled by 'Saints' and 'Stars'. The construction of those 30 'Castles', ten in each of the years 1932, 1934 and 1935, was to a large extent a matter of accountancy, and was justified in the following manner.

Each year a sum of money had been set aside to cover the depreciation of locomotives, and to allow for their renewal after an appropriate working life; and in the years of which I am now writing most new Great Western locomotives were built out of the Renewals Fund. As a *quid pro quo* the account expected the annual programme of new construction to be balanced by the withdrawal of at least an equal tonnage of old locomotives. In the ordinary way 'Saint' and 'Star' class 4—6—0s were first-class assets, good for any number of further years of service; but the times were far from 'ordinary', and in the stringent financial circumstances economies in running the railway had been made, as in war-

time, by making certain groups of locomotives work longer mileages between repairs. The top-line engines like the 'Castles' and 'Kings' were always maintained at concert pitch, but the lesser lights suffered, and it is always the older members of a class that suffer most in such circumstances. Thus the situation developed that a number of 'Saints' and 'Stars' began to need very extensive repairs. The fund was low, but on the other hand the Renewals Fund was in a healthy state; so it was a logical accounting step to scrap the older engines needing heavy repairs, and build new engines to replace them. 'Castles' were the only and obvious replacements. In consequence, between the years 1931 and 1935 twenty 'Saints' and ten 'Stars' were scrapped. The 'Stars' concerned were:

4001	*Dog Star*	Jan	1934
4002	*Evening Star*	June	1933
4005	*Polar Star*	Nov	1934
4006	*Red Star*	Nov	1932
4008	*Royal Star*	June	1935
4010	*Western Star*	Nov	1934
4011	*Knight of the Garter*	Nov	1932
4024	*The Dutch Monarch*	Feb	1935
4027	*The Norwegian Monarch*	Oct	1934
4029	*The Spanish Monarch*	Nov	1934

THE GWR STARS, CASTLES & KINGS

The new 'Castles' built from 1932 onwards had sufficient differences from the originals as to be given a new designation, and they were known as the '5013' class. Their names were all pleasing and euphonious, and for the most part well known. *Wigmore Castle* revived memories of the old 7 ft 8 in single that ran off the road on Box Tunnel, and two were 'poached' from the territory of other railways, namely, *Corfe Castle* and *Rhuddlan Castle*. These thirty new engines replacing scrapped 'Saints' and 'Stars' were:

5013	*Abergavenny Castle*
5014	*Goodrich Castle*
5015	*Kingswear Castle*
5016	*Montgomery Castle*
5017	*St Donats Castle*
5018	*St Mawes Castle*
5019	*Treago Castle*
5020	*Trematon Castle*
5021	*Whittington Castle*
5022	*Wigmore Castle*
5023	*Brecon Castle*
5024	*Carew Castle*
5025	*Chirk Castle*
5026	*Criccieth Castle*
5027	*Farleigh Castle*
5028	*Llantilio Castle*
5029	*Nunney Castle*
5030	*Shirburn Castle*
5031	*Totnes Castle*
5032	*Usk Castle*
5033	*Broughton Castle*
5034	*Corfe Castle*
5035	*Coity Castle*
5036	*Lyonshall Castle*
5037	*Monmouth Castle*
5038	*Morlais Castle*
5039	*Rhuddlan Castle*
5040	*Stokesay Castle*
5041	*Tiverton Castle*
5042	*Winchester Castle*

There were one or two superficial details by which the '5013' class could be distinguished from the '4073' class, such as the shaping of the front casing over the inside cylinder valve chests, and the introduction of a compartment above the centre and trailing coupled wheel splashers on the left-hand side, to accommodate the fireirons. This latter had first been fitted on No 4085 *Berkeley Castle*, as a trial, and it became standard from No 5013 onwards. There was also an alteration to the springing, omitting the compensating beams between the springs. The most important design change, which

was the reason for a new class designation, was in the boiler and firebox. In the '4073' class, to get the maximum possible firebox heating surface and grate area the water spaces between the inner and outer fireboxes had been made narrower than standard, and complaints had been made about the difficulty of cleaning this narrow space. In the '5013' class the water space was increased to normal; the number of small tubes was reduced from 201 to 197, and the grate area was reduced to 29·4 sq ft from the original 30·3 sq ft. On locomotives worked as were the Great Western four-cylinder 4—6—0s this reduction in grate area was of no consequence. The normal practice was to run with a deep fire built up 'hay-cock' fashion, and it was an ability to burn coal economically in such conditions, rather than mere grate area that governed the capacity of Great Western locomotives.

It was on the 1934 batch of 'Castles', commencing with No 5023 *Brecon Castle*, that a very important improvement in constructional methods was introduced. The performance of a locomotive, and its general reliability in service, depend to a large extent upon the accuracy with which the engine is built, and particularly the alignment of the frames, axle-box guides and cylinders. At Swindon, as nearly everywhere else, the traditional method of alignment with wires, centre-pop and trammels had hitherto been used. In the 1930s the German State Railways were making use of Zeiss precision optical gear for lining up locomotive frames, and the experience of that administration was that the time of lining up was cut to between one-quarter and one-third of that previously taken. Furthermore, a locomotive so treated would run a greater mileage between repairs than previously. This method was studied by the engineers of the Great Western Railway, and after modification of the Zeiss apparatus to suit production methods at Swindon it was adopted as standard practice for all new and repaired locomotives.

The basis of the apparatus was a telescope mounted within a tube, arranged so that it could be pivoted in vertical or horizontal planes by two dials. When these two dials were both set at zero, the telescope was in exact central alignment with its external tube—which was set with a self-centring spider—in the front bellmouth of one cylinder, and by an adaptor in the stuffing box at the back of the cylinder. A spirit-level ensured that the vertical and horizontal axes were correct, and a measuring surface set level with the front cylinder face by a straight edge provided zero for distance. The overall width across each pair of horns was measured by

*Down two-hour Birmingham express : engine No 5081 'Penrice Castle',
later renamed 'Lockheed Hudson'*

a vernier, after which a sighting scale was clamped to each horn in turn and the scale read through the telescope. The sighting scale was similar to a surveyor's staff and the reading gave the distance of the cylinder axis to the outside edge of the horn. The distance plus half the width over that pair of horns gave the distance to the theoretical centre line of the engine. If that sum did not amount to the same total at each horn, the cylinder axis was not parallel with the centre line of the line. A certain tolerance could be allowed there and the telescope pivoted horizontally until its centre was parallel with the engine centre line; but if the correction would have been beyond the allowed limit it would have been necessary to cut down some stiffeners or cross stays and reset the frames.

Assuming that the telescope was set parallel with the theoretical centre line of the engine, the sighting scale was removed and a collimator, clamped to a tube in such a way that it was dead at right-angles to the axis of the tube, was supported at the driving horn, the tube being right across the frame between both driving horns. The tube was held in a stand, the top of which could be moved vertically or horizontally to or from the cylinder, and through an angle horizontally. The collimator was an optical apparatus carrying two sets of cross scales illuminated by an electric lamp, and had the property of accepting at zero on its infinite scale only rays parallel with the telescope. If on sighting from the telescope the telescope cross lines cut the horizontal and vertical lines of the infinite scale of the collimator at zero, then the telescope and collimator were truly parallel, though not necessarily at the same place. How much they were out of plane could be read by focussing the telescope on the infinite scale of the collimator and reading the graduations. The horizontal, vertical and angular adjustments provided for in the collimator stand allowed the latter to be brought easily into alignment with the telescope. As the collimator was then parallel with the telescope and was fixed accurately at right-angles to the collimator cross-tube, it followed that the cross-tube was then between the driving horns at right-angles to the cylinder axis.

A dial indicator was used to obtain the distance of each horn cheek from the collimator cross-tube, and the latter was traversed longitudinally until it was central between the driving horns. A length gauge with dial indicator from locating points on the telescope tubes and the collimator tube gave a direct reading of the distance from the cylinder face

Up Swansea and West Wales express approaching Patchway : engine No 5046
'Clifford Castle', later renamed 'Earl Cawdor'

to the centre of the driving horn, and from the collimator cross-tube a locating stud on each frame was set at a definite distance from the horn centre. Length gauges enabled further locating studs to be set at each of the other horns, ie, 'leading', 'intermediate', and 'trailing', and from those similar measurements could be made to each of the corresponding horn cheeks. By means of the accurate rods and the dial indicator, all those measurements could be easily read to within a thousandth of an inch, although the total length between the leading and trailing horn centres might have been as much as 20 ft.

Thus a very accurate survey of the salient points of a locomotive frame could be made expeditiously, and from this decisions taken as to the amount of corrections to be made. I have dwelt on the process at some length because it proved the very cornerstone of Swindon constructional practice. It enabled valve gear parts to be made with precision, with an absolute minimum of clearance when new, so that newly out-shopped locomotives ran with the quietness of sewing machines. Such was the tightening up of clearances possible as a result that the situation became one that was vividly described by one

ex-Great Western man, after nationalisation when the differing practices of other famous locomotive manufactories came under review. This engineer said: 'We scrap at the amount of clearance they start with'. Dimensions previously maintained to within an accuracy of plus or minus 0·010 in were henceforth made to within an accuracy of plus or minus 0·002 in. This apparatus was used on older engines as they went through the works, and it is not without significance that the twenty engines of the 'Castle' class numbered between 5023 and 5042 quickly gained the reputation of being the best yet, of the whole class. No 5030 *Shirburn Castle* achieved the remarkable record of running 420,000 miles before the removal of the boiler from the frames. This engine had, of course, received intermediate repairs.

The policy of maintaining older engines as far as possible in a first-class state of repair, and the standardisation of methods at Swindon led to a number of 'Castle' features being incorporated in 'Stars' from time to time. There did not seem to be any overall policy with regard to these changes, and something like the putting of 'new wine into old bottles', as it were, resulted in improvisation at times of general overhaul. All the 'Stars' had new cylinders in the course of their lives, many of them more than once. To extend their lives, some engines had liners in their cylinders; but the maximum to which 'Star' cylinders could be bored out was $15\frac{5}{8}$ in diameter, and if the cylinder diameter was not to be reduced below 15 in the maximum thickness of liner was only $\frac{5}{16}$ in. This thickness permitted of only one rebore, at overhaul, and this particular expedient was quickly judged to be not worth the candle.

From 1929 onwards thirteen of the 'Stars' received new outside cylinders with outside steampipes, similar to those of the 'Castles'. The original outside cylinders were fed by steam pipes which emerged from the rear of the smokebox saddle between the frames. To accommodate the outside steampipes the piping in the smokebox had to be altered, and a hole cut in each side of the smokebox. This was all very well if one could be certain that a modified boiler was available for fitting to an engine with new cylinders and outside steam pipes. But this cut right across the principle of having standard boilers that could be fitted to any engine. Furthermore, the 'Star' boiler was normally interchangeable with those of the 'Saints' and the '28XX' 2—8—0s. The smokeboxes were not interchangeable, and until worn out stayed with their boilers. Inevitably

there were times when in the course of ordinary repair work a modified boiler had to be fitted to a non-modified engine, and then in the case of the 'Stars' a sharply-curved steampipe was fitted to connect the smokebox aperture with the flange on the cylinder casting between the frames. In retrospect it is a little difficult to see the justification for fitting 'Castle' type cylinders to 'Stars', if for nothing else than the lack of standardisation it introduced. Only the most comprehensive individual costing records would show if any economies were effected. Certainly there is no record of any improved performance on the road. By the beginning of the 1930s the 'Stars' were past their prime in any case. All their finest work, as recorded in Part I of this book, was done with the original layout of cylinders and piping.

The drawing which is reproduced on the following page has been prepared from a Swindon drawing dated March 1929. The first engine to be so treated was No 4024, in February of that year, so that the arrangement drawing, as was not infrequently the case, was a record of what had been done rather than an instruction to the shops. The alterations to the smokebox were such as could quite readily have been made without a drawing. The other twelve engines that received 'Castle' type

West to North express near Patchway: engine No 4043 'Prince Henry', with outside steampipes

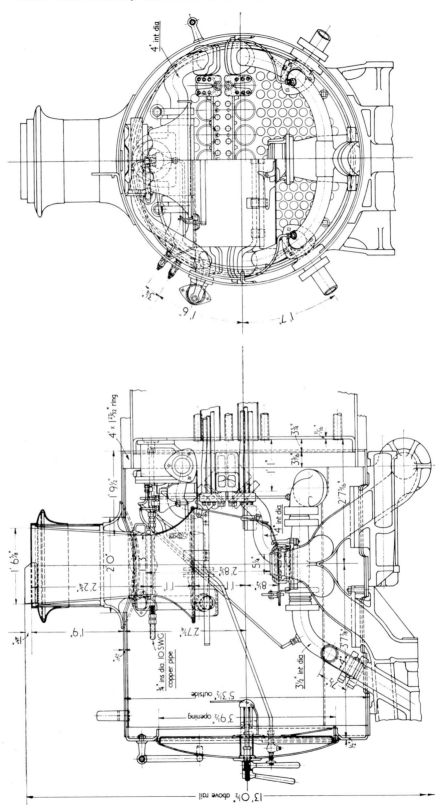

Smokebox layout of 'Star' class engine fitted with 'Castle' type cylinders and outside steampipes

cylinders were:

4040	*Queen Boadicea*	Feb	1930
4057	*Princess Elizabeth*	Apr	1930
4001	*Dog Star*	Oct	1930
4035	*Queen Charlotte*	Jan	1931
4043	*Prince Henry*	Oct	1931
4053	*Princess Alexandra*	Oct	1933
4049	*Princess Maud*	Feb	1935
4048	*Princess Victoria*	Oct	1938
4052	*Princess Beatrice*	Apr	1939
4060	*Princess Eugenie*	Aug	1944
4051	*Princess Helena*	Dec	1944
4055	*Princess Sophia*	May	1945

Two of the engines so equipped, namely the first one No 4024, and No 4001 *Dog Star*, were among the earliest engines of the 'Star' class to be scrapped. The case history at the end of this book refers to those engines which at one time or another received modified boilers, while retaining their old cylinders, and therefore had the so-called 'elbow' pipes. Engine No 4002 *Evening Star* had this arrangement as early as December 1929, when there was only one engine running with 'Castle' type cylinders, rather suggesting that at first boilers were being modified more quickly than new cylinders were being manufactured. But when a complicated procedure like this is set in motion the subsequent peregrinations of individual boilers provide a field for endless research for those who are so minded. It was seemingly a case of improvisation and expediency rather than a definite development in locomotive design, and as such it can be left without further comment. It can be added, however, that I had an excellent run behind the modified 4002 *Evening Star*, in June 1930, on the 7.50 pm from Birmingham to Paddington with a heavy train of 445 tons. While the work was not up to the most brilliant standards of the 'Stars' it was certainly very good. Curiously enough the train was worked down from Chester by No 4040 *Queen Boadicea*, which had been fitted with 'Castle' cylinders only four months earlier. The latter engine was stationed at Wolverhampton, and was much in demand on the sharply timed trains on the north road. I had several other good runs behind her that summer.

Reverting to the 'Castles' proper, an important accessory introduced as standard on the 1935 batch was the speedometer. Many times my motoring friends have expressed astonishment that for so many years speedometers were unheard of on British locomotives, and although speed restrictions were laid down for many parts of the line, their observance was left to the driver's judgment.

Furthermore, there were few trackside indications to show what the speed limits were. With the older and lighter engines considerable liberties were often taken, and it must be confessed that some of the most spectacular achievements of the 'Stars' included violations of speed orders, as when the driver of No 4055 *Princess Sophia* on the 12 noon up from Birmingham took Banbury station at a completely unchecked 80 mph instead of the stipulated 60 mph! With engines of the size and weight of the 'Kings' more rigid control was necessary, and following some experiments made on 'Castle' class engines Nos 5003 and 5008 in 1933-4, a very simple device was standardised, and in a short time fitted to all engines of the 'Castle' and 'King' classes.

The arrangement adopted as standard consisted of an alternating current generator driven direct from the driving wheel, and a voltmeter in the cab, which had a scale graduated to read in miles per hour. The dial was of 5 in diameter and was fixed on a corner of the firebox just below the driver's look-out window. It was mounted on Sorbo rubber blocks to absorb vibration, and insulated from the effects of heat by fibre washers. The drive to the ac generator was from a small return crank incorporated in the crank-pin washer of the right-hand trailing coupled wheel. A block on that crank engaged in a slotted link, mounted on a spindle carried on the same centre line as the coupled-wheel axle by a bracket suspended from the footplate. The slot was long enough to allow for the greatest possible displacements of the coupled wheel relative to the footplate bracket. The drive was transmitted through bevel gears to the generator, the armature of which ran on a vertical axis at $2\frac{1}{2}$ times the driving axle speed. An armoured cable conveyed the alternating current to the voltmeter in the cab, first passing through a rectifier, so that the voltmeter gave a unidirectional reading for both directions of running. Like most forms of speedometers they were not always accurate; but in many thousands of miles riding on the footplate of Great Western locomotives I did not come across one that was seriously out. If there was an error it was usually that they read high; although it was a fault on the safe side, it sometimes led to slight losses of time, from drivers assuming that they were travelling faster than was actually the case.

An amusing interlude in the history of both 'Castle' and 'King' classes began in the early months of 1935. Certain German and American locomotives intended for high-speed running had been streamlined, to lessen the air resistance, and the first of the Gresley 'P2' class, the *Cock o' the North* had an

Engine No 5005 'Manorbier Castle', with original layout of streamlined fairings

exterior form that could be so described, although the front-end included a considerable air-pocket. In 1935 Great Western Railway would be celebrating its centenary, and certain members of the Locomotive Committee of the Board were anxious that the company should be obviously 'with it' in this latest trend of locomotive engineering practice. Collett thought otherwise, but orders being orders something had to be done about it. He had a paper-weight model of a 'King' on his desk. An office boy was sent out to buy some plasticine from a toy shop, and then Collett in a few minutes determined the shape the new streamlining should take by rubbing plasticine across the front and down the sides of the running plates, round the cylinders, and filling the spaces behind chimney and safety valve covers

where eddies occur. A hemispherical 'blob' was stuck on the front of the smokebox. Then the model thus decorated was sent to the drawing office, and a draughtsman was given the job of producing the necessary working drawings, for both a 'King' and a 'Castle'. I regret to add that the whole exercise was regarded as something of a joke, and the seal was set upon it when a popular music hall and radio comedian visited Swindon Works and in a BBC broadcast referred to the 'engine that looks as if it had Teddy Brown welded on the front' (Teddy Brown was the leading fat-man comedian of the day).

The engines thus decorated were Nos 6014 *King Henry VII* and 5005 *Manorbier Castle*. Light-heartedness apart, they were the very first British

The up Bristolian near Ashley Hill hauled by the semi-streamlined No 6014
'King Henry VII', shrouding over cylinders removed

*Paddington - South Wales excursion near Patchway : engine No 5005 'Manorbier Castle',
with shrouding over cylinders removed*

locomotives to have definite streamlined fairings added to them. They preceded the 'A4' Pacifics of the LNER by about six months. It was perhaps typical of Collett that in shunning the limelight he missed a priceless opportunity of stealing the thunder of the LNER. A fully streamlined 'King' or 'Castle', accompanied by some appropriately faster running, would have gone far to keep the Great Western Railway in the forefront, when there was every sign of ground being lost to the northern lines. Had Collett seized his opportunity, when *Silver Link* appeared in September 1935 it would inevitably have been a case of 'another streamlined locomotive'. The illustrations of engines 5005 and 6014 show what a half-hearted attempt was made. The casings round the cylinders were soon found to be an encumbrance and a liability. The inside motion on the Great Western 4-cylinder 4—6—0s was difficult enough to get at anyway without a shrouding round the outside! On occasions there was overheating of the motion. The shrouding round the cylinders was removed in the autumn of 1935, and one by one the incongruous fairings were removed, and the whole episode quietly forgotten.

Authority was given for the construction of ten new 'Castles' in 1936, and for fifteen in 1937. These were to the standard '5013' class, but twenty-one of these engines achieved a modicum of distinction by being renamed *en bloc*, in 1937. In fact some of the engines of the 1937 batch bore their original names for no more than a few weeks. It was a complete break with tradition, in that none of the new names were those of 'Castles'. Oddly enough, this chain of events was set in motion by a change in the premiership of Great Britain. Shortly after the Coronation of King George VI, Stanley Baldwin retired, and duly created an Earl went to the House of Lords. Naming locomotives after political characters has its pitfalls, as the Great Central found to its cost; but Baldwin was in a different case altogether. Before he entered politics he had been a director of the GWR; his father was chairman of the company from 1905 to 1908, and there had been a 'Bulldog' class 4—4—0 named *Stanley Baldwin* for many years. On his elevation to the peerage the Great Western sought to honour him, and engine No 5063 which had gone into traffic in June 1937 as *Thornbury Castle* was renamed *Earl Baldwin* only a month later.

This gesture had immediate repercussions, because the GWR already had a class of 4—4—0s named after Earls, some of whom were directors of the company, and with the naming of a 'Castle' after Earl Baldwin it was felt inappropriate that

Engine No 5069 'Isambard Kingdom Brunel'

famous hereditary titles should exist on the useful, but definitely hybrid 4—4—0s of the '32XX' class. These latter were built, or rather rebuilt for the Cambrian section, using the 'Duke' type of boiler on a 'Bulldog' frame. More recently they have been familiarly known as the 'Dukedogs'. The names of these twenty engines 3200 to 3219 were transferred one by one to the 'Castles' Nos 5043 to 5062, and the original nameplates of these latter went into store at Swindon. All the 1936 batch was renamed, together with thirteen of the 1937 batch, though why it should have been necessary to rename 5064 *Tretower Castle* and 5065 *Upton Castle* as *Bishops Castle* and *Newport Castle*, ex Nos 5053 and 5058 respectively, is difficult to understand. The only engines of the 1937 batch that were not renamed at the time were 5066 *Wardour Castle* and 5067 *St Fagans Castle*.

The year 1937 was also notable for the decision to replace certain of the 'Abbey' series of 'Stars' by 'Castles'. Certain of the former engines needed new cylinders, and so a lot number was issued authorising the construction of ten new 'Castles' in replacement. The frames of the original engines were, however, in good condition so to some extent they were rebuilds. A batch of numbers in the general 'Castle' series was set aside for these replacements, namely 5083 to 5092, and using the old names the numbers were allocated to correspond with the original numbers—4063 becoming 5083, 4066 becoming 5086, and so on. The rebuilding was spread over 3½ years. The first to be treated was *Reading Abbey* in April 1937 and the last was *Tintern Abbey* as late as 1940. It was curious that the two earliest engines of the 'Abbey' series were left out

of this procedure. Nos 4061 *Glastonbury Abbey* and 4062 *Malmesbury Abbey* survived to be among the very last 'Stars' withdrawn. The two engines were only outlasted by that great veteran 4056 *Princess Margaret*.

Ten 'Castles', Nos 5068 to 5077, were built in 1938, and another ten, 5078 to 5082 and 5093 to 5097, in 1939; and twelve out of these twenty engines were subjected to renaming in 1940-1, but for a very different reason to that concerning the 5043-62 series. In the wave of intense pride and patriotism that accompanied the achievements of the Royal Air Force during the Battle of Britain the Great Western interpreted popular sentiment by renaming twelve engines of the 'Castle' after aircraft, the names of which were household words by the end of 1940. The engines chosen were 5071 to 5082, and it was remarkable that all the 'Castle' names displaced were with one exception being displaced for the second time. It was only *Drysllwyn*, used for the first time on No 5076, that did not have that curious distinction. All those displaced names went into storage for the duration of the war, but all were eventually used on post-war 'Castles'. While on the subject of names, mention must be made of the happy choice of *Isambard Kingdom Brunel*, and *Sir Daniel Gooch* for engines 5069 and 5070, built in 1938. Full details of the naming and renaming of these engines is contained in the appendix. A final point to be mentioned before concluding Phase Two of the 'Castle' saga is that with engine No 5044, in March 1936, a chimney 3 in shorter than previously was fitted. This gave a greatly improved appearance, and this change was gradually extended to the whole class.

CHAPTER 15

PERFORMANCE : 1930-1939

DURING the late 1930s the standards of day-to-day locomotive performance on the Great Western Railway remained very high. In general, there were perhaps not those dazzling feats of individual enginemen that highlighted the golden age of the 'Stars', as recorded earlier in Chapter 6; but all-round achievement was highly satisfactory. I was not travelling on the line myself quite so frequently in this period. My home was then in Hertfordshire, and although I had business interests in Chippenham my visits were occasional rather than regular. On the other hand train running was very comprehensively documented by the logs of a number of experienced recorders: by A. V. Goodyear and G. P. Antrobus on the Birmingham line; by R. E. Charlewood; by Sir James Colyer-Ferguson, who

was then at Oxford; and of course by Cecil J. Allen, who was travelling frequently to Chippenham and Bristol. Added to these were my own holiday journeys to Cornwall, and later some travelling on the West to North route via the Severn Tunnel. During all this period the 'Stars' continued to play an important part. With the building of more 'Castles' they had certainly been displaced from their earlier crack duties, but transferred to more distant depots, such as Worcester, Landore and Shrewsbury, they took over workings previously entrusted almost entirely to 'Saints'. The story of performance during the ten-year span of this chapter is therefore of all three classes of four-cylinder 4—6—0.

First then, to the 'Stars'. The inauguration of

Engine No 6005 'King George II', with indicator shelter

Up two-hour Bristol express near Stoke Gifford : engine No 4015 'Knight of St John'

the 'Bristolian' express in the centenary year of the GWR with its 1¾-hour schedule rather stole the thunder of the once-celebrated two-hour Bristol expresses; but there were drivers at Bath Road shed prepared to show that even with 'Stars', rather than 'Castles' or 'Kings', they could equal the speed achievements of their Old Oak counterparts on the 'Bristolian' itself. One such worthy got his chance when the 11.45 am up got a late start of 8½ min from Bristol. The brilliant result is tabulated herewith. Indeed No 4007 *Rising Star*, with a load well above the usual 'Bristolian' rake was driven at 'Bristolian' speed until all the lost time had been recovered. The schedule of the 'Bristolian' was then 78 min to passing Reading. After that there was no need for further hurry, and the 31·7 miles from Reading to Acton took 27 min 50 sec. Despite a final signal check the train reached Paddington 2¾ min early. There would have been not the slightest difficulty in running from Bristol to Paddington in 105 min or less, on such form as this, with an engine then thirty years old.

The insertion of stops at Bath, in place of the previous slip portions in the working of the two down two-hour Bristol expresses increased their difficulty of operation, with non-stop running between Paddington and Bath, 106·9 miles, booked in 102 min. Furthermore, the 11.15 am down included a heavy slip portion for Oxford, detached at Didcot. The engine workings were varied, so that occasion-

ally one had a 'Castle' or a 'King', but just as frequently a 'Star'. One could well imagine Churchward's heart glowing at the thought that his successors had sufficient confidence in the older engines to put 'Stars' on to the job, when the gross load well exceeded 400 tons for the first half of the journey. Two really splendid runs are tabulated,

GWR 11.45 am BRISTOL—PADDINGTON
Load : 267 tons tare, 280 tons full
Engine : 4007 *Rising Star*

Dist miles		Sch min	Actual m s	Speeds mph
0·0	TEMPLE MEADS .	0	0 00†	—
1·6	Stapleton Road .		5 02	—
9·1	Coalpit Heath .		14 40	56
13·0	Chipping Sodbury		18 49	60
17·6	Badminton .	24½	23 27	60
27·9	Little Somerford		31 40	82
34·7	Wootton Bassett .	41	37 26	54*
40·3	SWINDON .	47	43 01	66
51·1	Uffington .		52 36	78
61·1	Steventon .	65	58 58	81
64·5	DIDCOT .	68	61 28	83
72·9	Goring .		67 38	76
81·6	READING .	83½	74 32	65
93·4	Maidenhead .	94½	85 18	70
99·1	SLOUGH .	100	89 59	easy
108·5	Southall .	109	98 05	
113·3	Acton .		102 22	
116·3	Westbourne Park .	116	104 30	
—			sigs	
117·6	PADDINGTON .	120	108 43	

* Speed restriction
† Departure from Bristol 8½ min late

	GWR 11.15 am PADDINGTON—BATH							
Engine No				4035			4072	
Engine Name				Queen Charlotte			Tresco Abbey	
Load to Didcot tons E/F				394/420			436/460	
Load to Bath tons E/F				263/280			298/310	
Dist miles			Sch min	Actual m s	Speeds mph		Actual m s	Speeds mph
0·0	PADDINGTON . .		0	0 00	—		0 00	—
1·3	Westbourne Park . .			3 07	—		3 07	—
—				—	—		pws	
9·1	Southall		11	12 59	—		13 39	—
18·5	SLOUGH		20	21 58	68		22 45	67
24·2	Maidenhead . . .			27 13	67		28 05	65·5
31·0	Twyford . . .			33 20	67		34 06	—
36·0	READING . . .		36	37 52	68		38 26	70
44·8	Goring . . .			45 37	70·5		46 14	—
53·1	DIDCOT (slip) . .		51½	52 50	—		53 54	65
60·4	Wantage Road . .			59 15	69		60 30	—
66·5	Uffington			64 39	—		66 00	—
71·6	Shrivenham . . .			69 17	66		70 22	70
77·3	SWINDON . . .		75	74 23	—		75 21	—
82·9	Wootton Bassett . .			79 17	—		79 54	77
87·7	Dauntsey . . .			83 11	82		83 31	85·5
94·0	CHIPPENHAM . .		90	88 06	—		88 24	—
98·3	Corsham . . .			92 08	60		92 29	62
101·9	Box			95 17	78		95 36	76·5
104·6	Bathampton . . .			97 34	—		97 50	—
106·9	BATH		102	99 53			100 37	

with engines 4035 *Queen Charlotte* and 4072 *Tresco Abbey*. The schedule, in its point-to-point times, was somewhat uneven in its demands, booking 66 mph from Slough to Didcot after a very sharp initial 20 min from Paddington to Slough.

Thereafter the slightly uphill length from Didcot to Swindon was booked at only 61·7 mph after the load had been reduced by about 140 tons. With such heavy trains as 420 and 460 tons the drivers of these two engines were justified in not attempt-

Bristol - Paddington express in Sonning cutting : engine No 4007 'Rising Star'

GWR: OXFORD—PADDINGTON

Run No				1		2		3		4	
Engine No	.	.	.	4038		4018		4049		4017	
Engine Name	.	.	.	Queen Berengaria		Knight of the Grand Cross		Princess Maud		Knight of Liege	
Load, tons E/F	.	.	.	314/330		330/350		337/360		387/415	
Dist miles			Sch min	Actual m s		Actual m s		Actual m s		Actual m s	
0·0	OXFORD	.	0	0	00	0	00	0	00	0	00
5·1	Radley	.		7	25	7	15	7	25	7	34
10·6	Didcot East Junc	.	12	12	57	12	26	12	34	13	07
14·9	Cholsey	.		17	47	17	25	17	10	17	48
18·7	Goring	.		21	00	20	30	20	27	21	07
—				—		sigs		—		pws	
21·9	Pangbourne	.		23	45	23	59	23	15	25	18
27·4	READING	.	27½	28	25	29	52	27	52	31	01
32·4	Twyford	.		32	35	34	01	32	01	35	11
39·2	Maidenhead	.		38	05	39	30	37	23	40	35
44·9	SLOUGH	.	42	42	50	44	00	41	57	45	09
50·2	West Drayton	.		47	05	48	02	46	11	49	31
54·3	Southall	.	49½	50	30	51	32	49	38	53	17
—				—		sigs		sigs		—	
57·7	Ealing	.		53	10	sigs		53	08	56	26
—				—		—		—		sigs	
62·1	Westbourne Park	.	56	57	00	—		58	07	60	37
63·4	PADDINGTON	.	60	59	45	61	19	60	20	63	21

ing to maintain strict time in the early stages even though it meant detaching their slip portions a little behind time at Didcot. Both engines attained maximum speeds of 70 mph on level track with their full loads, while *Tresco Abbey,* passing Didcot at 65 mph, gradually recovered to a full 70 mph on the rise to Shrivenham. Both engines were practically on time at Swindon, and ran fast onwards to Chippenham with maximum speeds of 82 and 85·5 mph on Dauntsey bank. After that the finish could be relatively easy.

The acceleration of the important 8.55 am express from Worcester to Paddington to make a 60-min non-stop run over the final 63·4 miles from Oxford, gave further opportunities for the 'Stars' to distinguish themselves. This was a much heavier train than the 'flyers' from the Bristol direction, and the working was made more difficult by the slack necessary round the Didcot avoiding line. Taking account of this the point-to-point times were only 1½ min more than those of the 'Cheltenham Flyer' between Reading and Paddington. It will thus be appreciated that with 'Stars' instead of 'Castles', and loads varying between 330 and 415 tons there was little time in hand. Among the four runs I have selected for tabulation it was only *Queen Berengaria* that actually got through from Oxford to Paddington in under the hour, though the other three engines would have been punctual but for delays. On the second run *Knight of the Grand Cross* was

checked at Pangbourne, losing 2 min in running; but then some splendid running was made east of Reading with a maximum of 77 mph at Slough. The arrears of time would certainly have been made up but for the concluding checks. *Princess Maud,* with 350 tons, also did very well, with some even faster running east of Reading and a top speed of 79 mph at Twyford. but the signal check at Ealing was a bad one, and prevented strict timekeeping.

The remarkable performance of *Knight of Liege* in the last column requires special mention and analysis. The start out of Oxford, with 415 tons, was practically indistinguishable from the previous runs, with considerably lighter loads, and after negotiation of Didcot east curve speed was worked up to 72 mph before the Pangbourne re-laying check. After Reading the average speeds make impressive reading: to Twyford 72 mph, on to Maidenhead 75·6 mph, and over the next 5·7 miles to Slough 77·7 with a maximum of 79 mph—with a 'Star' hauling 415 tons! The permanent way slack had however cost at least 2½ min, and even though the speed continued to rule high, with an average of 68·2 mph right on to Ealing Broadway, time could not have been kept. As far as I can calculate, however, the net time was exactly 60 min. The principal feature of the run was of course the attained maximum on level track of 79 mph at Slough in the course of a long-sustained spell of high speed, averaging 74·5 mph from Twyford to West Drayton.

Down Cornish Riviera Express (15-car train) near Aldermaston :
engine No 6000 'King George V'

This indicates a drawbar pull of about $2\frac{1}{4}$ tons at 77 to 79 mph—well above Churchward's famous target of a drawbar pull of 2 tons at 70 mph.

Turning now to the 'Castles', the 'Cheltenham Flyer' schedule is so often quoted as a yardstick in referring to Great Western performance over the Bristol route that one naturally turns to it first. I am quite aware that enthusiasts whose sympathies lie elsewhere tend to write off what was once 'The World's Fastest Train' as a mere stunt in high-speed scheduling: a lightly loaded train, run by picked engines, on an easy downhill course with no intermediate speed restrictions. The impeachment, over 'an easy course', has been dismissed in Chapter 1 of this book, and there is no doubt that picked engines were used; but the main thing to remember

Up Torbay express near Burlescombe : engine No 6018 'King Henry VI'

about the 'Cheltenham Flyer' was that unlike the later high-speed trains in other parts of Great Britain, there was no strict limitation of load. The minimum was certainly no more than seven coaches; but neither traffic nor locomotive departments had any compunction about putting on a few extras, and loads of eight or nine coaches were of quite common occurrence. Furthermore, unlike every other high-speed train in the country the 'Flyer' ran six days a week. There was no easing of the schedule on Saturdays even in the height of the summer; indeed, some of my own fastest runs on the train were made on Saturdays.

The question of additional load on trains timed at such speeds raises to my mind a matter of principle. The attitude of the Great Western Railway was beyond praise in this respect. If traffic was accepted that involved extra coaches—and this applied also to the pre-war 'Bristolian'—then an all-out attempt was made to keep the time publicly advertised. Far otherwise was the policy adopted in more recent times, for on occasions when the going was likely to be difficult extra time was given in special working notices, not communicated to the public. Thus a train could, for example, be 10 min late by the published times, but driver and

guard could book 'right time'. This, of course, was nothing short of dishonesty. It had its repercussions sometimes. On one post-war occasion the traffic department wanted to attach two extra coaches to the down 'Bristolian'. The running authorities said they could only accept such a load if 10 min extra time was allowed. Covertly this was agreed. A 'King' class engine instead of the usual 'Castle' was put on to the job and a locomotive inspector instructed to ride on the footplate. Having got an excellent engine the driver and inspector scorned the extra allowance and without any difficulty ran the train to the normal time, to receive a severe reprimand for their pains!

This chapter is, however, about times when the old spirit of the Great Western Railway still flourished, and the accompanying table gives details of some cases of overload on the 'Cheltenham Flyer' leading up to one on which the driver came very near to keeping time with a load of 435 tons—*four hundred and thirty-five tons*! These conditions of heavy loading involve some of the finest high-speed running I have ever seen with the 'Castles', and they are deserving of close study. The table includes runs with seven, eight, ten, and finally thirteen-coach trains. Some very spectacular run-

GWR: THE CHELTENHAM FLYER

								1		2		3		4	
Run No								1		2		3		4	
Engine No								5055		5025		5018		5023	
Engine Name								*Lydford Castle*		*Chirk Castle*		*St Mawes Castle*		*Brecon Castle*	
Load, coaches								7		8		10		13	
Load, tons E/F								218/230		248/270		317/340		401/435	

Dist miles				Sch min	Actual m s		Actual m s		Actual m s		Actual m s	
0·0	SWINDON	.	.	0	0	00	0	00	0	00	0	00
5·7	Shrivenham	.	.		6	43	7	02	7	16	8	00
10·8	Uffington	.			10	22	11	01	11	19	12	17
16·9	Wantage Road	.			14	25	15	31	15	58	17	07
24·2	DIDCOT	.	.	21	19	13	20	44	21	22	26	15
32·6	Goring	.			25	02	26	48	27	36	31	44
35·8	Pangbourne	.			27	32	29	11	29	59	34	01
41·3	READING	.	.	34	31	47	33	17	34	08	36	06
46·3	Twyford	.			35	38	37	00	37	56	40	03
53·1	Maidenhead	.			40	33	41	50	43	04	45	20
					—		—		—		sigs	
58·8	SLOUGH	.		47½	44	39	45	50	47	22	52	20
64·1	West Drayton	.			48	26	49	41	51	24	57	19
68·2	Southall	.	.	54½	51	33	52	43	54	39	60	58
71·6	Ealing	.	.		54	10	55	13	57	12	63	48
					—		—		—		sigs	
76·0	Westbourne Park	.		61	59	00	59	19	60	41	68	35
77·3	PADDINGTON	.		65	61	49	62	15	63	04	71	41

Max speed mph	.	.	.	.	93·5		86·5		82		79
Location	.	.	.	.	Wantage Road		Maidenhead		Wantage Road Reading Ealing		Didcot

The up Bristolian, near Filton Junction : engine No 6027 'King Richa d I'

ning could be expected if a driver decided to 'have a go' with a seven-coach train, and the first run in the table, made on the very stormy New Year's Day of 1937 includes some very fast times. There was a strong south-west wind, with heavy rain, and while this might have been of some assistance in the early stages it was certainly not so when the line turns south at Didcot. Thus engine No 5055, then named *Lydford Castle*, made a very rapid start and worked quickly up to a maximum of 93·5 mph by Wantage Road. Then from 90 mph through Didcot the speed came down to 76·5 mph at Pangbourne. After the line had turned eastwards again, and there was some shelter in the cuttings, the speed rose again into the middle eighties and Southall was passed 3 min early.

The eight-coach train was again a rough winter occasion, when I was travelling through from Gloucester to Paddington, and the train was late in arriving from Cheltenham. The driver did his best to recover some time, but with an east wind and driving sleet for most of the way it was not possible to do much. To get through in $62\frac{1}{4}$ min in such conditions was splendid work. Apart from a brief drop to 79·5 mph after Goring water troughs the speed never fell below 80 mph at any point between Uffington and Hanwell, and the average speed over this 59·1 miles was 82·6 mph. Then comes a splendid run with a ten-coach train weighing 340 tons behind the tender, logged by Mr H. F. Maybank. The driver of *St Mawes Castle* on this occasion was Burgess, who did so well with *Manorbier Castle* on the record run with the down 5 pm from Paddington

on 6 June 1932. Shrivenham was passed at 71 mph, and a maximum of 82 was attained by Wantage Road. After that the speed fluctuated no more than slightly between further maxima of 82 mph at Reading and Ealing, and minima of 76·5 mph at Twyford and 76 at Hayes. An ability to attain and sustain 81-82 mph on level track with 340 tons load was demonstrated on this journey.

Lastly there is the astounding run of *Brecon Castle* with the 13-coach train of 435 trailing tons, also logged by Mr H. F. Maybank. Speed never quite reached 80 mph. The maximum was 79 mph, sustained on the faint descent between Steventon and Didcot; but a speed of 77·5 mph on the dead level approaching Reading indicated the remarkable drawbar horsepower of 1,070, and the fact that speed had averaged 76·8 mph from Uffington to Maidenhead shows clearly that this was no mere flash in the pan, achieved by mortgaging the boiler. It was a most splendid example of sustained steaming at a very high rate of evaporation. It was very unfortunate that so magnificent an effort, the product solely of a keen and resolute engine crew, and a first-class engine, should have been marred by signal checks. From a careful examination of all the figures I am doubtful if strict time would have been kept. I think they would have been a minute out on arrival; but what is a mere minute against such a display as this! Of course there was a pair of real sportsmen on the footplate. The driver, F. W. Street, had as fireman C. E. Brown, who in Western Region days was a top link driver of rare calibre, too, and gave me some fine runs.

177

Besides such running all other contemporary work of the 'Castles' naturally pales; but mention must be made of their work on the Cornish main line. At that time the load limit was fixed at the extraordinary figure of 420 tons tare. It must be admitted that this was expecting a little too much over such gradients, where it was quite impossible to balance the long uphill slogging by some really free running downhill. With loads of around 350 tons they managed the Cornish Riviera Express quite comfortably; but an engine designed for work like that just described on the 'Cheltenham Flyer' did not have an ideal valve setting for the Cornish banks. A two-cylinder engine with Churchward's setting of the Stephenson link motion would have been much better.

In the earlier part of this book some examples of outstanding work by 'King' class locomotives on the West of England main line were quoted. In the 1930s interest tended to shift to the Paddington—Birmingham service. For one thing, the introduction of the 1¾-hour trains between Paddington and Bristol in 1935 raised the natural question as to why Birmingham could not have an equally fast service. The distance was 7 miles shorter, and the

'King' class engines stationed at Wolverhampton included some of the finest units of the whole stud. These sentiments never got beyond a rather loud whispering campaign; but it was taken sufficiently seriously at Paddington and Swindon for some running diagrams to be prepared in the drawing office at Swindon to show how difficult it would be to operate a 105-min schedule, with a good paying load. Why the operating department insisted that nothing less than 300 tons tare would do, when the new Bristol express conveyed only 215 tons, was not explained. But it was all fairly obvious that the management did not want to do it.

The running diagrams which were published in *The Railway Gazette*, and which had been worked out in the fullest detail, were naturally based on the capacity of the 'King' class engines in continuous steaming. It is not possible to reduce to theoretical calculations that priceless attribute of the steam locomotive that enables a skilful driver and fireman to exact that extra effort on a bank, above the theoretical maximum, by mortgaging the boiler, possibly running down both pressure and water level, knowing that both can be recovered on the next downhill stretch. The Birmingham line in-

Birmingham and the North express topping Hatton bank : engine No 6017 'King Edward IV'

cluded a number of places where this could be done: Gerrards Cross bank, and the subsequent descent and slack through Wycombe; Saunderton bank, with Princes Risborough, and Ashendon to follow; Aynho slack following the ascent from Bicester to Ardley, and the Leamington stop before the attack on Hatton bank. The stretches where the engine was steaming hard continuously were relatively short; nothing to compare, for example, with the long, very slight, but absolutely continuous grind from Paddington up to Swindon, or the 20-mile pull from Exeter up to Whiteball Tunnel. The Wolverhampton drivers became experts to the last degree in running their own road to London, and although the pundits of the Swindon drawing office demonstrated that 400 tons was the optimum load for the Birmingham two-hour trains, these outstanding enginemen thought nothing of taking 500 tons out of Paddington, or, as described in Chapter 9, keeping time with a load of 475 tons throughout to Leamington—with a 'Castle'!

The runs I have chosen for inclusion here come mainly from the collection of G. P. Antrobus, who except at weekends and holiday times travelled on the 6.10 pm down from Paddington every day, for several years. I have chosen six truly superlative runs for discussion. On all of them circumstances demanded something above the average if time was to be kept, and it was entirely in the spirit of the No 1 link at Stafford Road shed, Wolverhampton, that a whole-hearted attempt to produce that extra would be made as a matter of course. First of all it will be seen that against a schedule time that was at first 91 min, and was later cut fractionally to $90\frac{1}{2}$ min, the net times varied between 83 and 87 min; furthermore, on the first and second runs with no more than moderate loads, by 6.10 pm standards, still faster times could clearly have been made had not the effects of the earlier delays been wiped out by Bicester. In view of my earlier comments about extracting the additional efforts from the locomotives, however, we must look to the uphill work. The Gerrards Cross and Saunderton inclines provide ideal data for horsepower calculations, because in the former case the hard initial section from Denham frequently results in the minimum speed occurring near Gerrards Cross station, and a slight acceleration afterwards, while from West Wycombe

Up West of England express on Fairwood troughs : engine No 6002
'King William IV'

179

THE GWR STARS, CASTLES & KINGS

GWR: PADDINGTON—LEAMINGTON

Run No			1	2	3	4	5	6
Engine No			6005	6017	6017	6008	6008	6008
Engine Name			King George II	King Edward IV	King Edward IV	King James II	King James II	King James II
Load, tons E/F to B'cester			357/380	403/425	415/445	472/505	476/505	474/510
to B'bury			327/347	367/388	380/407	436/465	445/470	437/470
to L'ton			293/315	298/315	314/335	366/390	374/400	369/400

Dist miles		Sch min	Actual m s	Actual m s	Actual m s	Actual m s	Actual m s	Actual m s
0·0	PADDINGTON	0	0 00	0 00	0 00	0 00	0 00	0 00
1·3	Westbourne Park		—	3 13	3 06	3 49	sigs	—
					sigs	sigs	sigs	sigs
3·3	Old Oak West Jc	7	5 41	6 54	7 31	7 40	6 43	6 35
			pws	pws	pws	pws		
7·8	Greenford	13	13 46	13 42	16 02	14 16	12 01	11 50
					pws			
10·3	Northolt Jc	15½	17 31	16 15	20 40	17 35	14 36	14 30
					pws			
14·8	Denham		21 45	20 21	27 57	22 15	19 04	19 00
17·4	Gerrards Cross		24 06	22 46	30 55	24 53	21 46	21 47
21·7	Beaconsfield		27 56	26 43	35 36	29 21	26 22	26 44
				pws				pws
26·5	HIGH WYCOMBE	32	32 24	31 12	40 64	34 04	30 44	32 07
31·5	Saunderton		38 05	36 56	45 56	39 53	37 04	38 08
34·7	PRINCES RISBOROUGH	42	41 02	39 56	49 10	43 18	40 28	41 29
40·1	Haddenham		45 09	44 11	53 00	47 25	44 30	45 34
44·0	Ashendon Jc	49½	48 33	47 49	55 57	50 53	47 35	48 49
50·4	Blackthorn		54 33	54 13	61 34	56 31	53 30	54 49
53·4	BICESTER	58½	56 56	56 57	63 59	58 59	55 58	57 25
57·2	Ardley		60 27	60 51	67 32	62 45	59 37	61 15
62·4	Aynho Jc	67	65 18	65 43	72 00	67 33	64 19	65 59
			sigs					
67·5	BANBURY	72	70 40	70 40	76 44	72 11	69 12	71 22
							pws	pws
71·1	Cropredy		74 22	74 14	79 52	75 24	73 31	76 21
76·2	Fenny Compton		78 54	78 58	84 15	79 53	79 01	81 40
81·2	Southam Road		82 45	83 16	87 47	83 40	83 02	85 35
83·6	Fosse Road		84 35	85 12	89 23	85 59	84 59	87 24
				pws		sigs	sigs	
87·3	LEAMINGTON	90½	88 26	89 27	92 59	90 45	89 23	91 08

Net time	min	84	87	83	86	86¾	86½

Principal speed mph:

	1	2	3	4	5	6
Denham	70	72	56	65	65	64
Gerrards Cross	65·5	64·5	52	58·5	57·5	55
Beaconsfield	68	66	56	58·5	56·5	54·5
Saunderton	61	61	54·5	53·5	52	51·5
Haddenham	83	82	91·5	87·5	90	85
Blackthorn	79	74	80	78	76	74·5
Ardley	62·5	59	63·5	60	62	59
Cropredy	64·5	63	69	66	52	54
Fosse Road	82	80	91	87	80	83

Calculated equivalent dhp:

	1	2	3	4	5	6
(a) Gerrards Cross bank	1,501	1,583	1,440	1,525	1,447	1,410
(b) Saunderton	1,642	1,815	1,785	1,761	1,694	1,676

the speed, on a good run, is usually rising slightly up the subsequent 1 in 164 grade to Saunderton.

Examination of the theoretical curves produced in the Swindon drawing office indicate that the uphill speeds were based on the maximum continuous steaming capacity of the 'King' class engine with a single fireman: a perfectly reasonable assumption in an exercise of this kind. With the 400-ton train the speeds shown on the graph are 57 mph at the upper part of Gerrards Cross bank and 50 mph at Saunderton. The gross load of such a train can be assumed as 420 tons behind the tender. The equivalent drawbar horsepowers involved are 1,250 and 1,380. In the classic trials of

*Up Torquay and Paignton express approaching Fairwood Junction, Westbury :
engine No 6011 'King James II'*

engine No 6001 in 1952, after that engine had been equipped with a 4-row superheater and modified draughting the equivalent dhp, when working at an evaporation rate of 30,000 lb per hr, with *two* firemen, was 1,500 at 50 mph and 1,370 at 60 mph. The equivalent dhp on the six runs tabulated have been very carefully calculated from the voluminous data compiled by Mr Antrobus, and in comparison with those of the Swindon diagram and of the tests with No 6001 they fairly make one rub one's eyes in wonder. Comparison of these efforts in relation to the continuous steaming results show the astonishing extent to which these Wolverhampton drivers were getting the 'extra' out of their engines. I need

hardly add that it is an achievement that would be utterly impossible with a diesel.

Every one of the runs tabulated is a classic in itself, but it is necessary to mention in particular some of their more outstanding features. On No 1, for example, look at the acceleration from 65·5 mph at Gerrards Cross to 68 mph before the Beaconsfield summit was topped, followed by 61 mph at Saunderton; but the power outputs were eclipsed on the truly phenomenal second run, with edhp values of 1,583 at Beaconsfield summit and 1,815 at Saunderton. On No 3 run, after heavy delays in the early stages, and passing High Wycombe 8 min late, a splendid attempt was made to regain lost time,

*The last 'King' to be built : No 6029 'King Stephen', later renamed
'King Edward VIII'*

and after another very big effort up Saunderton, 54·5 mph and an edhp of 1,785, there came the fastest sustained running of all six after Princes Risborough, with maximum speeds of 91·5 mph at Haddenham, and 91 mph at Fosse Road. Columns 4, 5 and 6 all relate to the working of loads exceeding 500 tons between Paddington and Bicester. They were all magnificent performances, and on the Gerrards Cross and Saunderton banks showed substantial 'extras' over both the theoretical and the 30,000 lb per hr figures for horsepower. Of these six runs it was only on the occasion that permanent way checks put the train 8 min late in passing High Wycombe that a late arrival occurred at Leamington.

One could continue discussion of these results indefinitely, following a variety of modes of analysis; but I think the figures themselves are enough to show that the 'King' class, in its original form, was an outstandingly successful locomotive design. It is important to appreciate that at the time these runs were made the locomotives had the original two-row low-degree superheaters, and the original draughting, with the jumper ring on the blast-pipe. Furthermore, Stafford Road shed, Wolverhampton, did not enjoy the choicest of coal supplies. They rarely received the finest grades of soft Welsh coal, more usually having to run with the best grades of local Staffordshire stuff. The secret of success was the tremendous spirit of pride in the job which permeated every grade of the service at Wolverhampton. I did not have the pleasure of making any footplate journeys in pre-war days, but from 1950 I rode with many drivers who had been main-line firemen in the great days of 1930-9, and in addition to the men whose driving feats are described in this chapter, Lewis, Glover, A. Smith, Jay, Brunsdon, and others, I have pleasurable memories of Curtis, the Macmillan brothers, Bert Griffiths, W. H. Shaw, and others of the post-war era.

CHAPTER 16

THE WAR YEARS

THE week-end of 2-3 September 1939 virtually marked the end of the Churchward era on the Great Western Railway. The network of high-speed express trains was suspended earlier than on other British railways because of the emergency measures needed for the evacuation of children from London, Birmingham and Liverpool; and although the subsequent 'phoney' period of the war did not result in any immediate physical disruption, such as was to come in the autumn of 1940, the fact that the rail-way as a whole and the locomotive department in particular were under Government control placed restraints upon the autonomy of Swindon such as had not previously been experienced. At the outbreak of war C. B. Collett was in his 69th year, but he carried on until the spring of 1941, when his retirement took place within a few weeks of the death of his great contemporary, Sir Nigel Gresley. Collett was succeeded by F. W. Hawksworth, who for many years had been Chief Draughtsman and

F. W. Hawksworth, Chief Mechanical Engineer 1941-9

Engine No 5071 as renamed 'Spitfire' in 1940 with the experimental 8-wheeled tender

who on John Auld's retirement became Principal Assistant to the Chief Mechanical Engineer. The succession, as always, on the GWR, was solid and secure. Hawksworth's immediate *entourage* were all men whom I came to know personally. F. C. Hall, one of the most charming of men, became Principal Assistant; W. N. Pellow was Outdoor Assistant and Locomotive Running Superintendent; K. J. Cook became Locomotive Works Manager; and H. Randle Carriage Works Manager. F. C. Mattingly was Chief Draughtsman, and a very brilliant young man, A. J. W. Dymond, became Personal Assistant to the CME, eventually to be entrusted with the nursing of various important new projects into fruition.

By the end of 1941 Hawksworth and his men certainly had their hands full of special tasks in connection with the war; but in this book, of course, I am concerned only with the story of 'Stars', 'Castles' and 'Kings'. War conditions certainly imposed a very heavy burden upon those responsible for the maintenance of all kinds of steam locomotives. At Swindon production of munitions was a first priority, and any practices that would prolong the intervals between visits to works of locomotives for repairs were adopted. There was inevitably a certain amount of 'patching up' done in repair work, and though this mainly concerned locomotives of lesser importance than the four-cylinder 4—6—0s it did affect them all to some extent. With the method of manufacture there was a certain thinning of the tubes at the bends of the superheaters, which in wartime conditions led to leaking; tubes were

The wartime livery of plain green, and crest on tender : engine No 4035 'Queen Charlotte'

184

The wartime livery on engine No 6029 'King Edward VIII'

patched, rather than replaced, and the butt-welding method used for insertion of new portions left flash at the joints.

On the road, much trouble was experienced with lower grades of coal. Great Western locomotives were more susceptible to the effects of poor coal than perhaps some of those on the northern lines, which had large superheaters, giving a high degree of superheat. But quite apart from fundamental causes of trouble such as this, there were difficulties arising from locomotives being sent out after inadequate servicing at the sheds, with boilers overdue for washout, smokeboxes uncleared of ashes, and blocked tubes. Against this rather gloomy picture I

Wartime and after—austerity grime! Engine No 4043 'Prince Henry' on
Paignton - Newcastle express near Dawlish Warren

The engine that never was ! An artist's impression of what the second Swindon 'Pacific' might have looked like

must record that even during the very worst days of the war I logged a number of excellent runs, with both 'Stars' and 'Castles', principally on the West to North route via the Severn Tunnel. A few of these runs are mentioned briefly at the end of this chapter. As the war years passed by there was ample evidence that no speedy return to a semblance or normality was likely once hostilities ended, and it appeared that some changes from traditional Great Western design were desirable. Experience was obtained, for the first time in the lifetime of most Swindon men, with locomotives of other than Great Western design: with the American-built Austerity 2—8—0, and with the LMSR Stanier 2—8—0, which all British railway companies were required to build in large quantities by the Ministry of War Transport.

The first outcome was the design of a superheater quite new to Swindon practice, and applied first on the new 'Hall' class engines of the '6959' class. This new design, with three rows of elements, was similar to the Schmidt, but incorporated the cherished Swindon feature of the regulator valve in it. In certain quarters outside the railway itself there was considerable doubt as to whether such a valve could be made steam-tight in high-temperature heaters, but this particular problem was satisfactorily settled. An improved feature was the elimination of the flat metal-to-metal joints by which the elements were attached to the heater in the standard 'Swindon' type of superheater. Initial reports from the running inspectors were very favourable. The 'Halls' with larger superheaters were reported to steam more freely, and the shed and works staff appreciated the new type of joints with the elements. The first batch of these engines was put into traffic in the summer of 1944, but in the meantime there had been stirrings in another direction altogether.

The Locomotive Committee of the Board had always included a number of directors who were genuinely interested in locomotives as such. Churchward, who was always on good terms with them, once said, in argument with Sir Aubrey Brocklebank: 'You're the only b—— director I've ever met who knew everything about valve gears!' The same august body had less success with Collett, and the 'sales resistance' he put up against their suggestions for a streamlined locomotive had the farcical result related in Chapter 14. In Hawksworth's time Captain Hugh Vivian was chairman of the committee, and as indicating his locomotive interests he was also chairman of Beyer, Peacock & Co Ltd. There is no evidence to suggest that he ever tried to get Hawksworth to try a Garratt; but war or no war there was

a feeling that the Great Western Railway ought to be making some preparations towards post-war traffic, and the resumption of high-speed running with heavy trains. The more progressive of the younger men in the Chief Mechanical Engineer's department felt that in any new development the principles of André Chapelon should be carefully heeded. During the war, with the accent on munitions production, and a policy of 'make-do-and-mend' prevailing in locomotive affairs, the drawing office, once Churchward's right hand throughout his brilliant development, had rather lost caste; but when the suggestion of a new 'Pacific' engine was made the opportunity was welcomed.

At the same time it seems to have been something of a 'cloak-and-dagger' business. Those concerned have told me that they had only the sketchiest of directives, from F. C. Mattingly. They were asked to put forward their ideas for a 'Pacific', and the only positive instruction issued in those early stages was that the boiler pressure was to be 280 lb per sq in. In response to requests for more information the reply was that standard practice was to be followed. A good deal of design work was done on the boiler. While bearing in mind all the basic features of Churchward's classic development the restriction in steam flow that to some extent handicapped the 'Kings' was eliminated, and a very high degree of superheat provided for. Two different schemes were worked out, using five-row and six-row superheaters respectively. In these preliminaries standard practice was certainly not followed, because provision was made for accommodating the regulator in a steam dome on top of the boiler. While preliminary work was thus being done on the boiler another draughtsman had taken the 'King' front-end, and completely streamlined the ports and steam passages in the Chapelon style.

Then, alas, those concerned had another visit from Mattingly, only the second he had paid while the project was live, and then it was to tell them to stop work. From that moment nothing more was done, and all that remained was a preliminary line diagram of what might have been Swindon's *chef d'oeuvre*. How the project originated in the first place, and how it was stopped one can only guess. Two points only may be put forward: it was essentially an express passenger engine (unlike Bulleid's 'Merchant Navy' class, officially designated 'mixed traffic'), and Authority probably frowned upon work expended on a super-express passenger locomotive in wartime. The second point is this: it would seem that hope was not entirely dead in the hearts of those who had initiated the project, when the

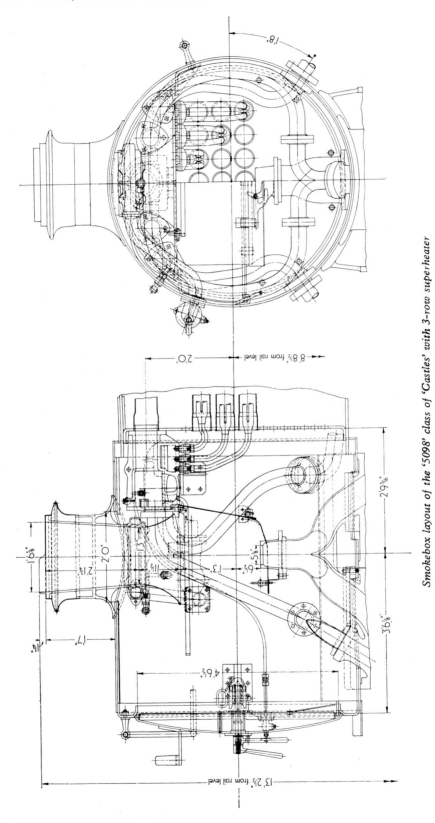

Smokebox layout of the '5098' class of 'Castles' with 3-row superheater

Post-war 'Castles' : engine No 7000 'Viscount Portal'

'County' class 4—6—0s appeared in 1945. These engines included two features quite out of normal context: the use of a boiler pressure of 280 lb per sq in, and the otherwise inexplicable introduction of an entirely non-standard coupled wheel diameter of 6 ft 3 in. Both these features were included in the stillborn 'Pacific'. Is it not a logical thing to guess that the 'County' was a guinea pig for the 'Pacific' which it was still hoped sometime to build?

I feel that a counter-suggestion that the 'County' was a definite attempt by Hawksworth to break away from the Churchward-Collett tradition, and that the new 4—6—0s were intended to be the post-war standard express passenger engine is quite fallacious. I have seen it suggested that 'Castle' building was resumed only after the 'Counties' had proved a 'failure'. This is quite at variance with the facts, for although the 'Counties' did not at first come fully up to expectations they did some very fine work, particularly on the more severely graded stretches of line, as in Cornwall and north of Wolverhampton. In any case the erecting shop switched straight over from 'County' to 'Castle' building within a matter of weeks.

The first post-war batch of 'Castles' was turned out in May and June 1946, bearing the numbers 5098-9, and 7000 to 7007. Except for Nos 7000 and 7003 they bore names that had twice previously been displaced. The two new names were *Viscount Portal*, the chairman of the GWR, on No 7000, and *Elmley Castle* on No 7003. Even then not all the twice displaced 'Castle' names were allowed finally to settle, as noted in the Case History of the 'Castles' (see Appendix). Engine No 7001 was renamed *Sir James Milne* in February 1948, and No 7007, the last express passenger engine to be built by the company, was renamed *Great Western*, and had the coat-of-arms on the driving wheel splasher beneath the nameplate. The thrice-displaced names *Denbigh Castle* and *Ogmore Castle* emerged once again in 1950. Almost at the end of the steam era No 7005 was renamed *Sir Edward Elgar* in August 1957 at the time of the centenary

of the great composer's birth. Apart from what might be termed the personalia of the new engines, they embodied certain important changes in design.

They were known officially as the '5098' class, and forty engines of this new series were built. Following the purely Great Western batch, in 1946, there were ten in each of the years 1948, 1949 and 1950 built to provide necessary replacements in express passenger motive power while the new British standard designs were being worked out. The principal difference from previous practice lay in the boiler, which had a three-row superheater of the type introduced on the '6959' series of 'Halls'. Engines with the modified superheater could readily be distinguished, on the right-hand side, by the longer casing over the oil pipe leading to the superheater header. The first two engines of the new series had the standard GWR sight-feed lubricators, but all subsequent engines had mechanical lubricators. The arrangement was not at first finalised, and several types of lubricator were tried, and in various positions. One of these latter was behind the outside steampipe, which of course made access to the inside motion more difficult than ever; but in later years the lubricators on most engines were moved ahead of the steampipe.

Mechanical lubrication brought problems of its own. In concordance with prevailing fashions elsewhere it was intended to take the responsibility for regulating oil supply out of the hands of the driver, and provide a carefully metered flow precisely to suit the needs of the engine. But the sight-feed hydrostatic lubricator was 'the breath of life' to Great Western enginemen; they had grown up with it, and were expert in its manipulation, and very soon there were complaints that the new engines were sluggish in comparison. The contrast was perhaps worsened because the first two of the new engines, Nos 5098 *Clifford Castle* and 5099 *Compton Castle* with sight-feed lubricators, were exceptionally powerful and free running. It was argued that with post-war systems of engine manning a driver would have no opportunities of finding out the vagaries of individual engines, and therefore could not use the old form of lubricator to advantage. This was the talk of backroom theorists. With any experienced driver it would not take ten miles of running for him to sense that an engine was sluggish, and adjust the lubricator to give a slightly faster rate of feed. It was perhaps not without significance that in the comprehensive series of dynamometer and stationary plant trials between engines of the '5013' and '5098' series of 'Castles' that No 5098 herself represented the latter series. One feels that on this account the results may not have been entirely representative of the work of the '5098' class, at any rate in its early days.

The 'County' class had a new type of tender with flush sides, and of welded construction. This was shown on the diagram of the proposed 'Pacific', but strangely enough it was not supplied on the first batch of the '5098' class 'Castles'. These had the old type, with the traditional flared top. The new type was subsequently used on the later batches of these engines, from No 7008 onwards, from 1948. Like the 'Counties' the new 'Castles' were fully lined out in the old style, and the use once again of the coat of arms with the letters GW on either side was a much pleasanter tender decoration than the totem used in the later 1930s.

While the construction of the first engines of the '5098' class did not actually take place in wartime the change in design from the '5013' series was certainly the result of wartime experience, and the next

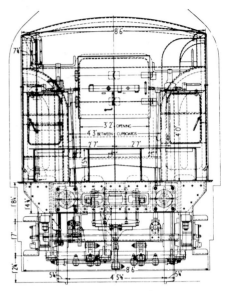

Tender cross-section

event in 'Castle' history also arose out of wartime and post-war austerity. It is difficult at this distance in time to appreciate the full severity of the coal situation as it came to affect all British railways in the years from 1944 onwards. It was particularly acute on the Great Western, which in pre-war years had been distinctly 'choosey' on the grades of coal purchased for locomotive purposes. Even in pre-war

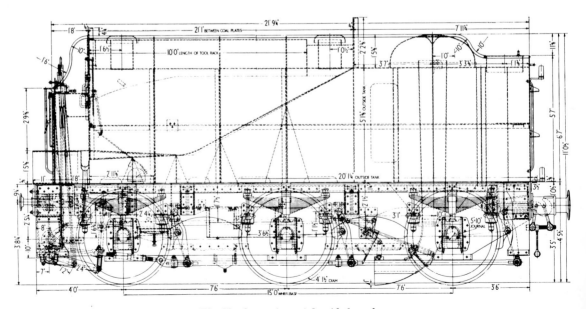

The Hawksworth straight-sided tender

The new-style tender attached to engine No 7033 'Hartlebury Castle'

years, however, it had not been plain sailing and the famous dispute with the South Wales coal owners over the price of coal had led to the threat to electrify the entire system *west of Taunton*. In the years of austerity following the second world war the management had to stomach the extraordinary situation of seeing much of the best Welsh coal earmarked by Government decree 'for export only' while Great Western engines, in South Wales above all places, struggled to make steam on dross imported from the USA!

The notable experiment in oil-firing eventuated from this situation. There was irony in its first application, to heavy mineral 2—8—0 engines of the '28XX' class working in South Wales, but the later extension of the scheme to include 4—6—0s

of the 'Hall' and 'Castle' classes savoured less of defiant propaganda, and had the making of a semi-permanent change in fuel provisioning. The management surveyed areas where coal was most expensive, through having to be conveyed over the longest mileage, and the thought developed of making Cornwall an all-oil-fired area. The workings were then entirely self-contained, and although many engines at Laira shed, Plymouth, worked both east and west of the Tamar it would not have been difficult to rearrange matters. The arrangement of the firebox is shown in the accompanying drawing. The burner, mounted at foundation ring level in a small chamber in the front of the firebox, was of the type in which oil flowed over a weir on to a ribbon of steam by which it was caught up,

Engine No 5091 'Cleeve Abbey', oil-fired, with small tender

191

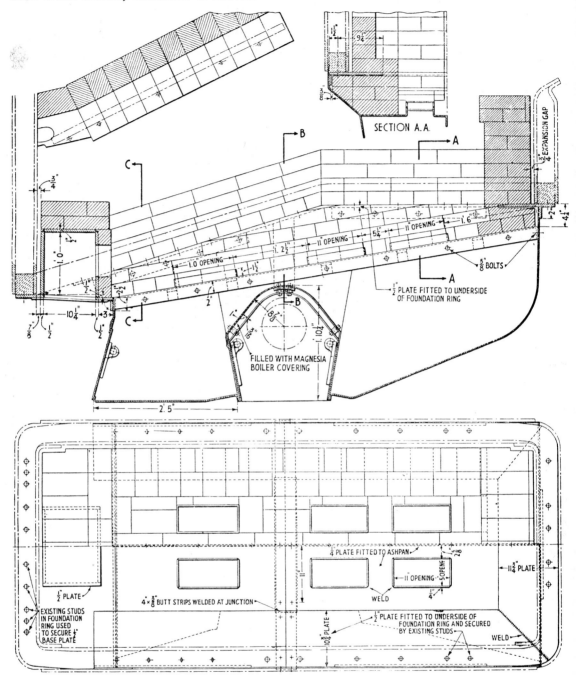

Layout of firebox : oil-fired locomotives

atomised and projected towards the back of the firebox at an inclination to the horizontal. The chamber carrying the burner had a small bottom damper door which could be preset to a suitable opening.

The floors of the firebox consisted of a steel plate in which were cut six rectangular holes giving a total air inlet of $2\frac{1}{4}$ sq ft. The normal type of ash-pan was modified to provide a suitable firepan; the original damper gear was retained. The air supply to the firebox through the orifices in the floor was controlled by opening or closing the damper doors in the firepan. Firebricks with a high alumina content were used to line the floor and the lower part

Cab layout on oil-fired 'Castle' class locomotives

of the firebox. The firehole door was redesigned to form a reasonably effective seal, and although easily opened was effectively locked when in the shut position. A peep-hole with cover was also provided.

Five engines of the 'Castle' class were so equipped, namely 100A1, 5039, 5079, 5083 and 5091. The first two mentioned were stationed at Old Oak Common, while 5083 and 5091 were at Bristol. All these four engines were kept close to headquarters for observation purposes, while 5079 *Lysander* returned to her home shed, Laira, to become—as one senior locomotive inspector put it—the 'flagship' of

the Cornish oil-fired fleet. I had some good runs with 5039 and 5091, and a dreadful one behind 100A1, which judging by the amount of black smoke emitted suggested either she was in dire trouble, or the crew were not familiar with oil firing. *Lysander* was a superb engine. I rode her in both directions between Plymouth and Penzance on the Cornish Riviera Express, and she gave me some excellent runs. Her steaming was rock-steady, and several times when pounding hard up the 1 in 60 gradients the firemen remarked that one just could not knock the needle off the red line indicating full

Engine No 5083 'Bath Abbey', oil-fired, with 4,000-gallon tender

boiler pressure.

The Great Western oil-firing project, which was conceived as a conversion scheme on a limited scale, not a general changeover from coal to oil firing, was noted by the Ministry of Fuel and Power; and in the midst of their own appalling difficulties over coal supply the Great Western scheme was hailed as an inspiration, and conversion on a national scale, and at huge expense, was initiated. Official hand-outs were issued detailing long lists of locomotives to be converted; millions of pounds of public money were spent in providing oil-fuelling plants. The propaganda was so loud and so widespread that at last another government department got to hear about it, and pointed out that we had insufficient foreign exchange to buy the necessary oil. The railways were nationalised by then, and the limited, logical and essentially practical Great Western development was terminated in the general debacle.

Before closing this chapter reference must be made to the details of wartime runs over the West to North route mentioned earlier. In general the 'Castles', with Walschaerts valve gear, did not show

up so well on the heavy banks as the 'Saints', which had monopolised this route for so long. Churchward's setting of the Stephenson link motion, with negative lead in full gear, gave a splendid distribution of steam when slogging hard at 30 mph on a 1 in 100 bank, and with one exception I have never noted 'Castle' hill-climbing to equal, let alone to surpass, the best achieved with the 'Saints'. Hill-climbing became of greater importance than ever during the war years, because for a long period speeds were limited to a maximum of 60 mph and any time lost uphill could not be regained by fast

GWR: PONTYPOOL ROAD—SHREWSBURY

Run No		1	2	3
Engine No	. .	5032	5086	5032
Engine Name	.	Usk Castle	Viscount Horne	Usk Castle
Load, tons E/F	.	416/450	392/420	411/460

Dist miles		Actual m s	Actual m s	Actual m s
0·0	PONTYPOOL ROAD		0 00	0 00
			pws	
1·6	*Little Mill Jc* .		4 50	3 05
6·8	Penpergwm . .		12 30	9 08
9·5	Abergavenny .		15 27	13 04
10·5	ABERGAVENNY JC		16 45	14 48
13·5	Llanvihangel .		23 07	22 56
21·0	Pontrilas . .		30 15	30 45
26·8	Tram Inn . .		36 09	36 35
			sigs	
33·5	HEREFORD .	0 00	48 25	46 50
4·2	Moreton-on-Lugg	7 35	7 50	8 12
7·5	Dinmore . .	11 25	11 37	12 14
10·2	Ford Bridge .	14 55	14 45	16 10
12·6	LEOMINSTER .	17 20	17 05	18 35
18·9	Woofferton .	23 40	23 48	26 17
23·5	LUDLOW .	28 50	28 42	31 45
28·1	Onibury . .	34 10	33 57	37 24
31·1	CRAVEN ARMS	38 05	37 47	41 27
38·2	CHURCH STRETTON	49 45	47 54	52 35
41·7	Leebotwood .	53 35	51 36	56 30
46·7	Condover .	58 15	55 35	61 00
			sig stop	sigs
51·0	SHREWSBURY	63 40	64 55	68 40
	Net times . .	63¾	41¼ + 61	46¾ + 66½

Engine No 5079 'Lysander', oil-fired, at Truro

running down the banks. I had several runs on the 7.30 pm 'Mail' out of Bristol, and one that remains particularly in my memory took place in the early autumn of 1940, when the Battle of Britain was at its height, and from Pontypool Road onwards we were running through a continuous 'Alert'. *Usk Castle* was the engine, and we got a remarkably clear road from Pontypool Road right through to Shrewsbury, where the 'Alert' was still on. In the blackout I was not able to log in detail until after Hereford, but from the accompanying table it will be seen that with a 450-ton train we were able to cover the 51 miles to Shrewsbury in 63¾ min. We certainly exceeded the temporary speed limit on the descent from Church Stretton, by momentarily touching 71 mph.

Later in the war, when the speed limit had been raised to 75 mph, I had an excellent run on this same train with engine No 5086 *Viscount Horne*. This was the rebuild of a 'Star' that had given me some grand runs in pre-war years, No 4066 *Malvern Abbey*. Despite a permanent way check at Little Mill Junction, which handicapped the start, this 420-ton load was taken up the Llanvihangel bank

with no lower speed than 26 mph on the 1 in 82, recovering to 28 mph on the 1 in 95 that leads to the summit. Even so, this falls behind a 'Saint' performance that I shall always remember, when No 2949 hauling 450 tons made speeds of 29 and 31 mph on these two stretches. As will be seen from the table, *Viscount Horne* was taken briskly down to Hereford and made a net gain of 8¾ min on the easy schedule then in force. Onwards to Shrewsbury, this engine did not show any great superiority over the work of *Usk Castle*, in air raid conditions, until Craven Arms was passed, and then there came a really fine culminating pull up to Church Stretton, with a minimum speed of 37 mph, against 27 mph by *Usk Castle*. Furthermore, we had a moment of real old-time running down to Shrewsbury, with a top speed of 82 mph near Condover. Other runs in this same period, with 5014 *Goodrich Castle*, 5077 *Fairey Battle* and 5060 *Earl of Berkeley*, all showed good work.

In the autumn of 1944 I had an engine pass for the 9.45 am from Newton Abbot to Shrewsbury, a duty worked on alternate days by Newton and Salop sheds, and usually provided with engines that were

Austerity fuel ! Saturdays only Wolverhampton - Paignton express at Langley Crossing, Chippenham : engine No 5055 'Earl of Eldon'

*High-speed ATC test run, 12 October 1947 : engine No 5056 'Earl of Powis'
at 86 mph near Twyford*

in first-class condition. I travelled on a Salop day, and once again we had *Usk Castle,* in positively regal condition. True, she was painted in unlined green, but the basic metalwork of her chimney cap and safety-valve cover had been bared, and not polished, but *burnished.* From the viewpoint of locomotive performance it was unfortunate that we had a heavy relief train just ahead, and suffered many signal checks until we were clear of the Newport area. Between Pontypool Road and Shrewsbury the conditions were somewhat different from those obtaining on the companion runs tabulated, in that this engine had worked through from Newton Abbot, and the others had come on fresh at Bristol. Thus although we were running well behind time the engine was not unduly pressed.

In view of my earlier remarks about 'Castle' performance on steep inclines, *Usk Castle* was worked in 35 per cent cut-off and full regulator from Abergavenny and yet fell to 20·5 mph on the worst part of the bank, and recovered only to 24 mph on the 1 in 95. Between Hereford and Church Stretton *Usk Castle* was working in 17 per cent with practically full regulator, and it was only when we had passed the junction with the one-time Bishops Castle line that cut-off was advanced to 25 per cent. Minimum speed at Church Stretton was 33·5 mph and maximum afterwards 76 mph.

In the up direction I had two runs with No 5072,

on the noon service from Shrewsbury, also a double-home turn. In between the two runs the engine had been renamed. In 1940 she was *Compton Castle,* and when I was on the footplate in 1944, *Hurricane.* Both runs included some good hill-climbing, and after I sent details of the second run to Swindon I learned some years later the excellence of the work caused such a surprise that a small team of engineers from the experimental section was sent to Shrewsbury to check the performance of this train and make sure I had not over-assessed the merit of the hill-climbing. Actually the 1944 run when I was on the footplate was not nearly as good as that of 1940, when No 5072 did not fall below 32 mph on the ascent to Church Stretton, against 27-8 mph, with cut-offs of 34 to 37 per cent when I was on the footplate. It was the same ascending from Hereford to Llanvihangel, with speeds at the summit of 34 and 30 mph, and most significant of all, 34 mph on that most trying 1 in 100 through Cattybrook tunnel to Patchway, against 28 mph, working in 32 per cent cut-off, on the 1944 run. Engine No 5072, as *Compton Castle,* certainly gave me some of the finest heavy-grade hill-climbing I have ever logged with a 'Castle'. The sustained speed of 34 mph maintained consistently on a successive of 1 in 100 banks involved the output of 1,350 edhp and probably needed the use of a cut-off of at least 40 per cent. This was grand for the year 1940.

196

CHAPTER 17

TESTING : OLD AND NEW METHODS

THE longevity of any particular locomotive class, or group of classes, is usually attributable to a variety of factors quite apart from its inherent qualities of design. In the case of the 'Castles' and 'Kings' the maintenance of those engines as first-class power units up to the final demise of steam traction on the Western Region was to a very large extent due to the energy, enthusiasm and engineering skill of one man who kept the flag of the GWR flying; yet he did so with such discretion and *bonhomie,* to back his precepts, as to carry the chief officers of the nationalised British Railways with him for much of the time. I refer, of course, to Sam Ell, who in 1947 was in charge of the experimental section of the locomotive drawing office. An extended reference to testing methods may seem a little beside the point in a history of a family of locomotive classes; but while Ell's work may not have prolonged the life of the 'Castles' and 'Kings' it most certainly kept them in top form to the very end, and effectively blocked any attempt there might have been to supersede them by alien types on the most important duties. Their eventual fall to the diesels was the result of politics, not engineering.

In the 1930s a great deal of very important spade work, little known outside Swindon, had been done towards making the process of locomotive testing more scientific. C. T. Roberts, who later became Chief Mechanical and Electrical Engineer of Scottish Region was, in dynamometer-car testing, feeling his way towards the principle of testing at constant rates of evaporation, while A. J. W. Dymond was charged with the task of modernising the stationary testing plant in Swindon Works. This latter project was an example of what one of his assistants once called the 'diabolical cunning' of C. B. Collett. Sir Nigel Gresley was a most persistent advocate of a national locomotive testing station, on the same lines as the celebrated French plant at Vitry-sur-

Seine. He got the support of Stanier in this, and when the question arose of securing some agreement for sharing expenses a suggestion was made that the Great Western might join in. The old Churchward plant, as Stanier knew it, was capable of absorbing no more than about 500 hp. Although he took little or no part in inter-railway discussions, Collett took care to keep himself very well informed, and when an official approach was made to the Great Western to participate in the project for a national testing station Gresley and Stanier were invited to come, or send representatives, to Swindon, and to their astonishment saw the plant completely modernised, and absorbing the all-out effort of a 'Saint' class engine No 2931 *Arlington Court,* at 70 mph! Obviously Swindon had no need to participate in the new project!

However it may have been attained Ell had, in 1947, a first-class tool at his disposal, while the pre-war work of C. T. Roberts with the dynamometer car needed not a great deal more than some finishing touches to form the basis of all post-war road testing on the Western Region. The

The 1948 Interchange Trials : engine No 6018 near New Barnet

197

*Engine No 6022 'King Edward III', with 4-row superheater. Tender is
lettered 'British Railways'*

corollary to Hawksworth's development of super-heating, first on the '6959' series of 'Halls' and then on the '5098' series of 'Castles' was the fitting of a four-row superheater on engine No 6022 *King Edward III*, and it was perhaps prophetic of things to come that this latter was the first engine I ever saw running on the Swindon stationary plant. That was in the summer of 1947, and at the beginning of the following year the Great Western, together with the other three British main-line railways, passed into national ownership, and became the Western Region. The new organisation was not three months old before the huge programme of locomotive inter-change trials was announced. Recalling the brilliantly spectacular performances put up by Great Western engines in previous interchange trials great things were expected from the 'Kings' and 'Halls' that participated, though there was disappointment that structure gauge restrictions precluded their use on the LMS and Southern lines covered on the trials. So far as this book is concerned only the work of the 'King' class engines Nos 6001 and 6018 is

*Engine No 6018 'King Henry VI' on clearance tests at Kings Cross
prior to test runs to Leeds*

198

involved.

It is very important to appreciate the background circumstances to these trials, as they affected the Western Region, before any comparison is made of the results attained with those from *Pendennis* and *Caldicot Castles* in 1925, and from *Launceston Castle* in 1926. In 1948 the Western Region management had no heart for nationalisation, a sentiment that was equally shared in the locomotive department at Swindon. There was none of the fiercely competitive spirit of some engine crews of other regions shown by the Great Western drivers in the running of any of the test trains, and superficial observers jumped to the conclusion that the 'King' class engines were past their day, and were overdue for superseding. The test trains were scheduled at the relatively slow speeds prevailing since the war. To engines in good condition they were an easy task, and the drivers of the 'King' class

engines concerned, encouraged to do no more than run their trains to time, made journeys that looked more or less of pedestrian quality. Compared with pre-war standards, and particularly with the magnificent work so consistently recorded by G. P. Antrobus on the Birmingham line, the performances were of little consequence. In the main series of interchange trials engine No 6018 was used on both the Western and on the Eastern Region lines.

Although a good deal was made of the fact that the 'King' class engine was being fired with coal having characteristics exactly the opposite of those normally used no trouble was experienced, and the official report contains this note: 'Engine steamed freely on coal having characteristics widely differing from that normally used on engines of the Western Region. Live steam injector only used, as steaming rate was usually less than the minimum supply rate of the 12 mm exhaust steam injector'. But the factor

The 1948 Interchange Trials : engine No 6018 on up Leeds express at Wakefield

PERFORMANCES OF WESTERN REGION 'KING' CLASS No 6018

Paddington—Plymouth route
DOWN: 20 and 22 April
UP: 21 and 23 April

Date	Location	Miles from Paddington	Mile post	Gradient 1 in	Speed mph	Recorded Pull tons	Recorded Dbhp	Equivalent Pull tons	Equivalent Dbhp	Cut-off per cent	Boiler pressure lb/sq in	Regulator position*
April												
20	Whiteball Tunnel	153·25	173·5	127R	26	6·7	1,082	8·1	1,253	30	235	1st valve $\frac{1}{4}$
20	Rattery	206·72	227	65R	31	5·0	927	7·1	1,310	30	230	$\frac{1}{2}$
21	Hemerdon Bank	219·5	239·75	42R	15	8·95	804	12·2	1,090	50	235	$\frac{1}{4}$
21	Long Sutton	128·0	128	264R	53	3·3	1,048	3·8	1,210	17	240	$\frac{1}{4}$
22	Wellington Bank	149·25	169·5	170R	45	4·3	1,159	5·1	1,380	25	230	$\frac{1}{4}$
22	Rattery Bank	205·75	226	90R	24	7·3	1,048	9·6	1,371	40	236	$\frac{1}{3}$
23	Stoke Canon	170·25	190·5	217R	48	3·6	1,034	4·2	1,210	20	245	Just open

* 2nd valve position shown except where otherwise stated

Kings Cross—Leeds route
DOWN: 18 and 20 May
UP: 19 and 21 May

Date	Location	Miles From Kings Cross	Miles From Leeds	Gradient 1 in	Speed mph	Recorded Pull tons	Recorded Dbhp	Equivalent Pull tons	Equivalent Dbhp	Cut-off per cent	Boiler pressure lb/sq in	Regulator position
May												
18	Wrenthorpe	177·0		91R	29·5	5·51	970	7·0	1,234	35	220	$\frac{1}{2}$
19	Abbots Ripton		122·3	200R	47·4	3·61	1,020	4·17	1,180	17	240	$\frac{1}{2}$
20	Wrenthorpe	177·0		91R	34·2	5·69	1,162	7·28	1,480	35	240	$\frac{1}{2}$
21	Hitchin		155·5	200R	48·3	3·65	1,053	4·20	1,212	20	235	$\frac{5}{8}$
21	Grantham		82·5	200R	36·0	4·91	1,055	5·74	1,055	25	230	$\frac{5}{8}$

RESULTS FROM MAIN SERIES OF INTERCHANGE TRIALS

	6018	6018
Engine No .		
Train and route .	DOWN: 1.30 pm Paddington—Plymouth North Road UP: 8.15 am Plymouth MB—Paddington	DOWN: 1.10 pm Kings Cross—Leeds UP: 7.50 am Leeds—Kings Cross

	Down	Down	Up	Up	Down	Down	Up	Up
Date .	20/4/48	22/4/48	21/4/48	23/4/48	18/5/48	20/5/48	19/5/48	21/5/48
Weight of engine (in wo) tons	135·7	135·7	135·7	135·7	135·7	135·7	135·7	135·7
Weight of train behind drawbar	Padding-ton	Padding-ton	Plym'th Mill Bay	Plym'th Mill Bay	KX 494·5	KX 495·0	Leeds 299·75	Leeds 299·75
tare tons .	482·00	482·00	330·15	330·15	Wake-field 366·75	Wake-field 367·75	Wake-neld 423·25	Wake-neld 427·25
(inc dynamometer car)	Newton Abbot 324·50	Newton Abbot 324·50	Newton Abbot 491·80 Reading 454·80	Newton Abbot 491·80 Reading 454·80			Don-caster 452·0 Gran-tham 491·0	Don-caster 456·0 Gran-tham 492·5
Train miles (actual) .	225·1	225·1	225·8	225·8	185·7	185·7	185·8	185·8
Ton miles exc weight of engine .	103,480	103,480	104,470	104,470	90,643	90,741	86,029	86,469
„ inc weight of engine .	134,020	134,020	135,110	135,110	115,840	115,941	111,242	111,682
Time, booked running min .	287	287	287	287	236	236	241	241
„ actual running min .	282·4	288·9	287·8	282·6	238·6	238·5	235·6	232·5
„ overall (inc stops) .	322·0	323·0	330·1	326·5	262·5	255·4	265·0	264·4
Speed mph average .	47·8	46·8	47·1	48·0	46·7	46·7	47·3	47·9
Work done hp hours .	2,820	3,220	2,897	2,841	2,773	2,921	2,321	2,338
Hp min/ton mile (train) .	1·635	1·867	1·664	1·632	1·834	1·932	1·619	1·622
Coal, total wt lb .	10,730	11,730	10,602	10,966	9,630	10,023	7,451	7,996
„ lb/mile .	47·66	52·11	46·96	48·56	51·85	53·93	40·12	43·01
„ lb/ton mile (exc engine) .	0·104	0·113	0·102	0·105	0·106	0·110	0·087	0·092
„ lb/ton mile (inc engine) .	0·080	0·088	0·078	0·081	0·083	0·086	0·067	0·072
„ lb/dbhp hour .	3·81	3·64	3·66	3·86	3·48	3·43	3·21	3·42
„ lb/sq ft grate/hr running time)	66·5	71·0	64·5	67·9	70·6	73·4	55·4	60·2
Water, total gallons .	8,145	8,510	7,910	8,029	7,985	8,285	6,989	7,389
„ gallons/mile .	36·2	37·8	35·0	35·6	43·0	44·6	37·6	39·8
„ lb/ton mile (inc engine) .	0·608	0·635	0·586	0·594	0·689	0·715	0·628	0·662
„ lb/dhp/hour .	28·87	26·42	27·30	28·26	28·82	28·35	30·12	31·61
„ lb water/lb coal (actual) .	7·59	7·25	7·46	7·32	8·29	8·27	9·38	9·24
Gross calorific value of coal (as rec'd) .	13,810	13,570	13,430	13,520	13,769	13,816	13,833	13,793
Btus/dhp hour .	52,600	49,400	49,200	52,200	47,800	47,400	44,400	47,200
Train miles under power .	192·9	193·1	195·6	196·1	157·2	161·5	162·4	162·4
Time under power, min .	238·0	247·7	247·0	243·8	200·6	205·3	200·8	197·1
No of signal and temporary pw checks	5	6	9	8	11	8	8	4
No of unbooked stops .			1		1			1
Average dhp (under power) .	711	780	704	699	830	854	693	712
Average db pull, tons (under power) .	2·45	2·79	2·48	2·43	2·95	3·03	2·39	2·41
Coal, lb/hour (running time) .	2,280	2,436	2,211	2,329	2,422	2,521	1,898	2,063
„ lb/hour (under power) .	2,705	2,842	2,575	2,699	2,878	2,928	2,227	2,431
„ lb/sq ft grate/hr (under power) .	78·9	82·9	75·1	78·7	83·9	85·4	64·9	70·9
Water, lb/hour (running time) .	17,310	17,670	16,490	17,050	20,080	20,850	17,800	19,060
„ lb/hour (under power) .	20,530	20,620	19,220	19,760	23,880	24,210	20,910	22,480
General weather conditions .	Fine and dry	Fine and dry	Stormy to fine	Fine and dry	Fine. Dry rail	Fine. Dry rail	Dull. Dry rail	Fine. Dry rail
Wind .	Westerly. Light air	Southerly. Fresh breeze	Easterly. Slight breeze	South Westerly. Slight breez	Easterly. Fair to strong	Easterly. Fair to fresh	Variable. Very light.	Northerly. Light

that contributed as much as anything to the difference in performance between Great Western engines of pre-war years and No 6018 in the interchange trials was the greatly reduced demands on the boiler. The 1.30 pm down from Paddington, for example, was allowed 45 min start-to-stop to Reading, and then 70 min for the ensuing 59·6 miles on to Westbury; while the 8.30 am up from Plymouth was allowed 113 min non-stop from Westbury to Paddington. Then there were start-to-stop runs of 53 min down and 55 min up over the 47·1 miles between Westbury and Taunton. If one compares these with the times made on an 'ordinary' run of pre-war days, as exemplified by the log of No 6000 on the Cornish Riviera Express shown on p 139, the astonishing disparity will be more than obvious! In addition to this there were numerous out-of-course checks, which interrupted the continuity of the steaming, and this affected the overall efficiency of the performance.

So much was made at the time of the difficulties under which Western Region locomotives were labouring through having to use unfamiliar coal that a second series of trials was run in November 1948 on which another 'King' class engine, No 6001, was fired with Welsh coal. Allowing for the difference in calorific value of the coals used, No 6001 showed a reduction of 6·4 per cent over No 6018 in coal consumption per dhp hr, though anyone familiar with locomotive running conditions would appreciate that such a difference, obtained in the course of runs on service trains, and trains moreover making such a modest demand on locomotive capacity, could easily arise from the difference between individual locomotives, or the driving techniques of the crews concerned, and have nothing whatever to

do with the nature of the fuel. As other observers pointed out, hard Yorkshire coal did not prevent *Pendennis Castle* from making some brilliant running in the interchange trials of 1925 on the LNER. In 1948 engine No 6018 put up some immaculate, if unspectacular, performances between Kings Cross and Leeds, and her basic coal consumption was actually better there than on her home ground between Paddington and Plymouth. Her best figure, of 3·21 lb per dhp hr on the 7.50 am up from Leeds on 19 May 1948 compares strikingly with the worst Plymouth figure, of 3·86 lb per dhp hr on the 8.30 am up on 23 April 1948. Between the two there is a 20 per cent difference, with the same engine, the same crew, and the same grade of fuel! Nevertheless the detailed reports of the interchange trials provide an interesting record of 'King' performance and they are set out in the accompanying tables. These include results from a contemporary series of tests run with the high-superheat 'King' No 6022.

In subsequent discussions with S. O. Ell, I remember how he emphasised the 'hit and miss' nature of testing on service trains without any scientific control of working on the footplate. In

Dynamometer-car test run, 19 May 1948 : No 6018 on up Leeds express leaving Hadley Wood Tunnel

RESULTS FROM TESTS WITH WELSH COAL

	'King' (low superheat) 6001				'King' (high superheat) 6022			
Class								
Engine No.								
Train and route	DOWN: 1.30 pm Paddington—Plymouth North Road UP: 8.15 am Plymouth MB—Paddington				DOWN: 1.30 pm Paddington—Plymouth North Road UP: 8.15 am Plymouth MB—Paddington			
	Down	Down	Up	Up	Down	Down*	Up	Up
Date	23/11/48	25/11/48	24/11/48	26/11/48	14/12/48	16/12/48	15/12/48	17/12/48
Weight of engine (in wo) tons	135·7	135·7	135·7	135·7	135·7	135·7	135·7	135·7
Weight of train behind drawbar tare tons (inc dynamometer car)	Paddington 480·6 Newton Abbot 326·2	Paddington 480·6 Newton Abbot 326·2	Plymouth 329·9 Newton Abbot 485·05 Reading 452·25	Plymouth 332·25 Newton Abbot 487·4 Reading 452·25	Paddington 481·0 Newton Abbot 322·5	Paddington 445·8 Exeter 290·6	Plymouth Mill Bav 325·0 Newton Abbot 478·4 Reading 443·3	Plymouth Mill Bav 326·6 Newton Abbot 480·0 Reading 413·0
	(Tare)	(Tare)	(Tare)	(Tare)	(Tare)	(Tare)	(Tare)	(Tare)
Train miles (actual)	225·1	225·1	225·8	225·8	225·1	225·1	225·8	225·8
Ton miles exc weight of engine	103,270	103,270	103,320	103,760	103,230	92,280	101,770	100,990
„ inc weight of engine	133,810	133,810	133,950	134,390	133,770	122,830	132,410	131,630
Time, booked running min	287	287	288	288	287·0	259·0	288	288
„ actual running min	305·0	305·6	289·4	289	304·1	278·7	294·4	302·4
„ overall (inc stops)	334·2	337·5	326·4	329·5	340·0	293·2	332·0	350·6
Speed mph average	44·3	44·2	46·8	46·9	44·4	48·4	46·0	44·8
Work done hp hours	2,891	2,762	2,870	2,935	3,245	2,902	2,800	2,959
HP min/ton mile (train)	1·680	1·604	1·666	1·697	1·886	1·887	1·651	1·758
Coal, total wt lb	10,030	10,002	10,046	10,354	10,266	10,254	9,214	10,224
Net coal (gross less train heating)	9,426	9,402	9,502	9,795	9,718	9,765	8,620	9,559
„ lb/mile	41·88	41·77	42·08	43·38	43·17	43·37	38·18	42·34
„ lb/ton mile (exc engine)	0·091	0·091	0·092	0·094	0·094	0·106	0·085	0·095
„ lb/ton mile (inc engine)	0·070	0·070	0·071	0·073	0·073	0·080	0·065	0·073
„ lb/dhp hour	3·26	3·40	3·31	3·34	2·99	3·37	3·08	3·23
Gross coal, lb/sq ft grate/hr (running time)	57·5	57·3	60·7	62·7	59·05	64·4	54·75	59·14
Water, total gallons	9,102	9,147	9,326	9,416	9,209	9,206	8,193	8,901
Net water (gross less train heating)	8,554	8,599	8,822	8,907	8,718	8,767	7,665	8,322
„ gallons/mile	38·0	38·2	39·1	39·5	38·73	38·94	33·94	36·85
„ lb/ton mile (inc engine)	0·639	0·643	0·659	0·663	0·652	0·714	0·579	0·632
„ lb/dhp hour	29·59	31·14	30·74	30·35	26·9	30·2	27·4	28·12
„ lb water/lb coal (actual)	9·07	9·14	9·29	9·10	8·97	8·98	8·89	8·71
Gross calorific value of coal (as rec'd)	14,920	14,940	14,800	14,760	14,850	14,720	14,310	14,490
Btus/dhp hour	48,600	50,900	49,000	49,300	44,500	49,500	44,000	46,800
Train miles under power	190·7	198·3	196·0	190·4	192·5	207·8	185·4	185·8
Time under power, min	255·3	261·9	245·1	238·3	253·7	248·7	239·9	242·5
No of signal and temporary pw checks	3	4	3	5	3	3†	4	6
No of unbooked stops					1	4		2
Average dhp (under power)	680	633	703	739	767	700	700	732
Average db pull, tons (under power)	2·54	2·33	2·45	2·58	2·82	2·34	2·53	2·67
Net coal, lb/hour (running time)	1,855	1,846	1,970	2,033	1,917	2,102	1,757	1,897
„ lb/hour (under power)	2,216	2,154	2,326	2,466	2,298	2,356	2,156	2,365
Gross coal, lb/sq ft grate/hr (under power)	68·7	66·8	71·7	76·0	70·8	72·1	67·2	73·8
Net water, lb/hour (running time)	16,830	16,890	18,290	18,490	17,200	18,870	15,630	16,510
„ lb/hour (under power)	20,110	19,710	21,600	22,430	20,620	21,150	19,170	20,590
General weather conditions	Misty at start	Fine and dry	Greasy rail at start. Fine	Greasy rail at start. Fine	Stormy. Wet rail	Fine. Dry rail. Fog later	Fine. Greasy rail	Fog patches. Greasy rail
Wind	Northerly to Easterly. Light breeze	S.E. Light breeze	East. Light air—light wind	South. Light air	Southerly to Westerly. Moderate breeze	South to S.W Light air	West. Light air—light breeze	Westerly to Northerly. Light air

* 5.30 pm train ex-Paddington † plus continuous signal checks from Taunton to Norton Fitzwarren, and from Rattery to Wrangaton

PERFORMANCES: ENGINES 6001 AND 6022

'King' Class (low superheat) No 6001

Paddington—Plymouth route
DOWN: 23 and 25 November
UP: 24 and 26 November

Date	Location	Miles from Paddington	Mile post	Gradient 1 in	Speed mph	Recorded Pull tons	Recorded Dbhp	Equivalent Pull tons	Equivalent Dbhp	Cut-off per cent	Boiler pressure lb/sq in	Regulator position*
Nov												
23	Wellington Bank	150·75	171	90R	38	5·0	1,135	6·05	1,372	30	230	Just open
24	Hemerdon Bank	219·50	239¾	42R	14	9·4	786	12·63	1,056	55	244	1st valve full
24	Dainton Bank	198·25	218½	38R	25	6·5	973	8·83	1,318	35	250	Just open
24	Stoke Canon	168·75	189	217R	48	3·3	948	4·85	1,390	25	230	1st valve ⅞
24	Silverton	166·50	186¾	219R	51	3·8	1,159	4·43	1,350	22	245	1st valve ⅞
24	Bruton Bank	112·75	127	98R	48	4·0	1,148	5·08	1,457	22	240	1st valve full
24	Bruton Bank	110·50	125	140R	42	4·4	1,102	5·37	1,330	25	230	1st valve full
25	Wellington Bank	150·75	171	90R	36	4·5	967	5·39	1,160	25	230	1st valve full
26	Hemerdon Bank	219·50	239¾	42R	15	8·7	780	11·93	1,070	55	240	Just open
26	Cullompton—Tiverton S	159·75	180	155R	31	6·1	1,131	6·98	1,292	30	240	1st valve full

* 2nd valve position shown except where otherwise stated

'King' Class (high superheat) No 6022

Paddington—Plymouth route
DOWN: 14 and 16 December
UP: 15 and 17 December

Date	Location	Miles from Paddington	Mile post	Gradient 1 in	Speed mph	Recorded Pull tons	Recorded Dbhp	Equivalent Pull tons	Equivalent Dbhp	Cut-off per cent	Boiler pressure lb/sq in	Steam chest pressure lb/sq in
Dec												
14	Strap Lane	105·75	120	409R	49·9	3·45	1,030	3·89	1,160	20	236	214
14	Whiteball	152·75	173	80R	30·5	6·1	1,112	7·49	1,364	30	230	210
14	Dainton Bank	197·00	217¼	41R	33·6	5·0	1,003	7·34	1,472	35	215	185
15	Hemerdon Bank	220·25	240½	42R	20·5	7·5	921	10·42	1,281	45	232	210
15	Keinton Mandeville	120·50	120½	330F	63·5	2·75	1,042	3·18	1,206	20	240	200
15	Pewsey	76·00	76	234R	60·0	2·5	896	3·7	1,325	17	220	200
16	Aldermaston	45·00	45	480R	50·1	3·5	1,042	3·64	1,086	15	240	225
16	Clink Road Jc	99·25	113¼	151R	56·5	3·0	1,012	3·56	1,200	15	240	225
16	Whiteball	151·00	171¼	90R	42·8	4·2	1,078	4·95	1,266	22	225	203
16	Whiteball	151·75	172	86R	35·3	4·85	1,025	6·06	1,275	22	230	210
16	Whiteball Tunnel	153·25	173½	127R	29·7	5·6	995	6·84	1,213	25	225	205
17	Hemerdon Bank	219·75	240	42R	17·5	8·0	837	11·2	1,169	45	235	205
17	Dainton Bank	199·75	220	76R	46·75	3·5	978	5·06	1,440	30	240	180
17	Savernake	71·00	71	198R	56·0	2·9	968	3·59	1,197	20	230	205

The 1948 Interchange Trials : engine No 6018 'King Henry VI' on one of the preliminary runs, passing Beeston Junction with an up Leeds express

marked contrast to the 'hit or miss' trials of 1948 were the fascinatingly precise results that he obtained with engine No 5098 *Clifford Castle* on the stationary test plant. It was often considered that measurement of coal consumption per dhp hr eliminated much of the variation in driving technique and effects of incidental delays, and reduced engine performance to a common yardstick by which direct comparison could be made between one locomotive and another. This was certainly not so, as clearly shown by the carefully controlled test results from

COMPARISONS WITH INTERCHANGE TRIALS

The equivalent values shown in column (3) are based on :

South Kirkby Hards, dry :		14,400 btu/lb	
Blidworth Hards, dry :		13,940 btu/lb	
Abergorki, dry :		15,100 btu/lb	

	Interchange trials South Kirkby coal (actual) (1)	Additional tests Abergorki coal (actual) (2)	Additional tests Abergorki coal (S. Kirkby equivalent) (3)	Decrease per cent Col 3 compared with Col 1 (4)
'King' Class (low superheat)				
Lb/train mile	48·82	42·28	44·33	9·2
Lb/train ton mile .	0·082	0·071	0·074	9·8
Lb/dhp/hr .	3·74	3·33	3·50	6·4
Lb/sq ft grate /hr (runn'g time) . .	67·5	59·6	62·6	7·3
'King' Class (high superheat)				
Lb/train mile		41·23	43·23	
Lb/train ton mile . .		0·070	0·074	
Lb/dhp/hr .		3·10	3·25	
Lb/sq ft grate /hr (runn'g time) . .		57·7	60·5	

Up Worcester express near Tilehurst : engine No 5090 'Neath Abbey'

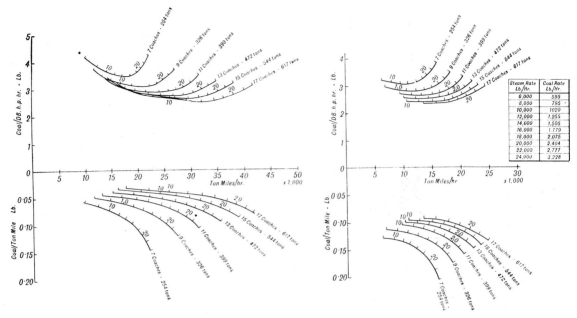

Steam Rate Lb./Hr.	Coal Rate Lb./Hr.
6,000	595
8,000	795
10,000	1,020
12,000	1,255
14,000	1,505
16,000	1,779
18,000	2,075
20,000	2,404
22,000	2,777
24,000	3,228

Performance of engine No 5098 'Clifford Castle'

one individual engine. In the graphs reproduced above the coal consumption figures are shown for running on level track and on a rising 1 in 200 gradient. From these graphs certain tables have been prepared. The first, relating to level track, shows the speed for the most economical use of fuel in a variety of loading conditions. From this table it will be seen that with a light load of 254 tons tare the most economical speed is 71 mph, whereas with a heavy load of 472 tons it is 58·5 mph. But then notice the difference in basic coal consumption: 3·5 against 2·8 lb per dhp hr on a 1 in 200 gradient. This would be below traffic needs, and a second table shows the results with the firing rate increased to 86 lb per sq ft of grate area per hr.

Another interesting study brought out from the graphs reproduced is the coal consumption involved in the haulage of various loads at a uniform speed

Up Cheltenham express near Twyford: engine No 5057 'Earl Waldegrave'

North to West express ascending Dainton Bank : engine No 5058 'Earl of Clancarty'

of 65 mph on level track.

It is also interesting to extract the details of performance that could be expected with those same five loads when No 5098 was steamed up to her maximum rate of evaporation, namely 24,000 lb of steam per hr.

From the above it would certainly seem that on a number of celebrated pre-war occasions 'Castles' were being steamed very near to their limit, on the Cornish Riviera Express, in days before the construction of the 'Kings', and on the 'Cheltenham Flyer'.

Engine 5098: LEVEL TRACK Firing rate 57 lb per sq ft of grate area per hour			
Load behind tender (tons tare)	Speed mph	Coal per dhp hour (lb)	Coal per train mile (lb)
254	71	3·5	25
326	64·5	3·17	27·5
399	60·5	2·95	29·5
472	58·5	2·8	30·25
544	55	2·7	32·5

Engine 5098: 65 mph ON LEVEL TRACK		
Load behind tender (tons tare)	Coal per dhp hour (lb)	Coal sq ft of grate area per hour (lb)
254	3·6	49·5
326	3·2	49·5
399	3·0	56
472	2·95	67
544	2·95	77

Engine 5098: RISING 1 in 200 GRADIENT Firing rate 86 lb per sq ft of grate area per hour			
Load behind tender (tons tare)	Speed mph	Coal per dhp hour (lb)	Coal per train mile (lb)
254	60	3·6	45
326	55	3·3	49
399	50	3·15	54
472	45	3·0	60
544	40	2·85	67·5

Engine 5098: 24,000 lb of steam per hour LEVEL TRACK			
Load behind tender (tons tare)	Speed mph	Coal per dhp hour (lb)	Coal per train mile (lb)
254	86·5	4·3	37·5
326	82	3·8	39·2
399	78·75	3·5	41·8
472	73·75	3·2	45·0
544	69·5	3·1	45·0

OCEAN MAIL SPECIALS: 1949
Engine: 5098 *Clifford Castle*

Date		26/8/49		13/9/49	
Load ton tare		303		338*	
Dist miles		Time min	Av sp mph	Time min	Av sp mph
0·0	Plymouth Dock Gates .	0		0	
0·9	North Road .	3	18·0	3	18·0
24·0	Totnes .	36	42·0	37	40·8
32·8	Newton Abbot .	49 (pass)	40·6	49 *arr*	43·8
				52 *dep*	
52·9	Exeter .	73	50·3	76½	49·3
83·7	Taunton .	104	59·6	110	55·2
111·2	Castle Cary .	129	66·0	134½	67·4
131·8	*Heywood Rd Jc*	153	51·4	154½	61·8
160·0	Bedwyn .	179	65·0	182	61·5
190·4	Reading .	208	62·9	209½	66·4
226·4	Paddington .	243†	61·7	247½	56·9

* Bank engine No 5060 Plymouth to Newton Abbot
† Net time 239 min

Reverting to engine No 5098 there was no doubt she was a star engine at that time and these details of test performance can be supplemented by some details of her work in regular service. In 1949 she was much in demand for 'Ocean Mail' specials from Plymouth, and on 26 August 1949 she made the first post-war run from North Road to Paddington in the even four hours. There was another very fast run just over a fortnight later, with a heavier train that required an assistant engine over the South Devon line. Mr Hawksworth was kind enough to give me copies of the inspectors' reports on these two journeys, and from the accompanying table it will be seen that the times were 170 min (167 min net) from Exeter to Paddington with 303 tons tare, and 171 min with 338 tons.

Only a few days after the second of these two runs I had the opportunity of riding this same engine myself on the 9.45 am West to North express throughout from Newton Abbot to Shrewsbury. I have set out the logs in full detail, but a summary of the running gave the following interesting results.

Some examples of actual working are interesting in view of the test performances recorded in the comprehensive series of Swindon trials.

1. Stoke Canon to Sampford Peverell: average speed 56·3 mph; cut-off 24 per cent full regulator.
2. Level track, Brent Knoll: 64 mph; cut-off 19 per cent full regulator.
3. Acceleration up Filton bank, 1 in 75 from dead start at Stapleton Road: 21 mph; cut-off 45 per cent full regulator.

Plymouth - Liverpool express leaving Teignmouth : engine No 7000 'Viscount Portal'

WESTERN REGION: 9.45 am NEWTON ABBOT—BRISTOL

Load: 13 coaches, 421 tons tare, 460 tons full
Engine: 4-cyl 4—6—0 No 5098 *Clifford Castle*
Driver: Nickless; Fireman: Williams (Salop shed)

Dist miles		Sch min	Actual m s	Speed mph
0.0	NEWTON ABBOT .	0	0 00	
1.0	*Milepost 213* .		3 06	
4.8	Teignmouth Old Quay		7 55	54 (max)
5.1	Teignmouth .	8	8 50	
0.0		0	0 00	
1.3	Parsons Tunnel Box .		2 54	
2.8	Dawlish . . .	6	5 39	
0.0		0	0 00	
1.7	Dawlish Warren .		3 21	43.5/48
3.7	Starcross .		5 53	45 (slack)
7.4	Exminster . .		10 04	59 (max)
11.3	St Thomas's . .		14 15	
12.2	EXETER ST DAVID'S .	18	16 15	
0.0		0	0 00	
1.3	Cowley Bridge Jc .		2 58	
3.4	Stoke Canon .		5 58	49.5
7.2	Silverton . .		10 17	56/54.5
8.4	Hele . .		11 33	57.5
12.6	Cullompton .		15 51	60
14.8	Tiverton Jc .		18 14	55/60.5
16.6	Sampford Peverell .		20 03	59.5
18.9	*Milepost 175* .		22 37	48.5
			sigs pw	
19.9	Whiteball Box .	26	24 50	
20.9	*Milepost 173* .		27 02	28
23.7	Wellington .		29 43	78
26.9	*Milepost 167* .		32 06	84
28.8	Norton Fitzwarren .		33 38	70.5
30.8	TAUNTON .	38	37 08	
0.0		0	0 00	
4.7	Cogload .		6 47	55.5
			pw slack	15
10.6	*Milepost 152* .		15 38	58
11.5	BRIDGWATER .	15	17 10	
0.0		0	0 00	
2.5	Dunball . .		4 37	50
6.3	HIGHBRIDGE .	9	8 33	60.5
9.1	Brent Knoll .		11 15	63
12.5	*Milepost 139* .		14 36	64.5
13.6	Uphill Jc .	17	16 05	
15.2	WESTON-SUPER-MARE	21	19 59	
0.0		0	0 00	
2.3	Worle Jc .	5	4 47	
7.1	YATTON .		10 51	58 (max)
13.2	Flax Bourton .		17 42	49 45.5
15.4	Long Ashton .		20 30	58 (max)
17.2	Parson Street .		22 48	
			sigs	
19.1	BRISTOL (TEMPLE MEADS)	26	27 45	

4. Llanvihangel bank, 1 in 95: speed 22 mph; cut-off 38 per cent full regulator.

The above data shows both the strength and the weakness of the 'Castle' engine particularly when it came to climbing a heavy bank.

WESTERN REGION: 12.34 pm BRISTOL—SHREWSBURY

Load: 13 coaches, 421 tons tare, 460 tons full
Engine: 4-cyl 4—6—0 No 5098 *Clifford Castle*
Driver: Nickless; Fireman: Williams (Salop shed)

Dist miles		Sch min	Actual m s	Speed mph
0.0	BRISTOL (TEMPLE MEADS)	0	0 00	
1.6	Stapleton Road .	6	5 12	
0.0		0	0 00	
0.9	Ashley Hill .		2 53	
2.1	Horfield . .		6 43	21
3.2	Filton Jc . .	8	9 33	slack
8.0	Pilning . .		15 47	67.5/61.5 66
14.1	Severn Tunnel West Box .	23½	22 54	
14.9	SEVERN TUNNEL JC .	26	25 11	21
20.9	Llanwern .		33 23	57
			pw slack	10
24.0	Maindee East Jc .	38	37 53	
26.4	Caerleon .		43 09	45
29.2	Llantarnam .		47 28	34.5
			pw slack	10
31.0	Pontynewydd .		53 18	26
33.4	*Milepost 32½* .		59 32	23
33.7	PONTYPOOL ROAD	56	60 55	
0.0		0	0 00	
1.6	Little Mill Jc .		2 42	59
4.2	Nantyderry .		5 29	51/56
6.8	Penpergwm .		8 29	60/46
9.5	Abergavenny .	12	12 23	
13.5	Llanvihangel .	22	23 00	17.5/22
15.9	Pandy . .		25 54	74 (max)
21.0	Pontrilas .	31	30 22	57 (min)
26.8	Tram Inn .		36 20	63
30.1	Red Hill Jc .	41	39 52	
33.5	HEREFORD .	47	45 15	
0.0		0	0 00	
1.7	Shelwick Jc .	4½	4 30	
4.2	Moreton-on-Lugg .		7 31	55.5 58
7.5	Dinmore .		11 02	46 (min)
10.2	Ford Bridge .		14 14	63
			pw slack	
12.6	LEOMINSTER .	16½	18 22	15
15.8	Berrington .		23 47	50
18.9	Woofferton .	23½	27 19	65
23.5	Ludlow .	29	32 00	53
25.7	Bromfield .		34 20	53.5
			sigs	40
28.1	Onibury .		37 10	43.5 36
31.1	CRAVEN ARMS .	38	41 33	49
34.0	*Milepost 17* .		45 29	41
35.6	Marsh Brook .		47 47	42.5
36.7	*Milepost 14½* .		49 27	38.5
			pw slack	15
38.2	CHURCH STRETTON .	49	52 40	
			sig checks	
51.0	SHREWSBURY .	71	73 52	

Some of the starts from the many intermediate stops showed off to remarkable effect the surefootedness of Great Western 4—6—0 locomotives; from Teignmouth, in heavy rain, we passed Parsons

Tunnel Box, 1·3 miles in 2 min 54 sec, and the working was thus:

Start		75 per cent cut-off
In 150 yd	45	,,
In ½ mile	35	,,
In 0·9 mile	25	,,

During this start there was no suspicion of slipping. Another factor that must be taken into account in assessing this interesting performance was the extremely 'intermittent' character of the demands

Engine 5098: NEWTON ABBOT—SHREWSBURY	
Length of journey	216·5 miles
Booked time, including stop . .	367 min
Left Newton Abbot . . .	3 min late
Arrived Shrewsbury . . .	6½ min late
Actual time including stops . .	370½ min
Booked running time . . .	312 min
Actual running time . . .	319 min
Net running time . . .	295 min
Net average speed	44 mph
Water consumption	38 gall per mile
Coal consumption (estimated) .	40-42 lb per mile
Coal per sq ft of grate area per hour of running time .	56 lb
Max estimated dhp at 61 mph .	1,450

upon the locomotive. From Taunton to Pontypool Road, for example, we covered only 81·1 miles in 154 min and during that time the regulator was open for only 100 min. That our average coal consumption was only 40-42 lb per mile in working a 460-ton train in these circumstances was a remarkable tribute to the efficiency of the locomotive. Of course I could quickly sense, from my footplate experience, that *Clifford Castle* was quite a 'star' engine, and her working was impeccable throughout; but even with this reservation the run, following up the test details previously recorded, is a great tribute to the latest version of the 'Castle' class. With the hydrostatic lubricator she was very free running, as instanced by the maximum speed of 84 mph down Wellington bank and the rapid acceleration from Llanvihangel summit to 74 mph before Pandy. At the same time one notes, with significance, the rather laboured ascent from Abergavenny to Llanvihangel.

The tests in which engine No 5098 was pitted against the 'standard' engine No 5087, and the first 'Castle' to be fitted with a 4-row superheater, No

Paignton - Manchester express on Teignmouth sea wall : engine No 4000 'North Star'

5.55 pm Paddington - South Wales express near Cholsey : engine No 5049
'Earl of Plymouth' with the author on the footplate

5049 *Earl of Plymouth* paved the way for the full-scale testing carried out later under the auspices of the British Railways Board. The alteration of No 5049 did not materially improve the performance. The heating surface of the superheater was increased to 393 sq ft, and the final steam temperature was raised to about 660 deg F. I was able to make a round trip from Swindon to Paddington and back on this engine, and these gave the following results:

Engine 5049: SWINDON—PADDINGTON		
Train . . .	2.11 pm up	5.55 pm down
Distance . . .	77·3 miles	77·3 miles
Gradient (average) .	1 in 1,510 (falling)	1 in 1,510 (rising)
Booked time .	89 min	87 min
Load tons tare .	400	439
Load tons gross .	430	470
Actual time . .	86 min 42 sec	88 min 50 sec
Checks (number) .	ONE	ONE
Net time . .	$83\frac{1}{2}$ min	$86\frac{3}{4}$ min
Net average speed .	55·7 mph	53·5 mph
Maximum speed .	65 mph	62 mph
Water consumed (tender gauge) .	1,650 gall	2,300 gall
Water per train/mile .	21·3 gall	29·7 gall

It will be seen that the booked speeds of the two trains were in inverse ratio to the loads and haulage effort involved, though on the down journey in making a running average of 58 mph over the 55·7 miles from Slough to Marston East Box the cut-off

was not advanced beyond 17 per cent and the regulator was kept about 3/5ths open on the main valve. It will be noticed also how closely the speed corresponded with the most economical working rate for this weight of train as given in the table on page 65. If the performance of No 5049 can be considered similar to that of the 'King' class engine with a 4-row superheater, and an evaporation of about $8\frac{3}{4}$ lb of water per lb of coal taken as typical, the coal consumption on this round trip of mine can be taken as $24\frac{1}{2}$ lb per train mile on the 2.11 pm up, and 34 lb per mile on the 5.55 pm down. Nevertheless, the performance of No 5049 did not justify any further conversions at that time, and the engine merely remained as one of the 'star' performers at Canton (Cardiff) shed.

Arising from the methods used in carrying out the tests, and the comprehensive nature of the performance data secured and collated, their practical application was demonstrated in what was then termed 'scientific train timing', and a supplement to the report on the trials with engine No 5098 showed the results of such timing applied to non-stop running between Newport and Paddington in various conditions of loading. Bearing in mind that any 'scientifically' prepared schedules must serve day-to-day conditions, an explanation of the 'basic' and 'recovery' classes of duty must be noted. The

'5098' CLASS
TIME SCHEDULES: NEWPORT—PADDINGTON
Load: 11 cars, 363 tons tare, 400 tons full

Duty	Basic	Recovery	High
Steam rate lb/hr under power*	16,000	18,000	20,000
Coal rate lb/hr under power*	1,779	2,075	2,404

Dist miles		Time min	Time min	Time min
0·0	NEWPORT	0	0	0
9·8	Severn Tunnel Jc	13½	13	12¾
10·6	Severn Tunnel West	15	14½	14¼
20·3	Patchway	32½	31	29¾
21·4	Stoke Gifford	34½	33	31½
33·4	Badminton	50½	47¾	45¼
50·5	Wootton Bassett	66¾	63¼	60
56·1	Swindon	73	69¼	65½
76·9	Steventon	91¾	87	82¼
80·3	Didcot	94½	89¾	84¾
97·4	Reading	109¾	104	98½
102·4	Twyford	114½	108½	102¾
109·2	Maidenhead	120¾	114½	108½
114·9	Slough	126	119½	113¼
124·3	Southall	135	127¾	121
132·1	Westbourne Park	142¼	134¾	127¾
133·4	PADDINGTON	146¼	138½	131½

Max speed at Little Somerford	mph	77·0	81·0	83·0
Average speed Swindon-Southall	mph	66·0	70·0	73·8

* Time under power taken as 97 per cent total running time

'5098' CLASS
TIME SCHEDULES: NEWPORT—PADDINGTON
Load: 13 cars, 429 tons tare, 470 tons full

Duty	Basic	Recovery	High
Steam rate lb/hr under power*	16,000	18,000	20,000
Coal rate lb/hr under power*	1,779	2,075	2,404

Dist miles		Time min	Time min	Time min
0·0	NEWPORT	0	0	0
9·8	Severn Tunnel Jc	13¾	13½	13
10·6	Severn Tunnel West	15¼	15	14½
20·3	Patchway	34¾	33½	31½
21·4	Stoke Gifford	37	35½	33½
33·4	Badminton	54½	51½	48½
50·5	Wootton Bassett	71	67¼	63½
56·1	Swindon	77¾	73¾	69½
76·9	Steventon	97¼	92¼	87
80·3	Didcot	100	95	89½
97·4	Reading	116½	110¼	103¾
102·4	Twyford	121½	115	108
109·2	Maidenhead	128¼	121¼	113¾
114·9	Slough	133¾	126½	118½
124·3	Southall	143¼	135½	126¾
132·1	Westbourne Park	150¾	142¾	133½
133·4	PADDINGTON	154	146½	137¼

Max speed at Little Somerford	mph	75·0	77·0	82·5
Average speed Swindon-Southall	mph	62·5	66·2	71·4

* Time under power taken as 97 per cent total running time

North to West express near Penpergwm: engine No 5073 'Blenheim'

'basic' is the rate which shows the greatest economy in working, and which is two-thirds of the practical maximum continuous steaming rate of the engine. It was then considered that all locomotives of the class which were fit for the road should have been able to recover time to the extent shown by the difference between the 'basic' and 'recovery' duty. Thus on the Newport—Paddington run a 'Castle' worked at 18,000 lb per sq in should have been able to make up roughly 8 min on the basic non-stop timing of the 146 min with a 400-ton load. Engines in good condition, working to 5/6ths of the maximum steaming capacity could make a non-stop run in 131½ min. The schedules are set out herewith, for both 400- and 470-ton trains, and it is the average speeds from Swindon that make such interesting reading. Average speeds of 73·8 mph are striking examples of the expectancy of performance in high steaming conditions, and will be referred to later in this book in connection with the accelerated services of 1954.

CHAPTER 18

NATIONALISATION UNDER WAY

MR Hawksworth remained in office at Swindon for the first two years of nationalisation, but on his retirement at the end of 1949 the organisation was completely changed, in accordance with the precepts being applied to British Railways as a whole. Instead of the one supreme head of the locomotive department the organisation was split into three, with a mechanical and electrical engineer, a carriage and wagon engineer, and a motive power superintendent. At first K. J. Cook, H. Randle and W. N. Pellow filled these offices. There had been much gratification among Great Western enthusiasts at the continuance of 'Castle' building after nationalisation; but until new standard designs were ready there was really no other course, in

providing replacements for superannuated express passenger engines, unless of course British Railways had wanted really to set the heather on fire around Swindon by planting pre-grouping engines of alien design upon the Western Region. In authorising the construction of more 'Castles', and also 'Halls' and 'Manors' high authority left Swindon to its own devices to the extent of permitting the continued use of the Great Western style of numberplate on the cab side, though on the engine front the painted figures on the buffer beam were replaced by cast numberplates on the smokebox door, in the Midland and LMS style. It so happened, however, when working express trains that were carrying their reporting numbers the large

Falmouth - Paddington express passing Teignmouth : engine No 4081 'Warwick Castle'

Engine No 6028 'King George VI' in bright blue livery, at Bath

plates mounted on the smokebox door hid the engine number, and with its removal from the buffer beam the engines of these trains looked anonymous from the front.

There was also the vexed question of painting. Very soon after nationalisation Lord Hurcombe asked R. A. Riddles what colour he was going to paint the BR engines. As a good North Western man Riddles replied 'black'. The noble lord was horrified, and so there began the series of experiments with different colours. Some of the 'Kings', in common with engines of other regions in the '8P' power classification, were painted in Prussian blue with red lining—reminiscent of the Great Eastern; while some of the 'Castles' appeared in a pale green. This latter was set off by a lining out scheme in the LNWR style, and looked positively bilious! At first the basic idea was to have something different from anything that had gone before. Riddles tried to get his black by having one of the LMS 'Princess Royal' Pacifics magnificently turned out in the full LNWR style, but the first decision was that the '8P' engines should be in Caledonian blue, though with black underframes. On the 'Kings', retaining their polished brass safety valve covers and copper chimney tops, the famous blue

looked a thorough misfit. Sir Felix Pole, who by that time was quite blind, said he was glad to be spared of the sight of a 'King' in blue! But to the delight of all Western supporters the historic Brunswick green of the GWR was chosen for the second-line express passenger engines, though with just enough variation in the lining out for it to be said that it was *not* Great Western. After a relatively short time the 'Kings' also reverted to Brunswick green—and so did the 'Pacifics' of the other regions.

The 1948 batch of 'Castles', Nos 7008 to 7017, in addition to having the straight-sided tender, included one non-Castle name that gave great satisfaction, No 7017 *G. J. Churchward*. In a book like this I need not enlarge upon the appropriateness of such a name. Engine No 7013 *Bristol Castle* became the object of some controversy in February 1952. In that month King George VI died, and it was desired to use the engine *Windsor Castle* for the Royal funeral train. Unfortunately the historic 4082 was not at that time in a suitable condition for so important a duty, and so the name and numberplates were transferred to No 7013, together with the commemorative plaques relating to the Royal visit to Swindon in 1924 when King George V drove the engine from the works to the station. It

Engine No 7011 'Banbury Castle' in experimental pale green livery

Up South Wales express near Llanharan : engine No 5027 'Farleigh Castle'

was, of course, immediately noticed that the engine hauling the funeral train of King George VI was not the real 4082, but an engine belonging to the '7000' series, and the management of the Western Region had some awkward moments explaining what they had done! To them, no doubt, one 'Castle' was as good as another; but it needed no more than a schoolboy spotter, let alone an adult locomotive enthusiast to note the deception. The name and number remained on the real 7013 until that engine was withdrawn in February 1965, but the commemorative plaques were removed a little time after the special Royal Train working. The real 4082, as 7013, survived almost as long, and was not with-

Engine No 7017 'G. J. Churchward' showing the earlier WR tender style

*The last 'Castle' built, No 7037, prior to the naming ceremony on 15 November 1950
by HM the Queen, when Princess Elizabeth*

drawn until September 1964, after a life of forty years.

The 1949 batch, 7018 to 7027, all had true 'Castle' names, and all retained their bestowed names during their comparatively short lives. The last lot, 7028 to 7037, came out in May-August 1950, and the last one of all was the subject of a special naming ceremony on 15 November 1950. Until that day the engine ran without a name. On that day Queen Elizabeth II, when Princess Elizabeth, paid a visit to Swindon Works on the occasion of the golden jubilee of the borough of Swindon, and Her Royal Highness not only performed the naming ceremony of engine No 7037 *Swindon*, but also followed the precedent set by her grandfather,

in 1924, by driving a locomotive from the works to the station. This latter engine was appropriately No 4057 *Princess Elizabeth*. 'Stars' were getting a little scarce by that time, but with the exception of No 4051 all the 'Princesses' were still running. At the time it was thought that No 4057 would probably be among the last to go, though in actual fact it was her last overhaul and she was withdrawn in February 1952.

Mention of No 4057 brings me back to the 'Stars' in general, and the story of their last twenty-odd years must now be recorded. Although the changes were no more than superficial their appearance altered considerably. Many engines of the class acquired 4,000-gallon high-sided tenders. In 1936

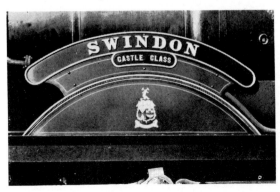

Engine No 7037

Engine No 4073

for a short time the old eight-wheeled bogie tender built for *The Great Bear* ran attached first to No 4045 and then to No 4022, while shortly after World War II No 4043 had the experimental eight-wheeled Collett tender which had been built in 1931. Then there was a change in chimneys. The chimney originally put on to the 'Grange' class was also used on 'Stars' from 1939 onwards. This was 1 ft 9 in high, as compared with the true 'Star' chimney which was 1 ft 11¾ in. The 'Grange' chimney looked much better in combination with the shorter variety of safety-valve cover which was coming into general use; but what with shorter chimneys, outside steam pipes and 4,000-gallon tenders, the 'Stars' began to look like 'Castles'. The distinguishing feature remaining was, of course, the cab.

During the war the 'Stars' were painted plain black, while the original 'King' series, renamed 'Monarchs' in 1927, were the victims of the changing pattern of the war itself. In 1940 seven of the original ten engines remained, and they bore names as follows:

4021	*British Monarch*	
4022	*Belgian Monarch*	(5/40)
4023	*Danish Monarch*	(11/40)
4025	*Italian Monarch*	(6/40)
4026	*Japanese Monarch*	(1/41)
4028	*Roumanian Monarch*	(11/40)
4030	*Swedish Monarch*	(11/40)

The figures in brackets indicate when these names were removed, and from these dates one can identify events connected with the war. Eventually only No 4021 retained a name. The others spent their last ten to twelve years nameless, with the legend 'Star Class' painted in small letters on their central splasher. After the war the remaining 'Stars' were eventually repainted in the lined green used on the Castles', 'Counties', and later on the 'Halls' as well.

Engine No 7007

A total of forty-seven 'Stars' remained to enter national ownership in January 1948, though eight engines of the class were withdrawn sufficiently early after that date as not to receive smokebox numberplates. Engine No 4004 *Morning Star* was the only one to be withdrawn in 1948, only the second of the class since September 1940, when No 4067 *Tintern Abbey* had been converted to 'Castle' class and renumbered 5087. The only post-war withdrawal in Great Western days was No 4014 *Knight of the Bath* in 1946. Three more, all 'Knights', were all that the year 1949 claimed; but more general withdrawal began in 1950, with seven scrapped in that year, and sixteen in 1951.

In 1950 the allocation of the class was:

Bristol (Bath Road)	9
Gloucester	1
Laira (Plymouth)	1
Landore (Swansea)	5
Oxford	1
Shrewsbury	5
Stafford Road (Wolverhampton)	6
Swindon	6
Westbury	3

By that time 'Stars' were rarely to be seen on first-

The last 'Castle' built: No 7037 'Swindon', carrying the arms of the borough

Engine No 4042 'Prince Albert' as running with 'elbow' steampipes in 1949

class express work, though in the immediate post-war period, before there were many of the new 'Castles' at work, certain engines which were in first-class condition were put on to some important turns. A case in point was the Stafford Road engine No 4031 *Queen Mary*, which for several weeks in 1946 worked the Wolverhampton-Penzance express, when it was restored after the war, as between Wolverhampton and Newton Abbot. The engine worked through, but was re-manned in each direction at Bristol. The Bath Road engines were perhaps the exception to the general rule, and in those post-war years were frequently on the London expresses. In the autumn of 1949 I made the round trip from Bristol to Paddington and back on the footplate of No 4042 *Prince Albert* with the impressive results to be described later; but in those years of austerity one of the finest and most unexpected of all my journeys with 'Stars' came one Friday evening in the summer of 1947 when I was

bound for Cardiff and joined the 5.55 pm from Paddington at Swindon. This was usually a 'Castle' turn, worked moreover by engines in the immaculate condition then characteristic of the Canton top-link; but on this occasion an enormous train of fourteen coaches, absolutely packed and weighing at least 510 tons behind the tender, arrived from Paddington behind No 4030 looking very shabby and dilapidated.

I feared the worst, although the train arrived very little behind time; and then the driver proceeded to coax a marvellous performance out of this old 'crab'. The 5·6 miles to Wootton Bassett, where speed was reduced for the junction, took 9 min 37 sec, and then, after touching 67 mph at Little Somerford, the $8\frac{1}{2}$ miles of continuous 1 in 300 to Badminton were climbed at a minimum speed of 48 mph before the stop. Over the last four miles speed averaged 52, 50·5, 49·5 and 49 mph respectively. The 22·7 miles from Swindon took 28 min 45

9 am Bristol - Paddington express : engine No 4091 'Dudley Castle'

Liverpool - Plymouth express near Dawlish : engine No 5078 'Beaufort'

The up 'Dutchman', 8.30 am Plymouth to Paddington, passing Teignmouth :
engine No 6024 'King Edward I'

sec. Speed rose to 67 mph again down the descent from Badminton, but with such a load the driver was not risking an unassisted climb out of the Severn Tunnel and we stopped at Pilning Junction to take a bank engine. The run finished with a smart spurt on the level from Newton to Cardiff, 11·7 miles in 16¼ min start-to-stop. The edhp on the Badminton ascent was about 1,100—very good indeed for an obviously run-down 'Star'.

Reverting to the gradual demise of the class, by the end of 1951 there were no engines of the 'Star' and 'Knight' series left in traffic, though fortunately No 4003 *Lode Star* had by that time been scheduled for preservation. The year 1952 saw another twelve of them withdrawn, and by the end of 1954 there were only three left: the two unrebuilt 'Abbeys' 4061 *Glastonbury Abbey* and 4062 *Malmesbury Abbey*, and No 4056 *Princess Margaret*. These three engines led a remarkably active life in their last year, and in the following chapter there are details of some splendid runs I was able to make on their footplates. *Princess Margaret* in particular was a great favourite among the enginemen at Bath Road; in fact one driver once remarked to me: 'She's the best "Castle" we've got!' She was so good that I tried to persuade High Authority to put her on the up 'Bristolian', but it would not be risked. Eventually, as the last working 'Star', she was withdrawn in October 1957, and with her ended one of the greatest locomotive sagas in history. She was not the longest lived of them all, despite her 43 years and 3 months; *Lode Star* and *Rising Star*, each with 44 years 5 months held the record, while *Knight of the Grand Cross* and the original 'Kings' *Edward* and *George* each just topped 43 years. Engine No 4021, the first of the two last mentioned, held the record for mileage covered, 2,035,000, a notable achievement.

CHAPTER 19

LAST WORK OF THE 'STARS'

IN the years 1949 to 1956 I had eight unforgettable footplate runs, and although the engines concerned were allocated to enable me to study their workings no special preparations were otherwise made. The engines were working in the links concerned; it was just that the locomotive authorities were kind enough to see that they were on the jobs selected on the days I had my footplate passes. In this way I rode *Prince Albert* on the 9 am Bristol to Paddington, returning with the 1.15 pm; *Princess Charlotte* on the 7.15 am Plymouth to Paddington; *Malmesbury Abbey* on the up 'Merchant Venturer', returning with the down West of England 'Postal' special; and finally *Princess Margaret* on various turns from Bristol, to Paddington and to Newton Abbot.

It was as long ago as 1949 that I imagined I was making my last footplate journey on a 'Star' engine. No 4042 *Prince Albert* was then newly out-shopped from Swindon, and allocated to Bath Road shed, Bristol, she was doing some fine work. It was arranged for me to ride her on the morning round trip from Bristol to Paddington and back. The return working on the 1.15 pm down was then quite a hard turn with a train of 350 to 400 tons, and allowed 114 min for the 106·9 miles non-stop from Paddington to Bath. It was this latter run that provided the principal source of interest, because the up run, though also made non-stop from Bath, was allowed 5 min more. The engine was as near-perfect as one could expect a steam locomotive to be, and

Last duties : engine No 4038 'Queen Berengaria' on Westbury - Swindon stopping train near Chippenham

on the eastbound run we made the journey in 118 min 26 sec with a load of 430 tons. This included a bad signal delay at Reading, and the net average speed was 57 mph. Details of the down journey are set out in the accompanying table, and although a load of ten coaches weighing 365 tons gross behind the tender would not be considered a heavy load for a 'Star', in the circumstances that developed it was substantial enough.

We got a bad start out of Paddington, with signals causing a slowing to 10 mph at Old Oak East, and a permanent way check at West Drayton. From there onwards, however, we got an absolutely clear road to Bathampton. As will be seen from the log the combined effect of the two initial checks was to put us 5 min late through Slough. Just beyond that station the driver used 18 per cent cut-off for a while, with full regulator; but this did not give the speed required and a mile beyond Maidenhead he advanced to 20 per cent. From this change the controls remained completely unchanged for 50 miles. I cannot recollect ever having seen running conditions on a steam locomotive remain constant for so long. The boiler pressure was maintained between 210 and 225 lb per sq in, though I must add these were the extremes; the more usual variation was between 215 and 220 lb per sq in. This steady and excellent working was gradually regaining lost time, and we passed Swindon only 1 min late.

Then the steaming was eased. Cut-off was reduced to 15 per cent just after Swindon, and at Hay Lane, adjacent to the 80th milepost and the summit of the line, the driver changed over to the first valve of the regulator. This gave us a splendid concluding spurt, with a top speed of 82 mph at Dauntsey. The finish was hindered by signal checks, though we were able to stop in Bath just short of the public arrival time of 3.10 pm. The net time,

WESTERN REGION:
1.15 pm PADDINGTON—BRISTOL
Load: 10 coaches, 340 tons tare, 365 tons full
Engine: 4-cyl 4—6—0 No 4042 *Prince Albert*
Driver: Clark; Fireman: Bishop (Bristol Bath Road shed)

Dist miles		Sch min	Actual m s	Speed mph
0.0	PADDINGTON .	0	0 00	
1.3	Westbourne Park .		3 10	
			sigs	10
5.7	Ealing Broadway .		10 37	50
9.1	Southall . .	12½	14 27	54.5
10.9	Hayes . . .		16 28	57.5
			pw slack	
13.2	West Drayton .		20 20	10
16.2	Langley . .		24 25	55
18.5	SLOUGH . .	22	27 07	59
21.0	Burnham (Bucks) .		29 36	61
24.2	Maidenhead . .	28	32 55	58.5
31.0	Twyford . .	35	39 45	62
36.0	READING . .	40	44 27	66
38.7	Tilehurst .		46 53	65
44.8	Goring . . .		52 32	64.5
48.5	Cholsey . .		55 57	66
53.1	DIDCOT . .	58	60 13	66
56.5	Steventon . .	61½	63 25	63
60.4	Wantage Road .		67 09	62
66.5	Uffington . .		73 13	60
71.6	Shrivenham . .		78 17	61.5
77.3	SWINDON . .	83	83 56	62
82.9	Wootton Bassett .		89 10	68
85.3	Incline Box .		91 15	70.5
87.7	Dauntsey .		93 12	82
91.0	*Milepost 91* .		95 45	76
94.0	CHIPPENHAM .	100	98 19	67
98.3	Corsham . .		102 33	58.5
101.9	Box . . .		105 54	71.5
			sigs	
104.6	Bathampton . .		108 25	
			sig stop	
106.9	BATH . .	114	114 43	
1.0	Oldfield Park .		2 27	
4.5	Saltford . .		6 51	53.5
6.9	Keynsham . .		9 27	61
9.8	St Anne's Park .		12 36	
			sigs	
11.4	BRISTOL . .	18	17 10	

however, was no more than 106½ min, and I was most interested to see that our point-to-point time of 53 min 52 sec for the 58 miles from Reading to Chippenham was a shade faster than the sectional timing of this train in 1939, when the schedule was 102 min from Paddington to Bath, with a load generally much under 300 tons. The water consumption was 31 gallons to the mile, with a coal consumption of about 35 lb per train mile. The average consumption of the complete round from Bristol to Paddington and back was only 31 gallons of water per mile, and this was enough to give us net average speeds between Paddington and Bath of 57.2 mph going up, with 430 tons, and of 60.2 mph on the return, with 365 tons. This was indeed an excellent all-round performance.

In 1950 engine No 4054 *Princess Charlotte* was

Engine No 4062 'Malmesbury Abbey', with straight-sided tender temporarily attached

stationed at Laira. She was newly overhauled and was in spanking condition. She was frequently used on the 7.15 am from Plymouth to Paddington, and on one of these occasions I rode on the footplate. While I was unfortunate with the weather, which was very wet and miserable, I was very fortunate in my driver and fireman. Fred Gould was one of those born enginemen who never wasted a pound of steam, while Eric Warr was one of those enthusiastic souls who was prepared to shovel his heart out if necessary, but had also the innate sense of enginemanship that enabled him to match his efforts to his driver. Between them they treated me to a performance that was astonishing in its economy in fuel. The engine was in perfect mechanical condition, and with a load of 345 tons we could have made some quite record running; but there was no need, and there was nothing of the exhibitionist about Fred Gould. The only spell of any length where the engine was worked at all hard was on the rise to Whiteball, and then only in 20 per cent cut-off, increased to 25 on the final pitch past Burlescombe.

After Taunton the engine was worked in 15 per cent cut-off the whole way to Paddington, except for a brief increase on the later stretches of the Bruton bank. Even with this there were lengthy stretches where the regulator was very far from fully opened. As will be seen from the log we were keeping very closely to our booked point-to-point times. The signal checks descending the Kennet Valley were not severe and did not affect our running times by more than about $1\frac{1}{4}$ min. We had a comfortable minute in hand at Reading, and with easy running and observance of the slight speed restriction then in force through Slough we were $2\frac{1}{2}$ min early at Southall. We did not need the lavish amount of recovery time then provided on the last stretch and so stopped in Paddington $6\frac{3}{4}$ min early. There was nothing spectacular about this fine run except the coal and water consumption. A careful check on the tender gauge indicated a usage of about 24 gallons per mile, the coal consumption was about 27 lb per mile—a perfect exposition of a Churchward locomotive at its finest.

In the 1950s those of us with an eye to the older locomotives of the Great Western stud were constantly delighted as successive engines of the 'Star' class were given 'heavy-general' overhauls at Swindon, and came out glittering as if brand new. Such apparitions were certainly growing fewer, but those that did emerge could certainly show a good deal of their finest form. By the year 1952 I felt that the time had probably come to make a 'last journey' on a 'Star', and one summer evening Authority kindly put No 4062 *Malmesbury Abbey* on to the Bristol evening round trip to Paddington and back. Going

7.15 am Plymouth - Paddington express in Sonning Cutting : engine No 4054
'Princess Charlotte'

8.54 am EXETER—PADDINGTON
Load: 10 cars, 324 tons tare, 345 tons full
Engine: 4054 *Princess Charlotte*
Driver: F. Gould; Fireman: E. Warr (Old Oak)

Dist miles		Sch min	Actual m s	Speed mph
0·0	EXETER . .	0	0 00	—
3·5	Stoke Canon . .		7 07	43·5
7·2	Silverton . .		11 30	53
12·6	Cullompton . .		17 17	60
14·8	Tiverton Jc . .		19 47	51/58
19·9	*Whiteball Box* .	25	25 37	44·5
23·7	Wellington . .		29 11	75
30·8	TAUNTON . .	38	36 37	
2·4	*Creech Jc* . .	4	4 38	47·5
8·0	Athelney . .		10 47	60·5
11·9	*Curry Rivel Jc* .		14 50	60
17·2	Somerton . .		20 42	50
25·5	Alford . .		28 44	69
27·6	CASTLE CARY .	30	30 44	60·5
31·0	Bruton . .		34 24	50·5
34·4	*Milepost 122¾* .		39 05	34
40·4	*Blatchbridge Jc* .	45	45 33	67·5
42·4	*Clink Road Jc* .	47½	47 29	57
45·7	*Fairwood Jc* .	51	50 39	65·5
48·1	*Heywood Road Jc* .	54	53 14	eased
55·8	Lavington . .		61 29	60·5
61·6	Patney . .	69	68 13	48·5
67·4	Pewsey . .		74 13	61·5
72·6	Savernake . .	81	80 04	53·5
76·3	Bedwyn . .	85	83 54	61·5
84·2	Kintbury . .		91 29	66
			sigs	40
89·6	NEWBURY . .	98	97 07	
97·9	Aldermaston . .		105 30	67
			sigs	
106·7	READING . .	116	114 51	
111·7	Twyford . .	122	121 01	60
118·5	Maidenhead . .	129	127 32	66
124·2	SLOUGH . .	135	133 04	60*
129·5	West Drayton .		138 10	64
133·6	Southall . .	145	142 27	57
137·0	Ealing Broadway .		145 42	64
142·7	PADDINGTON .	160	153 12	

Net time: : Taunton—Paddington 152 min
Estimated coal consumption 27 lb per mile
* Speed restriction

5.25 pm BRISTOL—PADDINGTON
'The Merchant Venturer'
Load: 9 cars, 294 tons tare, 315 tons full
Engine: 4062 *Malmesbury Abbey*
Driver: W. Hares; Fireman: D. Howlett (Bristol)

Dist miles		Sch min	Actual m s	Speed mph
0·0	TEMPLE MEADS	0	0 00	
1·7	St Annes Park . .		4 20	48
			pws	40
4·6	Keynsham . .		8 12	55 (max)
11·5	BATH . .	17	16 40	
2·3	Bathampton . .		4 16	50
5·0	Box . .		7 12	63
8·6	Corsham . .		11 16	46·5
11·9	*Milepost 95* . .		14 36	65
12·9	CHIPPENHAM .	19	16 07	
3·0	*Milepost 91* . .		4 49	55·5
6·3	Dauntsey . .		8 19	58
			sigs	15
11·1	Wootton Bassett .		15 15	
			sigs	
16·7	SWINDON . .	24	23 05	
5·8	Shrivenham . .		8 04	64·5
10·8	Uffington . .		12 37	72
			pws	47
				60
16·9	Wantage Road .		19 02	
			pws	15
21·8	Steventon . .	25	25 30	55·5
24·2	DIDCOT . .	28½	28 51	64·5
28·8	Cholsey . .		33 07	66
38·6	Tilehurst . .		42 05	69
			sigs	
41·3	READING . .	46	45 40	
3·0	*Milepost 33* . .		5 17	55
			pws	40
5·0	Twyford . .	8	7 36	
11·8	Maidenhead . .	15	14 05	68
15·0	Burnham . .		17 24	71
17·5	SLOUGH . .	21	19 46	56*
22·8	West Drayton . .		25 01	64·5
26·9	Southall . .	30	29 32	60*
30·3	Ealing Broadway .		32 18	70·5
34·7	Westbourne Park .	39	36 18	
36·0	PADDINGTON .	45	39 05	

* Speed restrictions

up on the 'Merchant Venturer' the load was not so heavy as I could have wished for; but there were several permanent way slacks in operation and there were still restrictions to full speed running at both Slough and Southall. Again I was fortunate in having another splendid pair of enginemen in W. Hares and D. Howlett of Bath Road shed, Bristol.

In making a number of footplate runs on up expresses from Bristol I have always found it traditional to take things very easily to Bath, while the fire is still a bit 'green'; but having got the boiler conditions nicely settled down Hares made a thrilling run to Chippenham. Less than a mile from the start the cut-off was fixed at 25 per cent, and there it stayed till we emerged from Box Tunnel. The result was a rapid acceleration to 63 mph at

Box, and a climb through the tunnel, with its awkward 2 miles at 1 in 100, without speed falling below 46½ mph. Cut-off was reduced to 15 per cent at Corsham, and we made a very smart run into Chippenham. On restarting, the cut-offs were 25 per cent after one mile, and 15 per cent in another mile, which produced a rapid acceleration to 55·5 mph at the crossing of the River Avon, at Milepost 91.

From Swindon onwards 15 per cent was the normal running position, and Driver Hares used longer cut-offs only for brief moments in accelerating from checks. With so good an engine, and a load of no more than 315 tons behind the tender we naturally had things very comfortably in hand all the way. As on my run with No 4054 we gained substantially

*The up Merchant Venturer near Thingley Junction : engine No 4062 'Malmesbury Abbey',
with the author on the footplate*

on time in the final approach to Paddington, and arrived 6 min early. With the numerous intermediate stops, and various out-of-course slowings, there was not the same opportunity for continuous highly economical steaming as with No 4054. On this up journey from Bristol to Paddington the water consumption averaged 31 gallons per mile, and the coal about 36 !b per mile. This was good enough, but on the return journey I was to see the working of this splendid engine in a still more favourable light. As usual she took the West of England 'Postal', and I recall with amusement the slight air of suspicion with which police and postal officials scrutinised my footplate pass and allowed me to enter the platform!

This time we had a heavier load, while a succession of checks gave us a late start of 5½ min from Reading. This provided our driver and fireman the opportunity to give an immaculate display of 'Star' performance. In getting away the cut-off was reduced to 25 per cent in one mile, and to 15 per cent at Pangbourne. After that Hares drove entirely on the regulator. From Pangbourne successive readings of boiler pressure gave 220, 218, 220, 215, 220, 215, after which I stopped taking notes of what was absolutely rock-steady steaming. The reserve capacity of the engine was shown when the regulator was opened a little wider near Uffington, and the speed which had dropped to 59 mph on the long gradual rise quickly picked up to 63 mph before Shrivenham. The downhill dash after Wootton Bassett, with its maximum speed of 82 mph on Dauntsey

bank, was made on the easiest of steaming, and with quite a quiet finish we reached Bath a minute early. The water consumption on the trip showed an average of 26 gallons per mile between Paddington and Bath, and the coal consumption was about

10.10 pm PADDINGTON—BATH West of England Postal Special Load: 11 vans, 312 tons tare, 345 tons full Engine: 4062 *Malmesbury Abbey* Driver: W. Hares; Fireman: D. Howlett (Bristol)				
Dist miles		Sch min	Actual m s	Speed mph
0·0	PADDINGTON .	0	0 00	
			sigs	
1·3	Westbourne Park .	3	4 08	
5·7	Ealing Broadway .		10 28	53
9·1	Southall .	12½	14 07	57
18·5	SLOUGH .	22	23 23	66
24·2	Maidenhead .	28	28 50	62
			pw sigs	
36·0	READING .	41	45 30	
5·5	Pangbourne .		8 05	61
12·5	Cholsey .		14 32	66
17·1	DIDCOT .	20	18 47	65
20·5	Steventon .	23½	21 51	66
24·4	Wantage Road .		25 30	64
27·9	Challow .		28 58	60
30·5	Uffington .		31 36	59
35·5	Shrivenham .		36 36	63
41·3	SWINDON .	45	42 15	61
46·9	Wootton Bassett .		47 31	68
51·7	Dauntsey .		51 30	82
58·0	CHIPPENHAM .	62	56 32	68
62·3	Corsham .		60 37	60
65·9	Box .		63 48	76
68·6	Bathampton .		66 14	
70·9	BATH .	76	69 37	

224

8.30 am Bristol - Paddington express at Langley Crossing, Chippenham : engine No 4056
'Princess Margaret', with the author on the footplate

30-31 lb per mile.

These runs on *Malmesbury Abbey* were made on 5 June 1952, forty-five years after the first introduction of the four-cylinder 4—6—0s, and thirty-nine years after the finalisation of the design with superheaters and 15 in diameter cylinders. Then I thought these must surely be my last runs on 'Stars' in first-class express work, and at the time I felt happy that what I expected to be the finale had been such a good one. Nevertheless, on a raw winter's morning towards the end of 1955 I was waiting on Bath station ready to board yet another 'Star', No 4056 *Princess Margaret*. It was the 8.53 am to Paddington this time, with a 325-ton load, and another fine pair of enginemen in Driver Giles and Fireman Andress. We got a bad start, and after a succession of checks were stopped dead at Box, right at the foot of that nasty ascent through the tunnel. We made an excellent restart; cut-off was back to 37 per cent in ½ mile, and was further reduced to 27 per cent soon after we had entered the tunnel. We steadily gathered speed. There was an occasional slip, but it was well controlled by the driver, and we emerged at 30 mph. Then the use of 20 per cent cut-off brought a quick acceleration to 64 mph before the Chippenham stop. The run thence to Paddington is tabulated herewith.

With a minute or so of lost time to regain the engine was hustled away, with 30 per cent cut-off after 1¼ miles, 22 per cent at Milepost 91, and a reversion to 24 per cent at Dauntsey. This gave us a truly splendid start. The engine, like all the 'Stars' featured in this chapter, was a perfect 'Rolls-Royce' of an engine, riding beautifully, and responding vigorously to every adjustment of the controls. After the checks through Swindon she was worked up in

20 per cent cut-off with the first valve of the regulator, and gave us a steady 75 mph down through the Vale of the White Horse. Then came checks: adverse signals to 30 mph in the approach to Didcot, and a very heavy permanent way check to 10 mph at Pangbourne. Then we were away again and by Reading working in 20 per cent cut-off, regulator three-quarters open, and doing 65 mph. This work-

9.19 am CHIPPENHAM—PADDINGTON
Load: 9 cars, 310 tons tare, 325 tons full
Engine: 4056 *Princess Margaret*
Driver: Giles; Fireman: Andress (Bristol)

Dist miles		Sch min	Actual m s	Speed mph
0·0	CHIPPENHAM	0	0 00	
3·0	*Milepost 91*		4 58	56
6·3	Dauntsey		8 19	61·5
8·7	*Incline Box*		10 54	51·5
11·1	Wootton Bassett		13 27	58·5
			sigs	30
16·7	SWINDON	21	20 16	
22·5	Shrivenham		26 05	67·5
27·5	Uffington		30 28	71
33·6	Wantage Road		35 30	75
39·5	Steventon	41	38 40	75
			sigs	30
40·9	DIDCOT	44	42 18	
45·5	Cholsey		47 03	67·5
48·2	Goring		50 17	71·5
			pws	10
58·0	READING	61½	62 18	65
63·0	Twyford		66 42	72
69·8	Maidenhead	73	72 11	75
75·5	SLOUGH	78	76 48	76/73*
80·8	West Drayton		81 10	72
84·9	Southall	88	84 39	71·5
88·3	Ealing Broadway		87 53	66·5
			pw sigs	
92·7	Westbourne Park		92 55	
94·0	PADDINGTON	101	96 38	

Net time 88½ min
* Speed restriction

225

*Up Cheltenham, Gloucester and Bristol express in Sonning Cutting :
engine No 4022 unnamed (formerly 'King William')*

ing continued to Maidenhead, where with the speed just topping 75 mph cut-off was reduced to 15 per cent. Thenceforward a brisk and practically un-delayed finish brought us into Paddington $2\frac{1}{2}$ min early. The net time from Chippenham was, how-ever, no more than $88\frac{1}{2}$ min—a start-to-stop average of 63·7 mph. This fast run was made on a water consumption averaging 30 gallons per mile from Chippenham to Paddington, and a coal consumption of 35-36 lb per mile.

Three weeks later on 26 November 1955 I did have my very last runs on a 'Star' class engine. Once again it was No 4056 *Princess Margaret*, and this time on the 6.45 am North to West mail from Bristol to Newton Abbot. It was a raw, frosty morning, with mist in places, and we pulled out of Temple Meads with eleven coaches and vans, a gross load of 340 tons behind the tender. There was rime on the rails, and the engine was at first inclined to slip; but Driver Connett took her gently up to Flax Bourton, on 25 per cent cut-off and a partly opened regulator, and we topped the bank at 45 mph. The first signs of dawn were showing as

we got into speed, and touched 64 mph at Yatton, and then observing the severe slack at Worle Junction we clocked into Weston-super-Mare dead on time. After the very bad permanent way check before Uphill Junction we got splendidly into speed, and along this level stretch I saw the same kind of driving as on the other 'Stars': 16 per cent cut-off, regulator just over half open, giving us 63 mph on the level. There was rather more varia-tion in the boiler pressure on this trip, and I have notes of 200 lb per sq in; but we were running very comfortably to time, and the generous recovery allowance between Highbridge and Bridgwater more than retrieved the time by which we had overstayed our schedule at Weston.

Station business was heavy on this early-morning mail train, and we were standing for $9\frac{1}{2}$ min at Bridgwater, instead of the allotted 5 min. Further-more, there is little margin in the run forward to Taunton, and we needed 18 per cent cut-off from about $2\frac{1}{2}$ miles out of Bridgwater. At Taunton the engine was re-manned, and we left just over 1 min late for the attack on Wellington. Our new driver

226

6.45 am BRISTOL—EXETER
Load: 11 cars, 326 tons tare, 340 tons full
Engine: 4056 *Princess Margaret*
Driver, to Taunton: Connett; Fireman: Graves (Bristol)
to Exeter: Palmer; Fireman: Parsons (Taunton)

Dist miles		Sch min	Actual m s	Speed mph
0·0	TEMPLE MEADS .	0	0 00	
1·9	Parson Street . .		5 40	
5·9	Flax Bourton . .		11 04	45
12·0	YATTON . .		16 53	64
16·8	*Worle Jc* . .	22	21 46	20*
19·1	WESTON-SUPER-MARE .	26	26 08	
			pws	5
1·6	*Uphill Jc* . .	3	5 08	
6·1	Brent Knoll . .		10 58	55
8·9	HIGHBRIDGE .	14	13 51	60
12·7	Dunball . .		17 33	63
15·2	BRIDGWATER .	27	20 48	
3·5	*Fordgate Box* . .		6 04	52/56
6·8	*Cogload* . .		9 40	52·5
9·1	*Creech Jc* . .		11 59	61·5
11·5	TAUNTON .	16	15 30	
2·0	Norton Fitzwarren .		4 15	45·5
7·1	Wellington . .		10 52	52
8·9	*Milepost 172* . .		13 08	
			sigs	28
9·9	*Milepost 173* . .		15 25	
10·9	*Whiteball Box* . .	17	17 40	26·5
15·9	Tiverton Jc . .		23 02	70·5
18·2	Cullompton . .		25 04	63/58*
23·6	Silverton . .		30 23	65
27·3	Stoke Canon . .		33 49	68
			sig/stop 4½ ft	
30·8	EXETER .	40	44 04	

* Speed restrictions

used 20 per cent from Norton Fitzwarren, and 25 per cent from Poole siding (a mile short of Wellington). We were going splendidly up the bank when we sighted Beam Bridge 'distant' on. After closing the regulator speed dropped to 28 mph before the signal cleared, and then with 45 per cent cut-off at first, reduced to 35 at the entrance to Whiteball tunnel we made a lovely ascent: surefooted, with a thrilling, staccato exhaust and holding 26½ mph through the tunnel. This was excellent work with a load of 340 tons. An easy run down to Exeter, on 15 per cent cut-off with the first valve only, would have given us an early arrival, but for a prolonged signal stop outside. I have not tabulated the continuation of the run round the coast to Newton Abbot: we had two permanent way checks and took 28 min 37 sec for these 20·2 miles in place of the 26 min scheduled. The intermittent character of the performance demanded on this turn, and the heavy work needed on Wellington bank are reflected in the coal and water consumption, which were estimated at 42 lb per mile and 35 gallons per mile.

I returned from Newton on No 4056 working the 11.34 pm West to North express, with a load of 375 tons behind the tender, with yet a third crew. Those who claim that the immaculate performance of Great Western locomotives was the

Wolverhampton - Weymouth (Saturdays) express near Castle Cary : engine No 4061 'Glastonbury Abbey'

*West to North express entering Temple Meads, Bristol : engine No 4056 'Princess Margaret',
with the author on the footplate*

outcome of the most selective manning may well be confounded by the results I noted with *Princess Margaret* in that one day! We kept exact time round the coastal section in this direction—26 min 3 sec to be precise—and then set out on the remarkable run tabulated. Driver Iles had opened out to full regulator by Exeter Riverside box. Cut-off was 25 per cent from Cowley Bridge Junction and 21 per cent from Stoke Canon. After that the working was

unchanged until we were over Whiteball summit. The most telling comment I can make about this ascent is to refer readers back to Chapter 9, where on page 114 I detailed the record run of *Caldicot Castle* with the up Cornish Riviera Express during the Interchange Trials of 1925. The times achieved on that rather exceptional occasion were 6 min 14 sec to Stoke Canon; 15 min 33 sec to Cullompton; and 23 min 31 sec to Whitehall Box. More than thirty years later with an almost identical load (375 against 380 tons) *Princess Margaret* fractionally *surpassed* those times! All the way up the bank the boiler pressure was well sustained, never below 210 lb per sq in, and mostly at 215 to 220 lb per sq in.

After that remarkable exhibition we had the usual succession of 'fits and starts'. The level running after Taunton was all made on 15 per cent cut-off, mostly with full open regulator; but we had a magnificent finish, from Weston. After the usual slow negotiation of Worle Junction the driver worked in 20 per cent cut-off with full regulator—hard going!—and this took us up to 63 mph at Yatton, prior to clearing the Flax Bourton bank at the fine minimum speed of 57 mph. Signals were slightly against us in the approach to Bristol, but we had the satisfaction of finishing dead on time. And this really was my last footplate trip on a 'Star'. The fuel and water consumption was naturally heavier on a run of this quality, and the average water consumption between Newton Abbot and Bristol was exactly 40 gallons per mile; the coal consumption was 47 to 48 lb per mile. The veteran locomotive had nevertheless showed herself mistress of the job, and in equalling *Caldicot Castle* between Exeter and Whiteball had an outstanding piece of work to her credit.

12.7 pm EXETER—BRISTOL
Load : 11 cars, 350 tons tare, 375 tons full
Engine : 4056 *Princess Margaret*
Driver : Iles (Bristol)

Dist miles		Sch min	Actual m s	Speed mph
0·0	EXETER . .	0	0 00	
3·5	Stoke Canon . .		6 07	48
7·2	Silverton . .		10 16	56·5
12·6	Cullompton . .		15 37	63
14·9	Tiverton Jc . .		17 56	54·5/61
19·9	*Whiteball Box* . .	26	23 29	44·5
			pws	30
23·7	Wellington . .		29 12	72
			pws	30
30·8	TAUNTON . .	37	37 13	
2·4	*Creech Jc* . .		3 55	55
4·7	*Cogload* . . .		6 20	60
8·0	*Fordgate* . . .		9 21	67
11·5	BRIDGWATER .	15	13 05	
2·5	Dunball . .		4 40	50
6·3	HIGHBRIDGE .	9	8 37	60
9·1	Brent Knoll .		11 18	65
13·6	*Uphill Jc* . .	17	15 48	
			pws	5
15·2	WESTON-SUPER-MARE .	20	20 58	
2·3	*Worle Jc* . . .	4	4 30	20*
7·1	YATTON . .		10 39	63
13·2	Flax Bourton .		16 35	57
15·4	Long Ashton .		18 50	62
			sigs	
19·1	TEMPLE MEADS .	25	25 05	

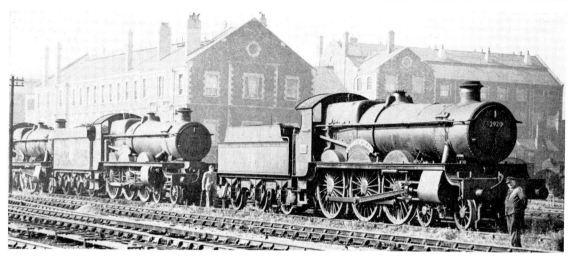

The last line-up? Engines 2920 'Saint David' and 4056 'Princess Margaret'
outside Swindon works. Actually it proved not to be the
last time for No 4056

Engine No 4003 'Lode Star' on road transporter en route for
Swindon Municipal Museum

CHAPTER 20

IMPROVED DRAUGHTING

IN the years immediately following the retirement of F. W. Hawksworth 'Castles' and 'Kings' continued to do good work on the schedules then prevailing. At times, indeed, some of the newest 'Castles' put up some performances that could be called phenomenal. But for a variety of reasons such standards of performance could not be relied on always. Difficulties in servicing and the quality of coal supplies made necessary some intensive research work to improve the steaming of the whole stud of ex-Great Western locomotives. As a matter of policy the accent was to be on increased steam production. The quality of performance that I have described in the foregoing chapter, dealing with the 'Stars', showed Great Western working at its pre-war finest. It was certainly not attainable by *any* engine, on *any* fuel that might be supplied. As a supplement to those farewell performances of the 'Stars', in ideal conditions, I must describe in detail an altogether exceptional performance with a 'Castle' that I logged personally in 1950. It indicates what was probably the optimum working rate of the '5098' class, as originally built. The engine in question was, of course, fitted with the then standard mechanical lubricator.

I had a footplate pass for the 3.30 pm from Paddington to Plymouth, and secured an excellent record. There was nothing unusual about it; just top-class performance by an engine in first-class condition. It was nothing more than one would expect from a good 'Castle'. I stayed overnight in Plymouth and returned next morning to Chippenham, travelling by the 8.30 am London express as far as Westbury. This was the return working of the crew with whom I had ridden the previous day, but normally provided with a 'King'. Engine No 7036 *Taunton Castle* had done us so well that Driver Cook asked for her again. He was reminded that the load would be 'fourteen' from Newton Abbot, but that caused neither him nor Fireman Hughes any concern. So, from Exeter, with a load

of exactly 500 tons behind the tender, I commenced to log the running. My footplate pass did not apply to the up journey but in good conditions I was able to record a maximum of data.

The opening run to Taunton was good enough in all conscience, with an attained maximum speed of 59 mph at Cullompton, and a speed of 50 mph held to within 2 miles of Whiteball summit. After that, with a fast run down the bank and a maximum speed of 82 mph below Wellington we more than

10.3 am EXETER—WESTBURY
Load: to Taunton, 14 cars, 460 tons tare, 500 tons full
to Westbury, 15 cars, 490 tons tare, 535 tons full
Engine: 7036 *Taunton Castle*
Driver: A. Cook; Fireman: L. Hughes (Old Oak)

Dist miles		Sch min	Actual m s	Speed mph
0·0	EXETER . .	0	0 00	
1·3	*Cowley Bridge Jc* .		3 41	
3·5	Stoke Canon . .		6 45	48·5
7·2	Silverton . .		11 05	55·5/53
12·6	Cullompton . .		16 45	59
14·8	Tiverton Jc . .		19 16	50·5/57·5
17·9	*Milepost 176* . .		22 43	51·5
19·9	*Whiteball Box* . .	25	25 29	37·5
23·7	Wellington . .		29 19	77·5
26·9	*Milepost 167* . .		31 47	82
			pws	15
30·8	TAUNTON . .	38	36 50	
2·4	*Creech Jc* . .	4	4 30	51
8·0	Athelney . .		10 18	62/59
11·9	*Curry Rivel Jc* .		14 17	61·5
17·1	Somerton . .		19 54	53/63·5
20·5	Charlton Mackrell .		23 14	57
22·7	Keinton Mandeville .		25 26	66·5
27·5	CASTLE CARY .	31	30 03	58
29·1	*Milepost 128* . .		31 39	60
30·1	*Milepost 127* . .		32 42	56
31·1	Bruton . .		33 44	50·5/52·5
32·1	*Milepost 125* . .		35 04	48
33·1	*Milepost 124* . .		36 21	46·5
34·1	*Milepost 123* . .		37 45	40
	Milepost 122¾ (Summit) .			34·5
40·4	*Blatchbridge Jc* .	46	44 16	72
42·4	*Clink Road Jc* .	48½	46 01	64·5
45·7	*Fairwood Jc* . .	52½	49 01	72
47·2	WESTBURY . .	55	51 39	

Liverpool - Plymouth express just over Whiteball summit : engine No 7029 'Clun Castle'

kept time to Taunton, despite a permanent way slack to 15 mph near Norton Fitzwarren. Then, however, there was yet another coach to be added, and the locomotive staff at Taunton had an assistant engine ready to couple on ahead of No 7036. But Driver Cook and his fireman disdained any such assistance, and we went forward with the tremendous load of 535 tons. It was then that the work became so completely outstanding. I was very sorry not to be on the footplate, and so able to record every detail of the working, but it was evident from the times and speeds that Cook was to some extent conserving his efforts so as to make maximum performance uphill. For example, the running from Creech Junction to Curry Rivel Junction, largely on level track, was good though not unusual; but then came the astounding climb of Somerton bank where the minimum speed of 53 mph on 1 in 264 was steadily sustained for more than a mile. The edhp rose from 800 at Curry Rivel Junction to 1,360 at the top of the bank.

After Castle Cary the engine was worked in 25 per cent cut-off, with full regulator, and the ascent of the Bruton bank was a masterpiece in itself. As will be seen from the log the 5 miles between mileposts 128 and 123 occupied only 6 min 6 sec, and yet the average gradient between these two points is 1 in 122. Making careful allowance for the loss in kinetic energy in the train, due to the deceleration from 60 to 40 mph, the average edhp during that strenuous 6 min works out at 1,600. The experimental section at Swindon has reported that the maximum they had noted with a 'King' when making up time in revenue-earning service was 1,440. *Taunton Castle* surpassed this, and it is probable that the actual cut-offs used were greater than those indicated on the scale, and reported to me by Driver Cook. In any case, the run provides yet another example complementary to those with 'Kings' on the Birmingham route detailed in Chapter 15, of a steam locomotive being worked intermittently at far higher steaming rates than the boiler could continuously sustain. The practical result was that this enormous train was brought into Westbury 3¼ min inside schedule time. It will be appreciated with what regret I left the train at Westbury, to catch the local connection to Chippenham.

The research into methods of increasing the steaming capacity of locomotives was directed towards both 'Castles' and 'Kings', and also to the 'Hall' and 'Manor' classes of two-cylinder 4—6—0. It was later applied to the 'Counties' as well. But in view of the very comprehensive test data subsequently published in S. O. Ell's paper to the Institution of Locomotive Engineers principal interest, so far as this book is concerned, centres upon the 'Kings'. As originally designed, with a jumper top to the blastpipe, this latter was 7 in below the centre

231

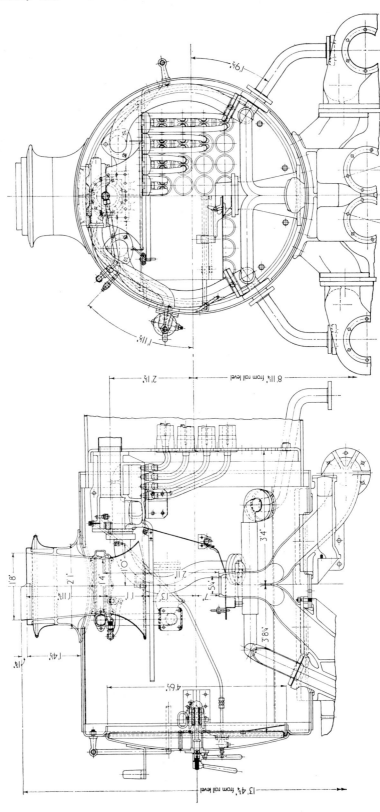

'King' class : the original 4-row superheater layout as applied to engine No 6022 'King Edward III'

line of the boiler. The throat of the chimney, 1 ft 4 in diameter, was 2 ft 11 in above this, and above the throat the chimney tapered out to 1 ft 8 in diameter at the top. This was the arrangement on the 4-row superheater boiler fitted to engine No 6022 in 1947. At that time there were no arrangements for self-cleaning in the smokebox. For servicing the latter were considered essential in British Railway days, and as the wire mesh would necessarily offer some resistance to the flow of flue gases from the tubes to the chimney it was evident that means had to be provided for sharpening the blast. At first it was thought that this would seriously interfere with the economical work of the engine, but careful studies indicated that any such deterioration would be more than counteracted by the improved steaming capacity effected. The drawings on pages 90 and 92 show successive stages in the development of the blastpipe and chimney proportions.

In the studies that took place at Swindon it was found that in single blastpipe designs the upper limit of the boiler was approached, and sometimes actually fixed in good designs by the limiting discharge rate of the orifice. It proved so in the re-draughted 'King'. It was estimated that when the self-cleaning plates were fitted the draughting limit

and the front-end discharge limit would approximately coincide. The blastpipe and chimney proportions used as a first-approximation in design proved remarkably accurate, and the modified arrangements fitted to two 'King' class engines, 6001 and 6017 in the autumn of 1952, won golden opinions from the operating staff in ordinary revenue-earning service. A similar change was also made to engine No 5025 of the 'Castle' class. The design was, however, not ultimately finalised so far as the 'Kings' were concerned until engine No 6001 *King Edward VII* was put on to the stationary test plant at Swindon, for 'full dress' trials, in the spring of 1953. Ell's work in this respect is an object lesson for all time in the history of locomotive design. By small, well-considered changes, very cheaply carried out, the boiler limit of continuous evaporation was advanced to more than 30 per cent above its normal working rate. On the heaviest pre-war duties the 'Kings' had been required to steam continuously at rates of about 25,000 to 26,000 lb per hr for periods of about one hour on end; against this the modified 6001, with the small adjustment shown desirable in the stationary tests, had a front-end limit of no less than 33,600 lb per hr. The 'runs' on the stationary plant, some of which I was able to observe per-

Engine No 6001 'King Edward VII' at 75 mph on the stationary plant

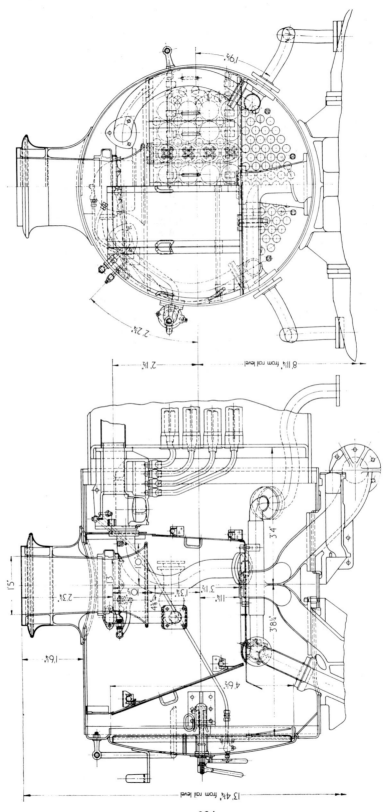

'King' class : modified smokebox layout with improved draughting developed on No 6001

*Engine No 6001 'King Edward VII' with dynamometer car ready for the
classic controlled road tests of 1953*

sonally, were impressive enough; but the interpretation in the form of load haulage on the road was thrilling beyond measure. The tests runs were made between Reading and Stoke Gifford sidings, and as the special trains had to be given paths amid the ordinary traffic of the day they were timed at con-

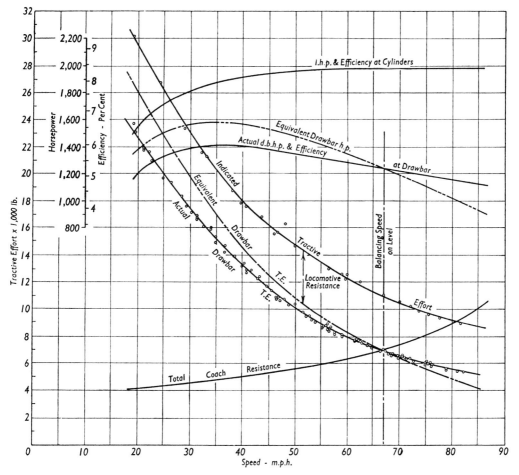

Test results : steam rate 28,700 lb per hour

235

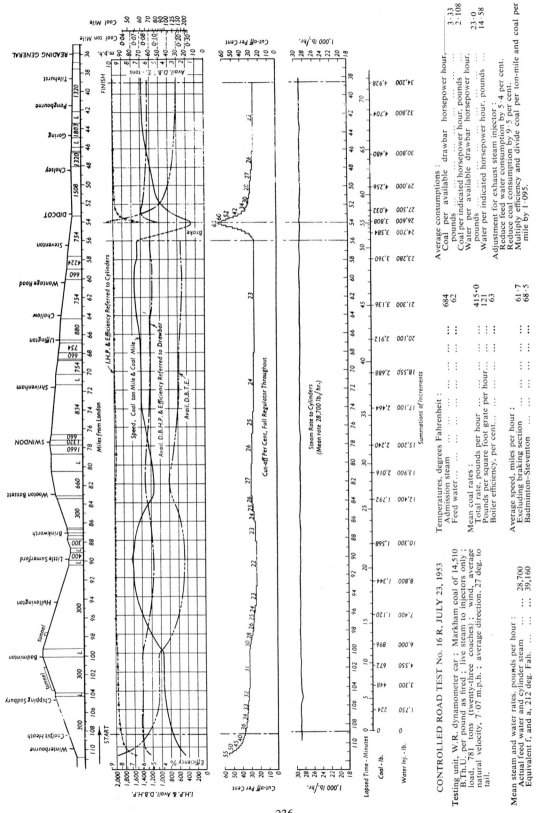

CONTROLLED ROAD TEST No. 16 R, JULY 23, 1953

Testing unit, W.R. dynamometer car ; Markham coal of 14,510 B.Th.U. per pound as fired ; live steam to injectors only ; load, 781 tons (twenty-three coaches) ; wind, average natural velocity, 7·07 m.p.h. ; average direction, 27 deg. to tail.

Temperatures, degrees Fahrenheit :				
Admission steam	...	...	...	684
Feed water...	...	...	...	62
Mean coal rates :				
Total rate, pounds per hour	...	...	415·0
Pounds per square foot grate per hour...	...	121
Boiler efficiency, per cent...	...	...	63
Average speed, miles per hour :				
Excluding braking section	...	...	61·7
Badminton-Steventon	...	...	...	68·5

Mean steam and water rates, pounds per hour :
Actual feed water and cylinder steam 28,700
Equivalent f, and a, 212 deg. Fah. 39,160

Average consumptions :
Coal per available drawbar horsepower hour, pounds ... ... 3·33
Coal per indicated horsepower hour, pounds ... 2·108
Water per available drawbar horsepower hour, pounds ... ... 23·0
Water per indicated horsepower hour, pounds ... 14·58

Adjustment for exhaust steam injector :
Reduce feed water consumption by 5·4 per cent.
Reduce coal consumption by 9·5 per cent.
Multiply efficiency and divide coal per ton-mile and coal per mile by 1·095.

temporary express passenger speed, and loaded so as to demand high rates of steaming. In these circumstances the test trains reached a maximum formation of 25 coaches, and a little short of 800 tons tare.

The accompanying diagram shows in graphical form the performance on a run from Stoke Gifford to Reading with a load of 23 coaches, 781 tons tare, when the steaming rate was 28,700 lb per hr. The test at constant steaming rate began on passing Coalpit Heath station, at a speed of about 38 mph, and it finished near Tilehurst. The average speed, excluding the section on which the train was being braked to observe a 15 mph speed restriction, was 61·7 mph; and this tremendously hard work, including a maximum speed of 81 mph at Little Somerford, was performed on a coal consumption of 3·33 lb per dhp hr. The complete analysis of the

performance is given in a second diagram, which shows a series of inter-related graphs prepared from this one test. It will be seen from this latter graph that the maximum indicated hp was a little below 2,000, while the relation between the actual dhp measured in the dynamometer car and the 'equivalent' value, after a correction for gradient, is clearly shown. In these steaming conditions the balancing speed on level track with this particular train was 67 mph. In comparing this with the actual speed run down the slight gradients in the Vale of the White Horse it will be appreciated how markedly those gradients can assist the running. The speed in the neighbourhood of Wantage Road was 77 mph.

It was my privilege to ride in the dynamometer car when an even heavier load was conveyed, and the steam rate was a full 30,000 lb per hr. There was an admixture of some lighter stock, however,

*Mr S. O. Ell (right) with the author at Stoke Gifford prior to the
run detailed on page 238*

Engine No 6001 with 25-coach test train approaching Swindon at 60 mph

and the 25 coaches included in the rake had a tare weight of 796 tons. On both these runs we had a clear road throughout. They were made on weekdays amid the ordinary traffic, and a considerable wait was necessary at Stoke Gifford before a path was available for the return trip. In anticipation of this the outward test was ended at Badminton so that opportunity would be available to let down the

fire before the long period of waiting. The outward run was thus of approximately one hour's duration, and to provide roughly comparable conditions the return test was ended at the 49th milepost. Remark-

WR DYNAMOMETER CAR CONTROLLED ROAD TEST
Load: 25 cars, 796 tons tare, 798 tons full
Engine: 6001 *King Edward VII*

Dist miles		Time m s	Speed mph
0·0	*Scours Lane Jc* . .	0 00	Pass slowly 10 mph
0·9	Tilehurst . . .	2 25	
2·7	*Milepost 39½* . .	Start of test	
3·8	Pangbourne . .	6 48	47
7·0	Goring . . .	10 40	53·5
10·7	Cholsey . .	14 44	56
15·3	DIDCOT . .	19 32	58
18·7	Steventon . .	23 03	58
22·6	Wantage Road . .	27 02	60
26·1	Challow . .	30 36	59
28·7	Uffington . .	33 16	59
31·2	*Knighton Crossing* .	35 51	58·5
33·8	Shrivenham . .	38 26	61·5
39·5	SWINDON . .	44 09	60
42·2	*Hay Lane Box* .	46 45	64·5
45·1	Wootton Bassett .	49 43	66/50★
51·9	Little Somerford .	56 14	72
56·4	Hullavington .	60 36	57·5
58·2	*Milepost 96* . .	62 30	54
60·2	*Milepost 98* . .	64 44	53
62·2	Badminton . .	67 02	52 end of test
70·7	Coalpit Heath .	75 22	65·5
74·2	*Stoke Gifford West* .	80 02	

★ Speed restriction

WR DYNAMOMETER CAR CONTROLLED ROAD TEST
Load: 25 bogies, 796 tons tare, 798 tons full
Engine: 6001 *King Edward VII*

Dist miles		Time m s	Speed mph
0·0	*Stoke Gifford East Box* dep	0 00	
0·75	*Milepost 110¾* .	3 48	
1·5	*Milepost 110* .	5 25	
1·6	Winterbourne .	5 45	
3·0	Coalpit Heath .	8 09	
4·3	*Westerleigh Jc* .	10 18	40
6·9	Chipping Sodbury .	13 58	42.5/45
11·5	Badminton . .	20 06	45·5
17·3	Hullavington . .	25 58	72
21·8	Little Somerford .	29 32	78
24·5	Brinkworth . .	31 47	71
28·6	Wootton Bassett .	35 43	58
31·5	*Hay Lane Box* .	38 48	56
34·2	SWINDON . .	41 34	60
35·5	*Milepost 76* . .	42 52	62
37·8	*Marston East* .	45 00	64
40·0	*Milepost 71½* . .	47 00	68
42·5	*Knighton Crossing* .	49 13	67
45·0	Uffington . .	51 24	69
47·6	Challow . .	53 40	69·5
51·1	Wantage Road .	56 38	70·5
55·0	Steventon . .	59 57	71
58·4	Didcot . .	62 48	71
62·5	*Milepost 49* . .	66 20	69
65·0	*South Stoke Box* .	68 30	68·5
66·7	Goring . .	70 03	67
70·0	Pangbourne (41½) .	72 57	67
71·5	*Milepost 40* . .	74 25	60
72·8	Tilehurst . .	75 50	
73·5	*Scours Lane Jc* up Home . . arr	76 55	

ably fine and steady running was performed on both tests, as will be seen from the accompanying logs. The firing rate was approximately 4,000 lb per hr, and as this was well above the figure of 3,000 lb per hr generally considered the maximum for one fireman in continuous working, two firemen were carried. The enginemen concerned, all from Swindon shed, were Driver Hinder, with Firemen Shurmer and Green. The former did *all* the actual firing on the outward journey, and the latter on the return. The second fireman was available on each occasion to do all the various odd jobs that normally came within the duties of a steam locomotive fireman.

It was, of course, not envisaged that duties would regularly be undertaken by engines with the 'improved draughting' involving such efforts as these. It was that the enhanced maximum capacity with good coal provided a margin for recovery, and a margin for working on inferior fuel, and still possessed the capacity to operate service trains punctually. As mentioned earlier in this book a considerable point was made at the time of the 1948 interchange trials of the difficulties under which Great Western engines were working in having to use unfamiliar coals. The following results are therefore of great interest, as showing the difference in performance of the modified 'King' No 6001 when using a grade 1A soft coal and a grade 2B 'hard'.

R. A. Smeddle, Chief Mechanical and Electrical Engineer to 1962

Engine No 6001 : IMPROVED DRAUGHTING		
Coal:		
grade	1A	2B
pit	Markham	Blidworth
gross calorific value Btu/lb .	14.510	12.740
Steam rate, lb/hr . . .	24.900	22.730
Max ihp . . .	1.770	1.630
at speed mph . .	70–80	70–80
at cut-off per-cent . .	20–23	18–19
Max edhp . . .	1.340	1.210
at speed mph . .	35	33
at cut-off per-cent . .	30	28
Coal per ihp hr/lb . . .	1·70	1·84
Coal per dhp hr/lb . . .	2·24	2·48

With the re-draughted engines at their disposal accelerated schedules were planned to require continuous steaming rates of around 20,000 lb and from the foregoing table it will be appreciated that even with a grade 2B hard coal of much reduced calorific value a 'King' should have a comfortable margin in reserve. Not many weeks after the conclusion of this comprehensive series of 'full-dress' trials I had an opportunity of riding on engine No 6001 in ordinary service. The train was the up 'Cornish Riviera Express', nominally non-stop from Plymouth to Paddington; but with a substantial summer load an assistant engine had to be taken over the South Devon line, and the actual non-stop run to London was from Newton Abbot West. Details of the running are set out in the accompanying log. With a gross load of 425 tons behind the tender the effort required was naturally far below that put forth on the maximum test occasions. Furthermore, except for a momentary sight of an adverse 'distant' at Norton Fitzwarren the road was clear throughout, and the run was thus an exposition of economy in working.

In making an actual time of 174 min over the 173·5 miles from Exeter to Paddington a cut-off of 17 per cent was used throughout, except for two spells of about 5 min each: 20 per cent for the last 3 miles up to Whiteball summit, and 22 per cent from Bruton up to Brewham summit. Over the harder initial stage of the journey, between Exeter and Fairwood Junction the evaporation rate was approximately 18,000 lb per hr for an average speed of 62·25 mph, while on the remaining 97 miles to Paddington, using an average of only 23 gallons per mile the evaporation rate was only about 14,000 lb per hr. As will be appreciated from the log much of this 97-mile stretch was covered under very easy steam, and indeed the last appreciable firing took

Up Cornish express near Castle Cary, with 14-coach Saturday load: engine No 6009 'King Charles II'

| | | | UP CORNISH RIVIERA EXPRESS NEWTON ABBOT WEST—PADDINGTON Load: 12 cars, 396 tons tare, 430 tons full Engine: 6001 *King Edward VII* Driver: Hammett; Fireman: Henwood (Laira) | | |

Dist miles			Actual m s		Speed mph
0·0	*Newton Abbot West*	.	0	00	
0·2	NEWTON ABBOT	.	1	20	
5·4	Teignmouth	.	8	52	50
8·2	Dawlish	.	12	42	54
15·7	Exminster	. .	20	53	62
20·4	EXETER	. .	26	12	30*
23·9	Stoke Canon	. .	30	27	54
27·6	Silverton	. .	34	23	60
33·0	Cullompton	. .	39	42	64·5
35·2	Tiverton Jc	. .	41	57	57/64
40·3	*Whiteball Box*	.	47	20	47·5
44·1	Wellington	.	50	48	85
			sigs		60
51·2	TAUNTON	.	56	57	64·5
53·6	*Creech Jc*	.	59	10	67
59·2	Athelney	. .	64	20	63·5
62·9	*Curry Rivel Jc*	.	68	04	67
68·4	Somerton	. .	73	11	59
73·9	Keinton Mandeville	.	78	18	72
78·8	CASTLE CARY	.	82	42	58*/60
85·6	*Milepost 122¾*	.	90	31	44
91·6	*Blatchbridge Jc*	.	96	17	73/65
96·9	*Fairwood Jc*	.	100	59	69
99·3	*Heywood Road Jc*	.	103	15	62
107·0	Lavington	.	110	23	68
112·5	Patney	.	116	17	56
118·6	Pewsey	.	122	20	64·5
123·8	Savernake	.	127	42	58
127·5	Bedwyn	.	131	31	69
140·8	NEWBURY	.	143	47	easy
152·1	Theale	.	154	50	
157·9	READING	.	160	55	40*
169·7	Maidenhead	.	173	37	60
175·4	SLOUGH	.	179	19	60
184·8	Southall	.	189	01	
193·9	PADDINGTON	.	200	08	
	* Speed restrictions				

place at Newbury. From Reading inwards, indeed, we were just killing time. It must be added, however, that the running conditions were virtually perfect on a hot and calm summer's day and the engine fired with good quality Welsh coal. The average evaporation between Exeter and Paddington was about 15,500 lb per hr. It is, of course, not possible to relate this directly to the Swindon test results and read off from the graphs the corresponding coal consumption. On this service run the steaming was not uniformly maintained throughout; but making some allowance for the varying and intermittent character of the performance demanded the coal consumption would have been something less than 30 lb per mile. From my observations at Swindon stationary plant, from my journeys in the dynamometer car, and finally from personal experience on the footplate I formed the impression that No 6001 in her modified form was an extremely good engine.

I must mention also at this stage the work of some of the modified 'Castles', and particularly No 5025 *Chirk Castle* and No 7034 *Ince Castle*. I have tabulated three runs on Paddington-Bath non-stops made in 1953-4, on which some very fine work was done. Until June of the latter year the 1.15 pm down was allowed 106 min for the run, with a minimum load of ten coaches, and with two 15 mph permanent way checks en route it needed some smart work to keep time. Actually we did not quite manage it, but the main feature of the run was the very fast finish, with its maximum of 90 mph at Dauntsey and a time of only 24 min 48 sec for the last 29·6 miles from Swindon. This was the first post-war occasion on which I had noted a maximum speed of 90 mph in ordinary service on the Western, though from June 1954, when the substantial accelerations came into force, they became common enough.

The 5.5 pm down had an easier timing, but the tremendous energy shown on this trip arose from a slightly late start, because of the bursting of a carriage-warming hose at the last minute, and the need for its replacement. Driver Wilkins was one of the finest of all the Bristol enginemen of the day, and with such an engine as *Chirk Castle* we had wiped out the late start by the time we passed Reading. Despite two bad checks he was through Swindon in 81¾ min, and there was no need for undue haste afterwards. In making 75 mph on the level at Reading the engine was developing about 800 dhp. Wilkins was also the driver on the third run tabulated, which was made just before the accelerated times of June 1954 came into force. Then the 1.15 pm had its time cut to 97 min for the Paddington-Bath run, but with a normal load of only seven coaches. The succession of checks on this journey would have discouraged the majority of drivers, but not Wilkins!

First of all, through bad operating, we got a succession of checks out to West Drayton through a much slower train running ahead of us, and the time to Slough was as much as 25 min 25 sec. We

WR PADDINGTON—BATH							
Train		1.15 pm		5.5 pm		1.15 pm	
Engine No		7034		5025		7034	
Engine Name		*Ince Castle*		*Chirk Castle*		*Ince Castle*	
Loads tons E/F		335/350		341/370		360/380	
Driver (BRD)		Flowers		Wilkins		Wilkins	
Dist miles		Actual m s	Speeds mph	Actual m s	Speeds mph	Actual m s	Speeds mph
0·0	PADDINGTON	0 00		0 00		0 00 sigs	
9·1	Southall	12 24 pws	64·5 15	12 36	61	14 55 sigs	
18·5	SLOUGH	24 26	62	20 57	74	25 25	62
24·2	Maidenhead	29 52	66	25 47	71	30 42	67
31·0	Twyford	35 56	67·5	31 32	69·5	36 40	69
36·0	READING	40 18	70·5	35 45	75	40 57	72
41·5	Pangbourne	45 08	68	40 24 sigs	69·5 10	45 38	70·5 69
48·5	Cholsey	51 23	67	49 34	57	51 38 pw sigs	70 5
53·1	DIDCOT	55 36	64·5	54 06	64	59 20	
60·4	Wantage Road	62 17	65·5	60 59 sig stop	63·5	68 01	63·5
66·5	Uffington	68 03 pws	63·5 15	71 03	52	73 33 pws	69 25
71·5	Shrivenham	74 12		76 22	64·5	78 41	
77·3	SWINDON	82 08	63·5	81 45	66/58	85 39	64·5
82·9	Wootton Bassett	87 00	75	87 08	67·5	90 27	75
87·7	Dauntsey	90 35	90	91 04	81	94 01	92
91·0	*Milepost 91*	92 49	88	93 35	77	96 16 sigs	86·5 47·5
94·0	CHIPPENHAM	94 56	80	96 00	69·5	99 35	
98·3	Corsham	98 23	72/69	99 54	62·5	104 11	61
101·9	Box	101 24	74	103 10	69	107 23	72
104·5	Bathampton	103 57		105 35	67·5	109 44 sigs	68
106·9	BATH	106 56		108 12		113 15	
	Net times, min	99½		100		97½	

The Pembroke Coast Express in Sonning Cutting : engine No 7009
'Athelney Castle', with improved draughting

ran well thereafter, but it was after the very bad checks approaching Didcot that Wilkins really began to extend *Ince Castle*. Having been delayed thus far, and with the knowledge of another permanent way check ahead, any driver might have given up; speed was worked up to 69 mph on the rise to Uffington, requiring an edhp of about 950, and then having observed the Shrivenham restriction we simply *flew*. My previous maximum with this engine down Dauntsey bank was eclipsed by a top speed of 92 mph, but even then we did not get a clear road. The net time on this most enterprising trip was, however, not more than 97½ min—an average of about 66 mph start to stop. These runs with engines having the improved draughting were certainly the shape of things to come, after the June accelerations of 1954.

The practical results of all the work done at Swindon in 1953, and previously, on the subject of draughting were seen in the summer of 1954. The General Manager of the Western Region, K. W. C. Grand, was very anxious to restore pre-war speed,

and particularly by the 'Bristolian' express to a nonstop schedule of 1¾ hours between Paddington and Temple Meads in each direction. R. A. Smeddle had given the utmost encouragement to Ell in all the development work carried out, and by the summer of 1953 he was quite confident that the 'King' class engines with improved draughting could do the job, in any ordinary conditions of weather and fuel that were likely to occur. But the operating authorities were very sceptical, and a good deal of 'sales resistance' was offered to the proposed accelerations. The general manager was, however, quite resolute, and for the summer service of 1954 a number of other accelerations were planned on the Bristol route, to be worked by 'Castle' class engines with improved draughting. The schedules were worked out in detail by the staff of the experimental department at Swindon, under S. O. Ell, and while the normal point-to-point times were laid down in accordance with steaming rates now shown to be eminently practical recovery margins were also built in, at intervals, to provide for permanent

The Sunday Cornish Riviera Express, diverted via Chippenham :
engine No 6023 'King Edward II'

way slowings, and other occasional delays. The general principle adopted was that 4 min recovery time should be included at approximately 50-mile intervals. On the Bristol service, therefore, the 105-min 'Bristolian' schedule would include 8 min recovery time, and thus envisage a running time of 97 min as regularly practicable. With the seven-coach train proposed no difficulty was anticipated with 'King' class engines in making a 'net' average of 73 mph start-to-stop.

In May 1954 what could be termed as a 'dress rehearsal' for the accelerated 'Bristolian' was staged,

except that the working conditions were in certain respects more strenuous. The run was to be virtually a continuous one, with a special train routed via Bath, North Somerset Junction and Stapleton Road, and returning to Paddington via Filton and Badminton. Brief stops were scheduled in the Bristol area; but for engine and crew it was a continuous working. It was planned to run at a maximum recovery level, and to make the test as representative of ordinary conditions as possible no special arrangements for engine or crew were permitted. The first top-link Old Oak crew available

Another view of the diverted Sunday Cornish Riviera, approaching Chippenham :
engine No 6004 'King George III'

243

High-speed dynamometer-car test run, 30 April 1954, passing West Ealing at 70 mph :
engine No 6003 'King George IV'

for a special train was allocated, and similarly the first available 'King' with improved draughting. I was invited to join the party in the dynamometer car that day, and enjoyed yet another enlivening experience of Western Region running. Although no special arrangements were made the crew actually called, Driver Wasley and Fireman French, were very much on their mettle, and Mr Grand himself rode on the footplate on the outward half of the journey.

The logs of these interesting runs are set out in the accompanying tables. The load was slightly heavier than that proposed for the restored 1¾-hour 'Bristolian' timing, which was to be seven coaches, with a tare weight of 235 tons; but with full passenger loading the gross load of the service train was expected to be about 250 tons, whereas the test train carried only the staff of the experimental department, and a number of other railway officers.

On the outward journey 4 min recovery time was included in the schedule between Reading and Didcot, and also between Bath and the terminating point at Dr Days Bridge Junction. Generally speaking, the train was run very closely to the planned schedule, having regard to the unfamiliarity of the driver and fireman with the continuous high-speed running of this kind. There was a certain unevenness in the effort, which resulted from variations in the steaming; but taken all round it was a splendid first try. With only one check we should, according to the planned schedule have been 4 min early at Dr Days Bridge Junction. As it was we were 3¼ min early. Notable speeds were the maximum of 84 mph on the level at Didcot, an acceleration to 81·5 mph up the slight rise to Uffington, and the maximum of 96·5 mph on Dauntsey bank.

Dr Days Bridge Junction was reached at 12.35 pm and after a brief stop there we proceeded to

HIGH SPEED TEST RUN: 30 APRIL 1954 10.55 am PADDINGTON—BRISTOL Load: 8 cars, 253 tons tare, 260 tons full Engine: 6003 *King George IV* Driver: Wasley; Fireman: French (Old Oak)				
Dist miles		Sch min	Actual m s	Speed mph
0·0	PADDINGTON .	0	0 00	
5·7	Ealing . . .		7 26	68·5
9·1	Southall . .	11	10 18	72
13·2	West Drayton .		13 43	75
18·5	SLOUGH . .	17½	17 51	75
24·2	Maidenhead .	21½	22 14	80
31·0	Twyford . .	27	27 24	82/74*
36·0	READING . .	31	31 23	75
41·5	Pangbourne .		35 54	72
48·5	Cholsey . .		41 21	80
53·1	DIDCOT . .	48	44 44	84
60·4	Wantage Road .		50 04	79·5
66·5	Uffington .		54 38	81·5
			pws	18
71·5	Shrivenham .		59 39	
77·3	SWINDON . .	67	65 44	72
82·9	Wootton Bassett .		70 03	82
87·7	Dauntsey . .		73 20	96·5
94·0	CHIPPENHAM .	79	77 33	78
98·3	Corsham . .		80 51	80
101·9	Box . .		83 30	82
106·9	BATH . .	88½	88 17	35*
113·8	Keynsham . .		94 57	75
117·9	*Dr Days Bridge Jc* .	102½	99 19	
Net time 96 min * Speed restriction				

HIGH SPEED TEST RUN: 30 APRIL 1954 12.53½ pm STAPLETON ROAD—PADDINGTON Load: 8 cars, 253 tons tare, 260 tons full Engine: 6003 *King George IV* Driver: Wasley; Fireman: French (Old Oak)				
Dist miles		Sch min	Actual m s	Speed mph
0·0	STAPLETON ROAD . .	0	0 00	
3·2	Filton Jc . .	5	5 10	
11·4	Chipping Sodbury .		13 30	66
16·0	Badminton . .	18	17 47	63·5
26·3	Little Somerford .		25 25	93
33·1	Wootton Bassett .	30½	30 22	65*
38·7	SWINDON . .	35½	35 03	79
49·5	Uffington .		42 51	87
55·6	Wantage Road .		46 59	90/88·5
62·9	DIDCOT . .	56	51 52	92·5
67·5	Cholsey . .		54 57	86
71·3	Goring . .		57 56	eased
80·0	READING . .	68	64 31	82/77
91·8	Maidenhead . .	76½	73 01	90
			eased	81
97·5	SLOUGH . .	81	77 08	84
102·7	West Drayton .		80 52	86
106·9	Southall . .	87½	84 13	73
110·3	Ealing . .		86 53	77·5
			pws	
114·7	Westbourne Park .		92 55	
116·0	PADDINGTON .	101½	95 35	
Net time 93½ min				

Stapleton Road, from which we started away on our high-speed return trip to Paddington only 18½ min after our arrival at Dr Days Bridge Junction. This proved to be another splendid run, despite certain incidental difficulties with steaming—not different, however, from conditions that might be expected in ordinary service. The initial timing requiring speeds of no more than 64-6 mph up the 1 in 300 to Badminton was planned to give a little respite to the crew of an engine starting from cold from

The high-speed test run of 30 April 1954, passing Hullavington on the return journey at 86 mph

The down Bristolian passing Chippenham : engine No 6015 'King Richard III'

Bristol, as in the case of the up 'Bristolian' in normal service, and the maximum speed subsequently attained at Little Somerford was frequently exceeded later in regular working. From Swindon onwards, however, a most competent display of sustained fast running was made. The average speed of 83·8 mph over the 64 miles from Swindon to West Drayton included the observance of slightly restricted speed between Goring and Reading, and again through Twyford station. The final permanent way check cost 2 min, and left a net time of 93½ min—exactly corresponding to the 8 min recovery time included in the 101½-min schedule. While the day's round in which we travelled from Paddington to Bristol and back between the hours of 10.55 am and 2.29 pm was an exhilarating experience—an overall average speed of 66·2 mph inclusive of the stops in the Bristol area—the exact-

The up Bristolian near Hullavington : engine No 6009 'King Charles II'

ness of the timekeeping was a triumph for the testing staff at Swindon, no less than for the enginemen who thus had the opportunity of participating in this dress rehearsal. The accelerated times came into force in June 1954, and with the exception of the down and up 'Bristolian' they were all worked by 'Castle' class engines. The principal onus fell upon Bath Road shed, Bristol, in those first months and several 'Castles' in specially good condition were drafted thence. These included 5027, 5057, 5063, 5077 and 5096, and added to engines like 5025 and 7034 made a fairly puissant stud. As expected the 'Kings' handled the accelerated 'Bristolian' with ease. In the very first week I clocked No 6015 *King Richard III* from Temple Meads to Paddington in 96 min 12 sec start-to-stop, and although running thus at maximum recovery standard was neither usual nor necessary the train was frequently 5 min early in arriving at Paddington. The temptation to enginemen to attain very high speeds when recovering time was stimulated by the lifting of the speed limit altogether on certain stretches of the line where the permanent way was in particularly good shape. The working timetables included the statement, referring to these stretches, that the speed might be 'as high as necessary'. This was a plain invitation to 'have a go', and over the years a number of instances were recorded of speeds closely approaching 100 mph by both 'Castle' and 'King' class engines.

Dist miles		Sch min	Actual m s		Speed mph
77·3	SWINDON	67	65	31	69
80·0	*Hay Lane Box*		67	38	79
82·9	Wootton Bassett		69	44	85
84·0	*Milepost 84*		70	30	88
85·0	*Milepost 85*		71	11	89
86·0	*Milepost 86*		71	50	95
87·0	*Milepost 87*		72	27	102·5
87·75	Dauntsey		72	53½	
89·0	*Milepost 89*		73	39	98
90·0	*Milepost 90*		74	16	95
91·0	*Milepost 91*		74	55	91·5
			eased		
94·0	CHIPPENHAM	79	77	00	80

The highest speed I noted personally with a Great Western four-cylinder 4—6—0 was on the down 'Bristolian' with the normal seven-coach train and engine No 6018 *King Henry VI*. The accompanying log shows the relevant part of this journey, following recovery from a permanent way slowing east of Swindon. The maximum was 102·5 mph and very fortunately Kenneth Leech was at Dauntsey on this occasion and photographed the train, 'in the act' as it were. I am aware that several claims have been made subsequently of considerably higher speeds for 'King and 'Castle' class engines fitted with twin blastpipes and chimneys; but none of these claims have the supporting weight of evidence to enable them to be accepted as absolute fact. They are discussed in Chapter 21.

The up Bristolian near Hullavington at 85 mph : engine No 5076 'Gladiator',
with the author on the footplate

VITAL DYNAMOMETER CAR TESTS

IN studying what proved to be the final series of dynamometer car test runs with the Great Western four-cylinder 4—6—0s it is extremely important that the practical background should be fully appreciated. By some observers of locomotive performance it has been assumed that they were carried out principally to determine the ultimate capacity of the 'King' and 'Castle' class engines, but this is certainly not so. They were conducted on an urgent basis by practical railwaymen faced with the need to provide enhanced and more reliable all-round motive power, and if possible to devise alterations to design that could be made within the provisions of a strictly limited budget. They were definitely not a series of academic studies conducted in the style of remote back-room researches. Time was vital, and throughout the entire series the operating, motive power and chief mechanical engineer's departments worked in the closest liaison. Furthermore, it was

essential in providing for the working of the traffic that the accelerated timings proposed should be capable of achievement by *any* engine of the class— not by a few picked, carefully nursed units. This principle was, of course, not so readily applicable to the entire 'Castle' class, but the aim was certainly to make it applicable to all thirty of the 'Kings'. The schedules had to be capable of observance by an engine in the most run-down condition that was permitted in traffic.

To provide the necessary data for working out the new schedules the engine chosen for the original series of tests with the improved draughting had been one with not the best of reputations, No 6001. The draughting alterations described in Chapter 20 turned it into an extremely puissant machine, if not an exceptionally speedy one, by the standards set by other engines of the class, and when the time came for the 1955 trials another 'run of the mill'

'King George IV' with final form of single chimney
Down Saturday West of England express near Castle Cary: engine No 6003

Dynamometer car test, 10 March 1955, with Cornish Riviera Express near Reading West : engine No 6013 'King Henry VIII'

engine—very far from a 'star' performer—was chosen for the exceedingly arduous tests with the 'Cornish Riviera Express'. The high management of the Western Region wished to accelerate that most famous of trains to a four-hour schedule between Paddington and Plymouth, and the operating department were of the opinion that no existing Western Region locomotives were capable of the job, with the maximum load desired, of fourteen coaches from Paddington to Heywood Road, and twelve from there to Plymouth. Mr Smeddle and his staff were quite confident that the 'Kings' with improved draughting could do it; but to prove the point a series of dynamometer car test runs was arranged, in which the 'Kings' were to be pitted against 'Pacifics' of other regions. It was originally proposed to have both Eastern and London Midland 4—6—2s on test, and in addition to run the 'BR8' 4—6—2 No 71000 *Duke of Gloucester*, which was then on trial at the Swindon stationary testing plant. Eventually, however, the only stranger to run the 'Limited' was the LMR 'Duchess' class 4—6—2 No 46237 *City of Bristol*; the performance of the 'BR8' 4—6—2 on the stationary plant provided

ample data for her likely performance between Paddington and Plymouth to be accurately assessed.

In this book, it is, of course, the performance of 'King' class engine No 6013 *King Henry VIII* with which I am concerned. The runs made on the four successive days 8-11 March 1955 are of immense importance, not only including the hardest sustained efforts ever made by a 'King' class engine in all the history of the class, but including features of such deep significance as to initiate the further development which was ultimately to prove the final phase of the 'Castles' and 'Kings'. There were to be no unduly favourable conditions in these trials. The choice of a week in early March ran the risk of rough weather, and the engine chosen for test was an average member of the class, with a considerable mileage since last overhaul. As will be apparent from the photograph of the down train on 10 March she had a bad steam leak from the left-hand outside cylinder valve gland. I rode down to Plymouth in the dynamometer car and witnessed the magnificent performance detailed in the accompanying table. It was at that time the fastest run ever made between Paddington and Exeter, and the details of coal and water consumption show that it was made with good economy. My invitation was extended to the final up journey on the following day; but unfortunately an engagement on Tyneside necessitated my returning to London on the same evening, and I therefore missed the experience of witnessing the altogether extraordinary run that was made on Friday 11 March 1955. Then the load was one of twelve coaches throughout from Plymouth to Paddington but a strong easterly wind made those twelve coaches pull like fourteen in normal weather conditions, and the task of maintaining the accelerated schedule was made exceedingly onerous. The gross load behind the tender was actually 420 tons, but the equivalent load, in calm weather, would have been nearer 480 tons.

From all previous accounts of engine performance on the up road between Exeter and Paddington the task of working such a load over that 173.5 miles in 165 min will be appreciated as an extremely

CORNISH RIVIERA EXPRESS
Dynamometer Car Test Run
Load: to Heywood Road, 14 cars, 460 tons tare, 490 tons full
to Newton Abbot, 12 cars, 393 tons tare, 420 tons full
Engine: 6013 *King Henry VIII* (ID)
Driver: Shave; Fireman: Mitchell (Old Oak)

Dist miles		Sch min	Actual m s	Speed mph
0.0	PADDINGTON .	0	0 00	
1.3	Westbourne Park .		3 16	
5.7	Ealing . .		8 55	57.5
9.1	Southall . .	12½	12 20	61
13.2	West Drayton .		16 22	63
18.5	SLOUGH . .	21	21 00	70
24.2	Maidenhead .	26	25 51	71
31.0	Twyford . .	32	31 31	70
36.0	READING . .	37	35 58	40*
			pws	20
44.8	Aldermaston . .		46 37	64.5
53.1	NEWBURY . .	55	54 10	66/62.5
58.5	Kintbury . .		59 02	66
61.5	Hungerford . .		61 49	62
66.4	Bedwyn . .	68	66 17	67
70.1	Savernake . .	72½	70 04	50
75.3	Pewsey . .		74 48	78/75
81.1	Patney . .	82½	79 14	82
			pws	40
86.9	Lavington . .		84 00	
94.6	Heywood Road Jc .	93	91 08	72/65
97.0	Fairwood Jc .		93 10	72
100.3	Clink Road Jc .		96 04	62
102.3	Blatchbridge Jc .	100½	97 48	71
108.5	Milepost 122¾ .		103 11	60
115.1	CASTLE CARY .	113½	108 49	77/65*
122.0	Keinton Mandeville		112 46	77.5/74
125.8	Somerton . .		117 00	82/75
130.8	Curry Rivel Jc .		120 53	83
138.0	Cogload . .		126 25	72/73
142.7	TAUNTON . .	136½	130 18	70.5
146.6	Milepost 167 .		133 39	66
148.6	Milepost 169 .		135 30	62.5
149.8	Wellington . .		136 45	60
151.6	Milepost 172 .		138 39	46
152.6	Milepost 173 .		140 02	39
153.6	Whiteball Box .	149	141 37	37.5
158.6	Tiverton Jc .		146 18	77
160.9	Cullompton . .		148 15	eased
166.4	Silverton . .		153 01	80 (max)
170.0	Stoke Canon .		155 54	
173.5	EXETER . .	167½	159 14	45*
			pws	15
178.2	Exminster . .		165 59	
			pws	30
188.5	Teignmouth . .		178 44	
193.7	NEWTON ABBOT	192	186 15	

Net times: to passing Exeter, 156 min
to stopping at Newton, 178 min
* Speed restrictions

CORNISH RIVIERA EXPRESS
Dynamometer Car Test Run
Load: 12 cars, 393 tons tare, 420 tons full
Engine: 6013 *King Henry VIII*
Driver: F. Bolt; Fireman: E. Knapman (Laira)

Dist miles			†Actual m s	Speed mph
0.0	EXETER . .	.	0 00	pass slowly
3.5	Stoke Canon .	.	4 13	52.5
7.2	Silverton .	.	8 22	58.5
12.6	Cullompton .	.	13 34	65
14.9	Tiverton Jc .	.	15 40	60/66
19.9	Whiteball Box .	.	20 38	53.5
23.7	Wellington .	.	23 52	80
28.8	Norton Fitzwarren	.	27 49	71
30.8	TAUNTON .	.	29 27	74
38.8	Athelney .	.	35 45	77.5
42.5	Curry Rivel Jc .	.	38 40	75
48.0	Somerton .	.	43 29	65/71.5
53.5	Keinton Mandeville	.	48 15	67/75
58.4	CASTLE CARY .	.	52 31	53
			pws	17
61.8	Bruton .	.	59 00	46
65.2	Milepost 122¾ .	.	63 32	42
71.2	Blatchbridge Jc .	.	68 53	78
73.2	Clink Road Jc .	.	70 29	73
76.5	Fairwood Jc .	.	73 02	81
78.9	Heywood Road Jc .	.	75 02	70
86.6	Lavington .	.	81 28	76
92.1	Patney .	.	86 41	64.5
98.2	Pewsey .	.	91 41	73
103.4	Savernake .	.	96 20	61
107.1	Bedwyn .	.	100 00	easy
112.0	Hungerford .	.	104 35	62*
115.0	Kintbury .	.	107 19	70
120.4	NEWBURY .	.	111 43	79
123.9	Thatcham .	.	114 27	80
126.7	Midgham .	.	116 52	58*
132.3	Theale .	.	121 46	74.5
137.5	READING .	.	127 45	37*
142.5	Twyford .	.	132 52	68
149.3	Maidenhead .	.	138 28	74
155.0	SLOUGH .	.	143 07	74.5
160.3	West Drayton .	.	147 28	71
164.4	Southall .	.	151 12	70
167.8	Ealing .	.	153 51	71.5
			sigs	
172.2	Westbourne Park .	.	159 38	
173.2	PADDINGTON .	.	162 04	

Overall time from Plymouth, 241 min
† Times from passing Exeter slowly
* Speed restrictions

The Swindon dynamometer car in 1955, looking rearwards showing dials for direct indicating of horsepower

difficult one. It entailed the almost unprecedented firing rate of 4,000 lb of coal per hour between Exeter and Reading. Had not the engine crew thrown themselves into the task with might and main it would have been impossible. More than this, it would, even so, have been impossible had not Inspector Andress, who was riding on the footplate, worked like a Trojan in getting coal forward. This is one case where the running details, as given in the accompanying log, are not self-explanatory; but a comparison of the performances on 10 and 11 March go some way towards clarification.

Diagrams plotted in the drawing office of the experimental section at Swindon, showing the working over three sections where the engine was being steamed continuously hard for long periods, are reproduced herewith, namely from Exeter to Whiteball, from Taunton to Castle Cary, and from Heywood Road Junction to Savernake. On these diagrams are plotted the speed, the actual dhp

DOWN CORNISH RIVIERA EXPRESS: 10/3/55 Paddington—Newton Abbot	
Average net steam produced by boiler .	26,950 lb/hr
Firing rate	3,245 lb/hr
Average dhp	
under power	978
actual	828
Coal per dhp/hr	
inclusive of auxiliaries . . .	3·32 lb
exclusive of auxiliaries . . .	3·21 lb
Average speed (actual) . . .	62·5 mph

UP CORNISH RIVIERA EXPRESS: 11/3/55 Exeter—Reading	
Running time	127·6 min
Average speed	64·7 mph
Power time	117·3 min
Total coal	8,240 lb
Firing rate	4,210 lb/hr
Net steam rate	29,835 lb/hr
Average dhp	1,020
Coal per dhp/hr	
inclusive of auxiliaries . . .	4·13 lb
exclusive of auxiliaries . . .	4·00 lb

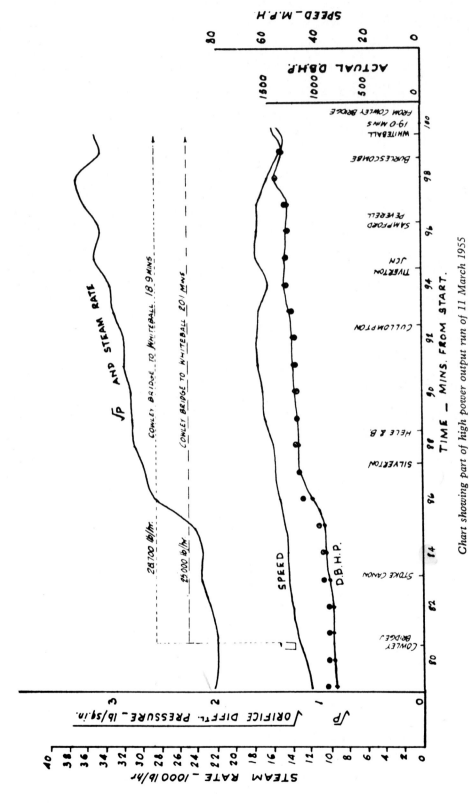

Chart showing part of high power output run of 11 March 1955

The Swindon dynamometer car in 1955, looking forward from integrator table

uncorrected from gradient, and the steam rate. Lines are drawn on the diagram to show the steam rate of 25,000 lb per hr, corresponding to the maximum firing rate it is considered that a single fireman could sustain continuously, and to a steam rate of 28,700 lb, which is considered to be attainable intermittently for recovery purposes. On clearing the area of restricted speed through Exeter, and beginning to settle down into express speed, it was soon clear that the adverse weather conditions were having a seriously hampering effect and soon after Stoke Canon a telephone message from the dynamometer car to the footplate initiated a marked stepping up of the effort. From there onwards a comparison of the actual steam rate with the 28,700 lb maximum recovery rate shows the outstanding nature of the effort developed. Near Burlescombe a peak of 37,000 lb per hr was attained, with an actual dhp, on 1 in 115, of 1,440. Corrected for gradient

this gave an equivalent figure of 1,860.

Between Creech Junction and Keinton Mandeville the steam rate was continuous above 30,000 lb per hr for 18 min, with a maximum of 34,000, with the edhp at 1,400 near Somerton. The third diagram shows the magnificent effort made between Heywood Road Junction and Savernake, when the fireman and Inspector Andress were both beginning to feel the physical strain of such an effort. On the 1 in 222 gradient from Lavington to Patney the minimum speed was 64 mph; the steam rate rose to a peak of 34,500 lb per hr, and the actual dhp recorded at 1,300 corresponded to an 'equivalent' value of 1,535. To keep up this kind of performance with little intermission, from Exeter to Reading, was a positively heroic effort on the part of Driver Bolt and Fireman Knapman of Laira shed. In addition to Inspector Andress I must also mention the engineer from the testing staff who was also on

253

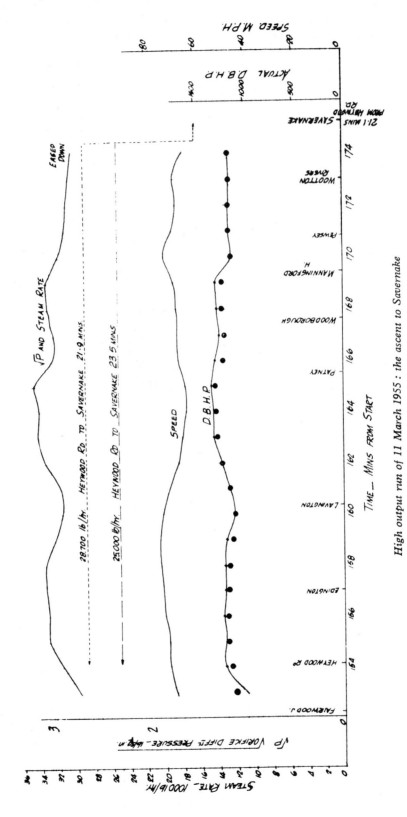

High output run of 11 March 1955 : the ascent to Savernake

Engine No 6015 'King Richard III' with double chimney

the footplate on this memorable occasion, for he became well known to enthusiasts in connection with the working of preserved locomotives: the ever-cheerful Ernest Nutty. Heroics apart, however, those graphs showed, in the greatest clarity, a weakness in the design of the 'King' class engines

as re-draughted. The steam rate is proportional to the square root of the back pressure, and this can be read off, to a different scale, from the three diagrams. It will be seen that there were times when this back pressure rose to about 10 lb per sq in.

Experience was available at Swindon showing the

Engine No 6015 on the Cornish Riviera Express on the run detailed on page 118

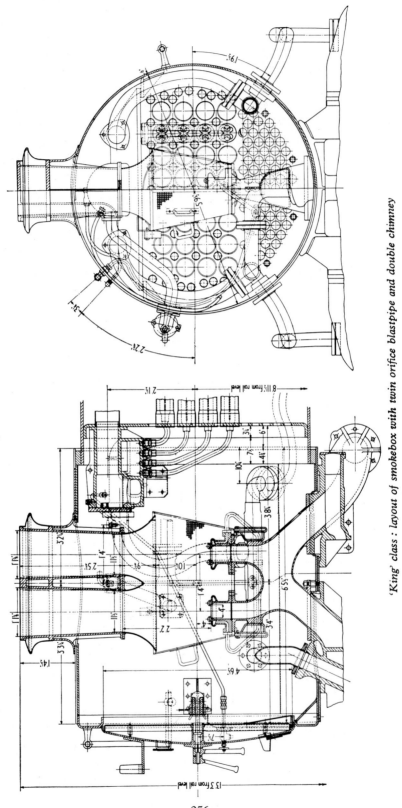

'King' class : layout of smokebox with twin orifice blastpipe and double chimney

effect of twin orifice blastpipes, and the working of the LMR 'Duchess' class 4—6—2, and of the 'BR8' showed that the arrangement of twin blastpipe and chimney had the effect, on those engines, of permitting a high rate of evaporation with a low back pressure. The smokebox of the 'BR8' engine had in fact been worked out at Swindon, and the two blastpipes were each those of a '2301' class 0—6—0—the celebrated 'Dean Goods'—which had an outstandingly successful arrangement of draughting. Smeddle, therefore, decided to try the effect of a double-blastpipe on a 'King'.

The lay-out of the smokebox incorporating the double blastpipe as worked out by Sam Ell is shown in the accompanying drawing. It was extremely successful in removing the limitations to evaporation imposed by the former single-chimney draughting arrangement. Henceforth the maximum continuous rate was limited only by the capacity of the grate to burn fuel. The efficiency of draughting was improved, enabling the orifice discharge pressure to be reduced to one-third of that of the single chimney arrangement, and this, of course, resulted in a considerable reduction in back pressure on the pistons, and a freer running locomotive. It was found possible to reduce the 'pull' on the fire and to achieve uniformity of air distribution over the firebed. Although this is to some extent anticipating the results of the test runs about to be described it was found in general that the double-chimneyed engines showed a 7 per cent economy in coal consumption over the single-chimneyed high-superheat 'Kings' with improved draughting. This economy was observed by the locomotive testing staff in the working of comparable revenue-earning express passenger services.

At this time also the 'Kings' were being fitted with new cylinders, and the historian can look back a little wistfully to what might have been achieved had the opportunity been taken of introducing the improved, internally streamlined design of cylinders sketched out for the projected 'Pacific'. The British locomotive world was already well aware of the astonishing improvement wrought by a comparable process on the LMSR 'Royal Scots', when the rebuilt version was produced, in 1943. In combination with the modified smokebox and blastpipe arrangements internally streamlined cylinders would have resulted in a veritable 'Super King'. The change would have required entirely new patterns and coreboxes, and the extra cost would have been considerable. The enhanced power might have been too much for the existing frame design to withstand, as it proved to be in the case of the Chapelon rebuilt

The original form of self-cleaning screens on the double-chimneyed 'Kings'

4—8—0s on the PO Midi Railway in France. The frames of the 'Kings' were partially renewed by welding on new front portions, ahead of the motion plate. This was, of course, just a renewal of the original design, and did not involve any strengthening or other modification.

Engine No 6015 *King Richard III* was the first to have the modified smokebox arrangement, and reports from the running inspectors were so enthusiastic that Sam Ell fixed up a trip on the Cornish Riviera Express, on which he was accompanied by Inspector W. Andress. The driver was W. Potter, the senior driver at Old Oak Common; essentially a 'safe' man, regularly entrusted with Royal Trains, but not at all the kind of man one would associate with all-out attempts on speed records. This suited Ell's purpose admirably, which was to see for himself how the modified engine performed when worked in the same way as the single-chimneyed engines were, when making maximum speeds of 85 mph. Ell and Inspector Andress rode No 6015 on Monday 26 September 1955, and on the following day Ell reported to Mr Smeddle thus:

THE GWR STARS, CASTLES & KINGS

Engines of the 'King' class have benefitted very substantially from improved draughting, but tests revealed that the internal resistance at high rates of evaporation and high speeds could be reduced by fitting a double chimney design with these special proportions. The greatest benefit would be found in the freedom with which the engine would run at high speeds and improvement in power then available.

Engine No 6015 has recently been fitted, and after an initial period on the 11.15 am ex Paddington was tried yesterday, September 26th, on the Cornish Riviera. This run revealed that the substantial improvements expected were attained. On stretches where high speeds of about 85 mph are normally obtained, speeds rose on engine No 6015 to over 100 mph with the same engine working. On stiff bank working, the reduced back pressure was reflected in a marked improvement in engine performance. Steaming in general was entirely satisfactory. Water consumption was relatively low and coal consumption reduced by the reduced tearing action on the fire by the double chimney.

I attach a log of the run, from which it will be seen that the engine was easily capable of recovering time from the several severe restrictions, and two of these signal checks. A third severe check at Totnes brought the train to a stand for 9 min, but the arrival at Plymouth was no more than 8 min late.

LOG OF CORNISH RIVIERA 10.30 AM PADDINGTON TO PLYMOUTH, MONDAY 26/9/55

Engine No 6015: Load 331 tons/10 vehicles throughout

			Booked	Actual
Paddington	.	d	10.30 am	10.30 am
Westbourne P	.	p	10.33	10.33
Southall	.	p	10.42	10.45
Slough	.	p	10.49½	10.51
Maidenhead	.	p	10.54½	10.56
Twyford	.	p	11.00½	11.01½
Reading	.	p	11.06	11.08
Newbury	.	p	11.24½	11.24
Bedwyn	.	p	11.37½	11.37
Savernake	.	p	11.41½	11.41
Patney	.	p	11.51½	11.50
Heywood Road Jc	.	p	12.02 pm	11.59
Blatchbridge	.	p	12.09	12.06 pm
Castle Cary	.	p	12.22	12.19
Creech	.	p		12.41
Taunton	.	p	12.46	12.45
Wellington	.	p		12.53
Whiteball	.	p	12.57	12.58
Exeter	.	p	1.15	1.17
Newton Abbot	.	arr	1.40	pass 1.44½
		dep	1.43	
Dainton	.	p	1.49½	1.50
Totnes	.	p	1.56½	arr 1.56
				dep 2.05
Brent	.	p	2.07½	2.18
Hemerdon	.	p	2.20	2.30
Plymouth (North Rd)	.	arr	2.30	2.38

Signal and engineering delays . . .	27 min
Late arrival at Plymouth	8 min
	—
Recovery by engine	19 min
Max recovery allowed in schedule . .	9 min
	—
Recovery above max recovery allowance .	10 min
	—

TRS 15 mph Ladbroke Grove } 1 min
TRS 50 mph O.C.C. East

TRS 50 mph Twyford East 2 min
Signal check Reading East

TRS 75 mph Patney - Lavington
Max speed 103 mph Lavington

Max speed 100 mph Curry Rivel
TRS 30 mph Alford H 4 min
Signal check Creech 2 min
TRS 15 mph Wellington 3 min

TRS 10 mph City Basin } 4 min
TRS 30 mph Teignmouth

TRS 30 mph Totnes
Signal check stopped 9 min

The speeds were carefully observed by stopwatch, and as Ell remarks, showed that where the single-chimneyed engines attained speeds of 85 mph the modified engine was running at 100 mph. He was so pleased with these results that he suggested that his chief assistant, H. Tichener, should also have a trip. This was quickly arranged, and on Thursday 29 September Tichener and Inspector Andress arrived at Paddington to ride No 6015 on the 'Limited'. Quite fortuitously Driver Potter was again on the job, and before leaving he confided to his 'passengers' that he might be able to do even better than on the Monday. And where both observers on the Monday had clocked 103 mph—just prior to the commencement of a slight permanent way restriction to 75 mph near Patney—Andress clocked one quarter mile, at 106½ and one at 108¾ mph. The stop-watch was not reset after the second reading, and was taken to Swindon and shown to Ell on the following day. Then the rumours began to get around: the popular press got hold of one version, and 116 mph was quoted in print, and eventually through the exaggerations of certain ultra-ardent Great Western fans the speed got at one stage to 130 mph! In one version reported personally to myself at Swindon the locality (110 mph) was given as Langport. Recent research, how-

St Ives to Paddington express (Saturdays) passing Wolfhall Junction, Savernake :
engine No 6017 'King Edward IV'

ever, and fresh conversations with those actually involved, has brought this documentation to light, and the 108½ is thus revealed as a reading from one stop-watch observer. The average for ¾ mile was 107½ mph.

This reported speed has since become the subject of some controversy; certain erudite analysts have claimed that it was impossible. I was not there, and there is no supporting evidence of point-to-point times; but Sam Ell was one of the most highly disciplined experimental engineers I have ever met, and I am sure that professional etiquette would have restrained him from making any exaggerated claim. I am quite prepared to admit that a few isolated stop-watch readings might have given figures a half or even 1 mph out; but not more than that. As to the 'impossibility' of such a figure, the increased freedom of the double-chimneyed engines gives the lie to any such assertion. As described in Chapter 20

of this book I logged in great detail a rapid acceleration to 102·5 mph with a single-chimneyed 'King' on Dauntsey bank, and I certainly do not see any theoretical reason why a much freer running engine should not have travelled at higher speed between Somerton and Curry Rivel Junction. There is unfortunately no absolute proof either way—only the word of an experimentalist of the highest integrity.

In May 1956 another engine, No 6002 *King William IV*, was put through a series of trials, first on the West of England road, and later between Paddington and Wolverhampton. Through Mr Smeddle's kindness I was able to accompany three of these runs, and was able to witness at first hand not only some very fine running but also some features of the performance that were of marked significance in comparison with the working of the single-chimneyed engines. My three runs were made on the 3.30 pm Paddington to Plymouth, on

Engine No 6017 'King Edward IV' with the tapered form of double chimney

Engine No 6002 'King William IV' (double chimney) passing Teignmouth

seven months earlier I had ridden on the footplate of engine No 6015 *King Richard III*, on the down 'Cornish Riviera Express', and logged a performance of outstanding merit. A reference to this personal experience may appropriately precede the description of the test runs. This was one of those occasions when the incidence of delays might well have seemed to put completely out of the question any chance of running the 'Cornish Riviera Express' to Plymouth in the even four hours. An abbreviated log of this journey is set out in the accompanying table.

Before the start it was known that three permanent way slacks were required. These were expected to cost about 9 min in running, and without unduly forcing the pace an attempt was made in the early stages to get some time in hand. With cut-offs of 15 per cent on the level to Reading, and 15 to 17 per cent up the Kennet Valley, 5 min had been gained on this fast timing to Patney. Then we ran into heavy fog, and instead of detaching our Weymouth slip coach at Heywood Road Junction we had to feel our way into Westbury and stop. This

the up 'Cornish Riviera Express', and on the 3 pm Birmingham Snow Hill to Paddington; but some

CORNISH RIVIERA EXPRESS
Load: to Westbury, 11 cars, 362 tons tare, 390 tons full
to Plymouth, 10 cars, 327 tons tare, 350 tons full
Engine: 6015 *King Richard III* (double chimney)
Driver: Newcombe; Fireman: Hawker (Laira)

Dist miles		Sch min	Actual m s	Speed mph	Dist miles		Sch min	Actual m s	Speed mph
0·0	PADDINGTON .	0	0 00		130·9	*Curry Rivel Jc* .		132 01	82
5·7	Ealing .		8 54	58·5	138·1	*Cogload* . .		137 32	73
9·1	Southall .	12	12 21	64				pws	15
13·2	West Drayton .		16 04	69	142·8	TAUNTON .	136	143 54	55
18·5	SLOUGH .	19½	20 23	75	144·8	Norton			
24·2	Maidenhead .	24½	25 00	73		Fitzwarren .		145 54	63
31·0	Twyford .	30½	30 34	74				pws	15
36·0	READING .	36	35 01	(slack)	149·9	Wellington .		153 32	60
44·8	Aldermaston .		44 11	68	153·7	*Whiteball Box* .	147	157 39	47
53·1	NEWBURY .	54½	51 43	64/68	158·7	Tiverton Jc .		162 03	78·5
58·5	Kintbury .		56 23	70	161·0	Cullompton .		163 54	eased
61·5	Hungerford .		59 05	60*	166·4	Silverton .		168 16	80 (max)
66·4	Bedwyn .	67½	63 31	67½	170·1	Stoke Canon .		171 10	
70·1	Savernake .	71½	67 19	eased	173·6	EXETER .	165	174 41	
75·3	Pewsey .		72 00	79/74	178·3	Exminster .		179 27	68
81·1	Patney .	81½	76 29	83·5	188·6	Teignmouth .		191 06	eased
			fog stop		193·8	NEWTON			
94·6	*Heywood Road Jc*	92	92 56	66		ABBOT .	190	197 38	25*
95·6	WESTBURY arr		95 03		194·9	*Aller Jc* .	.		56
	dep		96 53		195·6	*Milepost 216* .		200 05	
97·1	*Fairwood Jc* .	94	99 41	52	196·6	*Milepost 217* .		201 21	
100·4	*Clink Road Jc* .	97	103 24	53·5	197·6	*Dainton Box* .	197	203 20	26
	Blatchbridge .			69	202·3	Totnes .	204½	209 31	54
108·4	*Milepost 122¾* .		110 35	60·5	205·2	*Tigley Box* .		213 50	26·5
111·8	Bruton . .		113 31	75	207·0	*Rattery Box* .		217 39	34
115·2	CASTLE CARY .	112	116 28	60*	209·3	Brent . .	215½	220 49	50
			pws	15	218·9	*Hemerdon Box* .	230	231 47	63 (max)
120·1	Keinton				221·8	Plympton .		234 09	72 (max)
	Mandeville .		123 02	58·5	224·1	Lipson Jc .		237 11	
125·6	Somerton .		127 51	76/70	225·6	PLYMOUTH .	240	239 50	

* Speed restrictions

led to a delay of 12 min and made us $4\frac{1}{2}$ min late on passing Castle Cary with all three permanent way slacks yet to come. Yet, as will be seen from the log, with excellent work throughout we were able to make a punctual arrival in Plymouth, having effected a net gain of no less than 21 min on schedule. This was certainly a most impressive example of the work of the double-chimneyed engines; for although the load was relatively light, by the standards of this route, in the early stages the concluding load of 327 tons tare is fairly close to the maximum permitted to an unassisted 'King' over the South Devon line. Throughout the trip No 6015 in her modified condition gave every impression of a very strong and free-running engine. The water consumption was a total of 7,800 gallons, equal to 35 gall per mile, and an evaporation of 19,500 lb per hr. This, of course, was a long way below the maximum capacity of the locomotive.

Coming now to the full dress trials of engine No 6002, in May 1956, detailed logs are shown of the journeys that I experienced personally. These do not show in the bare times speeds achieved any features of performance that would not have been expected, either with the single-chimneyed engines with improved draughting or indeed from the original design in pre-war conditions of fuel and maintenance; but in the dynamometer car there were some points of significance. Furthermore, the results obtained a year earlier with the 'Duchess' class 4—6—2 of the London Midland Region were available for comparison. The latter was by common consent one of the most advanced designs in regular service in Great Britain at the time, and in the heavy duty imposed by test conditions on the Cornish Riviera Express both the 'Pacific' and the 'King' were well extended. The first test run with 6002 was made on the 3.30 pm express, which had a rather easier timing, but conveyed the full load as far as Exeter. There was the additional interest that with the reduced load from that station onwards no assistance was taken over the South Devon line, and one could see from the dynamometer car the effects of the Dainton and Rattery inclines.

To Taunton the train was run at the point-to-point times of the four-hour Cornish Riviera Express reaching Taunton stop in 133 min 14 sec against the 136 min to pass of the latter train. The engine appeared to develop the effort easily, and as will be seen from the log there was no actual dhp in excess of 1,150. From the restart a fine effort was made up Wellington bank, with 475 tons, and the 1,200 actual dhp approaching Whiteball Tunnel was equal to 1,540 'equivalent'—an excellent figure at 42 mph.

The later form of self-cleaning screen developed at Swindon

Over the South Devon line very consistent outputs of 1,100 to 1,250 actual dhp were shown on the banks, and with a load of 278 tons tare, 295 tons full this gave us minimum speeds of 30 mph at Dainton, 29.5 mph at Tigley, after a maximum of only 48 mph through Totnes, and an attained maximum of 40 mph at Rattery summit. With very easy running afterwards and a bad signal check at Plympton, we ran the 61.8 miles from Exeter to Plymouth in 69 min 33 sec instead of the 75 min booked to this train.

THE GWR STARS, CASTLES & KINGS

On the return journey by the Cornish Riviera Express on the following day we were double-headed as far as Newton Abbot, and then made the excellent run tabulated. We were working to the regular 4¼-hour schedule, and in good weather conditions had no particular need for hurry. The point that interested me above all others on this run was the striking difference in back pressure, as compared with that on the single-chimneyed 'Kings'. On the Bruton bank, where the engine was being worked hard the maximum difference in pressure across the orifice did not exceed 1¾ in of mercury. This

represented a smokebox vacuum of 9 in and a pressure of 4½ lb per sq in. In recovering from the Lavington permanent way check, where for a brief period the engine was being worked really hard, developing 1,300 actual dhp on a 1 in 222 gradient,

3.30 pm PADDINGTON—EXETER
Dynamometer Car Test Run
Load: 449 tons tare, 475 tons full
Engine: 6002 *King William IV* (double chimney)

Dist miles		Sch min	Actual m	s	Speed mph	Actual dhp
0·0	PADDINGTON	0	0	00		
1·3	Westbourne Pk	4	3	07		
5·7	Ealing		8	37	59	
9·1	Southall	13	11	51	66	
13·2	West Drayton		15	31	69	
18·5	Slough	21	19	53	74	
24·2	Maidenhead	26½	24	35	72	
31·0	Twyford	33	30	17	71	
36·0	READING	38	34	43	40*	
			pws		15	
41·3	Theale		42	58	59/64	1,150
46·8	Midgham		48	12	60*	1,000
53·1	NEWBURY	57½	54	28	64/61	
58·5	Kintbury		59	35	66	1,000
61·5	Hungerford		62	24	60*	
66·4	Bedwyn	71½	67	07	64	1,100
70·1	Savernake	76	71	05	45†	950
75·3	Pewsey		75	39	79/75	1,050
81·1	Patney	87	80	23	80·5	1,000
			pws		75*	
86·9	Lavington		84	43	87	950
94·6	Heywood Rd Jc	98	90	14	75	nil
100·3	Clink Rd Jc		95	08	61·5	1,000
102·3	Blatchbridge Jc	105	96	49	70·5	900
108·3	Milepost 122¾		102	32	58	
115·1	CASTLE CARY	108	50	67/56*	
120·0	Keinton Mandeville		113	10	72/68	870
125·5	Somerton		117	46	76/70	1,000
130·8	Curry Rivel Jc		121	49	84	
138·0	Cogload		127	21		
142·7	TAUNTON	148	133	14		
2·0	Norton Fitzwarren		3	43	51	1,100
7·1	Wellington		9	16	58	1,200
9·9	Milepost 173		12	32	42	1,200
10·6	Whiteball Box	16	14	00	41·5	
15·9	Tiverton Jc		18	46	74/68	
18·2	Cullompton		20	37	74	
				pws	15	
27·3	Stoke Canon		31	15	66	1,200§
29·5	Cowley Bridge Jc	35	33	23		
30·8	EXETER	37	35	38		

* Speed restrictions, regular
† After slack to 50 mph at Grafton
§ In accelerating from slack

UP CORNISH RIVIERA EXPRESS
Dynamometer Car Test Run
Load: 12 cars, 391 tons tare, 420 tons full
Engine: 6002 *King William IV* (double chimney)

Dist miles		Sch min	Actual m	s	Speed mph	Actual dhp
0·0	Newton Abbot West	0	0	00		
0·2	NEWTON ABBOT		1	10		
5·4	Teignmouth		7	55	50	
8·2	Dawlish		11	14	52	
15·7	Exminster		19	20	62	800
20·4	EXETER	24½	24	50	10*	
23·9	Stoke Canon		30	07	54	950
27·6	Silverton		34	07	60/55	
33·0	Cullompton		39	08	61	1,000
35·3	Tiverton Jc		42	00	54/58	900
40·3	Whiteball Box	48½	47	37	46	1,200 (max)
44·1	Wellington		51	01	82/79	
49·2	Norton Fitzwarren		54	47	84	
			sigs		58	
51·2	TAUNTON	59	56	42		
53·6	Creech Jc		58	52	72	800
59·2	Athelney		63	34	68	820
62·9	Curry Rivel Jc		66	57	72	
68·4	Somerton		71	45	60/70	950
71·6	Charlton Mackrell		74	43	64	930
73·9	Keinton Mandeville		76	42	70·5	800
78·8	CASTLE CARY	85	81	00	63	1,100
85·6	Milepost 122¾		88	18	45	1,000
91·6	Blatchbridge Jc	100	93	55	76	850
93·6	Clink Road Jc	102	95	32	72·5	
96·9	Fairwood Jc	105	98	07	77·5	
99·3	Heywood Rd Jc	107	100	03	70	1,000
107·0	Lavington		106	30	71·5	1,000
			pws		25	
112·5	Patney	121	115	18	56	1,300 (max)
118·6	Pewsey		120	54	66	1,000
123·8	Savernake	131	126	10	56	750
127·5	Bedwyn	136	129	45	70	
132·4	Hungerford		134	18	60*	700
135·4	Kintbury		137	04	71	
140·8	NEWBURY	147	141	27	77/73	
144·3	Thatcham		144	16	75·5	
147·1	Midgham		146	47	60*	
152·7	Theale		151	54	69	800
			sigs		30	
157·9	READING	163½	159	31		800
162·9	Twyford	169	165	09	69	900
			pws		15	
169·7	Maidenhead	174½	173	37	45	850
175·4	SLOUGH	179½	179	32	66	800
184·8	Southall	189	187	54	68	880
188·2	Ealing		190	52	68	
193·9	PADDINGT'N	202	199	10		

Net time 192 min
* Speed restriction

262

Dynamometer car tests with engine No 6002, having double chimney :
the 3.30 pm ex-Paddington passing Reading

the back pressure was less than 6 lb per sq in, and for the rest of the ascent to Savernake it was approximately 3 lb per sq in. This clearly indicated a much freer running engine than the single-chimneyed type, and fully justified the predictions made for the change. A considerably faster run was made on the dynamometer car test run two days later, with the same engine and load. There were little differences in time to Exeter, but after that the second journey drew ahead, with overall times of 53 min 51 sec to Taunton; 76 min exactly to Castle Cary; 94 min 2 sec to Heywood Road; and 152 min 57 sec to Reading. Although the effort was then somewhat eased the arrival at Paddington was in 188 min 25 sec from the Newton start—thus practically observing the special four-hour schedule operated in the 1955 trials with engine No 6013. In calm weather, however, there was a great difference in the effort required, as will be seen from the accompanying table.

Within my own experience in the dynamometer car, by far the hardest work demanded of No 6002 came on the trip with the 3 pm up from Birmingham. Schedule-wise this could have been an easy duty, but through a piece of faulty operating we were stopped for 13 min at Banbury Junction, and so left Banbury on our 67·5-mile run to Paddington some 16 min late. With a load of 434 tons tare this gave plenty of opportunity for some hard running. The immediate start out of Birmingham was quite gentle, but then we got away in great style, reaching 78 mph at Lapworth, passing Hatton somewhat faster than usual, and then touching 88 mph before Warwick. Climbing the Southam Road bank we did well, showing a back pressure of less than 4 lb per sq in, when developing 1,320 edhp at 50 mph, and then there came the succession of checks from Ironstone sidings onwards. On the continuation run to Paddington an allowance of 86 min would have been absurdly easy in comparison with pre-war running standards on the Birmingham route, even with **two**

UP CORNISH RIVIERA TESTS		
Year	1955	1956
Engine No . . .	6013	6002
Type	Single Blastpipe	Double Blastpipe
Load, tons tare . . .	393½	391
Average speed mph . .	64·7	64·7
Firing rate lb/per hr . .	4,210	2,800
Net steam rate lb per hr . .	29,835	20,800
Average dhp . . .	1,020	799
Coal per dhp hr (lb) exclusive of auxiliaries . .	4·0	3·5

'KING' AND LMR 'DUCHESS' CLASS COMPARISON OF TESTS RESULTS OF WR LOCOMOTIVES ON 'CORNISH RIVIERA'—WESTERN REGION

		WR 'King' Class No 6002				LMR 'Duchess' Class No 46237			
Date		28/5/56	29/5/56	30/5/56	31/5/56	17/5/55	18/5/55	19/5/55	20/5/55
Total coal	lb	11,083	10,232	11,997	10,460	13,601	12,759	14,427	12,859
Trip coal	lb	9,761	8,910	10,675	9,138	11,758	10,916	12,584	11,016
Trailing ton miles		98,500	97,100	103,800	97,100	104,700	97,700	96,380	105,200
Total water	lb	77,000	69,000	83,500	70,800	91,050	91,400	99,400	94,100
Work done on trailing load dhp	hrs	2,706	2,709	3,213	2,675	3,263	3,052	3,074	3,349
Total coal/trailing ton mile	lb	·112	·106	·116	·108	·130	·130	·150	·122
Total water/trailing ton mile	lb	·783	·711	·804	·729	·870	·943	1·032	·895
Total coal/dhp hr	lb	4·09	3·78	3·73	3·91	4·17	4·18	4·7	3·84
Total water/dhp hr	lb	28·4	25·5	26·0	26·5	27·9	30·0	32·4	28·1
Trip coal/dhp hr	lb	3·60	3·29	3·33	3·41	3·50	3·58	4·12	3·29

bad permanent way checks to be observed; but the late start was, for test purposes, fortuitous, and we had some really hard running.

The first significant item was the descent from Ardley to Blackthorn, where the engine was steamed hard. The figure of 1,150 dhp shown in the log was on topping Ardley summit, but the effort dwindled only a little as the speed rose from 56 mph at Ardley station to 86 mph at Blackthorn. At the latter point the back pressure was only 2 lb per sq in. A careful observance of the speed restriction was made at Ashendon Junction following which a big effort was transiently registered: 1,400 actual dhp and a back pressure of $4\frac{1}{2}$ lb per sq in. Some of the hardest work of all came in recovering from the Princes Risborough slack, up the 1 in 167 to Saunderton. At the summit speed was 35 mph; the actual dhp showed an equivalent value on this gradient of 1,470, and the back pressure was $7\frac{3}{4}$ lb per sq in. This was one of the highest registered with No 6002; but even this was low compared with the figures shown on certain stretches by No 6013 in the 1955 tests. Perhaps the most significant comparison between the single- and double-chimneyed engines, so far as these tests are concerned lies in the 900 dhp developed by No 6002 at 86 mph at Blackthorn, and the closely similar figure of 950 at 87 mph at Lavington on the down 3.30 pm express. In the full dress trials on No 6001 the actual dhp figure at 86 mph when 'all-out', two firemen and making a steam rate of 28,700 lb per hr was only 900. At Blackthorn No 6002 had the regulator eased back to give only 190 lb per sq in steam chest pressure. This shows clearly the great improvement in performance at high speed made by the introduction of the double chimney.

One of the most interesting results of the several stages of improved draughting on the 'Kings' is the comparison that the performance of the final version affords with the LMSR 'Duchess' class 'Pacific'. The overall results of the Cornish Riviera tests, in May 1955 with the 4—6—2 *City of Bristol* and in May 1956 with No 6002, are tabulated herewith, and on the strength of trip coal per dhp hour the advantage lies slightly with the 'King'. It was these results that convinced the Western Region management that there was no need to look beyond the indigenous Swindon design for locomotives to work the accelerated services. Authorisation was given for the whole class to be rebuilt with double chimneys, and the work was completed with No 6008 *King James II* in December 1958.

For some time previous to the 'King' trials, 'Castle' class engines had taken over the working

3 pm BIRMINGHAM—PADDINGTON
Dynamometer Car Test Run
Load: 434 tons tare, 470 tons full
Engine: 6002 *King William IV* (double chimney)

Dist miles		Sch min	Actual m s		Speed mph	Actual dhp
0·0	BIRMINGHAM					
	(SNOW HILL)	0	0	00		
3·2	Tyseley	5½	5	18	54	1,200
7·0	Solihull	12½	9	10	60	900
10·4	Knowle	12½	12	12	69	800
12·9	Lapworth		14	16	78	500
17·1	Hatton	18	17	38	72	700
21·3	Warwick		20	40	88	
23·3	LEAMINGTON	24	23	19		
1·1	*Milepost 105*		3	10		1,200
6·1	Southam Road		9	25	50/49	1,000
11·2	Fenny Compton		14	42	63/54·5	950
16·2	Cropredy		19	42	72	700
			sig stops			
19·8	BANBURY	25	41	37		
3·5	King's Sutton		5	48	56	
5·1	*Aynho Jc*	9½	7	29	60	
			pws		25	
10·3	Ardley	18½	15	38	45	1,150
14·1	BICESTER		18	58	80	950
17·1	Blackthorn		21	02	86	900
20·1	Brill		23	14	73/77	
23·4	*Ashendon Jc*	33½	26	00	61★	1,150
27·4	Haddenham		29	38	71	1,400
32·8	PRINCES					
	RISBORO'	44	35	08		
			pws		15	
	Summit				35	1,300
36·0	Saunderton		42	30	53	1,250
38·7	West Wycombe		45	30	62 (max)	
41·0	HIGH					
	WYCOMBE	54	48	28	40★	1,100
45·8	Beaconsfield		54	11	56	900
50·1	Gerrards Cross		58	11	73	600
52·7	Denham	68	60	12	82	500
57·2	Northolt Jc	72	63	41	75	500
59·7	Greenford	74	65	35	78	
62·9	*Park Royal*		67	58	65	
64·2	*Old Oak West Jc*	78	69	36	45★	
66·2	Westbourne Pk	82	72	23		
67·5	PADDINGT'N	86	75	18		

Net time 68¼ min from Banbury
★ Speed restrictions

ABOVE. Engine No 7018 'Drysllwyn Castle' being fitted with twin blastpipe and chimney

BELOW. Engine No 6000 'King George V' in final form

Engine No 7018 'Drysllwyn Castle' as first fitted with double chimney, and 3-row superheater

of the 'Bristolian' express in both directions. This gave much better utilisation of motive power, as the engine of the down train returned to London on the 12 noon up express from Temple Meads, and the engine of the up express returned on the 7.50 pm down from Paddington. Such was the success attained with the first 'Kings' fitted with double chimneys that a parallel development was commenced with the 'Castles'. Engine No 7018 *Drysllwyn Castle* was selected as the 'guinea pig'. She had been very much of a black sheep, but was taken in hand by Sam Ell and his staff, and as fitted with a double chimney in May 1956, showed vastly

improved performance, while retaining her original three-row superheater. The black sheep thereupon became a veritable 'flower of the flock', and following dynamometer car tests on the Torbay Express was allocated to Bristol Bath Road shed to work the up 'Bristolian'. Once again I had the privilege of personal participation in these notable developments. On 26 July 1956 I rode down from Paddington to Torquay in the dynamometer car behind No 7018, and on 9 August 1956 rode the engine from Bristol to Paddington in 97 min 8 sec start-to-stop. The log of the dynamometer car test run on the Torbay Express is appended herewith.

Dynamometer car test run with the Torbay Express : engine No 7018
ascending Goodrington bank

THE TORBAY EXPRESS
Dynamometer Car Test Run
Load: 9 cars, 310 tons tare, 330 tons full
Engine: 7018 *Drysllwyn Castle* (double chimney)
Driver: Way; Fireman: Rutherford (Newton)

Dist miles		Sch min	Actual m s		Speed mph
0·0	PADDINGTON .		0	00	
5·7	Ealing . . .		9	04	60 (max)
			sigs		45
9·1	Southall . .		12	26	
18·5	SLOUGH . .		21	49	71
			sigs		20
			pws		20
36·0	READING . .	38	47	35	
44·8	Aldermaston .		56	59	65
53·1	NEWBURY . .		64	39	68/64
58·5	Kintbury . .		69	27	71
61·5	Hungerford . .		72	05	61★
66·4	Bedwyn . .		76	39	66
70·1	Savernake . .		80	40	46
			pws		10
75·3	Pewsey . . .		86	10	
81·1	Patney . . .		93	28	70·5
86·9	Lavington . .		97	52	87
94·6	*Heywood Road Jc* .	94½	103	18	77/72
97·0	*Fairwood Jc* .		105	12	74
100·3	*Clink Road Jc* .		108	02	60
102·3	*Blatchbridge Jc* .		109	55	71
108·5	*Milepost 122¾* .		115	18	63
115·1	CASTLE CARY .		120	52	78/62★
122·0	Keinton Mandeville .		124	57	76/71
125·8	Somerton . .		129	23	78/74
130·8	*Curry Rivel Jc* .		133	08	88
138·0	*Cogload* . .		138	30	79
142·7	TAUNTON . .	140	142	12	72
144·7	Norton Fitzwarren .		143	52	70·5
149·8	Wellington . .		148	38	62
152·6	*Milepost 173* .		151	40	47·5
153·6	*Whiteball Box* .	152	152	58	46
158·6	Tiverton Jc .		157	16	84/70
160·9	Cullompton . .		158	55	83
			eased		65
166·4	Silverton . .		163	28	78
170·0	Stoke Canon . .		166	27	74
173·5	EXETER . .	170	169	54	

Net time 156 min
★ Speed restriction

There were a couple of severe permanent way checks in operation on the London side of Reading and with reaction from the slow running of other trains with close margins ahead we began getting signal checks no further out that Southall, and eventually we passed Reading 9½ min late. Then, except for a permanent way check near Pewsey we

got a clear road right through to Exeter and covered that 137·5 miles in 122 min 19sec to arrive on time. Quite apart from the pleasure of logging an exciting run the double-chimneyed 'Castle' gave ample evidence of her improved performance. Up the Kennet Valley we were registering 750 to 900 actual dhp, but one of the most remarkable demonstrations was that during the high speed sustained on the level after descent of the Lavington bank we registered a drawbar pull of 3·8 tons, and an actual dhp of 800 at 88 mph. The drawbar pull rose again to nearly 4 tons on the rise to Milepost 122¾, that time at 67 mph and developing an actual dhp of 950. During the fast running across the Langport cut-off with full regulator, and showing a steam and 3·8 tons, though the maximum of 88 mph on this stretch was attained under easier steam than the corresponding one on the level between Lavington and Edington: a 2·1 ton drawbar pull, and an actual dhp of 500.

The effort was stepped up to some purpose after Taunton, and the drawbar pull increased from 1·6 tons at Norton Fitzwarren to 3·5 tons at Wellington and finally to 4·5 tons entering Whiteball Tunnel. The engine was there working in 30 per cent cut-off line the drawbar pull varied between 1·8 temperature of 750 deg F. From Wellington to the tunnel the actual dhp lay between 1,000 and 1,050, with the equivalent value at 1,450 on the 1 in 80 gradient. A fast run down to Exeter wound up a most excellent performance. The principal comment to make is that this engine, with double blastpipe and chimney, showed herself capable of a power output at high speed little below that of the re-draughted single-chimneyed 'King' No 6001, when going 'all-out' on a steam-rate of 28,700 lb. *Drysllwyn Castle* as finally rebuilt was certainly an exceptional engine. When I rode her on the up 'Bristolian', only a fortnight later, she had a much easier task, even though running at full recovery rate throughout and arriving 8 min early. The water consumption was a little under 30 gallons per mile, and the firing rate only about 2,400 lb per hr. The impact of the 'King' tests with No 6002 and the successful running of No 7018 are discussed in the following chapter.

CHAPTER 22

1958 AND AFTER

IN February 1958 the Western Region of British Railways took delivery, from the North British Locomotive Company, of the first of an entirely new type of express passenger locomotive, the diesel-hydraulic D600. The fact that this particular class proved unsuccessful, and that the name of the pioneer engine *Active* proved something of a misnomer, is apart from the general theme of this book. But the fact remains, that the arrival of D600 at Swindon marked the first step in a programme involving the complete replacement of steam traction by diesel in the Western Region. This metamorphosis had been long foreseen, and all but the most diehard reactionaries were resigned to its inevitability. Few however foresaw the precipitous haste with which the change would ultimately be made. In February 1958 no 'Stars' remained in traffic; but only five Churchward engines rebuilt as 'Castles' had been withdrawn. The entire 'Castle' class proper was still in service, plus one rebuild, No 4037, and of course the 'King' class was then intact. Taken together there were, at that date, 196 four-cylinder 4—6—0 express locomotives in service. Eight years and four months later the last survivor of that famous stud was taken out of traffic.

There is a good deal of evidence to suggest that the 'plan' for the replacement of steam included a great number of loose ends. When substantial orders were placed for diesel-hydraulic locomotives it was announced that it was part of a plan for the complete replacement of steam *west of Newton Abbot*. It revived memories of the ill-fated Great Western scheme for oil-firing. But so far as the present book is concerned it seems quite evident that in 1958, and even later, a considerable life was envisaged for the 'Castle' and 'King' class locomotives, if only from the amount of money that was spent in keeping a high proportion of them tuned virtually to concert pitch.

During their later years the 'Kings' fell victims to a number of troubles, arising directly from their longevity. They were never anything but top link

engines. Apart from the brief periods when they were running in, after visits to Swindon for overhaul, they were consistently on the heaviest main-line work, and after thirty years troubles of a purely mechanical kind were almost inevitable. One of the most serious was the crop of fatigue cracks that developed in the bogies from January 1956. Repairs had been made by welding from time to time, but at this period the failures were sufficiently numerous for the whole class to be temporarily withdrawn from service until additional stiffening strips had been welded to the bogie frames. They were not out of traffic for long. Engine No 6012 was returned to service in the first week in February and the others followed quickly. During the emergency four Stanier 'Pacifics' were borrowed from the London Midland Region. There had been 'Duchesses' before on the Western Region; but this time the visitors included two engines of the 'Princess Royal' class.

While the repairs to the bogies were in the nature of 'patching up'—albeit, a thoroughly good and lasting job—other modifications were considered which were intended to prolong the life of the class for a further dozen years at least. Their early replacement did not appear to be foreseen in 1957-8. One of the most interesting developments was the proposal to fit roller bearings to all axles, and it went so far as the placing of an order with British Timken for complete sets of bearings for eight engines. The material was delivered at Swindon in 1957-8. Whether the substitution of roller bearings for the well-designed Swindon plain bearing would have increased the free-running qualities of the locomotives is a moot point; but it would almost certainly have reduced casualties from overheated bearings, which were becoming more frequent with the increased age of the locomotives. Unfortunately the work was never done.

The renewal of the front portion of the frames has been briefly mentioned previously. This had always been a source of some weakness in all the

Great Western four-cylinder 4—6—0 locomotives, though in stating this it must be appreciated that it is said in a relative sense only. The design as a whole was very sound, but when locomotives are in continuous heavy service for the number of years enjoyed by the 'Castles' and 'Kings', any weakness, however relative, will begin to show up in old age. When the front section of the frames needed renewal the remainder was usually fit for further use, and it was therefore the practice to cut the frames ahead of the leading coupled axle, and to weld on a new front section. By official reckoning this was considered to make the locomotives fit for a further twenty-five years of service! All thirty engines of the 'King' class had this renovation carried out, together with new cylinders. Another modification was the fitting of new outside steampipes. Movement of the outside cylinders, caused by flexing of the frames, caused breakages of the outside steampipes, and these were therefore redesigned to make them more flexible by omitting the original straight section, and increasing the radius of the end sections. The change was quite apparent, and with a modified front casing over the inside cylinders, associated with the renovated front frames, and the double chimneys, the 'Kings' certainly had something of a new look about them in their latter days.

Another interesting change concerned certain of the 'King' class engines stationed at Wolverhampton. From 1954 onwards these engines were fitted with 'Alfloc' water treatment equipment; this enabled them to run for thirty days between boiler washouts, and provided for more consistent steam-

The 1955 bogie contretemps : engine No 6013 minus bogie

ing because the heating surfaces collected less scale. Eventually the fitting of 'Alfloc' equipment extended to seventeen 'Kings': all the 1927-8 batch except 6003, 6004, 6010, 6018 and 6019, plus Nos 6020 and 6022. I had a footplate pass to ride No 6014, so equipped, on the 9 am up two-hour express; but on

Up West of England express climbing Bruton bank : engine No 6018 'King Henry VI'

The up Mayflower near Dawlish Warren : engine No 6004 'King George III'
with double chimney

the particular day there was unfortunately a derailment at Bicester which necessitated our diversion via Oxford. 'Kings' were not allowed to run between Ayhno and Didcot, and so we had to give up No 6014 at Banbury, and take instead a high-mileage 'Hall'.

Over the years the general scheme of allocation to sheds of the 'King' class engines had not varied very much. Until the end of World War II they had been divided, in varying numbers, between Old Oak, Newton Abbot, Laira and Stafford Road, and in 1947 it was interesting to find that the London allocation was at its smallest ever, while Newton Abbot and Laira were at their maximum. The figures were then 9, 5, 12 and 4. In December 1948 however Nos 6000, 6018 and 6019 were transferred

Kingswear - Paddington express leaving Whiteball Tunnel :
engine No 5055 'Earl of Eldon'

The down Torbay Express at Whiteball summit : engine No 7000
'Viscount Portal'

to Bristol. They were frequently on the 9 am up express to Paddington, while one of them worked on a triangular diagram from Bristol to Shrewsbury, Shrewsbury to Paddington and thence back to Bristol. The three engines did not stay at Bristol very long. In the summer of 1959 No 6019 was transferred to Newton Abbot for two months, and during that brief sojourn was the last 'King' to be stationed there. It was returned to Bristol in September 1949, and then with No 6018 went to Old Oak Common in July 1950. The pioneer engine No 6000 remained longest at Bristol and went to Old Oak Common in September 1952. From then until the autumn of 1961 the class was divided only between Old Oak, Stafford Road and Laira. In the exciting summer of acceleration on the West of England route, 1955, the allocation was Old Oak 14, Laira 10, Stafford Road 6.

When the diesels really began to get a hold on the West of England services the 'Kings' were gradually transferred away from Plymouth, and by the autumn of 1959 there were only two left, Nos 6013 and 6016. In February 1960, however, these were reinforced by the arrival of No 6002, though this was followed by the almost immediate transfer of No 6013 to Old Oak. In September 1960 No 6019 went to Cardiff Canton shed, and this was the prelude for the general transference of 'Kings' to Cardiff. In August 1961 six more of them arrived in Wales. This was their last home, and it lasted for less than a year, because in February 1962 withdrawal began, and by the end of that year the whole class had been taken out of traffic. The final allocation, as in January 1962, has a melancholy interest but is worth quoting:

Engine No	Shed
6000	Old Oak
6001	Stafford Road
6002	Laira (SRD 7/62 to 9/62)
6003	Canton
6004	Canton
6005	Old Oak
6006	Stafford Road
6007	Stafford Road
6008	Old Oak
6009	Old Oak
6010	Canton
6011	Stafford Road (OOC 9/62-12/62)
6012	Old Oak (SRD 4/62 to 9/62)
6013	Stafford Road
6014	Stafford Road
6015	Stafford Road
6016	Laira (SRD 7/62 to 9/62)
6017	Stafford Road
6018	Canton (OOC 6/62 to 12/62)
6019	Canton (SRD 3/62 to 8/62)
6020	Stafford Road
6021	Old Oak
6022	Stafford Road
6023	Canton
6024	Canton
6025	Old Oak
6026	Old Oak
6027	Stafford Road
6028	Old Oak
6029	Old Oak

The large accumulation at Stafford Road came to include some engines that were in store. Others came to be stored at Swindon. The last three, 6000, 6011 and 6018, were withdrawn in December 1962.

271

Down Saturday relief Cornish Riviera Express on Ratte y incline : engines 6002
'King William IV', which had worked the first part to Newton Abbot,
and 5099 'Compton Castle'

Of these No 6000 was saved for preservation, while No 6018 was taken out of store in April 1963 to work enthusiasts' special. Otherwise this was the end, and the end of one of the most famous steam locomotive classes the world has ever known. Engine No 6013 showed the highest total mileage, 1,950,162.

If the 'Kings' were approaching their end when the year 1958 opened, the last phase of the remarkable history of the 'Castles' was only just beginning, and it was a phase clearly intended to last a great deal longer than actually proved to be the case. The excellent results obtained with the double-chimneyed engine No 7018, and its fast running in regular service on the 'Bristolian', prompted a further development, in the combination of a double chimney with a 4-row superheater, on engine No 4090 Dorchester Castle. There had in the meantime

A distinguished nameplate : engine No 5017

been another rebuild with double chimney, No 5043 *Earl of Mount Edgcumbe*; but it was the performance of *Dorchester Castle* that really sparked off the final phase of 'Castle' history. After conversion No 4090 went back to her former shed, Old Oak Common, and was soon put on to the down 'Bristolian'. While there was not a great deal of difference in the maximum steaming capacity of the engine the increased freedom in running was most marked and made her very popular on that fast train. The running inspectors at Bristol, who were using No 7018 on the corresponding up train, also watched her performance. The earlier reputation of No 7018 as a black sheep had not entirely been effaced, and there were some inspectors who considered she was still not ideal. Bath Road shed certainly had some very splendid single-chimneyed engines, both of the 2-row and 3-row superheater varieties, and No 7018 was against strong competition.

Smeddle himself took a keen personal interest in the working of the double-chimneyed engines, and the success of No 4090 led to a further rebuilding of No 7018. In April 1958 that engine left Swindon not only with a four-row superheater but also with a lubricator setting that gave about 50 per cent more oil than standard. She then became a 'flyer' beyond compare, though so far as can be traced no other 'Castle' had this lubricator setting. Between the end of 1957 and December 1961 no fewer than sixty-four further 'Castles' received double chimneys, the last to be so modified being

OUTSIDE STEAM PIPES

Original shape on No 5017   *Modified shape on No 5018*

No 5078 *Beaufort*. The actual dates of the engines so converted are given in the Appendix dealing with the case histories of the three classes of four-cylinder 4—6—0. In view of the gathering impetus of dieselisation it was remarkable that conversions were continued during the year 1961, for by then withdrawal of the 'Castles' had begun, and by January 1961 eight of the '4073' and '5013' classes had been withdrawn, in addition to five of the re-builds from 'Stars'. During 1961 three more of the '4073' class were scrapped, while fifteen others were equipped with double chimneys. At that time, faced with the impending withdrawal of the entire 'King' class Smeddle envisaged the retention of a

Paignton to Paddington express climbing Bruton bank : engine No 5044
'Earl of Dunraven'

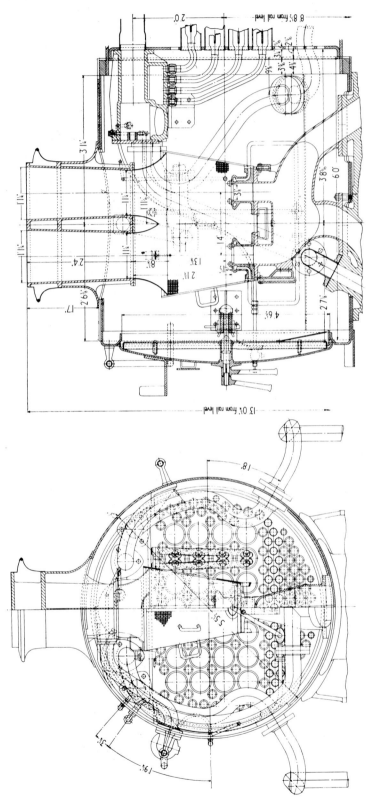

'Castle' class : arrangement of smokebox with twin-orifice blastpipe and chimney; 4-row superheater

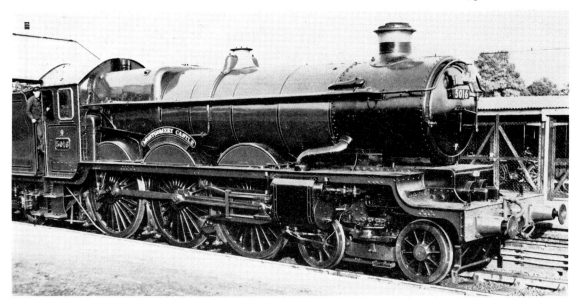

The standard '5013' class as running in early BR days :
No 5016 'Montgomery Castle'

reduced stud of 'Castles' equipped with every aid to efficiency that he could provide.

Looking at the double-chimneyed 'Castles' in more detail, the accompanying drawing shows the layout of the smokebox, and it is rather curious to notice the lack of internal streamlining of the passages leading to the twin-blastpipes. The flat surfaces, and almost square corners are very marked. This drawing also shows the form of spark-arrester devised at Swindon. It had been claimed that the original Churchward type of smokebox was partially self-cleaning on account of the spark-arresting baffles; whatever claims might have been made for it in this direction an enormous amount of ash used to collect, and I shall always remember seeing the smokebox door opened on the engine that had worked the up Cornish Riviera Express on arrival at Old Oak shed, and the deposit was almost up to the top of the blastpipe! After nationalisation a number of 'Castles' and 'Kings' were fitted with the LMSR type of self-cleaning baffles. These proved difficult to clean, and caused a slight loss of draught. Superficially also they were very unwelcome because they caused the train and the surrounding

Engine No 4087 'Cardigan Castle' at Laira sheds, June 1960

275

The up Bristolian passing Hullavington at 90 mph plus : engine No 7018
'Drysllwyn Castle'

countryside to be covered with a deposit of smoke-box char. The Great Western had always paid a high regard to the amenities of the countryside through which it passed, and the risk of crop fires and such like had always received the most serious consideration. At Swindon, therefore, an indigen-ous type of spark-arrester was developed, in the form of a basket round the blastpipe. It allowed small particles of char to pass but arrested the larger ones.

The double chimney, as originally fitted was not a handsome device. It was a built-up affair with flat sides, although incorporating the characteristic lip-top and copper adornment. These were later re-placed by a cast design of slightly elliptical cross section. It tapered outwards from the base, and some students of locomotive history have connected this detailed feature with Mr Smeddle's personal influence, recalling that he was a North Eastern man by training, and son of a North Eastern officer of long standing and high status. Quite apart from its shape, however, the double chimney sadly im-paired the graceful appearance of the 'Castles', particularly when seen broadside. The setting for-ward of the chimney caused this effect; but as will be appreciated from a study of the cross-sectional drawing it could not have been avoided. One must be content with the axiom 'handsome is as hand-some does', and the double-chimneyed 'Castles' in their freedom of running certainly had the advant-age over the standard ones of the post-war era. Whether or not any of them, even including the exceptional 7018 with her extra oil supply, could have surpassed an outstanding pre-war engine with hydrostatic-lubricators, and the jumper in pristine condition, is another matter.

The jumper ring could well have been a govern-ing factor if any deliberate attempt at a maximum speed record had been made with an engine of the '5013' class. This device was intended to lift at each exhaust beat when a locomotive was working hard at low speed, and lessen the chance of disturbance of the firebed. Experience suggested that the jum-

*Outside cylinder, showing detail of original
form of steampipe*

North to West express near Onibury : engine No 7017 'G. J. Churchward'

per-top was apt to remain lifted whenever a loco-motive was working hard, at whatever speed, and to remain lifted. One can well imagine that when 'Stars' and 'Castles' were working fourteen-coach trains of 500 gross tons or more, on the Cornish Riviera or Torbay Expresses, the going could be tremendously hard, continuously, for the first 1¼ hours out of Paddington. It is true that the blast

The down Torbay Express at Wolfhall Junction, Savernake :
engine No 7000 'Viscount Portal'

The up Cornishman climbing Hemerdon bank : engine No 7015
'Carn Brea Castle', with double chimney

might be softened at a time when the demand for steam was at a maximum, but the exhaust would be freer, and by lessening the back pressure permit of a higher indicated hp to be developed in the cylinders. The truth was that if the jumper ring remained continuously raised for any length of time it would become jammed with smokebox char and

seriously impair the steaming by keeping the blast-pipe orifice at its increased area just at a time when the smaller area was needed to produce draught.

The withdrawal of the 'Castles' began in March 1950 with No 100 A1 *Lloyds*. This, of course, was not a true 'Castle' in originally having been a rebuild of No 4009 *Shooting Star*. Three more rebuilds went in 1951-3, namely 111, 4016 and 4032. The historic No 4000 *North Star* was withdrawn in May 1957, and before she went I had enjoyed a brief but excellent run on her footplate from Wolverhampton to Shrewsbury, with the heavy 2.9 pm express. The last of the rebuilds, No 4037, survived until 1962. This engine had received new frames and almost to the end she was a favourite on the double-home turns between Newton Abbot and Shrewsbury. An excellent example of her work is quoted on p 286. The first true 'Castle' to be scrapped was No 4091 *Dudley Castle* in January 1959, though Nos 4073 and 4074 had actually been included in the Western Region withdrawal programme for 1955. Far from being withdrawn No 4073 continued in traffic until May 1960, while No 4074 got a double chimney in April 1959!

While R. F. Hanks was Chairman of the Western Region Board, and the succession of general managers were ex-Great Western men the old traditions were as secure as anything could be under nationalisation, and Smeddle received staunch backing from Paddington. But in January 1962 there was a

Engine No 7004 'Eastnor Castle' on train carrying
official mourners to Windso at the funeral
of King George V

Saturdays only West to North express near Whiteball summit :
engine No 7029 'Clun Castle'

great change. Roy Hammond went to the Eastern Region and in his place there arrived the fiery, iconoclastic S. E. Raymond. Within a matter of days cherished relics of former Great Western prowess were consigned to the vaults, and from the general manager's room there came an all-out campaign to try and eradicate all memories of the past. One important feature of this campaign was to secure for the Western Region the distinction of being the first region of British Railways to eliminate steam traction completely. Quite apart from any technical questions of motive power the chief mechanical engineer, for the first time in Swindon's history since the great Churchward-Inglis feud, found himself seriously at variance with the general manager, and in 1962 after only a few troubled and bitter

months Smeddle retired, to be stricken immediately with what proved to be a fatal illness.

In 1962 no fewer than fifty-four 'Castles' were withdrawn, including four, Nos 5008, 5019, 5027, and 5078, which had received double chimneys in 1961. In 1963 the slaughter was almost as great, with a further forty-nine condemned, and the year 1964 opened with only forty-six of the class still in service. A historian of the future, comparing this rate of demise with other features revealed in the case history of the 'Castle' might well rub his eyes and wonder what the impecunious nationalised British Railways were really about in those years from 1958 to 1963. But when propaganda gets a really firm hand logic and sound economics are apt to be cast to the winds.

CHAPTER 23

SWAN SONG

THE story of the elimination of steam traction on the express train services of the Western Region as told in Chapter 22 makes remarkable, if sad, reading; but 'Castles' and 'Kings' alike went down with flying colours, and in this final chapter an account must be given of some outstanding performances put up in those last eight years. In those years I was travelling regularly between Paddington and Bath, and quite apart from the interesting details of engine performance that I collected the reliability of the service in general was such as to be taken for granted in arranging business appointments, often with fairly tight margins. The series of travel diaries that I kept during those years gives the complete lie to the somewhat nauseating anti-steam propoganda issued from official circles in those years of transition. Whatever reasons may have been advanced for the superseding of steam it was certainly not unreliable on the London-Bath route. I have, nevertheless, written enough to place the capacity of the 'Castles' and 'Kings' beyond any doubt, and in this chapter I am concerned with certain performances in those last years that have features of special significance.

At that time the 7.45 am up from Bristol was something of a prestige business train. It had a 60-

Penzance - Wolverhampton express descending Dainton bank : engines No 5066 'Sir Felix Pole' (double chimney) and No 5065 'Newport Castle'

8.26 am CHIPPENHAM—PADDINGTON					
Engine No		6023		6003	
Engine Name		*King Edward II*		*King George IV*	
Load: to Didcot Coaches		12		13	
Tons E/F		426/460		443/480	
Load: to Paddington Coaches		11		11	
Tons E/F		391/420		373/405	

Dist miles		Actual m s	Speed mph	Actual m s	Speed mph
0·0	CHIPPENHAM	0 00		0 00	
		sig stop			
6·3	Dauntsey	15 45*	0	8 25	61
11·1	Wootton Bassett	24 15		13 44	47/55
16·7	SWINDON	29 45		19 20	
22·5	Shrivenham	34 30	77	24 19	74
27·5	Uffington	38 15	82	28 18	77·5
33·6	Wantage Road	42 48	80	32 58	79
40·9	DIDCOT	48 07	83·5	38 54	64†
45·5	Cholsey	51 29	82	42 54	76·5
52·5	Pangbourne	56 42	78·5	48 53	64†
58·0	READING	60 57	69†	53 34	71·5
63·0	Twyford	65 13	72	57 50	73
69·8	Maidenhead	70 49	73·5	63 11	76·5
75·5	SLOUGH	75 27	75	67 37	77
80·8	West Drayton	79 48	70·5	71 47	75
84·9	Southall	83 27	67	75 08	73·5
88·3	Ealing	86 22	69	78 08	
		sigs			
90·7	*Old Oak West Jc*	89 05		80 42	
92·7	Westbourne Park	93 07		84 31	
				sig stop 4 min	
94·0	PADDINGTON	96 35		93 57	

Net times	min	84	86

* Departure time   † Speed reductions

mph timing up from Chippenham, and was usually worked by a 'King'—very frequently No 6000. With a load of around 400 tons it was normally a fairly easy task, but I have tabulated herewith details of the running on two somewhat exceptional occasions. Both engines concerned were then fitted with double chimneys. On the first run, made in December 1958, we were stopped by signals at Dauntsey, and so took 29¾ min to pass Swindon. Then despite a load of 460 tons to Didcot, and 420 tons beyond, we went like the wind, and averaged 77·5 mph throughout from Swindon to Slough. Down the gentle descent through the Vale of the White Horse we ran at 82-3 mph, and although the pace was not so hot after the marked easing through Reading we nevertheless passed Southall, 78·6 miles from the start at Dauntsey, in 67 min 42 sec. Our actual start-to-stop run from Dauntsey to Paddington, 87·7 miles, was made in 80 min 50 sec inclusive of a final signal check. From Swindon eastwards we were running fully up to the standards required on the pre-war 'Cheltenham Flyer' and 'Bristolian' with double the load. On the second run we had a

heavier load from Chippenham, but a completely clear road to Old Oak Common. On this trip the average speed from Swindon to Southall was 73·3 mph and steam was shut off at the latter station, we having covered 84·9 miles from the dead start in 75 min 8 sec.

Out of a number of runs on the down 'Bristolian' it is perhaps no more than natural that two with the pioneer engine to have the combination of double chimney and four-row superheater should be outstanding. Generally speaking the down train was a harder proposition than the up 'Bristolian', with the long, faintly adverse stretch to Swindon, usually against the prevailing wind, and there were times when the ordinary 'Castles', with the improved draughting, had their work cut out to keep time. In April 1958 engine No 5060 *Earl of Berkeley* gave me a typical run in the single-chimneyed tradition. The start out of London was delayed and it took 22 min 33 sec to pass Slough. Then we averaged 76 mph over the next 58·8 miles on to Swindon, an extremely good piece of uniform running with a maximum of 80·5 mph approaching Reading, and

'Caerphilly Castle', when stationed at Bristol, and working the 9 am Temple Meads to Paddington, in Sonning Cutting

THE 'BRISTOLIAN'

Engine: 4090 *Dorchester Castle* (double chimney)
Load: 7 cars, 246 tons tare, 265 tons full

Dist miles	Driver (Old Oak)						Actual m s	Speed mph (W. Harris)	Actual m s	Speed mph (Jermy)
0.0	PADDINGTON	.	.	.	.	.	0 00		0 00	
5.7	Ealing	.	.	.	.	.	8 32	62.5	8 22	62
9.1	Southall	.	.	.	.	.	11 32	72	11 27	69
13.2	West Drayton	.	.	.	.	.	14 53	77	14 52	76.5
18.5	SLOUGH	.	.	.	.	.	18 55	79/74	18 51	80.5
24.2	Maidenhead	.	.	.	.	.	23 23	78.5	23 08	81
31.0	Twyford	.	.	.	.	.	28 26	82	28 12	76.5
							pws	15	pws	15
36.0	READING	.	.	.	.	.	33 33		33 38	
41.5	Pangbourne	.	.	.	.	.	38 47	75	39 34	71
48.5	Cholsey	.	.	.	.	.	44 11	77.5	45 03	80
53.1	DIDCOT	.	.	.	.	.	47 44	78	48 28	81
60.4	Wantage Road	.	.	.	.	.	53 20	77	53 59	78
66.5	Uffington	.	.	.	.	.	58 03	78	58 41	77
71.5	Shrivenham	.	.	.	.	.	61 49	79.5	62 36	76.5
									sigs	50
77.3	SWINDON	.	.	.	.	.	66 14	78	67 33	
82.9	Wootton Bassett	.	.	.	.	.	70 26	81.5	72 15	82
87.7	Dauntsey	.	.	.	.	.	73 47	95	75 33	95
91.0	*Milepost 91*	.	.	.	.	.	75 52	91	77 40	90
94.0	CHIPPENHAM	.	.	.	.	.	78 02	78	79 56	72
98.3	Corsham	.	.	.	.	.	81 23	75.5	83 24	76
101.9	Box	.	.	.	.	.	84 09	80/72*	86 08	79/76
106.9	BATH	.	.	.	.	.	88 34		91 03	
113.8	Keynsham	.	.	.	.	.	95 01	72	97 58	74
118.4	BRISTOL (TM)	.	.	.	.	.	100 47		103 45	
	Net times				min		98¼		99¾	

a minimum of 74·5 mph at Challow. The maximum at Dauntsey was 86 mph and Bristol was reached in 104 min 33 sec. Net time was exactly 100 min. This was an excellent performance in itself, and showed the remarkable consistency of steaming that distinguished the 'Castles' at their best. The two runs with No 4090 *Dorchester Castle*, however, showed a mastery over the schedule that the single-chimneyed engines did not possess.

There was a striking similarity in the work of two different drivers, both of whom I came to know well, and yet were widely differing personalities. In their running as far as Twyford there were no more than seconds in it, and both were sustaining over 80 mph on the 1 in 1,320 rise from Maidenhead. The two runs were made within a week of each other, and both suffered a heavy permanent way check at Reading. Both recovered to make average speeds of 78·3 and 77 mph over the 35·8 miles from Pangbourne to Swindon. The times over this stretch might well have been identical had not the second run experienced a signal check to 50 mph at Highworth Junction. Both trains passed the top of

'Clun Castle', passing Belle Isle, en route from Kings Cross to York, 1967

Dauntsey bank at 85 mph, and then again there was an astonishing correspondence over the next 6 miles between posts 85 and 91: 3 min 53 sec and 3 min 55 sec with maximum speeds of 95 mph on both runs. After that, with clear roads, neither driver had occasion to hurry unduly, and both trains arrived at Bristol comfortably within schedule time. Some

Her last journey and attracting little attention! No 4073 in the streets of Kensington, en route for the Science Museum

Sixtieth anniversary, 1904-1964 : No 4079 'Pendennis Castle' leaving Paddington on high speed run to Plymouth

months later I had a footplate pass to ride one of the double-chimneyed engines on this service, but the occasion was unfortunately marred by very bad weather, dense fog in places, and an exceptional delay due to a road accident having damaged one of the overbridges near Pangbourne.

I used frequently to travel by the 1.15 pm from Paddington, which also required some smart locomotive work to cover the 106·9 miles to Bath nonstop in a working time of 96½ min. With a slightly slower timing than the 'Bristolian' this train occasionally carried an extra coach, but out of many good runs there was not one that stands noticeably above the average of good 'Castle' performance in those last years. I have tabulated one, however, that has something of a sentimental interest in that one of the now-preserved engines, No 4079 *Pendennis Castle*, was involved. It was made just before Christmas 1957, and with an entirely clear road we stopped at Bath in 94¼ min from Paddington. There was nothing special about the performance except its complete steadiness of steaming, and an average speed against the slight gradient of 71·4 mph. The engine was in excellent form at that time, and on the various Bristol workings gave a number of sound runs. Inevitably one thinks of the age of the engine, though of course there would not have been much of the original machine left in 1957. Before she passed into the hands of her later owners

Dist miles	1.15 pm PADDINGTON—BATH Load : 7 cars, 250 tons tare, 265 tons full Engine : 4079 *Pendennis Castle*		Sch min	Actual m s		Speed mph
0·0	PADDINGTON	.	0	0	00	
5·7	Ealing	. . .		8	27	58
9·1	Southall	. .	11½	11	41	66
13·2	West Drayton	.		15	20	71
18·5	SLOUGH	.	19	19	40	73·5
24·2	Maidenhead	.		24	19	73·5
31·0	Twyford	.		29	49	74
36·0	READING	.	33	33	48	77
41·5	Pangbourne	.		38	18	70
48·5	Cholsey	. .		44	16	70
53·1	DIDCOT	.	49½	48	13	70
60·4	Wantage Road	.		54	28	69
66·5	Uffington	.		59	44	69
77·3	SWINDON	.	72	69	05	68·5
82·9	Wootton Bassett	.		73	42	75·5
87·7	Dauntsey	.		77	23	84
94·0	CHIPPENHAM	.	85	82	05	74
98·3	Corsham	.		85	48	64·5
101·9	Box	. .		88	48	79
106·9	BATH	. .	97	94	15	

Pendennis Castle was to appear still more vividly in the limelight, as will be told later in this chapter.

I now pass to what proved to be the very last years, and there is first a run made in April 1962 on the 60-min evening express from Oxford to Paddington. With a certain amount of encouragement from interested observers the more sporting of the drivers were showing what these engines could do, and the accompanying log illustrates the work of *Llandovery Castle,* when with a clear road the train of six coaches was brought into Paddington 7 min early. The average speed of 71·7 mph was slightly slower than that of the pre-war 'Cheltenham Flyer' over a route that was shorter and which included only 53 miles of uninterrupted fast running. The friend that logged this run told me that on the following day an even faster run was made by engine No 4082 *Windsor Castle.* This, of course, was the changeling (*née* 7013). The time claimed was 51 min though this has not been fully authenticated, other than my friend's testimony that he saw the train pass through Twyford, and the time by his watch was one min faster than on the previous day when he logged the run in detail. These last two experiences are enough to show the spirit that emulated the steam locomotive express drivers in those final years.

There are next two interesting runs logged respectively in 1960 and 1961 on the West to North route, on the Newton Abbot - Shrewsbury double-home turns. They show the work of both sheds concerned, and I have tabulated only the Hereford - Shrewsbury sections of the runs. The double-

Dist miles		Sch min	Actual m s	Speed mph
	5.30 pm OXFORD—PADDINGTON Load: 6 cars, 188 tons tare, 200 tons full Engine: 5001 *Llandovery Castle* (double chimney)			
0·0	OXFORD . .	0	0 00	
5·1	Radley . .		6 48	
7·3	Culham . .		8 37	82
10·6	*Didcot East Jc* .	11½	11 35	45*
14·9	Cholsey . .		15 48	
21·9	Pangbourne .		21 01	85
27·4	READING . .	25½	24 53	87
32·4	Twyford . .		28 27	82
39·2	Maidenhead .	35	33 13	87
44·9	SLOUGH .	39½	37 12	85
50·2	West Drayton .		40 50	83
54·3	Southall . .	46½	43 48	82
57·7	Ealing . .		46 12	87
			sigs	
62·1	Westbourne Park .		50 05	
63·4	PADDINGTON .	60	53 09	

chimneyed engine *Barbury Castle* was running punctually from Hereford, whereas the veteran No 4037, still with single chimney, was 9¼ min late through a succession of signal and permanent way checks from Bristol. The observer who logged the run of *Barbury Castle* was pardonably astonished by an arrival 14 min early, and spoke to the engine crew on arrival. The driver's only comment was: 'She's on form, so we let her run'. But a further incentive was, of course, that they were Salop men working home after a lodging turn! As a piece of engine performance it was splendid, particularly in the final minimum of 42 mph at Church Stretton, after several miles climbing at 1 in 112. On the

Restored to her former glory: No 4073 outside Paddington before transfer to the Science Museum

		Sch min	5095 *Barbury Castle* 386/410			4037 *The South Wales Borderers* 386/410		
	Engine No							
	Engine Name							
	Load: tons E/F							
Dist miles			Actual m s		Speed mph	Actual m s		Speed mph
0·0	HEREFORD	0	0 00			0 00 sigs		5
1·7	*Shelwick Jc*	5½	3 58			4 50		
4·2	Moreton-on-Lugg		6 50		60	7 46		60
7·5	Dinmore		10 21		55	11 21		53
10·2	Ford Bridge		13 14		61	14 33		64
12·6	LEOMINSTER	17	15 37		62	16 45		62
15·8	Berrington		18 50		57	19 48		60
18·9	Woofferton	24	22 00		72	22 47		71
23·5	LUDLOW	30	26 36		59	27 16		60
25·7	Bromfield		29 05		58	29 30		61
28·1	Onibury				49	32 03		50
31·1	CRAVEN ARMS	40	35 10		56	35 26		60
35·6	Marsh Brook		40 56		47	42 26 44 01		sig stop
38·2	CHURCH STRETTON	51¼	44 32		42	49 58		35
41·7	Leebotwood		48 18		70	53 40		73 (max)
44·6	Dorrington		50 42		81	56 13		
46·8	Condover		52 33			58 18 sigs pws		
51·0	SHREWSBURY	73	58 51			66 58		

companion run my friend rode on the footplate. For those who claim that excellent Great Western performance was only possible with good coal this run provides something of a poser, because the fuel was a mixture of dust and ovoids. Although the fire was getting dirty, after the long run up from Newton, the pricker livened it up quickly. Newton Abbot men were on the job, and engine No 4037 was justifiably a favourite on this arduous double-home turn. The steaming was free, with pressure entirely

North to West express near Kingskerswell : engine No 4037 'The South Wales Borderers'

between 210 and 220 lb per sq in except for some brief lapses quickly remedied with the pricker. Cut-offs were between 15 and 20 per cent with half-open regulator, until the unfortunate signal stop at Marsh Brook. From this recovery had to be made up a continuous gradient of 1 in 112, and with full regulator and 30 per cent cut-off a speed of 35 mph was attained. Despite this stop the recovery margin in the schedule after Church Stretton would have allowed a punctual arrival in Shrewsbury; but a succession of checks after Condover prevented this, and made the train 3¼ min late on arrival.

Early in 1962 proposals were on hand for accelerated service by the Paddington - Birmingham route, and the civil engineer required a high-speed test, with the 'white-wash' car to observe the condition of the track under really high-speed running. For some reasons which I am not concerned with

here the 'special' had to be steam-hauled. One of the double-chimneyed 'Castles', No 7030, was taken out of store at Old Oak, and duly prepared for the job. Very hard work was anticipated, even though the train consisted of no more than five vehicles, and Driver Pimm of Old Oak had two firemen with him, while Inspector Hancock also rode on the footplate. The accompanying logs are important, as embodying what is probably the fastest running ever made over this route, particularly on the return trip. The start of the outward journey was not unduly fast—in fact I have a log of my own on which Gerrards Cross bank was climbed at 64·5 mph by a 'Saint' class engine hauling 320 tons! But after High Wycombe *Cranbrook Castle* was driven to some purpose, and the minimum speed of 76 mph at Ardley was first class. In the circumstances one might have expected faster running between Banbury and Southam Road, and the severe schedule between High Wycombe and Leamington was not maintained.

There was a tremendous start out of Leamington. Warwick was passed at 60 mph and a maximum of 70 attained before entering upon Hatton bank. Then its 3¼ miles at 1 in 110 were climbed with no lower drop in speed than from 70 to 66 mph. After that the delays were too much for timekeeping.

HIGH SPEED TEST TRAIN: 15 MAY 1962
10.25 am PADDINGTON—WOLVERHAMPTON
Load: 5 cars, 176 tons tare, 180 tons full
Engine: 7030 *Cranbrook Castle* (double chimney)

Dist miles		Sch min	Actual m s	Speed mph
0·0	PADDINGTON	0	0 00	
3·3	*Old Oak West Jc*	6½	5 53	
7·8	Greenford		10 33	73
10·3	Northolt Jc	13	12 32	68
14·8	Denham		16 30	74
17·4	Gerrards Cross		18 51	66
21·7	Beaconsfield		22 38	78 (max)
26·5	HIGH WYCOMBE	26½	27 39	
5·0	Saunderton		6 48	67
8·2	PRINCES RISBOROUGH	10	9 50	62*
13·6	Haddenham		13 55	96
17·6	*Ashendon Jc*	16½	16 36	86
20·9	Brill		18 58	
23·9	Blackthorn		21 02	92
26·9	BICESTER	22½	23 09	83
30·7	Ardley	25½	26 05	76
35·9	*Aynho Jc*	30	30 18	85/65*
41·0	BANBURY	34	34 45	74
44·6	Cropredy		37 48	72/70
49·6	Fenny Compton		42 00	75/66*
54·7	Southam Road		46 04	87 (max)
60·8	LEAMINGTON	49½	51 45	
2·0	Warwick		3 04	70 (max)
6·2	Hatton	7	6 56	66/55*
10·4	Lapworth		11 01	75
12·9	Knowle		13 14	
			pws	15
16·3	Solihull		18 56	54
20·1	Tyseley	18	22 33	79/60*
23·3	BIRMINGHAM (SNOW HILL)	22	25 59	
25·9	Handsworth	28½	30 06	
30·7	Wednesbury		37 23	
			sigs	
35·9	WOLVERH'PTON	42	46 55	

Net times: High Wycombe - Leamington 50½ min
Leamington - Wolverhampton 38 min
* Speed restrictions

'Clun Castle' approaching Shap summit,
14 October 1967

K

There was a turn-round time of 1 hr 55 min at Wolverhampton, and then there commenced the hard run back to Paddington set out in the second table. Once again the schedule proved to be too tight on the central section, despite some most spectacular running. From the start at Leamington there was an acceleration to 68 mph up the 1 in 187 of Southam Road bank, and a maximum of 86 mph preceded a slight easing through Banbury. Even so 1¼ min had been lost to Aynho, and a further ½ min was lost despite the tremendous burst of speed from Bicester to Brill. My friend's claim of a maximum speed of 103 mph at Blackthorn is well authenticated, but one can note the very hampering effect of the Aynho slack, when properly observed, as the average speed from Cropredy to Brill was no more than 80·7 mph. I have seen an average of 75 mph over this same stretch with a 'Star' and 380

tons! But this included an entirely unchecked speed of 75 mph over Aynho Junction. Again the speed restrictions at Ashendon Junction and Princes Risborough were very hampering, and that 1¼ min by which the train was down at Aynho was not recovered by High Wycombe. The final dash for London included a second maximum of 103 mph and as the scheduled stopping times at both Leamington and High Wycombe were cut the latter station was left on time and Paddington reached 1 min early. To all who participated it must have been a very exciting day.

As related in Chapter 22, the year 1962 saw the virtual ending of the Great Western four-cylinder express passenger 4—6—0s in regular passenger service, but there was a number of special runs in farewell. One of the most interesting was the round trip from Paddington to Plymouth and back, organised by Ian Allan to mark the sixtieth anniversary of the ever-famous 'Ocean Mail' record run of 9 May 1904. At that late stage in the superseding of steam it cannot have been easy to find an adequate number of 'Castle' class engines capable of the efforts demanded; because it was to be no sentimental perambulation, but a succession of tremendously hard runs. In actual fact there were, in May 1964, only thirty-nine remaining in traffic. One of these, and an excellent engine too, was No 4079 *Pendennis Castle*, which scored such a triumph for the GWR in the inter-exchange trials of 1925, and she was chosen to make the down journey, non-stop to Plymouth, in the level four hours. On the return journey the route of the 'Ocean Mail' of 1904 was to be followed, via Bristol, and in addition to a very fast run in *City of Truro* style from Plymouth to Bristol the last stage was to be made in the fastest-ever steam schedule from Temple Meads to Paddington, via Badminton, in 100 min start-to-stop. The engines chosen for the return trip were the double-chimneyed 7029 *Clun Castle*, from Plymouth to Bristol, and a standard engine of the '5013' class, No 5054 *Earl of Ducie*, from Bristol to Paddington. It was hoped to reach 100 mph both down Wellington bank, and at Little Somerford. As on the Wolverhampton test runs of 1962 two firemen were to be carried on each engine.

The provision of the two firemen requires a little explanation. On these runs the demands for steam and the associated firing rates were not expected to be more than had been regularly sustained in the hey-day of the 'Castle' class engines, including the working of the 'Bristolian' express. And although the timing proposed for 9 May 1964 was 100 min, the former 105 min steam timing included 8 min

	HIGH SPEED TEST TRAIN: 15 MAY 1962

2.20 pm WOLVERHAMPTON—PADDINGTON
Load: 5 cars, 176 tons tare, 180 tons full
Engine: 7030 *Cranbrook Castle* (double chimney)

Dist miles		Sch min	Actual m	Actual s	Speed mph
0·0	WOLVERH'PTON	0	0	00	
5·2	Wednesbury . .		7	52	
10·0	Handsworth .	15	13	45	69
12·6	BIRMINGHAM				
	(SNOW HILL) .	20	17	08	38*
15·8	Tyseley . . .	24	20	54	70
19·6	Solihull . . .		24	02	80 (max)
			pws		15
23·0	Knowle . . .	29½	27	23	
25·5	Lapworth . .		31	54	86
29·7	Hatton . . .	34½	35	21	65*
33·9	Warwick . . .		38	38	84
35·9	LEAMINGTON .	40	41	10	
6·1	Southam Road .		7	15	68/78
11·2	Fenny Compton .		11	21	76
16·2	Cropredy . .		15	17	86
19·8	BANBURY . .	17	17	58	78*
24·9	*Aynho Jc* . .	21	22	14	80/65*
30·1	Ardley . . .	25	26	32	76
33·9	BICESTER . .	27½	29	07	98
36·9	Blackthorn . .		30	55	103
39·9	Brill . . .		32	53	85
43·2	*Ashendon Jc* .	34	35	42	61*
47·2	Haddenham . .		39	04	80
52·6	PRINCES				
	RISBOROUGH .	41½	43	31	62*
55·8	Saunderton . .		46	25	68
58·5	West Wycombe .		48	48	81/48*
60·8	HIGH WYCOMBE	50½	51	59	
4·8	Beaconsfield . .		5	15	68
9·1	Gerrards Cross .		8	21	91
11·7	Denham . . .	10½	10	01	103 (max)
16·2	Northolt Jc . .	13¾	13	11	
19·7	Greenford . .	15	14	40	
23·2	*Old Oak West Jc* .	18½	18	25	40*
			pws		15
25·2	Westbourne Park .	20½	21	55	
26·5	PADDINGTON .	26	25	15	

* Speed restrictions

288

Relief for a diesel : No 5024 'Carew Castle' on the northbound Devonian near Torre, in the autumn of 1960

recovery time, so that an overall time of 97 min was expected to be regularly attainable with any engine put on to the job. In 1964, however, the number of firemen who were regularly working on steam was very small. To fire a big locomotive on a crack duty needs not only physical strength and fitness, but that build-up of physical training so well known to the athlete. Men working as 'second man' on diesels could not fail to be lacking in that physical training, and when long sustained running at 85-90 mph was contemplated the provision of a reserve fireman on the footplate was no more than prudent.

The full story of that exciting day has been told in great detail in *The Railway Magazine;* but brilliant though much of the running was, at that late stage in history, it added nothing to the saga of 'Castle' performance, in that no fact of individual achievement surpassed what had been done previously—if not in precisely the same location then certainly in comparable circumstances. *Pendennis Castle* was going well until part of the grate collapsed and she had to come off the train at Westbury. *Clun Castle* distinguished herself by hauling the 265-ton train from Exeter to Whiteball Box in 17 min 19 sec, and going over the summit at 67 mph, but no *City of Truro* exploit was attempted on the Wellington side. Even so that 75·6 miles from passing Exeter to arrival in Bristol took only

62 min 19 sec against the 64 min 17 sec of the 4—4—0 engine in 1904. A real record was hoped for on the final stage, but a side wind proved troublesome. A brilliant start was made out of Bristol, but although the engine was pressed very hard down the 1 in 300 from Badminton the maximum attained was no more than 94 mph. Many times I have seen the up 'Bristolian' cross the overbridge across the main road near Hullavington aerodrome, and the 'Castles' always seemed to be flying effortlessly on the wings of the wind. While one could hear the beat, it was the beat of an engine working in ideal conditions. On 9 May 1964 at least one very experienced locomotive engineer who was at the lineside thought that the *Earl of Ducie* was being 'slaughtered', to use his own word. The overall time to Paddington was 95 min 33 sec, and the engine suffered no harm in the process; but this time fell a little short of the fastest 'Bristolian' record, when No 7018 *Drysllwyn Castle* in her 4-row superheat days made the run in 93 min 50 sec, including a maximum of 100 mph at Little Somerford.

This year of 1964 saw the virtual end of 'Castle' working so far as official Western Region activities were concerned. By the end of the year only eleven of them remained in traffic; but two of them, both participants in the runs of 9 May 1964, were purchased and preserved under private ownership. These were No 4079 *Pendennis Castle* and 7029 *Clun Castle*. The latter was the last to remain in passenger service, and worked the last steam-hauled train out of Paddington on 11 June 1965. Since then *Clun Castle* has become the most widely-travelled engine of the class. She was in good condition when she was taken out of traffic, and so needed no 'restoration' in the ordinary sense; but her new owners had her repainted in the full Great Western style of the early 1930s, with the company's name in full on the tender, and the coat of arms; with the number on the front buffer beam, and the cast plate removed from the smokebox door. She retained the double chimney with which she was fitted in October 1959. Although this splendid new turnout was stretching a point so far as strict historical accuracy was concerned, in that *Clun Castle*, built in May 1950, was never a Great Western engine, all will rejoice at the enterprise that resulted in her preservation.

Under various auspices *Clun Castle* has made a number of special runs, but one of the most interesting from the performance point of view was on Saturday 14 October 1967, organised by the North Western branch of the Locomotive Club of Great Britain—'Castle to Carlisle'. The outward run was

LOCOMOTIVE CLUB OF GREAT BRITAIN
14 October 1967
SPECIAL TRAIN: GARSTANG—CARLISLE
Load: 7 cars, 215 tons full
Engine: 7029 *Clun Castle* (double chimney)

Dist miles		Sch min	Actual m s	Speed mph
0·0	GARSTANG .	0	0 00	
			pws	10
5·9	Bay Horse .		12 57	52
7·2	Galgate . .		14 30	67·5 (max)
11·5	LANCASTER .	17	18 50	55*
14·6	Hest Bank .		21 30	77·5
17·8	CARNFORTH .	27	24 14	58*
21·0	*Milepost 9½* .		27 47	47
25·1	Milnthorpe .		31 44	67·5
30·6	OXENHOLME .	43	37 57	44/47
37·7	*Grayrigg* .		47 15	42·5
			pws	35
43·7	Tebay . .	65	55 05	56·5
46·7	*Scout Green* .		58 45	38
49·2	*Shap Summit* .	75	62 33	42
			sig stop	
51·2	Shap . .		70 00	
			sig stop	
62·7	PENRITH .	90	90 26	
	Carlisle No 13 Box .	114	109 50	pass slowly

made by the LNWR route and the return by the Midland. By the kindness of one of the participants, Mr J. M. D. Bateman of Todmorden, I am able to include the accompanying logs of the most interest-

'Clun Castle', under private ownership, at Kings Cross, 8 October 1967

'Clun Castle' passing Durran Hill Junction on leaving Carlisle for Hellifield

ing sections of the two runs. The load was a light one compared with that No 5000 *Launceston Castle* had been required to haul on the 10 am from Euston to Glasgow, as between Crewe and Carlisle, in the autumn of 1926; but the circumstances were very different in 1967, when steam-hauled trains were not popular on British Railways. *Clun Castle* did very well from the booked stop at Garstang, and the ascent of Shap, with an acceleration from 38 mph at Scout Green to 42 at the Summit, was

LOCOMOTIVE CLUB OF GREAT BRITAIN
14 October 1967
SPECIAL TRAIN: APPLEBY—HELLIFIELD
Load: 7 cars, 215 tons full
Engine: 7029 *Clun Castle* (double chimney)

Dist miles		Sch min	Actual m s	Speed mph
0·0	APPLEBY . .	0	0 00	
2·5	Ormside . .	.	4 05	61
5·3	*Griseburn Box* .	.	7 07	54
7·5	Crosby Garrett .	.	9 14	62
10·7	Kirkby Stephen .	.	12 41	55/48
14·0	*Mallerstang* . .	.	16 41	50/48
17·5	*Aisgill* . .	28	20 57	50
				65
20·6	Garsdale . .	.	24 20	
			pws	20
23·8	Dent . .	.	30 30	
25·9	*Dent Head Box* .	.	32 35	62·5/60
28·7	*Blea Moor* . .	40	35 25	64
30·0	Ribblehead .	44	36 30	70
34·8	Horton . .	.	40 44	70·5
36·4	*Helwith Bridge* .	.	42 05	72/65
40·8	Settle . .	.	46 03	72
42·7	*Settle Jc* .	64	47 47	55*
46·0	HELLIFIELD .	70	53 29	

* Speed restriction

remarkable. The descent to Carlisle was, however, subject to very heavy delay. On the return trip over the Midland line the train had a very easy timing to Appleby, and indeed also on the continuation to Hellifield; but fortunately those responsible were in the mood to 'have a go' over the mountain section, with the excellent results shown in the accompanying table. Speed did not fall below 48 mph on the longest stretches of 1 in 100 ascent, between Smardale viaduct, just south of Crosby Garrett, and the south end of Birkett Tunnel, and again after Mallerstang. On the final stretch there was actually a recovery from 48 to 50 mph on the 1 in 100 before Aisgill summit was reached.

Clun Castle had by that time also become a familiar object on the Eastern Region, having run a 'Castle to Newcastle' trip on 9 September 1967. Between these two outings of the Locomotive Club I myself travelled behind *Clun Castle* on an Eastern Region officers' special from Finsbury Park to Peterborough, on 26 September 1967, an occasion that I am not likely to forget, because on the following morning, travelling by the diesel-hauled 9.45 am from Paddington, I was involved in the high-speed derailment at Foxhall Junction!

Since the first edition of this book was published the situation regarding the survivors of this great family of locomotives has changed a little. *Lode Star* and *Caerphilly Castle* are safe as priceless museum pieces, but those in running condition have been joined by No 5051, preserved carrying its original name of *Drysllwyn Castle*, while, to the regret of many, *Pendennis Castle* is away in the arid regions of north-western Australia. While occult from the gaze of most of us, I know that there she is a much honoured symbol of the best in British steam locomotive practice; and having visited the Hamersley Iron Railway I can appreciate what a superb sight she makes in that iron-red terrain.

At home, while locomotives such as 5051, 6000, and 7029 are still in running condition, and it is hoped that they may soon be joined by 6024, one cannot ring down the final curtain. The place in history of the breed as a whole, extending from the construction of the *North Star* in 1906 to the runs of *Clun Castle* in 1967, now extends over a full sixty years, and Smeddle's final development of the 'Kings' placed those engines on a level of efficiency fully equal to that of the Stanier 'Duchesses'. It can only be regretted that the occasion never arose

for an all-out trial of the double-chimneyed 'King' in the same way that Nos 6001 and 6013 were tested, and that one of them was not given the chance to reveal her true maximum speed capabilities. Nevertheless, on the evidence provided by the test results included in this book, there is material for connoisseurs to analyse, discuss and debate the possibilities for many years to come. The sure-footedness of the Great Western 4—6—0 was proverbial. One feels that the logical development would have been a 4—8—0 rather than the suggestion of a 'Pacific'. In France, Chapelon demonstrated how it was possible to get a phenomenal power-output from a narrow firebox on his PO Midi rebuilt 4—8—0s. A Swindon 4—8—0, with all the refinements of the Smeddle era, and internally streamlined cylinders, is an intriguing proposition.

ACKNOWLEDGEMENTS

The author and publishers wish to express their thanks to the following for permission to use illustrations: Messrs F. J. Arthur, p 79; R. L. Blenkinsop, p 282; P. F. Bowles, p 166 bottom; E. D. Brinton, p 117 top, 185 bottom, 210, 213, 219; H. C. Casserley, p 214 bottom; G. R. L. Coles, p 163; E. S. Cox, p 103 bottom, 105; Derek Cross, p 270, 291; M. W. Earley, p 64, 72 top, 76, 101, 106, 107, 111, 112, 132 top, 134, 138, 140, 141, 143 top, 154, 158, 170, 173, 175 top, 196, 202, 205 bottom, 206, 211, 222, 226, 242, 249, 255 bottom, 263, 276 bottom, 278 bottom; R. J. Faux, p 283 top, 290; Peter W. Gray, p 207, 218 bottom right, 270 bottom, 272 top, 280, 286, 289; F. R. Hebron, p 103 top, 143 bottom; J. G. Hubback, p 215 top; K. H. Leech, p 149 right, 191 top, 195, 214 top, 216 top, 218 top, 218 bottom left, 220, 224, 225, 227, 228, 229 top, 231, 240, 243, 245, 246, 247, 248, 259 bottom, 269 bottom, 271, 273 bottom, 275 top, 276 top, 279; Locomotive Publishing Co Ltd, p 27 top, 77, 84 bottom; John K. Morton, p 286; O. S. Nock, p 113 bottom, 116, 194 bottom, 198 top, 208; Overend Press Agency, p 199; Real Photographs Ltd, p 27 bottom right, 32 bottom, 33 left and right, 40 top left and right, 41 top, 44 top and bottom, 53 top and bottom, 54, 55 58 left and right. 60, 65, 68, 69 bottom, 72 bottom, 73 bottom left and right, 75 top, 78 right, 85 top, 88, 89 bottom, 93 bottom, 99, 100, 102 bottom, 109 left and right, 113 top, 115, 117 bottom, 119 bottom, 132 bottom right, 136 bottom left and right, 158, 197, 221; P. J. T. Reed, p 16, 20 top, 28 bottom left, 35, 47, 149 left; R. C. Riley, p 216 bottom left and right, 217 top, 229 bottom, 260, 283 bottom, 284, 285; J. F. Russell-Smith, p 212, 244, 277 top; the late G. H. Soole, p 252, 255 top, 257, 259, 261, 264, 265, 268 bottom, 269, 272, 277, 279, 281 top; G. Wheeler, p 265 top. Acknowledgement is also made of photographs loaned from the author's collection, taken by the following: Messrs R. Brookman, p. 20 bottom; the late E. Little, p 84 top; the late F. E. Mackay, p 19, 29, 57, 59, 66, 69 top; the late W. J. Reynolds, p 41 bottom, 62, 75 bottom, 78 left, 89 top, 91, 98, 108, 118, 121 top, 132 bottom left, 142; the late Bishop Eric Treacy, p 205 top.

For the remainder of the illustrations indeptedness is expressed to British Railways, also for the drawings from which most of the diagrams have been prepared.

The plate on p 186 is reproduced from a painting by Victor Welch. The frontispiece is reproduced from a painting by Terence Cuneo, by courtesy of H. P. Bulmer & Co, Hereford.

CASE HISTORIES

'STAR' CLASS

No	Original Name	Built	Superheated	Outside steampipes Elbow	'Castle'	Withdrawn
4000	*North Star* (a)	4/06	11/09	R. Castle		11/29
4001	*Dog Star*	2/07	1/11		10/30	1/34
4002	*Evening Star*	3/07	8/09	12/29		6/33
4003	*Lode Star*	2/07	5/11	3/49		7/51 (j)
4004	*Morning Star*	2/07	1/11	3/46		4/48
4005	*Polar Star*	2/07	2/11			11/34
4006	*Red Star*	4/07	4/11			11/32
4007	*Rising Star* (b)	4/07	5/11	5/47		9/51
4008	*Royal Star*	5/07	12/11	7/33		6/35
4009	*Shooting Star*	5/07	10/12	R. Castle		4/25
4010	*Western Star*	5/07	5/07			11/34
4011	*Knight of the Garter*	3/08	3/08			11/32
4012	*Knight of the Thistle*	3/08	1/11			10/49
4013	*Knight of St Patrick*	3/08	12/11			5/50
4014	*Knight of the Bath*	3/08	10/10	9/35		6/46
4015	*Knight of St John*	3/08	9/10	12/48		2/51
4016	*Knight of the Golden Fleece*	4/08	11/09	R. Castle		10/25
4017	*Knight of the Black Eagle* (c)	4/08	11/09			11/49
4018	*Knight of the Grand Cross*	4/08	9/10	5/31		4/51
4019	*Knight Templar*	5/08	1/10	5/48		10/49
4020	*Knight Commander*	5/08	11/09	3/49		3/51
4021	*King Edward* (d)	6/09	6/09	7/48		10/52
4022	*King William* (d)	6/09	10/10	6/48		2/52
4023	*King George* (d)	6/09	9/12			7/52
4024	*King James* (d)	6/09	2/11		2/29	2/35
4025	*King Charles* (d)	7/09	1/11			8/50
4026	*King Richard* (d)	9/09	5/13	10/32		2/50
4027	*King Henry* (d)	9/09	6/12			10/34
4028	*King John* (d)	9/09	9/11			11/51
4029	*King Stephen* (d)	10/09	4/11			11/34
4030	*King Harold* (d)	10/09	1/13			5/50
4031	*Queen Mary*	10/10	Built	8/48		6/51
4032	*Queen Alexandra*	10/10	"	R. Castle		4/26
4033	*Queen Victoria*	11/10	"	4/40		6/51
4034	*Queen Adelaide*	11/10	"	6/32		9/52
4035	*Queen Charlotte*	11/10	"		1/31	10/51
4036	*Queen Elizabeth*	12/10	"	7/43		3/52
4037	*Queen Philippa*	12/10	"	R. Castle		6/26
4038	*Queen Berengaria*	1/11	"	8/32		4/52
4039	*Queen Matilda*	2/11	"	12/48		11/50
4040	*Queen Boadicea*	3/11	"		2/30	6/51
4041	*Prince of Wales*	6/13	"	10/47		4/51
4042	*Prince Albert*	5/13	"	5/48		11/51
4043	*Prince Henry*	5/13	"		10/31	1/52
4044	*Prince George*	5/13	"	10/46		2/53
4045	*Prince John*	6/13	"	1/46		11/50
4046	*Princess Mary*	5/14	"	1/49		11/51
4047	*Princess Louise*	5/14	"			7/51
4048	*Princess Victoria* (e)	5/14	"	8/32	10/38	1/53
4049	*Princess Maud*	5/14	"		2/35	7/53
4050	*Princess Alice*	6/14	"	6/46		2/52

No	Original Name	Built	Superheated	Outside steampipes Elbow	Outside steampipes 'Castle'	Withdrawn
4051	*Princess Helena*	6/14	Built		12/44	10/50
4052	*Princess Beatrice*	6/14	,,		4/39	6/53
4053	*Princess Alexandra*	6/14	,,		10/33	7/54
4054	*Princess Charlotte*	6/14	,,	10/45		2/52
4055	*Princess Sophia*	7/14	,,		5/45	2/51
4056	*Princess Margaret*	7/14	,,	8/49		10/57
4057	*Princess Elizabeth* (f)	7/14	,,		4/30	2/52
4058	*Princess Augusta*	7/14	,,	10/44		4/51
4059	*Princess Patricia*	7/14	,,			9/52
4060	*Princess Eugenie*	7/14	,,	12/30	8/44	10/52
4061	*Glastonbury Abbey*	5/22	,,	7/49		3/57
4062	*Malmesbury Abbey*	5/22	,,	3/50		11/56
4063	*Bath Abbey*	11/22	,,			3/37
4064	*Reading Abbey*	12/22	,,			2/37
4065	*Evesham Abbey*	12/22	,,			3/39
4066	*Malvern Abbey* (g)	12/22	,,			12/37
4067	*Tintern Abbey*	1/23	,,			9/40
4068	*Llanthony Abbey*	1/23	,,			11/38
4069	*Margam Abbey* (h)	1/23	,,			4/39
4070	*Neath Abbey*	2/23	,,	3/37		1/39
4071	*Cleeve Abbey*	2/23	,,			9/38
4072	*Tresco Abbey*	2/23	,,			3/38

Notes:
(a) No 40 (4000) was not added to stock until 6/06 and ran nameless until 9/06.
(b) No 4007 was renamed *Swallowfield Park* in 5/37.
(c) No 4017 was renamed *Knight of Liege* in 8/14.
(d) When the 'King' class was introduced in 1927, Nos 4021-30 were renamed as follows:

4021	*The British Monarch*	6/27
4022	*The Belgian Monarch*	6/27
4023	*The Danish Monarch*	7/27
4024	*The Dutch Monarch*	9/27
4025	*Italian Monarch*	10/27
4026	*The Japanese Monarch*	7/27
4027	*The Norwegian Monarch*	7/27
4028	*The Roumanian Monarch*	7/27
4029	*The Spanish Monarch*	7/27
4030	*The Swedish Monarch*	7/27

Nos 4021-4/6-30 had altered nameplates omitting 'The' fitted in October/November 1927. Names were removed from 4022 (5/40), 4023 (11/40), 4025 (6/40), 4026 (1/41), 4028/30 (11/40), and the words 'Star Class' were painted on the splasher.
(e) No 4048 was temporarily named *Princess Mary* for the Royal Wedding on 28/3/22.
(f) No 4057 was fitted with a small rectangular brass plate above the left-hand number plate in 1951, recording that the engine was driven by HRH Princess Elizabeth from Swindon Works to Swindon station on 15/11/50.
(g) No 4066 was renamed *Sir Robert Horne* in 5/35. The nameplates were removed in 7/37 and new plates *Viscount Horne* fitted in 8/37.
(h) No 4069 was renamed *Westminster Abbey* in 5/23.
(j) Preserved in the Great Western Museum, Swindon.
(k) The following engines carried 'half cone' boilers at various times between 1909 and 1921: 4000-2/4/6/9-16/8/21/3/4/6-9/34/5/40/5.

(l) The engines were allocated Swindon Works numbers and lot numbers as shown below: the works numbers of No 4045 and subsequent engines were not carried on the engine:

Engine Nos	Swindon Works Nos	Lot Nos
40 (4000)	2168	161
4001-10	2229-38	168
4011-20	2300-9	173
4021-30	2365-74	178
4031-40	2380-9	180
4041-50	2536-40	195
4046-60	2572-86	199
4061-72	2915-26	217

'CASTLE' CLASS

No	Original Name	Built	Double Chimney	Withdrawn
111	*Viscount Churchill*	9/24		7/53
4000	*North Star*	11/29		5/57
4009	*Shooting Star* (a)	4/25		3/50
4016	*Knight of the Golden Fleece* (a)	10/25		9/51
4032	*Queen Alexandra*	4/26		9/51
4037	*Queen Philippa* (a)	6/26		9/62
		Built		
4073	*Caerphilly Castle*	8/23		5/60 (o)
4074	*Caldicot Castle* (b)	12/23	4/59	5/63
4075	*Cardiff Castle*	1/24		11/61
4076	*Carmarthen Castle*	2/24		2/63
4077	*Chepstow Castle*	2/24		8/62

No	Original Name	Built	Double Chimney	Withdrawn
4078	*Pembroke Castle*	2/24		7/62
4079	*Pendennis Castle*	2/24		5/64 (p)
4080	*Powderham Castle*	3/24	8/58	8/64
4081	*Warwick Castle*	3/24		1/63
4082	*Windsor Castle* (c)	4/24		9/64
4083	*Abbotsbury Castle*	5/25		12/61
4084	*Aberystwyth Castle*	5/25		10/60
4085	*Berkeley Castle*	5/25		5/62
4086	*Builth Castle*	6/25		4/62
4087	*Cardigan Castle*	6/25	2/58	10/63
4088	*Dartmouth Castle*	7/25	5/58	5/64
4089	*Donnington Castle*	7/25		9/64
4090	*Dorchester Castle*	7/25	7/57	6/63
4091	*Dudley Castle*	7/25		1/59
4092	*Dunraven Castle*	8/25		12/61
4093	*Dunster Castle*	5/26	12/57	9/64
4094	*Dynevor Castle*	5/26		3/62
4095	*Harlech Castle*	6/26		12/62
4096	*Highclere Castle*	6/26		1/63
4097	*Kenilworth Castle*	6/26	6/58	5/60
4098	*Kidwelly Castle*	7/26		12/63
4099	*Kilgerran Castle*	8/26		9/62
5000	*Launceston Castle*	9/26		10/64
5001	*Llandovery Castle*	9/26	6/61	2/63
5002	*Ludlow Castle*	9/26		9/64
5003	*Lulworth Castle*	5/27		8/62
5004	*Llanstephan Castle*	6/27		4/62
5005	*Manorbier Castle*	6/27		2/60
5006	*Tregenna Castle*	6/27		4/62
5007	*Rougemont Castle*	6/27		9/62
5008	*Raglan Castle*	6/27	3/61	9/62
5009	*Shrewsbury Castle*	6/27		10/60
5010	*Restormel Castle*	7/27		10/59
5011	*Tintagel Castle*	7/27		9/62
5012	*Berry Pomeroy Castle*	7/27		4/62
5013	*Abergavenny Castle*	6/32		7/62
5014	*Goodrich Castle*	6/32		2/65
5015	*Kingswear Castle*	7/32		4/63
5016	*Montgomery Castle*	7/32	2/60	9/62
5017	*St Donats Castle* (d)	7/32		9/62
5018	*St Mawes Castle*	7/32		3/64
5019	*Treago Castle*	7/32	2/61	9/62
5020	*Trematon Castle*	7/32		11/62
5021	*Whittington Castle*	8/32		9/62
5022	*Wigmore Castle*	8/32	2/59	6/63
5023	*Brecon Castle*	4/34		2/63
5024	*Carew Castle*	4/34		5/62
5025	*Chirk Castle*	4/34		11/63
5026	*Criccieth Castle*	4/34	10/59	11/64
5027	*Farleigh Castle*	4/34	4/61	11/62
5028	*Llantilio Castle*	5/34		5/60
5029	*Nunney Castle*	5/34		12/63
5030	*Shirburn Castle*	5/34		9/62
5031	*Totnes Castle*	5/34	6/59	10/63
5032	*Usk Castle*	5/34	5/59	9/62
5033	*Broughton Castle*	5/35	10/60	9/62
5034	*Corfe Castle*	5/35	2/60	9/62
5035	*Coity Castle*	5/35		5/62
5036	*Lyonshall Castle*	5/35	12/60	9/62
5037	*Monmouth Castle*	5/35		3/64
5038	*Morlais Castle*	6/35		9/63
5039	*Rhuddlan Castle*	6/35		6/64
5040	*Stokesay Castle*	6/35		10/63
5041	*Tiverton Castle*	7/35		12/63
5042	*Winchester Castle*	7/35		6/65
5043	*Barbury Castle* (e)	3/36	10/56	12/63
5044	*Beverston Castle* (e)	3/36		4/62
5045	*Bridgwater Castle* (e)	3/36		9/62
5046	*Clifford Castle* (e)	4/36		9/62
5047	*Compton Castle* (e)	4/36		9/62
5048	*Cranbrook Castle* (e)	4/36		8/62

No	Name	Built	Double Chimney	Withdrawn
5049	Denbigh Castle (e)	4/36	9/59	3/63
5050	Devizes Castle (e)	5/36		8/63
5051	Dryslwyn Castle (e)	5/36		5/63 (q)
5052	Eastnor Castle (e)	5/36		9/62
5053	Bishop's Castle (e)	5/36		7/62
5054	Lamphey Castle (e)	6/36		11/64
5055	Lydford Castle (e)	6/36		10/64
5056	Ogmore Castle (e)	6/36	10/60	11/64
5057	Penrice Castle (e)	6/36	7/58	3/64
5058	Newport Castle (e)	5/37		3/63
5059	Powis Castle (e)	5/37		6/62
5060	Sarum Castle (e)	6/37	7/61	4/63
5061	Sudeley Castle (e)	6/37	9/58	9/62
5062	Tenby Castle (e)	6/37		8/62
5063	Thornbury Castle (e)	6/37		2/65
5064	Tretower Castle (e)	6/37	9/58	9/62
5065	Upton Castle (e)	7/37		1/63
5066	Wardour Castle (f)	7/37	4/59	9/62
5067	St Fagans Castle	7/37		7/62
5068	Beverston Castle	6/38	7/59	9/62
5069	Isambard Kingdom Brunel (g)	6/38	11/58	2/62
5070	Sir Daniel Gooch	6/38		3/64
5071	Clifford Castle (h)	6/38	6/59	10/63
5072	Compton Castle (h)	6/38		10/62
5073	Cranbrook Castle (h)	7/38	7/59	3/64
5074	Denbigh Castle (h)	7/38	9/61	5/64
5075	Devizes Castle (h)	8/38		9/62
5076	Dryslwyn Castle (h)	8/38		9/64
5077	Eastnor Castle (h)	8/38		7/62
5078	Lamphey Castle (h)	5/39	12/61	11/62
5079	Lydford Castle (h)	5/39		5/60
5080	Ogmore Castle (h)	5/39		4/63
5081	Penrice Castle (h)	5/39		10/63
5082	Powis Castle (h)	6/39		7/62
5083	Bath Abbey	6/37		1/59
5084	Reading Abbey	4/37	10/58	7/62
5085	Evesham Abbey	7/39		2/64
5086	Viscount Horne	12/37		11/58
5087	Tintern Abbey	11/40		8/63
5088	Llanthony Abbey	2/39	6/58	9/62
5089	Westminster Abbey	10/39		11/64
5090	Neath Abbey	4/39		5/62
5091	Cleeve Abbey	12/38		10/64
5092	Tresco Abbey	4/38	10/61	7/63
5093	Upton Castle	6/39		9/63
5094	Tretower Castle	6/39	6/60	9/62
5095	Barbury Castle	6/39	11/58	8/62
5096	Bridgwater Castle	6/39	1/59	6/64
5097	Sarum Castle	7/39	6/61	3/63
5098	Clifford Castle	5/46	1/59	6/64
5099	Compton Castle	5/46		2/63
7000	Viscount Portal	5/46		12/63
7001	Denbigh Castle (j)	5/46	9/60	9/63
7002	Devizes Castle	6/46	6/61	3/64
7003	Elmley Castle	6/46	6/60	8/64
7004	Eastnor Castle	6/46	2/58	1/64
7005	Lamphey Castle (k)	6/46		9/64
7006	Lydford Castle	6/46	5/60	12/63
7007	Ogmore Castle (l)	7/46	3/61	2/63
7008	Swansea Castle	5/48	6/59	9/64
7009	Athelney Castle	5/48		3/63
7010	Avondale Castle	6/48	10/60	3/64
7011	Banbury Castle	6/48		2/65
7012	Barry Castle	6/48		11/64
7013	Bristol Castle (c)	7/48	5/58	2/65
7014	Caerhays Castle	7/48	2/59	2/65
7015	Carn Brea Castle	7/48	6/59	4/63
7016	Chester Castle	8/48		11/62
7017	G. J. Churchward (m)	8/48		2/63
7018	Drysllwyn Castle	5/49	5/56	9/63

No	Name	Built	Double Chimney	Withdrawn
7019	*Fowey Castle*	5/49	9/58	9/64
7020	*Gloucester Castle*	5/49	2/61	9/63
7021	*Haverfordwest Castle*	6/49	11/61	9/63
7022	*Hereford Castle*	6/49	1/58	6/65
7023	*Penrice Castle*	6/49	5/58	2/65
7024	*Powis Castle*	6/49	3/59	2/65
7025	*Sudeley Castle*	8/49		9/64
7026	*Tenby Castle*	8/49		10/64
7027	*Thornbury Castle*	8/49		12/63
7028	*Cadbury Castle*	5/50	10/61	12/63
7029	*Clun Castle*	5/50	10/59	12/65 (p)
7030	*Cranbrook Castle*	6/50	7/59	2/63
7031	*Cromwell's Castle*	6/50		7/63
7032	*Denbigh Castle*	6/50	9/60	9/64
7033	*Hartlebury Castle*	7/50	7/59	1/63
7034	*Ince Castle*	8/50	12/59	6/65
7035	*Ogmore Castle*	8/50	1/60	8/64
7036	*Taunton Castle*	8/50	8/59	9/63
7037	*Swindon* (n)	8/50		3/63

(a) These engines were renamed as follows:
No 4009 was renumbered and renamed A1 *Lloyds* in 1/36. Additional plates with number 100 were fixed above the 'A1' in 2/36 and the buffer beam bore '100 A1'. For ordinary purposes the engine was known as No 100.
No 4016 was renamed *The Somerset Light Infantry (Prince Albert's)* and fitted with plaques of the Regimental Crest in 1/38.
No 4037 was renamed *The South Wales Borderers* in 3/37; the official naming ceremony took place on 14/4/37.
(b) An early official photograph shows No 4074 with the name spelt **Caldicott Castle**.
(c) In 2/52 the number and name 4082 *Windsor Castle* and the commemorative plaques were transferred to No 7013, and the number and name 7013 *Bristol Castle* was transferred to No 4082. The commemorative plaques were later removed from the new 4082.
(d) No 5017 was renamed *The Gloucestershire Regiment 28/61* in 4/54 to commemorate this Regiment's part in the Korean War.
(e) In 1937 it was decided to transfer the 'Earl' names originally allocated to 4—4—0s of the 32XX class to 'Castles' 5043-62. The 'Castles' received their new names as shown:

No	New Name	Date Altered
5043	*Earl of Mount Edgcumbe*	9/37
5044	*Earl of Dunraven*	9/37
5045	*Earl of Dudley*	9/37
5046	*Earl Cawdor*	8/37
5047	*Earl of Dartmouth*	8/37
5048	*Earl of Devon*	8/37
5049	*Earl of Plymouth*	8/37
5050	*Earl of St Germans*	8/37
5051	*Earl Bathurst*	8/37 (q)
5052	*Earl of Radnor*	7/37
5053	*Earl Cairns*	8/37
5054	*Earl of Ducie*	9/37
5055	*Earl of Eldon*	8/37
5056	*Earl of Powis*	9/37
5057	*Earl Waldegrave*	10/37
5058	*Earl of Clancarty*	9/37
5059	*Earl St Aldwyn*	10/37
5060	*Earl of Berkeley*	10/37
5061	*Earl of Birkenhead*	10/37
5062	*Earl of Shaftesbury*	11/37
5063	*Earl Baldwin*	7/37

Two of the names displaced by this renaming were transferred to the next two 'Castles' in serial order, as shown below:

No		
5064	*Bishop's Castle*	9/37
5065	*Newport Castle*	9/37

(f) No 5066 was renamed *Sir Felix Pole* in 4/56.
(g) No 5069 was built with nameplates of larger radius, which did not 'fit' the splashers. These were replaced by the standard pattern in 7/38.
(h) After the Battle of Britain in the autumn of 1940 Nos 5071-82 were given the names of famous aircraft of the time, as follows:

No	New Name	Date Altered
5071	*Spitfire*	9/40
5072	*Hurricane*	11/40
5073	*Blenheim*	1/41
5074	*Hampden*	1/41
5075	*Wellington*	10/40
5076	*Gladiator*	1/41
5077	*Fairey Battle*	10/40
5078	*Beaufort*	10/40
5079	*Lysander*	11/40
5080	*Defiant*	1/41
5081	*Lockheed Hudson*	1/41
5082	*Swordfish*	1/41

(j) Nos 7001-7 were renamed in commemoration of the passing of the Great Western Railway. No 7001 was renamed *Sir James Milne* in 2/48, after the last general manager of the company.
(k) No 7005 was renamed *Sir Edward Elgar* in 8/57, at the time of the centenary of the composer's birth.
(l) No 7007 was the last express passenger engine built by the Great Western Railway, and in 1/48 it was given the name *Great Western*. Transfers of the GWR coat of arms were put on the centre splashers soon afterwards.
(m) The nameplates of No 7017 were removed after the engine had been in service for a few days, and were replaced for the naming ceremony of 29/10/48.
(n) No 7037 ran nameless until the naming ceremony of 15/11/50.
(o) Preserved in the Science Museum, South Kensington, London.
(p) Preserved privately.
(q) Preserved privately as *Drysllwyn Castle*.

'KING' CLASS

No	Original Name	Built	Double Chimney	Withdrawn
6000	*King George V*	6/27	12/56	12/62 (d)
6001	*King Edward VII*	7/27	2/56	9/62
6002	*King William IV*	7/27	3/56	9/62
6003	*King George IV*	7/27	7/58	6/62
6004	*King George III*	7/27	7/58	6/62
6005	*King George II*	7/27	7/56	11/62
6006	*King George I*	2/28	6/56	2/62
6007	*King William III* (a)	3/28	9/56	9/62
6008	*King James II*	3/28	12/58	6/62
6009	*King Charles II*	3/28	5/56	9/62
6010	*King Charles I*	4/28	3/56	6/62
6011	*King James I*	4/28	3/56	12/62
6012	*King Edward VI*	4/28	2/58	9/62
6013	*King Henry VIII*	5/28	6/56	6/62
6014	*King Henry VII*	5/28	9/57	9/62
6015	*King Richard III*	6/28	9/55	9/62
6016	*King Edward V*	6/28	1/58	9/62
6017	*King Edward IV*	6/28	12/55	7/62
6018	*King Henry VI*	6/28	3/58	12/62
6019	*King Henry V*	7/28	4/57	9/62
6020	*King Henry IV*	5/30	2/56	7/62
6021	*King Richard II*	6/30	3/57	9/62
6022	*King Edward III*	6/30	5/56	9/62
6023	*King Edward II*	6/30	6/57	6/62
6024	*King Edward I*	6/30	3/57	6/62 (e)
6025	*King Henry III*	7/30	3/57	12/62
6026	*King John*	7/30	3/58	9/62
6027	*King Richard I*	7/30	8/56	9/62
6028	*King Henry II* (b)	7/30	1/57	11/62
6029	*King Stephen* (c)	8/30	12/57	7/62

(a) No 6007 was nominally withdrawn on 5/3/36 and renewed on 24/3/36.
(b) No 6028 was renamed *King George VI* in 1/37.
(c) No 6029 was renamed *King Edward VIII* in 5/36.
(d) Preserved as part of the National Collection
(e) Preserved privately

APPENDIX 2

NOMINAL VALVE EVENTS

	'Star', 'Castle' 'The Great Bear'	'King'
Valve diameter, in	8	9
Valve travel, in	$6\frac{7}{8}$	$7\frac{1}{4}$
Steam lap, in	$1\frac{5}{8}$	$1\frac{5}{8}$
Exhaust clearance, in	nil	nil
Lead, in	3/16	3/16
Cut-off in full gear, per cent	76·5	76·5

The lead of the 'Stars' and 'The Great Bear' was originally given as $\frac{1}{8}$ in but later official records showed it as 3/16 in.

The valve travel varied between inside and outside cylinders, the extremes being about $6\frac{3}{4}$ in inside and $7\frac{1}{2}$ in outside. The 'Stars' and 'Castles' had an average travel of about $7\frac{1}{8}$ in and the 'Kings' $7\frac{1}{4}$ in.

APPENDIX 3

BOILER DIMENSIONS

Engine Class	'Star'		'Castle'				'King'		'The Great Bear'		
Barrel:											
length	14 ft 10 in[1]		14 ft 10 in				16 ft 0 in		23 ft 0 in		
outside diameter, maximum and minimum	4 ft 13/16 in & 5 ft 6 in		5 ft 1 15/16 in & 5 ft 9 in				5 ft 6¼ in & 6 ft 0 in		5 ft 6 in & 6 ft 0 in		
Height of centre line	8 ft 6 in		8 ft 8½ in				8 ft 11¼ in		9 ft 0 in		
Firebox casing:											
length	9 ft 0 in		10 ft 0 in						8 ft 0 in		
width	5 ft 9 in		6 ft 0 in				6 ft 3 in		6 ft 6 in at top		
Firebox:											
length	8 ft 1 15/16 in		(a) 9 ft 2 7/16 in (b) (c) (d) 9 ft 1 15/16 in				10 ft 7⅞ in		7 ft 2⅜ in		
width	4 ft 9 in		5 ft 0⅛ in		4 ft 11⅞ in		5 ft 2⅛ in		5 ft 8⅝ in		
height	6 ft 6⅜ in		6 ft 8⅞ in		6 ft 8⅞ in		7 ft 0 3/16 in		6 ft 5 1/16 in		
Superheater: type	None	Swindon No 3	(a) Swindon No 3	(b) Swindon No 3	(c) Three-row	(d) Four-row	Swin- No 3	Four-row	Swindon No 1	Swindon No 3	Swindon No 3
Small tubes:											
number	250[2]	176[3]	201	197	170	138	171	115	141	147	147
outside diameter (in)	2	2	2	2	2	2	2¼	2¼	2½	2½	2½
Flues:											
number		14	14	14	21	28	16	32	21	14	14
outside diameter (in)		5⅛	5⅛	5⅛	5⅛	5⅛	5⅛	5⅛	4¾	5⅛	5⅛
Elements:											
number		84	84	84	84	112	96	128	84	112	84
outside diameter (in)			1	1	1¼	1¼	1	1¼	1⅜	⅞	1
Heating surface—ft^2:											
tubes	1,989[2]	1,687[3]	1,886	1,858	1,800	1,670	2,008	1,818	2,674	2,597	2,597
firebox	154	155[3]	164	163	164	163	194	195	182[5]	159	159
superheater elements		263[3]	263[4]	263[4]	313[4]	393[4]	313	489	545	506	399
TOTAL	2,143	2,105	2,313	2,284	2,277	2,226	2,515	2,502	3,401	3,262	3,155
Grate area—ft^2	27·1	27·1	30·3	29·4	29·4	29·4	34·3	34·3	41·8	41·8	41·8

Notes

1. 4 ft 10¾ in in early boilers.
2. The figures given refer to fifty boilers made between 4/06 and 10/08; in 1908 ten boilers were made with 247 tubes (1,966 ft^2), in 1908-9 fourteen boilers were made with 248 tubes (1,973 ft^2), and in 1909 four boilers were made with 301 tubes (2,093 ft^2). Most of these boilers were later superheated.
3. The figures given refer to 599 boilers made between 1922 and 1944; boilers made in 1909-11 had 166 tubes, except for the original boilers on Nos 4010-11, which had 165 tubes. The Cole superheater of No 4010 had eighteen flues of 4¾ in diameter and seventy-two elements of 1¼ in diameter, giving 269 ft^2; the Swindon No 1 superheater in No 4011 was similar, except for having 1⅜ in elements giving 300 ft^2. In 1914-19 108 boilers were made with Swindon No 3 superheaters with 112 elements in quadruple groups giving 330 ft^2. There were numerous small changes in the superheating surface of the No 1 boilers resulting from changes in the design or length of elements, for example from 2/52 the elements in the then standard pattern of the boiler were reduced from 263 ft^2 to 253 ft^2.
4. Shortening of the elements reduced the superheating surfaces as follows: Swindon No 3 to 253 ft^2, three-row to 302 and later to 295 ft^2, and four-row to 381 ft^2.
5. Including 24 ft^2 from four arch tubes of 3⅜ in diameter.

INDEX